115/12

D0994672

Tomorrow's Geography

for Edexcel GCSE Specification A

Book No.   St. Benedict's School
Geography Department

Name: _Harry Pass_

Form: _L5C_

CONDITION OF BOOK
AT START OF YEAR: NEW   GOOD   ADEQUATE

PLEASE LOOK AFTER THIS TEXT BOOK

Book No. **115/12**

St Benedict's School
Geography Department

NAME: _Shri Nallamothu_

FORM: _L5B_

endorsed by
edexcel

Tomorrow's Geography
for Edexcel GCSE Specification A

Third Edition

Mike Harcourt
Steph Warren

DL DYNAMIC LEARNING

HODDER EDUCATION
AN HACHETTE UK COMPANY

This material has been endorsed by Edexcel and offers high quality support for the delivery of Edexcel qualifications.

Edexcel endorsement does not mean that this material is essential to achieve any Edexcel qualification, nor does it mean that this is the only suitable material available to support any Edexcel qualification. No endorsed material will be used verbatim in setting any Edexcel examination and any resource lists produced by Edexcel shall include this and any other appropriate texts. While this material has been through an Edexcel quality assurance process, all responsibility for the content remains with the publisher. Copies of the official specifications for all Edexcel qualifications may be found on the Edexcel website – www.edexcel.org.uk

Every effort has been made to trace all copyright holders, but if any have been inadvertently overlooked the Publishers will be pleased to make the necessary arrangements at the first opportunity.

Although every effort has been made to ensure that website addresses are correct at time of going to press, Hodder Education cannot be held responsible for the content of any website mentioned in this book. It is sometimes possible to find a relocated web page by typing in the address of the home page for a website in the URL window of your browser.

Hachette UK's policy is to use papers that are natural, renewable and recyclable products and made from wood grown in sustainable forests. The logging and manufacturing processes are expected to conform to the environmental regulations of the country of origin.

Orders: please contact Bookpoint Ltd, 130 Milton Park, Abingdon, Oxon OX14 4SB. Telephone: (44) 01235 827720. Fax: (44) 01235 400454. Lines are open 9.00–5.00, Monday to Saturday, with a 24-hour message-answering service. Visit our website at www.hoddereducation.co.uk.

© Mike Harcourt and Steph Warren 2009

First published in 2001 by Hodder Education,
An Hachette UK Company
338 Euston Road,
London NW1 3BH

This third edition published 2009

Impression number   5
Year   2012 2011 2010

All rights reserved. Apart from any use permitted under UK copyright law, no part of this publication may be reproduced or transmitted in any form or by any means, electronic or mechanical, including photocopying and recording, or held within any information storage and retrieval system, without permission in writing from the publisher or under licence from the Copyright Licensing Agency Limited. Further details of such licences (for reprographic reproduction) may be obtained from the Copyright Licensing Agency Limited, Saffron House, 6–10 Kirby Street, London EC1N 8TS.

Illustrations by Oxford Designers and Illustrators Ltd and Pantek Arts Ltd.
Typeset in 11/13pt Myriad MM Regular by Pantek Arts Ltd, Maidstone, Kent
Printed in Italy

A catalogue record for this title is available from the British Library

ISBN: 978 0340 98376 8

Contents

Acknowledgements

The publishers would like to thank the following for permission to reproduce copyright material:
p.143 WaterAid, a true story from Ghana, www.wateraid.org; **p.288** Unique Caribbean Holidays, Sandals deluxe weddings package.

Photo credits
Cover: © Skyscan/J Farmar; **p.1** *tl* © Steph Warren, *tr* © Steph Warren, *bl* © Mike Harcourt, *br* THE KOBAL COLLECTION/POWER CORP/MUSE/MOONLIGHTING; **p.3** Imagery copyright Get Mapping Plc supplied by Skyscan.co.uk; **p.15** © Mike Harcourt; **p.16** © Mike Harcourt; **p.26** © Steph Warren, © Mike Harcourt, except *tl* © Piero Tonin/ www.CartoonStock.com; **p.29** © Mike Harcourt; **p.31** © Steph Warren; **p.34** *both* © Mike Harcourt; **p.41** © Stephen Dorey – Commercial/Alamy; **p.42** © Skyscan/J Farmar; **p.44** *l* © Lucy Phipps, *tr* © Steph Warren, *br* © Steph Warren; **p.46** © Angie Sharp/Alamy; **p.48** © John Farmar; Ecoscene/CORBIS; **p.50** *l* © Mike Harcourt, *tr* © Steph Warren, *cr* © Steph Warren, *br* © Steph Warren; **p.52** *all* © Mike Harcourt; **p.53** Data/image courtesy of the Channel Coastal Observatory; **p.54** *both* © Steph Warren; **p.55** *both* © Steph Warren; **p.57** *all* ©Environment Agency; **p.58** *all* © Steph Warren; **p.59** *c* © Steph Warren; **p.60** sannse (http://en.wikipedia.org/wiki/User:Sannse)/GFDL (http://en.wikipedia.org/wiki/GNU_Free_Documentation_ License); **p.61** *all* © Mike Harcourt; **p.64** © Mike Harcourt; **p.65** © Mike Harcourt; **p.66** *all* © Mike Harcourt; **p.67** *b* Dominic Tester; **p.68** *both* © Steph Warren; **p.69** *tl* Lucy Phipps, *br* © Steph Warren; **p.70** *both* © Steph Warren; **p.72** Daniel Berehulak/ Getty Images; **p.73** © Mike Harcourt; **p.76** © Steph Warren; **p.77** *t* © Mike Harcourt, *ct* © Richard Sheppard/Alamy, *cb* © Denny Rowland/Alamy, *b* © Mike Harcourt; **p.78** *t* © Mike Harcourt, *ct* © Mike Harcourt, *b* ©webbaviation.co.uk; **p.79** *t* © Edward Bent/Ecoscene, *b* © Mike Harcourt; **p80** *all* © Mike Harcourt; **p81** *all* © Mike Harcourt; **p.85** *t* © Steph Warren, *cr* Skyscan/© Air Images; **p.86** © Mike Harcourt; **p.88** © Stan Pritchard/Alamy; **p.90** © Wilmar Dik/World Pictures/Photoshot; **p.91** © John Peter Photography/Alamy; **p.92** © Mike Harcourt; **p.94** © Reuters/Corbis; **p.95** © epa/Corbis; **p.96** *t* © Michael Leckel/Reuters/Corbis, *b* ©Tourismusverband Paznaun – Ischgl; **p.97** *t* © Mike Harcourt, *b* © Thinkstock/Getty Images; **p.98** *l* © Mike Harcourt, *r* © Mike Harcourt; **p.105** © JUPITERIMAGES/Brand X/Alamy; **p.111** *t* © Hemis/Alamy, *b* © Roger Ressmeyer/CORBIS; **p.113** *t* Jeremy Horner/Panos Pictures, *b* © LE SEGRETAIN PASCAL/CORBIS SYGMA; **p.114** © Reuters/ CORBIS; **p.117** © david sanger photography/Alamy; **p.120** © ERIKO SUGITA/Reuters/Corbis; **p121** © Koji Sasahara/AP/PA Photos; **p.122** © LANDOV/PA Photos; **p.126** *both* © Steph Warren; **p.127** © Steph Warren; **p.128** *tr* © Werner Otto/Alamy, *bl* © imagebroker/Alamy; **p.129** © Steph Warren; **p.133** © Steph Warren; **p.134** *t* © Steph Warren, *b* © Stephen Saks Photography/Alamy; **p.137** *t* © Bye Bye Standby, *b* © Mike Harcourt; **p.138** © Aberdeen City Council; **p.139** *both* © Steph Warren; **p.143** *tr* © Mike Harcourt, *b* © Liba Taylor/Corbis; **p.144** *all* © Mike Harcourt; **p.145** © Chad Ehlers/Alamy; **p.152** *c* © Lou DeMatteis/The Image Works/TopFoto, *b* © Jodi Hilton/Corbis; **p.155** © Steph Warren; **p.156** © PhotoStock-Israel/ Alamy; **p.157** © Mike Goldwater/Alamy; **p.158** © Adrian Page/Alamy; **p.160** © Ed Kashi/CORBIS; **p.161** © Mike Harcourt; **p.162** *all* © Mike Harcourt; **p.165** © webbaviation.co.uk; **p.166** *tl* © ACE STOCK LIMITED/Alamy, *tr* © istockphoto_com/ Simon Kržič, *bl* © istockphoto_com/Brasil2, *br* © istockphoto_com/WillieB_ Thomas; **p.172** *both* © Mike Harcourt; **p.174** © Gregory Wrona/Alamy; **p.176** © Steph Warren; **p.178** *all* © Mike Harcourt; **p.179** Imagery copyright Get Mapping Plc supplied by Skyscan.co.uk; **p.180** © Steph Warren, © Mike Harcourt; **p.186** *both* © Steph Warren; **p.187** *both* © Steph Warren; **p.188** *all* © Steph Warren; **p.189** *all* © Steph Warren; **p191** © Steph Warren; **p.192** *all* © Steph Warren; **p.193** *both* © Steph Warren; **p.196** *tl* © JUPITERIMAGES/Brand X/Alamy, *tr* © Steph Warren, *b* © Steph Warren; **p198** © Walkers Snacks Ltd; **p.199** © Steph Warren; **p.202** © Steph Warren; **p.203** © Steph Warren; **p.204** © Mike Harcourt; **p.207** © Steph Warren; **p.209** *both* © Steph Warren; **p.211** *both* © Steph Warren; **p.214** Skyscan/© London Aerial; **p.215** © Mike Harcourt; **p.216** *t* © Skyscan/CLI, *b* © AA World Travel Library/Alamy; **p.220** © Steph Warren; **p.221** *both* © Steph Warren; **p.222** © Steph Warren, © Mike Harcourt; **p.225** © PCL/Alamy; **p.226** *tl* JORGEN SCHYTTE/Still Pictures, *c* © Reza; Webistan/CORBIS, *br* © Peter Turnley/CORBIS; **p.227** © BRENDAN BEIRNE/Rex Features; **p.232** © Eva-Lotta Jansson/Alamy; **p.233** © Lou Linwei/Alamy; **p.239** *t* Tibor Bognar/Corbis, *b* © Image Source Pink/Alamy; **p.241** © Lou Linwei/Alamy; **p.248** © Mike Harcourt; **p.249** © Mike Harcourt; **p.251** © Everett Kennedy Brown/epa/Corbis; **p.255** © Sipa Press/Rex Features; **p.260** © Steph Warren; **p.269** *both* © Mike Harcourt; **p.270** © Steph Warren; **p.271** © Mike Harcourt; **p.274** © Ken Welsh/Alamy; **p.278** *t* Imagery copyright Get Mapping Plc supplied by Skyscan.co.uk, *bl* © Mike Harcourt, *br* © Mike Harcourt; **p.279** *br* © Mike Harcourt; **p.285** *both* © Mike Harcourt; **p.286** © Mike Harcourt, © Steph Warren; **p.287** *l* © Jack Sullivan/Alamy, *r* © Philip and Karen Smith/ Photographer's Choice/Getty Images; **p.291** © Steph Warren; **p.293** (FREELENS Pool) Tack/Still Pictures; **p.294** LEILA GORCHEV/AFP/Getty Images; **p.295** *both* Lucy Phipps; **p.296** *t* Kate Findlay, *c* Kate Findlay, *b* © Steph Warren; **p.297** *both* © Steph Warren; **p.298** *both* © Steph Warren; **p.299** *all* © Steph Warren; **p.302** *all* © Footsteps Eco-Lodge, Gambia; **p.303** *all* © Footsteps Eco-Lodge; **p.305** © Mike Harcourt.

Maps on pp. 35, 36, 37, 38, 39, 40, 67, 69 and 70, reproduced fom Ordnance Survey mapping with the permission of the Controller of HMSO. © Crown copyright. All rights reserved. Licence number 100036470.

UNIT 1
Geographical Skills and Challenges

This unit has two chapters:

- **Chapter 1 Geographical Skills** looks at the geographical skills you need to succeed at GCSE Geography.

- **Chapter 2 Challenges for the Planet** explores the major challenges that the planet is facing – climate change and sustainability.

1 Geographical Skills

Learning objective – to study a range of geographical skills.

Learning outcomes
- To be able to use basic geographical skills.
- To be able to recognise and describe distributions and patterns of human and physical features.
- To be able to use and interpret Ordnance Survey maps.
- To be able to construct and interpret a variety of graphs, charts and maps.
- To be able to use geographical enquiry skills.
- To have knowledge of ICT and Geographical Information Systems (GIS).

A wide range of geographical skills are part of the study of geography including:
- basic
- cartographic
- graphical
- enquiry
- ICT
- Geographical Information Systems (GIS).

These skills will be explained in this unit and examples will be found throughout the book.

Basic skills

These are the skills that all geography students need and involve being able to draw sketches, label and annotate diagrams and interpret photographs for a variety of different situations.

What is the difference between a label and an annotation?

A label is a simple descriptive point. An annotation is an explanatory label. On Figure 1, the labels are in blue and the annotations are in red. The same principles apply for diagrams, maps, graphs and sketches.

How to draw, label and annotate sketches

To draw a sketch from a photograph follow these steps:

1. Draw a frame the size you want the sketch to be.

2. Lightly draw lines dividing the frame into four quarters. This will help with steps 3 and 4. The lines can be erased when the sketch is completed.

3. Draw in the most important lines such as rivers, coastline and the outline of the hills.

4. Draw in the less important features like woodland, settlements and communication lines. Do not make the sketch too detailed. It is not necessary to draw on every feature.

5. Add appropriate labels and annotations.

The sketch in Figure 1 is a drawing of Warkworth taken from the photograph in Figure 6 on page 216. It has been given descriptive labels and annotation with reasons explaining its site.

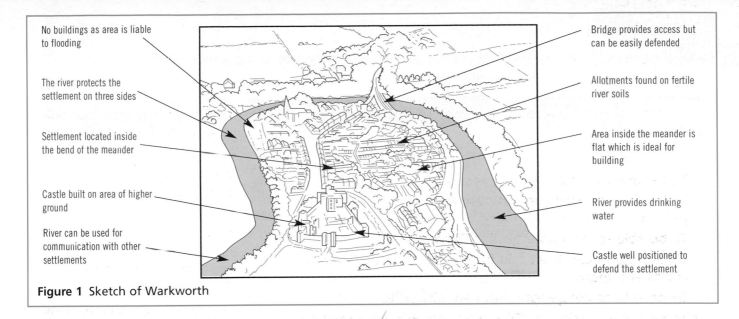

No buildings as area is liable to flooding

The river protects the settlement on three sides

Settlement located inside the bend of the meander

Castle built on area of higher ground

River can be used for communication with other settlements

Bridge provides access but can be easily defended

Allotments found on fertile river soils

Area inside the meander is flat which is ideal for building

River provides drinking water

Castle well positioned to defend the settlement

Figure 1 Sketch of Warkworth

How to interpret aerial, oblique and satellite photographs

Aerial photographs are taken from directly above. They are called 'bird's eye view' photographs because they show a picture taken as if looking down like a flying bird. Photographs which are oblique are taken from an angle and therefore show more detail such as the sides of buildings. Satellite images are pictures of the Earth taken from space. They can show patterns on a large scale such as the lights from urban areas on a continent or can zoom in to see small details such as cars on a street.

All of these different types of photographs show elements of the landscape which are not found on Ordnance Survey (OS) maps, such as types of crops being grown and the different uses of buildings.

When a photograph is interpreted it involves describing and explaining the physical and human geography which can be seen on the photograph. It is important when interpreting photographs that the writing is coherent and shows good literacy skills in expressing geographical points.

Figure 2 Interpretation of aerial photograph of Cambridge

Interpretation of aerial photograph

Physical features – relief: The land is very flat with no visible slopes. There are no rivers visible on the photograph. The soil is fertile due to the wide variety of crops being grown.

Human features – land use

Farmland: The fields are large if they are compared with the individual farm buildings shown on the photograph. They are mostly square and rectangular. This implies the use of large arable machinery. It is arable land with a wide variety of crops being grown – this can be seen by the different colours. There are also lines in the fields which show that machinery has been used. Because crops are growing in most of the fields the photograph must have been taken in the spring or summer. Most of the fields are divided by roads and ditches with the only exception being tree boundaries in the north-east of the photograph which are possibly being used as a wind break to protect the village of Landbeach.

Settlement: The village of Landbeach, which is clearly shown to the east of the photograph, is a linear settlement. For the length of the village there is only one house on each side of the road (the road number can be added by reference to the OS map). In the west on the map there are farms which display a dispersed land use pattern.

Cartographic skills

You will need to be able to recognise a number of different types of maps including atlas maps, sketch maps and Ordnance Survey (OS) maps.

Atlas maps

Atlases not only contain maps showing where places are but also show physical patterns such as the height of the land and human patterns such as population density. On atlas maps you will need to be able to recognise and describe distributions and patterns of both human and physical features. You will also need to be able to relate patterns of human geography to patterns of physical geography. This is shown with the two China maps, Figures 8 and 9, on page 237.

Sketch maps

The same steps should be followed as for drawing a sketch from a photograph.

Ordnance Survey maps

Studying OS maps will require you to possess a range of skills on which you will be tested. You may be asked to use map evidence in a number of different ways or use maps in association with photographs, sketches and written directions.

Symbols

You do not need to memorise the symbols that are used on OS maps because they will always be provided in the exam. We have reproduced them on the inside back cover of this textbook.

Grid references

You will need to be able to locate features using four and six figure grid references. Four figure grid references locate a square on the map and are usually used for large features such as area of a settlement or woodland. Six figure grid references locate a particular point on the map such as a church.

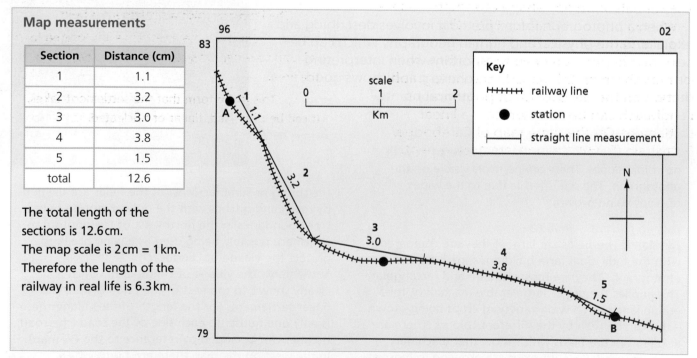

Map measurements

Section	Distance (cm)
1	1.1
2	3.2
3	3.0
4	3.8
5	1.5
total	12.6

The total length of the sections is 12.6 cm.
The map scale is 2 cm = 1 km.
Therefore the length of the railway in real life is 6.3 km.

Key
H++++++ railway line
● station
⊢———⊣ straight line measurement

Figure 3 Measuring distance between two stations on the OS map on page 37.

Measuring distances

You could be asked to measure distance as a straight or curved line. On a 1:50,000 OS map the grid lines are always 2 cm apart which represents 1 km on the ground. To measure a straight line distance between two points such as two churches in different villages:

- Use a ruler or the edge of a piece of paper.
- Mark on the piece of paper the location of the points or take the measurement with the ruler.
- Measure this distance against the scale line on the map.

To measure the distance along any curved line such as a road or a river, the curve should be split into straight sections. Figure 3 is a section of the railway line taken from the OS map on page 37 of this textbook. Notice how the line has been broken into straight sections. The straight sections can then be measured and converted into kilometres using the scale. The more straight sections that the curve is broken down into, the more accurate will be the final measurement.

Another way of measuring curved distances is with a piece of string which should be laid on the route to be measured. The length of the string can then be measured against the scale.

Site, situation and shape of settlements

The site, situation and shape of settlements are described in Unit 3 Chapter 11 Settlement Change, pages 214–228.

In this chapter you need to learn how to identify these on OS maps. In the cartographic section on the description of photographs, Landbeach can be seen, which is a linear settlement. On the same map of Cambridge, Bottisham (5460) is a nucleated settlement.

Compass directions

Map directions are given using the standard eight-point compass, as shown in Figure 4. In an examination, when an OS map is used, north will be taken as following the grid lines.

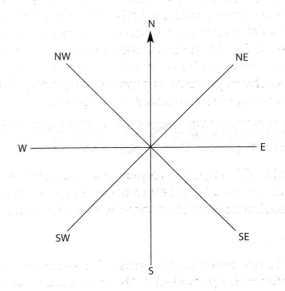

Figure 4 Eight-point compass

Site: The land on which a settlement is built.

Situation: This is where a settlement is located in relation to other physical and human features in the area.

Shape: This is the form that the settlement takes. It can be dispersed, linear or nucleated.

Cross-sections

Figure 5 shows how to construct a cross-section along the line X–Y. To construct the cross-section follow this procedure:

1   Place the edge of a piece of paper along the cross-section.

2   Mark the heights on the paper where the paper crosses the contour lines. Also mark the spot height which shows the top of the hill.

3   Remove the piece of paper with the heights marked on it. Place it on some graph paper. Draw a vertical scale and mark points on the graph at the correct height. Point A for example being marked at 200 m.

4   Join up the crosses to show the shape of the land. In this case it is a hill with a steep slope and a less steep slope.

You may be asked to identify certain physical or human features and locate them on the cross-section you have drawn or been given. In some instances you may be asked to explain your labels. Figure 6 shows how to annotate a cross-section. The cross-section has been made from the OS map of the Wye Valley on page 39.

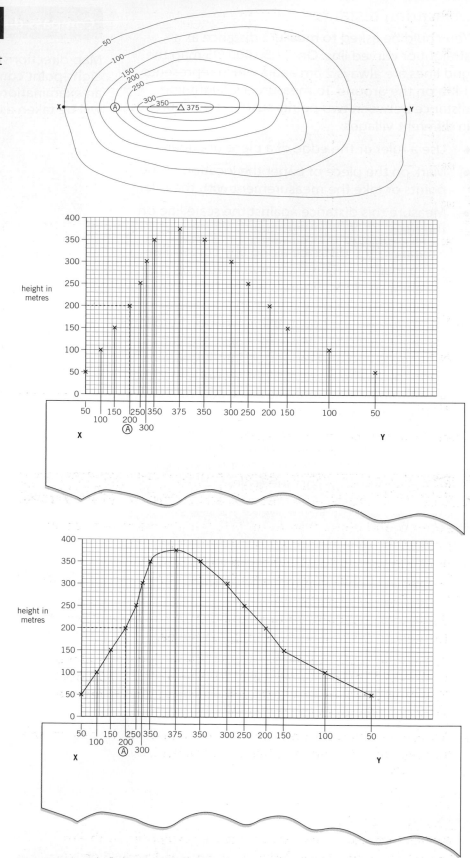

Figure 5 Constructing a cross-section

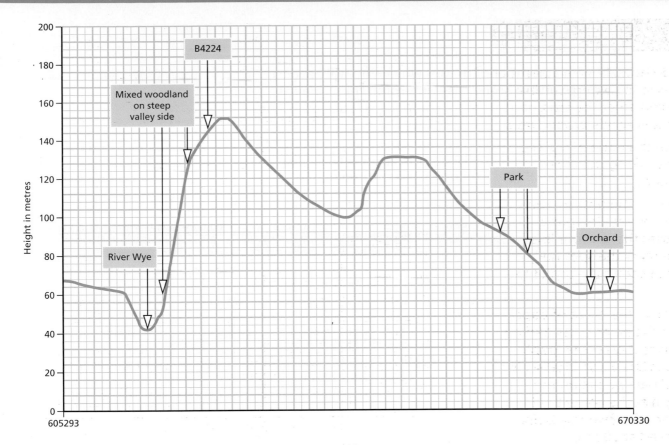

Figure 6 How to annotate a cross-section

Patterns of human and physical features

The human and physical features include patterns of vegetation (e.g. woodland), the land use (e.g. urban or rural) and communication networks (e.g. roads and railways).

If you are asked to describe a pattern or distribution on a map you should follow these steps:

1   Begin with a general statement about where the settlement is located on the map such as in the south-east.

2   Then go into greater detail, such as 'the settlement is along the lines of communication at the bottom of a steep slope'. This example mentions both a physical and human feature, although this is not necessary.

3   You should then be more specific and include in the answer the name of the road and the height of the land.

A description of the pattern of woodland on the Wye Valley map

Woodland is found in most areas of the map except the north-east. The land here is flat. The majority of the woodland is found on steep slopes along the rivers such as the river Wye. It is also found on the hill tops such as the long thin area of woodland on Marcle Hill from 629329 to 628370.

Graphical skills

You will be faced with a number of graphs which you will have to construct or complete and in some cases interpret. These graphs can be basic such as bar charts or more complicated such as isolines. The most frequently used graphical and mapping techniques are: bar charts, compound bar graphs, line graphs, pie charts, triangular graphs, flow lines, choropleth maps, isolines, proportional circles and rose diagrams. Some of these techniques are explained in this chapter.

Bar charts

Bar charts are one of the simplest forms of displaying data. Each bar is the same width but of varying length, depending on the figure being plotted.

- Simple bar charts are drawn with the bars at an equal distance apart and portray distinct data. As each bar represents a distinct piece of information they should each be a separate colour.

- Histograms are used to portray more continuous data, for example, rainfall on a climate graph. As these portray continuous data they should be coloured the same.

- In compound bar charts, the bar is subdivided on the basis of the information being displayed – the sectors of industry in different countries, for example, as shown by the compound bar chart in Figure 7.

- Another form of histogram is the population (age–sex) pyramid. This is constructed in a number of different ways, but usually as five- or ten-year age groups, with males on one side and females on the other. The lines are drawn horizontally and are the same width. The length of the bars is determined by the number of people in that age group or the percentage of the total population that age group represents.

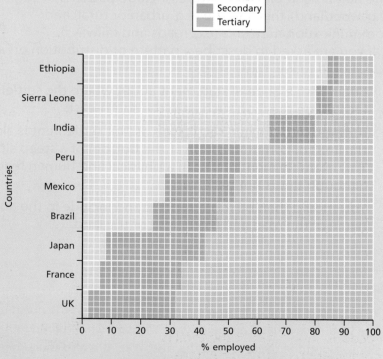

Figure 7 A compound or divided bar graph showing the sectors of industry in certain countries

Isolines

Isolines join places of equal value. Some special isolines are:

- contours which join places on a map which are of equal height

- isobars which are used on weather maps to join places of equal atmospheric pressure

- isohyets which join up places of equal rainfall

- isochrones which join up places an equal distance in time away from somewhere.

Some points to consider when drawing an isoline map are the following:

1 Isolines join up places of equal value.

2 Isolines cannot cross each other.

3 The interval between isolines must be the same, e.g. isochrone lines on the map have been drawn at five minute intervals. Contour lines on a 1:50,000 OS map are shown every 10 m.

Figure 8 uses isolines to join up places of equal time distance from a retail centre (isochrones).

Flow line maps

Flow line maps show movement between places. The direction of the line shows the direction of the flow. The thickness of the line shows the amount of the flow. It is essential when drawing flow lines to choose an appropriate scale and to keep the background as plain as possible to avoid clutter. The arrows in Figure 9 point in both directions showing that the total is a combination of both directions. The width of the arrow shows the number of people.

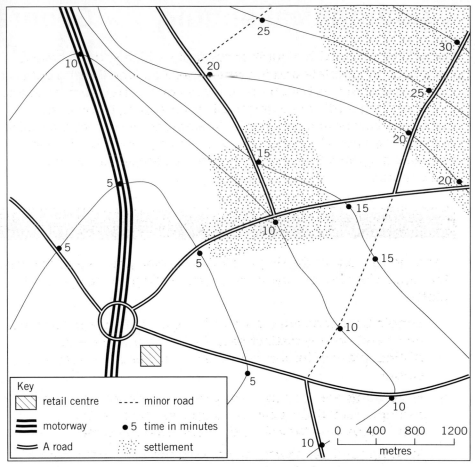

Figure 8 Isolines to join up places of equal time distance from a retail centre

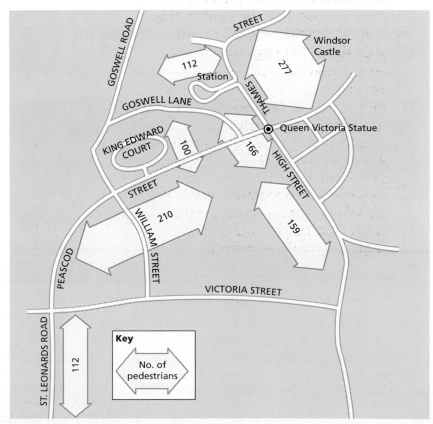

Figure 9 Pedestrian flows in Windsor

Geographical enquiry skills

These are skills which you will be using in Unit 4 Investigating Geography, which is the controlled assessment unit. Geographical enquiry skills may be tested in this unit by evidence provided on the examination paper which you will then have to describe, explain or interpret. You may also be asked about the appropriateness of data collection techniques that you have used to complete your fieldwork.

Geographical Information System (GIS) skills

A Geographical Information System (GIS) has a map as a base and layers of other information on top of it. This can be done by using tracing paper or clear acetate sheets, but is now more commonly done using computer databases. For example, Census data can be plotted onto a base map of an urban area to show characteristics such as crime rates and population structure. Examination questions could then be asked about the map that has been produced. You may also be asked for the advantages or disadvantages of GIS.

ICT skills

These will be tested in Unit 4 but may also appear in Unit 1 in a written form. You will not be expected to have access to a computer in the examination but may have to show your skill in using ICT. Questions could be asked on how to extract information from the internet or how to use databases such as the Census. The annotation of photographs is another skill which could be tested in the examination.

Ways that you could improve your geographical enquiry using GIS

- Study areas can be located and aerial photographs are provided for you.
- Graphs can be created on place mark spots either on a photograph or on a map from Google Earth™.
- Photographs can be uploaded onto Google Earth™ maps at a previously located place mark.
- Straight line distances can be measured using the Line tool and irregular lines with the Path tool.

Review

By the end of this section you should be able to:

- use basic geographical skills
- recognise and describe distributions and patterns of human and physical features
- use and interpret Ordnance Survey maps
- construct and interpret a variety of graphs, charts and maps
- use geographical enquiry skills
- use ICT and GIS in geographical enquiries.

Sample Examination Questions

Higher tier

1 Study the Ordnance Survey (OS) map of Cambridge on page 36.

  a Name the farms in grid square 4664. **(1 mark)**

  b What is the name of the linear settlement marked on the map that has a church with a tower, a public house and a telephone? **(1 mark)**

  c Describe the pattern of A roads in Cambridge. **(3 marks)**

2 Study the OS map of Warkworth on page 35.

  a Give the six figure grid reference for Alnmouth Station. **(1 mark)**

  b Find the level crossing in grid square 2306. What direction is the level crossing from Alnmouth station? **(1 mark)**

  c How far along the railway line is the level crossing from Alnmouth station? **(1 mark)**

  d Look at the area south of grid line 07. Where is most of the woodland found? **(1 mark)**

  e Look at the beach from grid line 05 to grid line 12. Describe the changing characteristics of the beach. **(3 marks)**

3 Study the two compound bar charts in Figure 10 on page 12.

  Use the following figures to draw a compound bar chart for Germany.

Primary	4%
Secondary	30%
Tertiary	66%

  (4 marks)

4 Study Figure 9 on page 9.

  a Where was the busiest flow of pedestrians in Windsor? **(1 mark)**

  b On the same day 50 people walked along Victoria Street. How wide would you draw the flow line to represent this data? **(1 mark)**

Foundation tier

1 Study the Ordnance Survey (OS) map of Cambridge on page 36.

  a How many farms are marked and named in grid square 4664? **(1 mark)**

  b Find Horningsea in grid square 4962. Name one service that can be found in the village. **(1 mark)**

  c Complete the following sentences which describe the pattern of roads in Cambridge. Use some of the words in the box.

five	nine	south	M11	east	north	M1
A603	seven					

  There are .... A roads that join in the centre of Cambridge.

  Cambridge has a ring road on the west and .... of the city.

  The ring road on the west is the .... **(3 marks)**

2 Study the OS map of Warkworth on page 35.

  a Give the six figure grid reference for Alnmouth Station. Choose from the list below

      111231

      249129

      231111

      129249 **(1 mark)**

  b Find the level crossing in grid square 2306. What direction is the level crossing from Alnmouth station? **(1 mark)**

  c How far along the railway line to the nearest kilometre is the level crossing from Alnmouth station? Choose from the list below.

      1 km

      3 km

      5 km

      7 km **(1 mark)**

  d Look at the area south of grid line 07. Where is most of the woodland found? **(1 mark)**

Sample Examination Questions

Higher tier (cont.)

c   Suggest one reason why a flow diagram is a good way of representing data.   (1 mark)

d   The pedestrian data could have been represented using a different presentation technique. Name a different presentation technique you could use and explain why it would be appropriate.   (2 marks)

5   ICT skills have been used to produce Figure 9. Say how ICT can be used to help and enhance the collecting and displaying of data. Reference to flow line maps will not receive credit.   (4 marks)

Total 25 marks

Foundation tier (cont.)

e   Look at the beach from grid line 05 to grid line 12.

Describe three characteristics of the beach.   (3 marks)

3   Study Figure 10 (below). It is a graph showing people employed in industry

Complete the paragraph using information from Figure 10.

This type of graph is called a................................. The percentage of people working in primary industry is 20% in .... In Taiwan there is ....% working in tertiary industry. In Mali only 3% work in .... industry.   (4 marks)

4   Study Figure 9 on page 9.

a   How many pedestrians walked along St Leonards Road?   (1 mark)

b   On the same day 100 people walked along Victoria Street. How wide would you draw the flow line to represent this data?   (1 mark)

c   Suggest one reason why a flow diagram is a good way of representing data.   (1 mark)

d   The pedestrian data could have been represented using a different presentation technique.

Name two different presentation techniques you could use.   (2 marks)

5   ICT skills have been used to produce Figure 9 on page 9. State four ICT skills you could use when collecting or displaying data. Reference to flow line maps will not get a mark.   (4 marks)

Total 25 marks

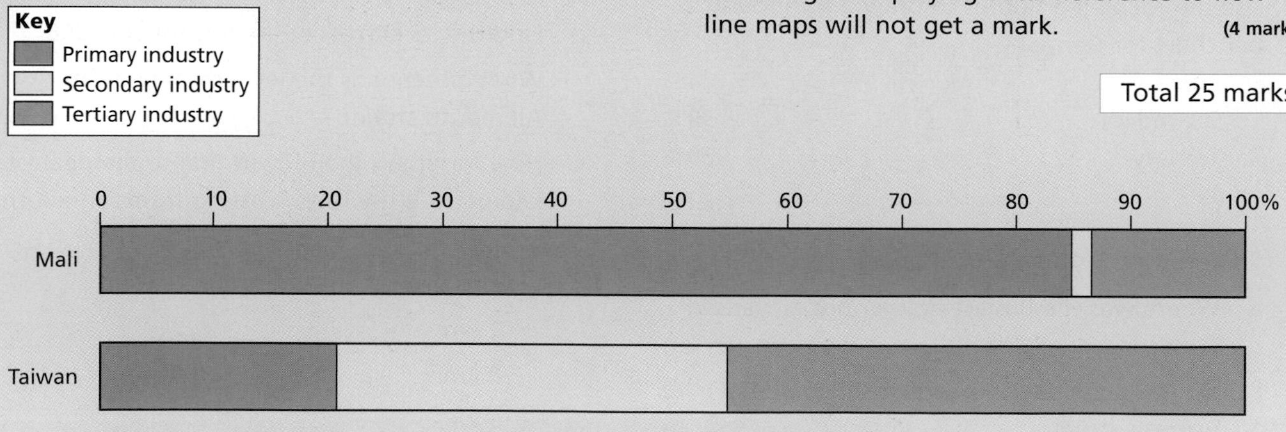

Key
- Primary industry
- Secondary industry
- Tertiary industry

	0	10	20	30	40	50	60	70	80	90	100%

Mali

Taiwan

Figure 10 Compound bar charts

The causes, effects and responses to climate change

> **Learning objective** – to study the causes and effects of climate change and how people have responded to the changes.
>
> **Learning outcomes**
> - To know how and why climate has changed since the last ice age.
> - To be able to discuss the causes of current climate change on a local and global scale.
> - To know the negative effects that climate change is having on the environment and people.
> - To be able to explain how people respond to climate change.

How has the world's climate changed since the last ice age?

The graph in Figure 1 shows the trend in the world's temperature since the end of the last ice age, approximately 10,000 years ago. The temperature since that time has increased by 6°C. Within this general trend, however, there have been a number of fluctuations. After the last ice age the temperature rose rapidly for the following 2,000 years. Between 4,000 and 8,000 years ago there were two warm periods interrupted by a colder spell. Another warm spell happened between the years AD800 and AD1200, which was known as the medieval warm period. There then followed the Little Ice Age where temperatures were below the long-term average for 600 years, ending in the late 1800s. In the past 100 years the temperature has begun to rise steadily, with greater increases since the 1960s. The temperature is projected to increase much more rapidly in the coming years, being 5°C warmer in 2100 than it is now.

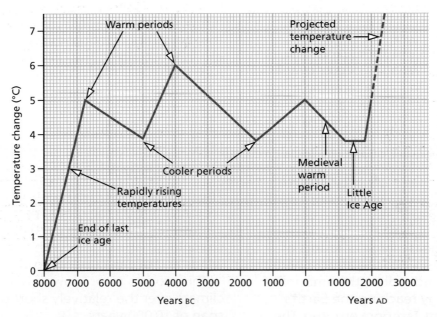

Figure 1 A graph of the world's temperature since 8000BC

Why has the world's climate changed since the last ice age?

The causes of long-term climate change can be either external, i.e. from space, or internal, from the ocean, land and atmosphere.

External factors which affect climate change

Solar output

This is energy that comes from the Sun. The energy that comes from the Sun changes over time. Measurements made in the 1980s showed that the total amount of solar energy reaching the Earth has decreased by 0.1 per cent. Although this is not much, if the trend continued for 100 years it could influence global climate. It has been predicted that a 1 per cent change in solar output could make the temperature rise or fall by between 0.5 and 1.0°C.

It is thought that the activity of sunspots on the Sun's surface affects solar output. There was a period of drastically reduced sunspot activity between 1645 and 1715 which might have been a cause of the Little Ice Age.

Orbital geometry

Orbital characteristics that are responsible for past and possible future climatic changes include:

1   The shape of the Earth's orbit around the Sun varies from nearly circular to elliptical and back to circular again every 95,000 years. Cold, glacial periods have occurred when the Earth's orbit is circular and warmer periods when it is more elliptical.

2   The tilt of the Earth's axis varies over time from 21.5° and 24.5°. This variation occurs over a 41,000 year time span. The greater the angle of the tilt, the hotter the summers are and the colder the winters are. When the angle is greater the Earth usually experiences warmer periods.

Internal factors which affect climate change

Volcanic activity

Volcanic eruptions release large amounts of sulphur dioxide and ash into the atmosphere. These act as a cloak and reduce the amount of solar (radiation) energy reaching the Earth's surface. In 1815 Mount Tambora erupted. The

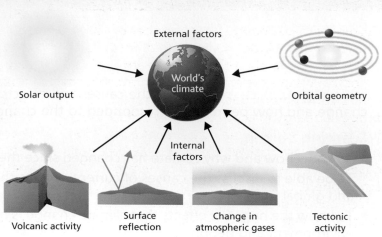

Figure 2 The factors that affect the world's climate

following year was unusually cold over much of the world with Europe having heavy snowfalls and frost throughout the summer; 1816 became known as 'the year without a summer'.

Surface reflection

During cooler periods when there is a larger amount of snow and ice on the Earth, global temperature will drop due to the snow and ice reflecting sunlight back to space. If the planet warms up, snow and ice will diminish, and the Earth will continue to get warmer.

Change in atmospheric gas

There is a clear relationship between the amount of carbon dioxide (CO_2) in the atmosphere and temperature variations. Carbon dioxide is one of the most important gases responsible for the greenhouse effect. The greenhouse effect keeps heat within the Earth's atmosphere by absorbing longwave radiation. Without the greenhouse effect, the average global temperature of the Earth would be minus 18°C rather than the present 15°C.

Tectonic activity

The movement of continents caused by plate tectonics affects the global pattern of atmospheric and ocean circulation; and the changing shape of the Earth's surface causes winds and ocean currents to change.

This process is too slow to have much effect on climate over the relatively short geological time span of 10,000 years.

The causes of current climate change on a local and global scale

Current climate change has a number of different causes; these include the burning of fossil fuels and the increase of methane in the atmosphere.

Fossil fuels are fuels which are produced from coal, oil and natural gas. These fuels are used to produce energy in power stations and to supply fuel to vehicles. In China 75 per cent of energy is produced from coal. When fossil fuels are burnt gases are released which build up in the atmosphere. One of these gases is carbon dioxide which contributes to the greenhouse effect causing climate to change. The generation of power accounts for 25 per cent of global carbon dioxide emissions. The use of fossil fuels to supply power to vehicles and to produce energy is dealt with in more detail in the sustainable section of this chapter.

Methane is a greenhouse gas; this means that it can trap heat within the Earth's atmosphere. It makes up 20 per cent of the greenhouse gases in the atmosphere and is 20 times more potent than carbon dioxide. Methane comes from organisms that were alive many years ago, recently dead rotting organisms and those alive today. Fossil methane which provides approximately 30 per cent of methane released into the atmosphere was formed underground many years ago. It comes to the surface when fossil fuels are mined.

Figure 3 A coal-fired power station

Modern methane comes from a variety of sources:

- wetlands including marshes and swamps
- the growing of rice
- landfills which contain rotting vegetable matter
- burning vegetation
- the bowels of animals.

The levels of methane in the atmosphere have been rising by 1.5 per cent a year for the past decade. This is due to:

- an increase in the mining of fossil fuels
- rising temperature, which causes an increase in bacteria emissions from wetlands
- an increase in rice production due to the growing population in rice producing countries
- an increase in the number of cattle and sheep for meat reflecting an increase in Western-style diets.

Figure 4 Rice paddies in China

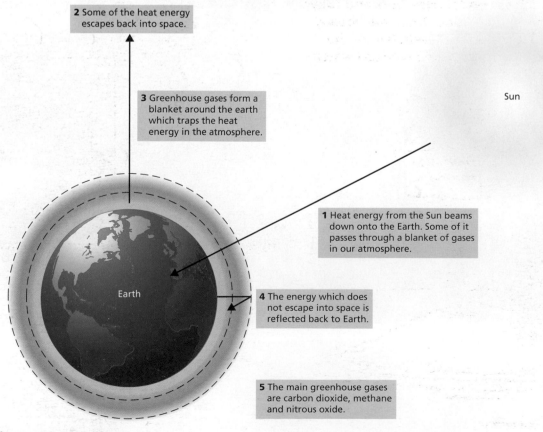

2 Some of the heat energy escapes back into space.

3 Greenhouse gases form a blanket around the earth which traps the heat energy in the atmosphere.

Sun

1 Heat energy from the Sun beams down onto the Earth. Some of it passes through a blanket of gases in our atmosphere.

Earth

4 The energy which does not escape into space is reflected back to Earth.

5 The main greenhouse gases are carbon dioxide, methane and nitrous oxide.

Figure 5 The greenhouse effect

The negative effects of climate change

Climate change has negative effects on the environment and people. These negative effects can be at both a local and a global scale. On a global scale there has been a change in crop yields, sea levels and glaciers.

Changing pattern of crop yields

Countries closest to the equator are likely to suffer the most as their crop yields will decrease. In Africa, countries such as Tanzania and Mozambique will have longer periods of drought and shorter growing seasons. They could lose almost a third of their maize crop. It is forecast that in India there will be a 50 per cent decrease in the amount of land available to grow wheat. This is due to hotter and drier weather.

Rising sea levels

Research published in 2007 by The Hadley Centre for Climate Change at Exeter, showed that between 1993 and 2006 sea levels rose 3.3 mm a year. This will lead to an 88 cm rise in sea levels by the end of the century. This rise will threaten large areas of low lying coastal land including major world cities such as London, New York and Tokyo.

Many islands in the Pacific Ocean are already being affected by rising sea levels. Two of the Kiribati islands are now covered with sea water.

People are also leaving other low lying coral atolls (islands) before they become engulfed by the sea.

Retreating glaciers

The vast majority of the world's glaciers are retreating (i.e. melting), some more quickly than others. This is thought by some to be due to the increase in temperatures caused by climate change. Research has shown that 90 per cent of the glaciers in Antarctica are retreating (see Figure 7). The melting of the glaciers at the poles could also affect ocean water movement. It is believed that melting ice in the Arctic could cause the Gulf Stream to be diverted further south. This will lead to colder temperatures in western Europe, matching the temperatures found across the Atlantic in Labrador at the present time. Temperatures are frequently below 0°C in the winter with averages of 8–10°C in July, which is 10°C cooler than the average UK summer temperature.

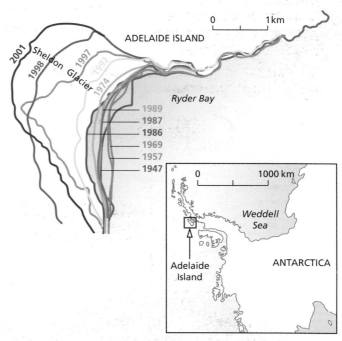

Figure 7 The retreat of the Sheldon glacier, Antarctica

Figure 6 Rising sea levels

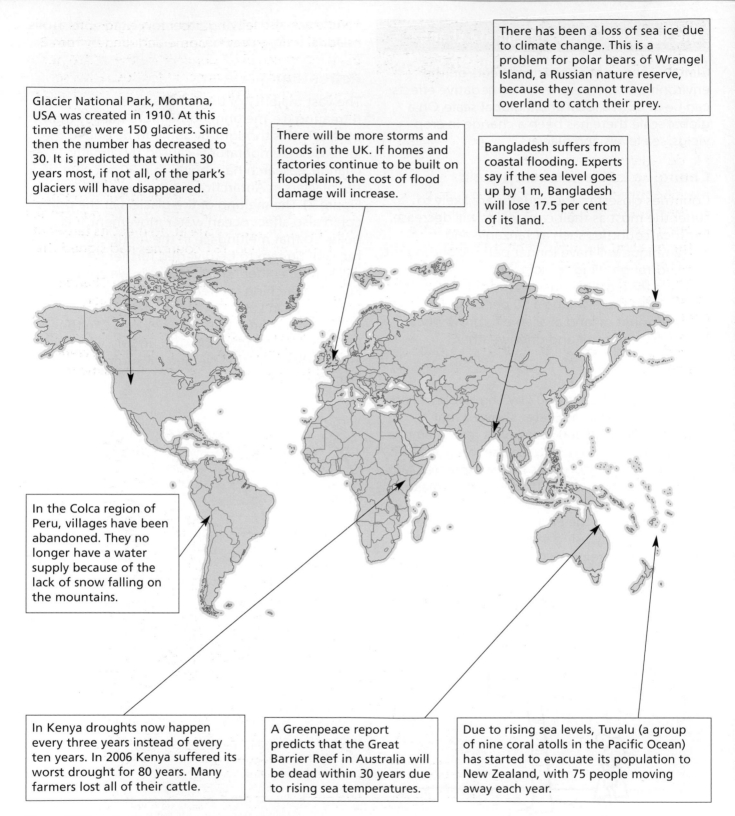

Glacier National Park, Montana, USA was created in 1910. At this time there were 150 glaciers. Since then the number has decreased to 30. It is predicted that within 30 years most, if not all, of the park's glaciers will have disappeared.

There will be more storms and floods in the UK. If homes and factories continue to be built on floodplains, the cost of flood damage will increase.

There has been a loss of sea ice due to climate change. This is a problem for polar bears of Wrangel Island, a Russian nature reserve, because they cannot travel overland to catch their prey.

Bangladesh suffers from coastal flooding. Experts say if the sea level goes up by 1 m, Bangladesh will lose 17.5 per cent of its land.

In the Colca region of Peru, villages have been abandoned. They no longer have a water supply because of the lack of snow falling on the mountains.

In Kenya droughts now happen every three years instead of every ten years. In 2006 Kenya suffered its worst drought for 80 years. Many farmers lost all of their cattle.

A Greenpeace report predicts that the Great Barrier Reef in Australia will be dead within 30 years due to rising sea temperatures.

Due to rising sea levels, Tuvalu (a group of nine coral atolls in the Pacific Ocean) has started to evacuate its population to New Zealand, with 75 people moving away each year.

Figure 8 The negative effects of climate change

The responses to climate change – from a local to a global scale

Global scale responses

Global agreements between nations

In June 1992 the United Nations held a meeting in Rio de Janeiro which has since been called the Earth Summit. This is because it was at this meeting that a number of decisions were made by the most powerful countries in the world about their response to climate change. The result of the meeting was the first international environment treaty which aimed to stabilise greenhouse gas emissions. This treaty lead to the Kyoto Protocol which was signed at the Kyoto conference in December 1997 and came into force in February 2005. Countries that signed and ratified the protocol agreed to cut greenhouse gas emissions by 5.2 per cent compared with 1990 levels globally. Each country agreed to a national limit on emissions which ranged from 8 per cent for the EU, 7 per cent for the USA, 6 per cent for Japan and 0 per cent for Russia. It also allowed increases of 10 per cent for Iceland and 8 per cent for Australia because they were not using all of their carbon allowance. In order to achieve their targets countries could either cut their emissions or trade with other countries in carbon. This means that a country could buy carbon credits from another country. For example, Iceland could trade 2 per cent of its carbon credits with the EU to enable the EU to meet its target of 8 per cent. By 2008, 181 countries had signed the Kyoto Protocol (see Figure 9).

In December 2007 a further Climate Change conference took place on the island of Bali, Indonesia where representatives of more than 180 countries were present. The result of the meeting was the Bali Roadmap in which initiatives were agreed to try to reach a secure future climate.

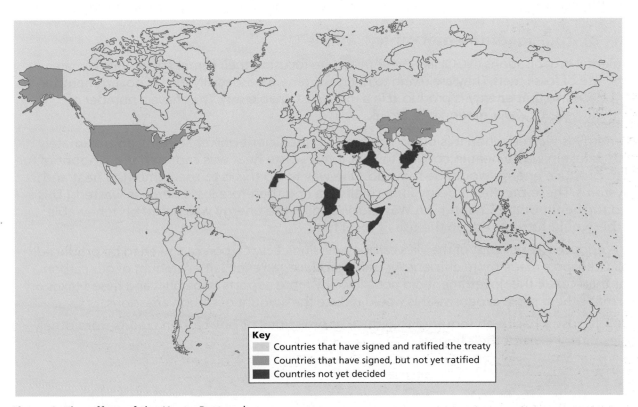

Key
Countries that have signed and ratified the treaty
Countries that have signed, but not yet ratified
Countries not yet decided

Figure 9 The effect of the Kyoto Protocol

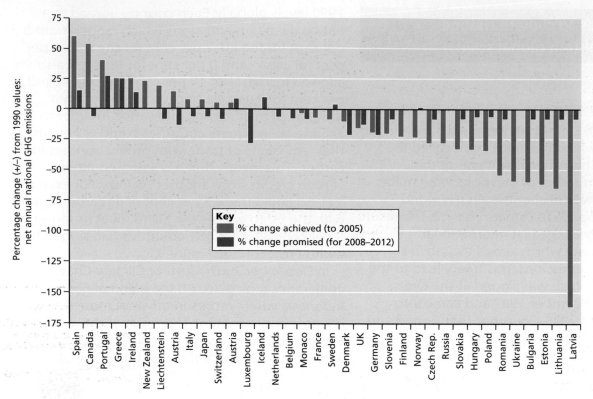

Figure 10 The 36 original Kyoto countries – what they had achieved by 2005 and what they promised to achieve by 2012

The actions of non-governmental organisations

Non-governmental organisations (NGO) like Greenpeace are focusing their campaign against climate change on the use of fossil fuels. They are trying to get governments, especially the UK government, to change their policies so that energy is produced in a more sustainable way. They have a number of solutions on their website: www. greenpeace.org.uk.

- A lot of energy is wasted when it is being produced in inefficient power stations; approximately two-thirds is lost in waste heat in cooling towers. If this waste heat was captured the amount of fuel needed to produce energy would be reduced. One way to do this is to use combined heat and power systems. These produce energy for a small area and therefore less energy is wasted. (This is discussed further in Unit 2 Chapter 7 A Wasteful World.) If the energy was based on renewable sources this would further reduce the use of fossil fuels.

- Transport produces 22 per cent of the UK's carbon emissions. Low carbon cars need to be produced and public transport made more efficient. Air traffic produces an even larger amount of our carbon emissions than cars. If the government did not allow any more airports to be built and raised taxes on flights to make them more expensive this would reduce the amount of carbon emissions.

- From 2005, industry has been required to reduce its emissions or buy carbon credits from other companies if they exceed their targets.

Local scale responses

By schools

'Livesimply' is a campaign which ran throughout the whole of 2007. It was initiated by the Catholic Church to encourage students to consider how they make choices in life. It provided a number of resources for schools which made students think about their impact on the world and sustainability.

Many schools are introducing energy efficient water and central heating systems run from renewable sources such as wind turbines or solar panels. (This is discussed further in Unit 2 Chapter 7.) Schools also have notices to switch off lights.

By local councils

The UK's target is to cut carbon emissions to 15 per cent below the 1990 levels by 2010 and 20 per cent by 2020. The government believes that the local councils are important in the reduction of carbon emissions as they have an influence on local home owners – 15 per cent of the UK's carbon emissions are produced by houses. Since April 2008 local councils' success in cutting carbon emissions has been one of their targets. To help them meet these targets the government has given them £4 million. The idea is for those local councils that have already introduced ideas to cut carbon emissions to help those that haven't. The six best councils are Eastleigh Borough Council, the City of London, Barking and Dagenham, Middlesbrough, Woking Borough Council and Worcestershire County Council. These councils have all introduced schemes which have cut carbon emissions. The changes can be as simple as giving away free low energy light bulbs or as sophisticated as Woking's CHP (combined heat and power) scheme. (This is dealt with in more detail in Unit 2 Chapter 7.)

By local interest groups

One such group is 'Manchester is my planet'. This group is running a 'pledge campaign' to encourage individuals to reduce their carbon footprint and become involved in a number of green energy projects. The group started in 2005 and works with the local council. There are now more than 20,000 individuals who have pledged to work towards a low carbon future. One of the initiatives is the Green Badge Parking Permit. People who own cars which have been recognised as having low carbon emissions can apply for a Green Badge Parking Permit which allows car owners to buy an annual parking permit for NCP car parks within Greater Manchester at a 25 per cent discount. The permit is valid for 12 months.

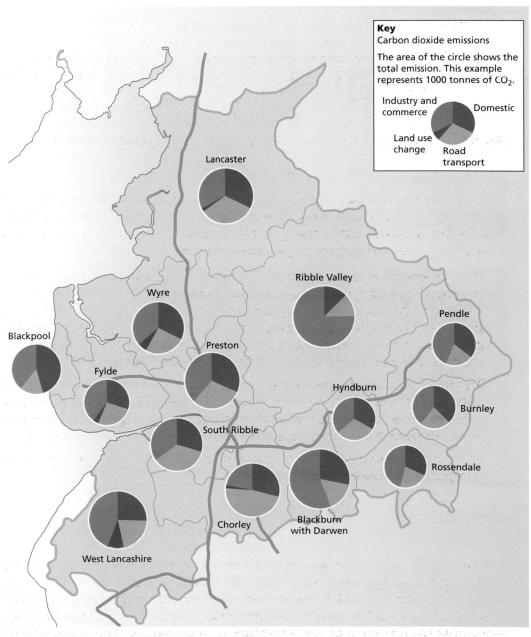

Figure 11 Carbon dioxide emissions in Lancashire

ACTIVITIES

Higher

1 Describe two factors which have caused climate to change since the last ice age.
2 Explain the greenhouse effect.
3 What is the Kyoto Protocol?
4 Why have so many countries signed the Kyoto Protocol?
5 The USA has signed the Kyoto Protocol but has not implemented it.
   Give reasons why.
6 Study Figure 8 on page 18. For each continent describe one effect of rising sea levels.

Extension

Use a search engine such as Google to research other initiatives which help to reduce carbon emissions. One which is useful is www.manchesterismyplanet.com

Foundation

1 Name one external factor which has caused climate to change.
2 Name two internal factors which have caused climate to change.
3 Rearrange the statements below to explain the greenhouse effect:
   Greenhouses gases form a blanket around the Earth which traps the heat energy in the atmosphere.
   The energy which does not escape into space is reflected back to Earth.
   Some of the heat energy escapes back into space.
   The main greenhouses gases are carbon dioxide, methane and nitrous oxide.
   Heat energy from the Sun beams down onto the Earth. Some of it passes through a blanket of gases in our atmosphere.
4 Study Figure 8 on page 18. Describe one effect of rising sea levels in Africa, South America, North America, Australia, Asia and Europe.
5 What is the Kyoto Protocol?
6 Why have so many countries signed the Kyoto Protocol?

Review

By the end of this section you should be able to:

- explain how and why climate has changed since the last ice age
- discuss the causes of current climate change on a local and global scale
- describe the negative effects that climate change is having on the environment and people
- explain how people respond to climate change.

Sustainable development for the planet

Learning objective – to study sustainable development.

Learning outcomes

- To learn definitions and interpretations of sustainable development.
- To be able to understand the policies of large organisations to make them more sustainable.
- To be able to explain the management of transport in urban areas.
- To be able to explain the effects of resource extraction from tropical rainforests and their management.

Definitions and interpretations of sustainable development

After decades of abusing the Earth's natural resources, concern grew about the effects that uncontrolled economic development was having on health and the environment. This led in 1980 to the United Nations releasing the Brundtland report.

It was this report that defined sustainable development as: 'development which meets the needs of the present without compromising the ability of future generations to meet their own needs.'

In order to formulate the definition of sustainable development the report focused on three areas:

- The conservation and enhancement of the environment by the development of new technologies.
- The achievement of social equality by developing countries being allowed to meet their basic needs of employment, food, energy, water and sanitation in a sustainable way.
- The economic growth of all countries in the world.

These ideas have been taken on and further developed over the past 30 years.

The values of the Brundtland report were reiterated in 1997 at a UNESCO meeting in Paris which made a further declaration regarding the responsibilities of the present generation towards future generations.

It stated that it was the responsibility of the present generation to bequeath to future generations an Earth which had not been irreversibly damaged by human activity. Natural resources should be used reasonably, life should not be harmed by modifications to ecosystems and that technological progress should not harm life on Earth.

A key area of sustainable development is that it should not hinder development but give a better quality of life both now and in the future.

In the UK four key sustainable areas have been identified.

- **Climate change and energy** – Reducing greenhouse gas emissions in the UK and worldwide while at the same time preparing for the climate change that cannot be avoided.
- **Natural resources** – The limits of the natural resources that sustain life, i.e. water, air and soil, are understood so that they can be used most efficiently.
- **Sustainable communities** – Places that people live and work in need to be looked after by implementing ideas such as ecotowns and green energy.
- **Sustainable consumption and production** – The ways that products are designed, produced, used and disposed of should be carefully controlled.

The development of policies by large companies to make them more sustainable

Large companies have realised that they must be more sustainable. They can achieve this in many different ways:

- during the manufacturing of the product
- in the recycling of packaging material
- by encouraging customers to recycle products
- by encouraging employees to be more sustainable in the workplace.

This desire to be more sustainable has led to other companies being developed which either produce equipment which allow waste products to be recycled or deal with the recycling of the products.

The food industry – Asda/Wal-Mart

The products which are sold in local Asda stores have travelled many miles. The last part of their journey is from a regional distribution centre. This is a large warehouse where products are stored until the local stores need them. They are then sent to the local stores by lorry. When the products arrive in the distribution centre they are packed in polythene and shrink wrap. The distribution centre in Didcot, Oxfordshire used to fill a skip four times a week and send it to a landfill site. This was costing Asda a lot of money and was not a sustainable way of dealing with the waste. The problem was solved by a company called Mil-tek that makes machines to bale plastic. They installed a large machine in the warehouse in Didcot. All of the waste plastic is now put into the baler and crushed to 10 per cent of its original size. The bales of plastic are collected once a week by a firm which recycles plastic. This is benefiting Asda which now receives money for the plastic instead of having to pay to have it taken away. It is also benefiting the environment because no plastic is being sent to landfill sites.

The communications industry – Nokia

Nokia are concerned that people do not recycle their old phones. This is a very serious situation, as more than 50 per cent of mobile phone users change their phone every year; 44 per cent of these old phones are left in drawers at home and are never used again. Nokia is trying to persuade people to hand in their old phones to recycling points because 100 per cent of the phone can be recycled. Old mobiles can be used in the manufacture of trumpets, park benches or even gold rings. If every mobile phone user recycled one phone it would save 240,000 tonnes of raw materials. Nokia are promoting this campaign in stores which sell their phones and with a very catchy jingle on their website – www. nokia.com. This website also gives information on where to find recycling points and the address to send the phone to if there is not a centre nearby.

A global company – General Electric

This is a large transnational corporation (TNC) which operates in many different countries. The company has introduced many policies to make it operate in a more sustainable way. One of their pledges is that by 2012 they will reduce fresh water usage by 20 per cent. This is expected to save 7.4 million cubic metres of water which is enough to fill 3,000 Olympic sized swimming pools. This will be achieved by assessing their water usage and improving their water recycling. Much of the water in their boilers and cooling towers will be recycled water.

Power generation – coal-fired power stations

Coal-fired power stations provide 38 per cent of the world's energy and in countries such as India and China they provide more than 50 per cent. This reliance on coal as an energy source and the resultant pollution means that coal-fired power stations need to be as efficient as possible in order to produce the least amount of pollution. Coal-fired power stations emit large amounts of carbon dioxide (CO_2), sulphur dioxide (SO_2) and nitrous oxide (N_2O). The emissions of these gases are a major contributor to both acid rain and climate change. The control of these emissions has been dealt with, with varying degrees of success.

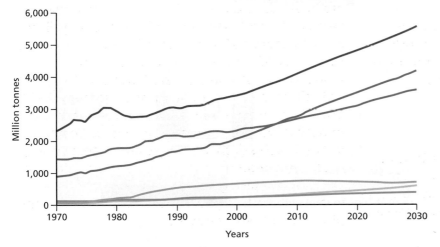

Key
- Coal
- Oil
- Gas
- Nuclear
- Hydro
- Other renewables

Figure 12 World energy usage 1970 to 2030

Carbon dioxide

One way of reducing CO_2 emissions is to make the power plant more efficient. Most power stations are only 36 per cent efficient. If this is raised to 40 per cent efficiency, CO_2 emissions drop by 25 per cent. The other way to deal with CO_2 emissions is to capture it from the flue gases. The technology to do this consists of amine scrubbers which use amine solutions to remove CO_2 from the waste gases. These can remove up to 98 per cent of CO_2 from the waste gases.

Sulphur dioxide

Many coal-fired power stations have systems which operate in the flue of the boiler to remove SO_2 emissions by about 60 per cent. If scrubbers are fitted into the flue the figure rises to about 95 per cent of the emissions being removed. In Germany all coal-fired power stations have scrubbers fitted but this is not the case in low income countries (LICs).

Nitrous oxide

Most power stations have systems fitted that will remove up to 70 per cent of nitrogen emissions.

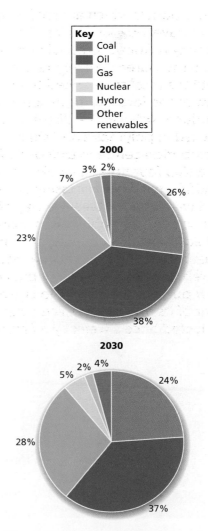

2000

2030

Figure 13 How energy is produced – 2000 and 2030

The use of video conferencing reduces a company's carbon footprint.

Hotel companies have a policy of only washing towels if the clients ask them to, therefore reducing water usage and soap powder.

Schools often have separate waste bins for paper and card in their classrooms. Pupils are also encouraged by signs to switch off lights. Most schools also have their computers controlled centrally so that a piece of software switches all the computers off and on in the school at set times.

The internet (email) is being used more to send information and documents. This means that less paper is being used. Many companies aim to become paperless in the future.

Large companies provide their employees with a variety of different bins to deal with waste products. There are not only bins for waste paper but also for other types of waste. There are notices to switch off lights and push taps in toilets to conserve water.

Tourist destinations provide a variety of ways to recycle waste.

Sustainable development in Dartmoor National Park

Figure 14 Sustainability in the workplace

The management of transport in urban areas

Sustainable transport involves maintaining the standard of transport that is required for society and the economy to function efficiently without placing too much pressure on the environment.

In the Sustainable Development Strategy for the UK, the government has stated that it will need to take action to control the rate of traffic growth, improve the performance of vehicles and make the public aware about the environmental impacts of polluting emissions from transport. People need to be encouraged to reduce their dependency on cars, but affordable alternative public transport systems must be available to allow them to do this.

In urban areas of the world there is a great dependency on the car as a means of transport. In both high income countries (HICs) and LICs people are becoming ever more dependent on private vehicles for moving around the city. Car ownership is growing most rapidly in LICs and HICs. In Delhi, India the number of vehicles in the city has grown from half a million in 1970 to more than 5 million in 2008.

Governments want people to give up using their cars and use public transport more frequently. The problem is that the car drivers will not use public transport until it is cheaper and more efficient.

It is imperative that this growing number of vehicles is managed to control the problems of congestion and pollution.

There are two ways to manage traffic in urban areas:

1 Respond to the increasing demand by building more roads. This might help congestion but will eventually lead to even more vehicles and an increase in pollution levels.

2 Reduce traffic with a range of sustainable schemes. A wide range of sustainable transport schemes has been introduced around the world to alleviate the problems of congestion and pollution.

Sustainable transport schemes

Congestion charging

Congestion charging is the practice of making motorists pay to travel into large urban areas during periods of heaviest use. The aim is to reduce the number of vehicles entering the city which will ease traffic congestion and therefore lower pollution emissions. It will hopefully lead to more sustainable forms of transport like walking, cycling or public transport being used.

The first city to introduce a congestion charge was Singapore. Motorists in Singapore have been charged to go into the central city area since 1974.

A number of other cities have now introduced congestion charging zones including Oslo, London and Stockholm.

London introduced the congestion charge in 2003. By 2008 it had had the following beneficial effects:

- Traffic levels have been reduced by 21 per cent.

- 65,000 fewer car journeys a day.

- An increase of 29,000 bus passengers entering the zone during the morning peak rush period.

- A 12 per cent increase in cycle journeys within the zone.

- 12 per cent reduction in the emission of nitrous oxide and fine particulates.

Durham, which introduced a congestion charge in 2002, has seen an 85 per cent drop in traffic entering the paying zone, and Stockholm's six-month trial period saw a 25 per cent decrease.

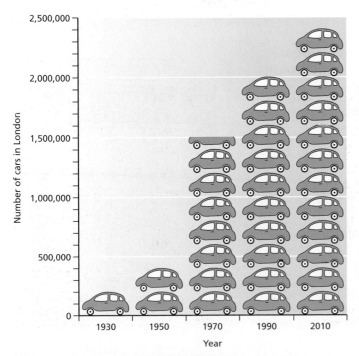

Figure 15 Increase in car ownership

Park and ride

Park and ride schemes allow shoppers to park their cars in large designated parking areas on the edge of the urban area and catch a bus into the town centre. Park and ride operates in 87 towns and cities in the UK. Parking is free but there is often a charge for bus travel to the city centre. The park and ride sites are usually located on the main routes coming into the urban area, so they are easily accessible for the greatest number of car users. There are environmental reasons for park and ride. Approximately 40 people will travel on one bus rather than in 40 individual vehicles, which means there will be much less congestion and pollution.

Cambridge park and ride

Cambridge has five park and ride sites covering all the main routes coming into the city (see Figure 16). The Madingly and Trumpington road sites are next to the M11 and the Milton and Newmarket road sites are close to the A14 giving easy access for motorists driving into Cambridge from the surrounding area. There are 4,500 parking spaces available. Double-decker buses carrying up to 70 passengers leave the parks every 10 minutes during the day from Monday to Saturday. It costs £2.20 per day to catch the bus into the city centre. The sites are well lit and have security systems operating during opening hours. There are waiting rooms, toilets and baby changing facilities.

Other sustainable transport schemes

There is a range of other sustainable transport schemes which can be used including:

- Car sharing where workers share lifts to work using their own cars. If half of UK motorists received a lift one day a week, vehicle congestion and pollution would be reduced by 10 per cent, and traffic jams by 20 per cent.
- Designated cycle and walking paths within the urban area. Milton Keynes is one of the best served urban areas in the UK with 273 km of cycle paths.
- Road lanes that only allow cars with at least two passengers to use them.
- Pedestrianised areas which restrict private vehicle access, but allow buses and trams to operate.
- Road lanes which give priority to buses, ensuring they get an easy passage through congested areas.
- Restricting car parking in central urban areas so motorists are forced to use public transport.

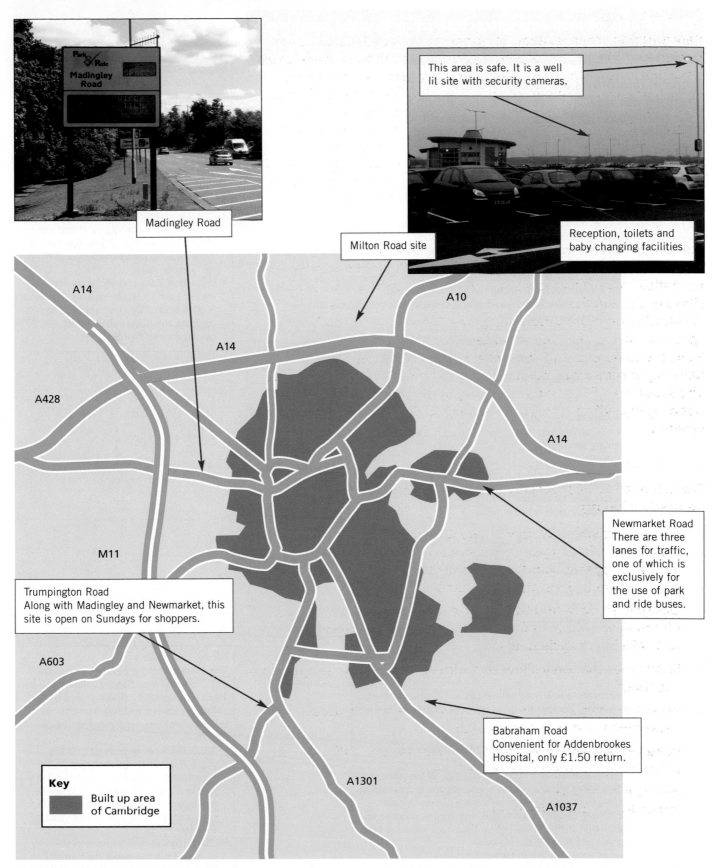

Madingley Road

This area is safe. It is a well lil site with security cameras.

Milton Road site

Reception, toilets and baby changing facilities

A14

A14

A10

A428

A14

M11

Newmarket Road
There are three lanes for traffic, one of which is exclusively for the use of park and ride buses.

Trumpington Road
Along with Madingley and Newmarket, this site is open on Sundays for shoppers.

A603

Babraham Road
Convenient for Addenbrookes Hospital, only £1.50 return.

A1301

Key
Built up area of Cambridge

A1037

Figure 16 Cambridge park and ride schemes

The effects of resource extraction from tropical rainforests and their management

Tropical rainforests are being destroyed at the rate of 32,000 hectares per day. The size of the remaining forest is about 5 per cent of the world's land surface. Much of the area which remains has been impacted on by human activities and does not contain its original biodiversity (see Figure 17).

Mining in Brazil
A variety of minerals are extracted from the Amazon Rainforest in Brazil.
Effects
- The Carajas iron ore mining project uses wood from the forest to power its pig iron plants, resulting in annual deforestation of 6100 km2 .
- Mercury is used in gold mining. The mercury is very toxic and is found in high concentration in fish. 90% of all fish caught in the gold mining region surrounding the River Tapajos is contaminated with mercury. If eaten it causes cancer and high miscarriage rates among the local tribespeople.
- In the state of Roraima there have been conflicts between gold prospectors and the indigenous Yanomamo Indians.

Logging in Cameroon
Large areas of the Cameroon have been cut down for commercial wood production.
Effects
- Roads built by the logging companies have opened up the forest for illegal loggers and commercial hunting. This has led to the slaughtering of mammals such as elephant, gorilla and chimpanzees whose meat is sold at high prices to restaurants.
- The Baka pigmies are often employed for a few days to show logging companies the best trees which unwittingly lead to them causing the destruction of their own environment.
- If the local Baka work in the sawmills they are not given protective clothing. The wood is often treated with toxic products against parasites and fungus which the workers can breath into their lungs.

Oil extraction in Ecuador
Oil is extracted from the Oriente region of Ecuador
Effects
- Toxic waste water mixed with crude oil seeps out of 600 unlined pits into the subsoil, polluting surrounding freshwater and farmland.
- Hydrocarbons are concentrated 200 – 300 times more in the water than is permissible in water used for human consumption. Stomach cancer is five times more frequent in oil exploitation areas and there are many more miscarriages amongst indigenous people such as the Huaorani.
- Many plants such as the periwinkle which can be used to cure childhood leukemia are now an endangered species.

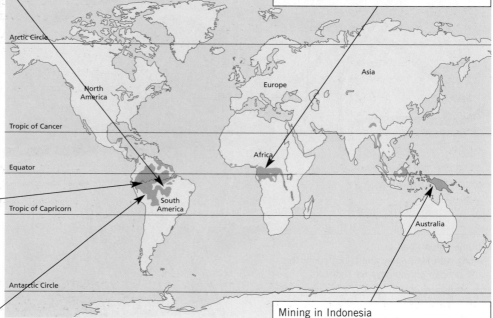

Gas project in Peru
In the Camisea region there is a large natural gas and pipeline project. Camisea is home to many Amazonian tribes including the Yine, Nanti and Nahua.
Effects
- Deforestation has caused drainage patterns to be altered, habitats destroyed and animal movements to be disturbed.
- It has also caused soil erosion and landslides resulting in the silting up of local rivers. Due to the silting there has been a decline in fish catches which has caused a rise in malnutrition particularly among children.
- The tribal people have caught diseases that they are not immune to. During the 1980s half of the Nahua people died from influenza and whooping cough caught from Shell employees.
- Only one in four of the Nanti live to be teenagers
- Many roads through the forest have been built due to the Camisea project. This has caused colonists to be attracted to the area who further destroy the forest by setting up farms.

Mining in Indonesia
The Freeport mining company mines gold and copper in West Papua, Indonesia since 1960. The company mines an area of 3.6 million hectares stretching from the coast to the central mountain range at Timika.
Effects
- 285000 tonnes of untreated mining waste is dumped into the River Aghawaghon every day. This pollutes the river and the coastal area by the river's mouth at Etna Gulf and poisons the fish. Local communities now have a shortage of water.
- The crocodiles and tortoises in the area of Teluk Etna Indonesia are currently on the brink of extinction due to pollution.
- The locals are exploited by being given the lowest paid jobs.

Figure 17 The effects of resource extraction from tropical rainforest

Tropical rainforest management

Tropical rainforests are being managed in different ways. One way is for the government of countries to take control of their forest areas. This can either be to ban any type of development or resource extraction, or to sustainably develop the rainforest areas. Another way is for non-governmental organisations (NGOs) to directly help local communities in rainforest areas.

French Guiana

The government of France, which controls the rainforest in French Guiana in South America, has refused to allow a gold mine. This was decided after an environmental assessment had been carried out. IAMGOLD, a Canadian mining company, wanted to mine gold in the Kaw Mountain area. This is close to a rainforest reserve and Kaw swamp which is a Ramsar-listed wetland. This area is home to 700 plant species, 100 different animals and 254 bird species. The open-cast mine would have affected the biodiversity of the area and put water containing cyanide into the Kaw swamp.

Costa Rica

Costa Rica is developing its rainforest in a sustainable way. One of the ways is through ecotourism. Many areas of the country have developed tourist facilities such as zip wiring and trails through the forest which are very popular with the tourists. Another way that Costa Rica is sustainably developing its forest is through its plant species. The Costa Rican government has allowed the American company Merck to look for plants which can be used to make medicines or fragrances for perfumes. The Costa Rican government will get a share of the profits of any products that are sold.

Malaysia

In Malaysia the government has rejected plans to build a coal-fired power plant at Silam, on the island of Borneo. It decided that the site was too close to the ecologically sensitive areas of Darvel Bay and Danum Valley. The government decided that it did not want to pollute the area and more environmentally friendly forms of energy would need to be found. The country has vast reserves of coal and other minerals such as gold. The government will not develop these resources at the expense of the rainforest which has many endangered species such as the orang-utan. Instead the government are going to develop ecotourism, emphasising the natural attractions such as world-class diving and the biologically diverse tropical rainforest.

Venezuela

Since 2008 the government of Venezuela has not issued any more permits to mine gold or diamonds in the Imataca Rainforest Reserve or anywhere else in the country. The country does not need to exploit the minerals for economic reasons, due to its oil reserves, therefore it can afford to conserve its forest area. This followed attacks on local people from illegal miners. The government will now protect both the biodiversity of the forest and the local people.

Madagascar

In 2001, Givaudan, a Swiss company, sent a team to Madagascar to survey for new fragrances. It developed 40 aromas which were then sold. The company shared the profits with local communities through conservation and development initiatives.

Figure 18 Ecotourism in Costa Rica

Ecuador

Oil has been extracted from the Amazon rainforest in Ecuador since the 1960s. The companies have done very little to manage the effects of the extraction. Recently the local indigenous people have taken the oil companies to court because of the destruction of their environment.

Texaco have agreed to pay $40 million to cover its share for cleanup of, among other things, some 160 of the 600 waste pits created. But the chief of the local Secoya tribe stated that $6 billion was needed to do the job properly.

Maxus Energy, the company that extracts oil from Yasuni National Park, has built an underground pipeline which has less of an environmental impact. They have provided schools for the local Huaorani and Quichua tribes and invested $60 million in environmental protection.

Bolivia

Another form of management is through carbon credits. Developing countries can set aside some of their forest and receive carbon credits. Industrialised countries can then buy these credits off the country and in this way the developing country earns money from its forest. The largest carbon credit project in the world is in Bolivia. The project is based in the Noel Kempff National Park which is an area of 1.5 million hectares and has been a UNESCO World Heritage Site since 2000. Bolivia has received £25 million by selling the carbon credits of this area. The money has gone straight to the communities who live in the areas as compensation. This means that they are no longer dependent upon logging and destroying the forest to farm to earn a living. The project is run by NGOs including the Friends of Nature Foundation and the Nature Conservancy.

Nature Conservancy

Nature Conservancy is an NGO which works with indigenous people in the Amazon Rainforest. The indigenous people now have the right to their land which is 20 per cent of the Amazon Rainforest. Nature Conservancy works with these people to help them develop the forest sustainably. They involve the whole community in their projects which usually start with ethnomapping. The first step is a satellite image of the area which the local people draw onto. They identify such things as natural resources, villages, and where illegal hunting, mining or logging takes place. This process can take many months. When it is complete it is taken away and digitised, then returned to the local people. The whole community then use the map to plan their use of the area.

In 2006 a training centre opened in Manaus, Brazil. The centre trains local people how to manage their areas; the first course is how to complete the ethnomapping exercise. Fifteen students are trained at a time and learn such things as GIS, remote sensing techniques, natural resource management and indigenous and environmental legislation. The students remain at the training centre for five months.

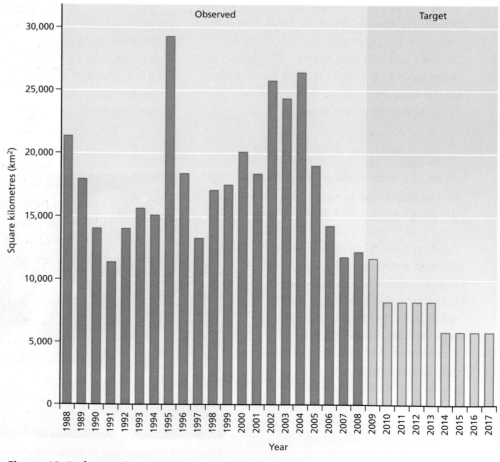

Figure 19 Deforestation in the Brazilian Amazon

ACTIVITIES

1 What is sustainable development?

2 Choose one area of business such as the communications industry. Explain the policies which have been developed by organisations in this industry to make them more sustainable.

3 Two ways that transport can be sustainably managed are explained in this chapter.

   a Choose one of them and explain why it is sustainable.

   b Developing alternative forms of public transport is another sustainable transport initiative that has been developed in Sheffield. Use the internet to help you describe and explain why using a tram network is a sustainable transport initiative.

Extension

Many other cities including Edinburgh and Manchester in 2008 have rejected charging vehicles to enter the city. Why have they done this?

Review

By the end of this section you should be able to:

- define and understand different interpretations of sustainable development
- understand the policies which large organisations implement to make them more sustainable
- explain the management of transport in urban areas
- explain the effects of resource extraction from tropical rainforests and their management.

Sample Examination Questions

Higher tier

1 Study Figure 1 on page 13. It shows how climate has changed in the past 10,000 years.

   a In the past 10,000 years, when was the world's temperature at its highest? **(1 mark)**

   b Describe the climate change in the past 10,000 years. Use data in your answer. **(4 marks)**

   c Many factors have caused the climate to change in the past 10,000 years. Explain how the Earth's movement in space can cause climate change. **(4 marks)**

2 Climate change has negative impacts on the environment. What impacts will rising sea levels have on the environment? **(2 marks)**

3 There have been many meetings by the governments of countries about climate change.

   The Kyoto Protocol and the Bali Roadmap were the results of two of these meetings. For any one meeting of governments concerning climate change that you have studied:

   State the main aims of the meeting and explain its successes. **(4 marks)**

Foundation tier

1 Study Figure 1 on page 13. It shows how climate has changed in the past 10,000 years.

   a How many degrees warmer was the Earth in the year AD2000 than in 8000BC? **(1 mark)**

   b The following paragraph describes the climate change in the past 10,000 years. Complete the paragraph. Use some of the words in the box.

5,000	slowly	200	highest	800	gradually
lowest	600	rapidly	3,000	4000	

   From 8000BC the temperature rose .... for 1,200 years. The climate has fluctuated. The .... temperature was 10,000 years ago when it was 5°C lower than the present temperature. There have been warm and cold periods. .... years BC was a warm period. The Little Ice Age lasted .... years. **(4 marks)**

   c Many factors have caused the climate to change in the past 10,000 years. The Earth's movement in space can cause climate change. Say whether the following statements are true or false.

Higher tier (cont.)

4   Study the photographs below in Figures 20 and 21. They show ways that large organisations are becoming more sustainable. Explain how these ways can make large organisations more sustainable. **(4 marks)**

5   Transport can be managed in urban areas to become more sustainable.

Chosen urban area ....

Explain how transport has been managed in a sustainable way. **(6 marks)**

Total 25 marks

Figure 20

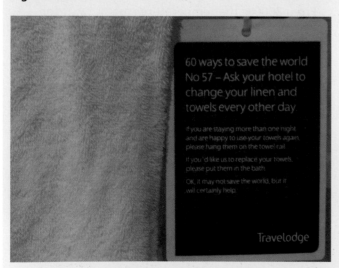

Figure 21

Foundation tier (cont.)

Statements	True	False
The shape of Earth's orbit around the Sun varies.		
The Earth's orbit around the Sun is star shaped.		
Cold, glacial periods have occurred when the Earth's orbit is circular.		
The Earth tilts on its axis.		

(4 marks)

2   Climate change has negative impacts on the environment. What impacts will rising sea levels have on the environment? **(2 marks)**

3   The Kyoto Protocol and the Bali Roadmap were global meetings about climate change.

Choose one of these meetings.

Chosen meeting...

a   What were the main aims? **(2 marks)**

b   Was the meeting successful? Explain your answer. **(4 marks)**

4   Study the photographs in Figures 20 and 21. They show ways that large organisations are becoming more sustainable.

a   What sustainable method is the organisation using in Figure 20? **(1 mark)**

b   Describe how the organisation in Figure 21 is trying to become more sustainable. **(3 marks)**

5   Transport can be managed in urban areas to become more sustainable. Study Figure 16 on page 29.

a   How many park and ride sites are there at Cambridge? **(1 mark)**

b   What has been done at Newmarket road to allow park and ride buses to flow easily? **(1 mark)**

c   How many of the park and ride sites are open on Sunday? **(1 mark)**

d   State one way that park and ride schemes are sustainable. **(1 mark)**

Total 25 marks

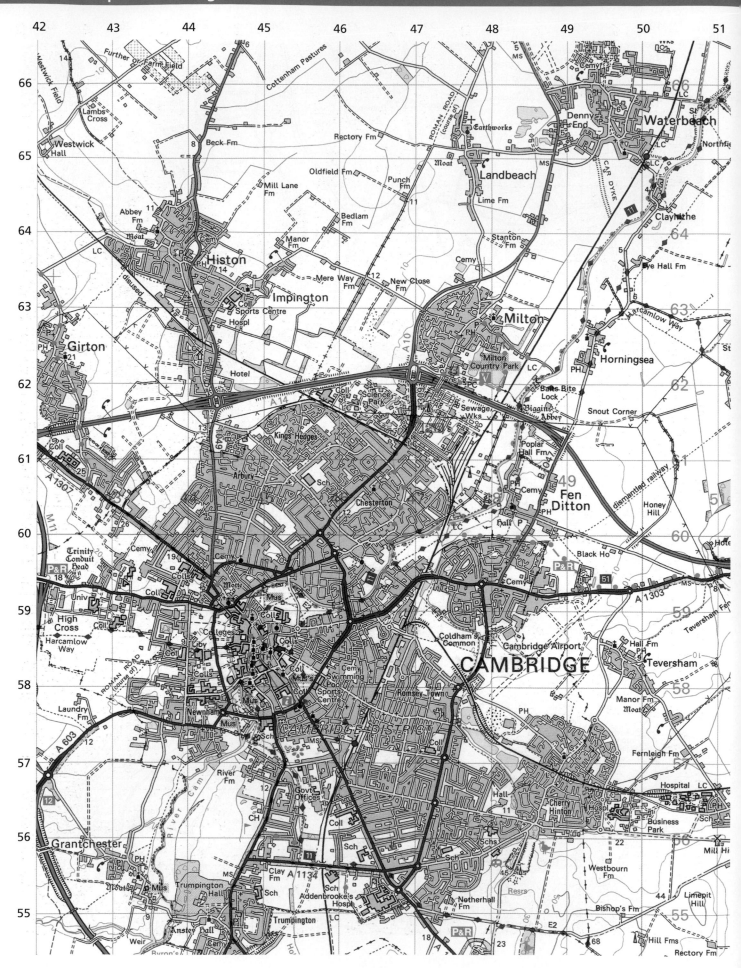

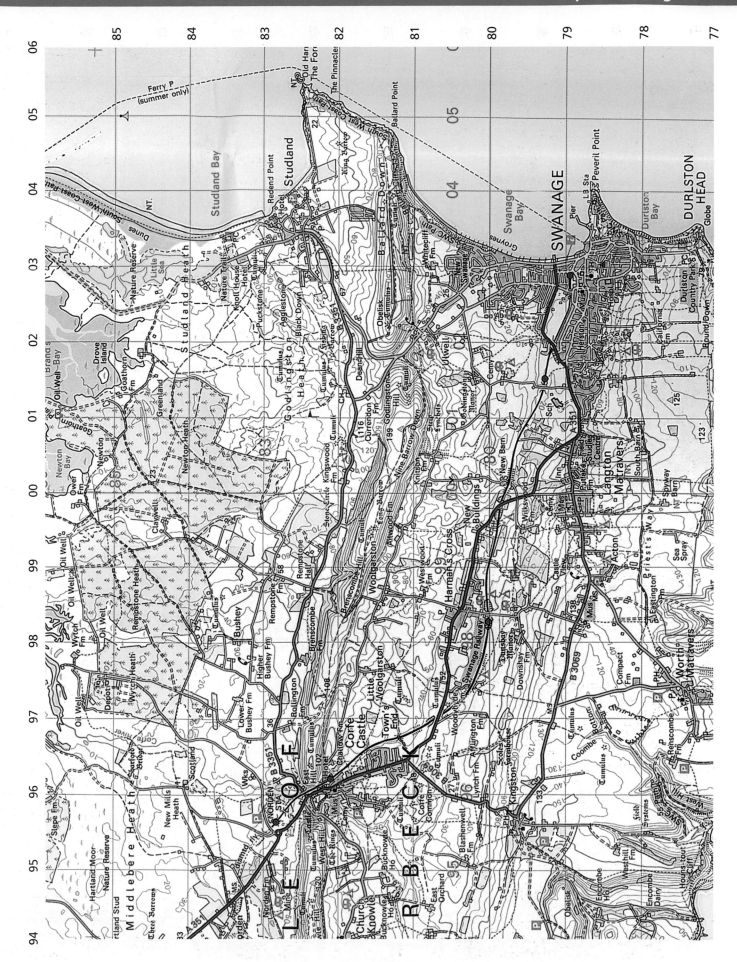

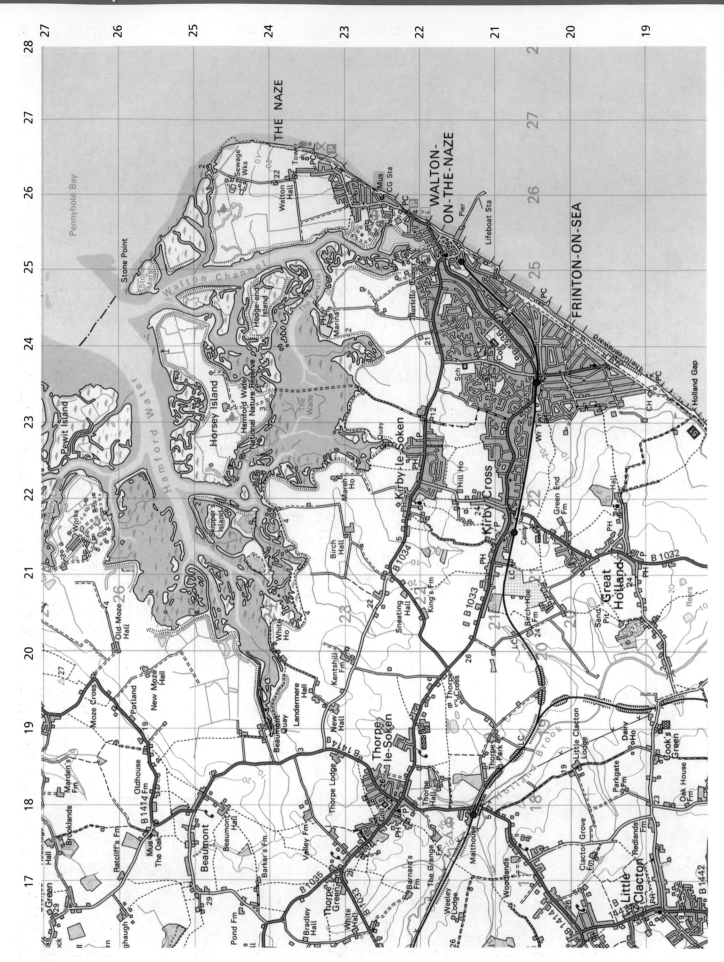

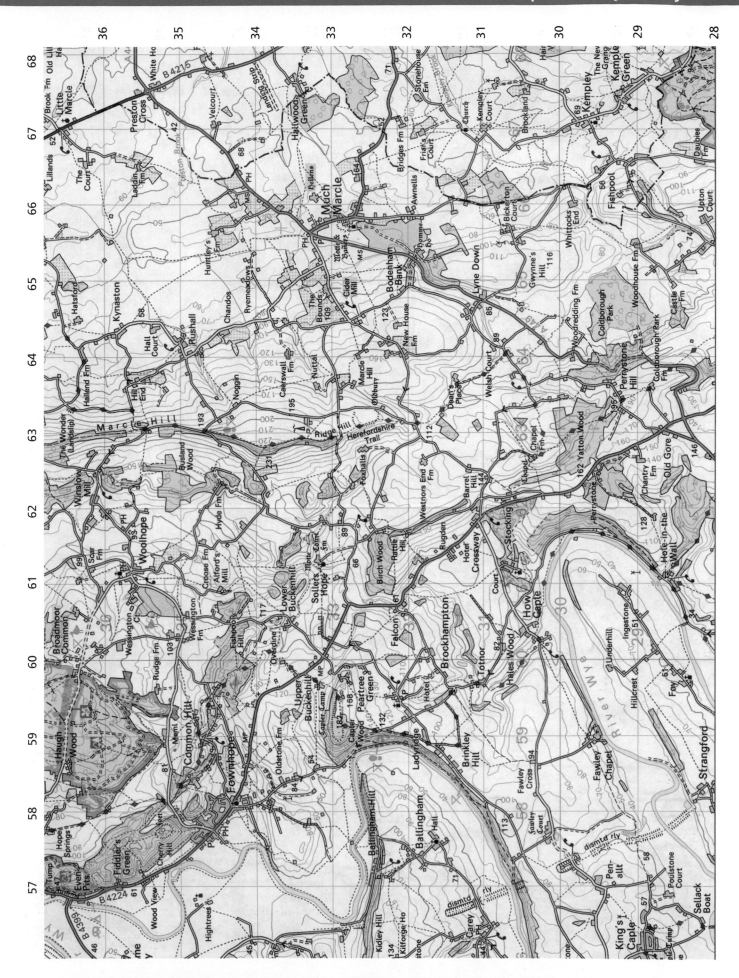

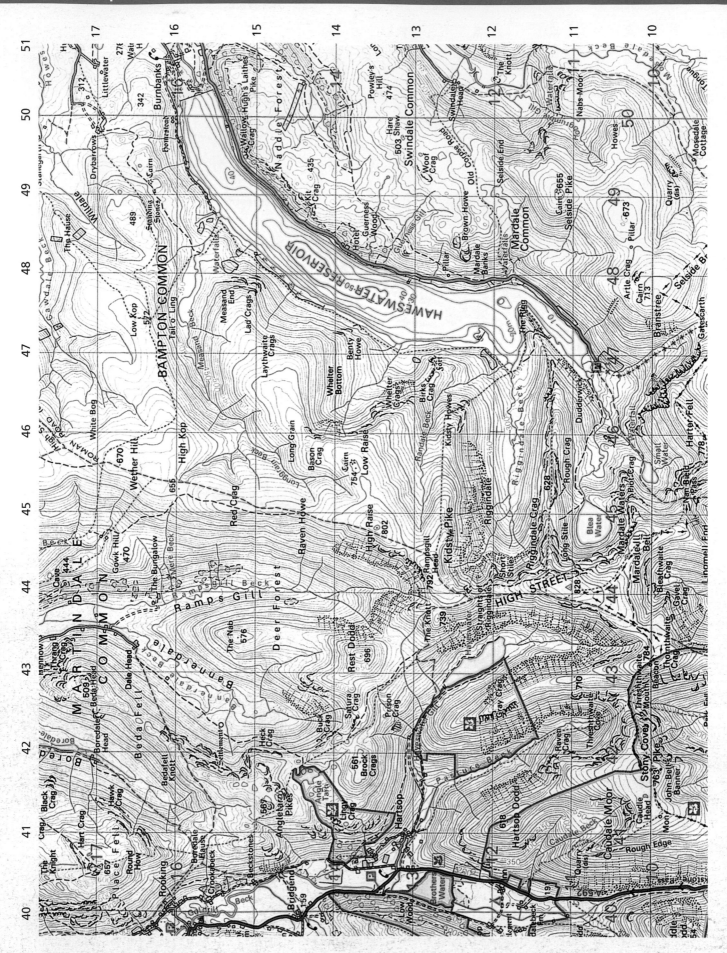

UNIT 2
The Natural Environment

This unit is about physical geography and environmental issues. There are six chapters.

- **Chapter 3 Coastal Landscapes:** the formation of some coastal landforms and how coastal areas are managed.

- **Chapter 4 River Landscapes:** the formation of some river landforms, how rivers flood and the ways flooding is prevented.

- **Chapter 5 Glaciated Landscapes:** the formation of some glaciated landforms and the ways that people use glaciated landscapes.

- **Chapter 6 Tectonic Landscapes:** the location, characteristics and management of earthquakes and volcanoes.

- **Chapter 7 A Wasteful World:** types of waste, how waste is recycled, sources of energy and their management.

- **Chapter 8 A Watery World:** how water is used in different countries, water inequalities, the management and conflicts of water.

3 Coastal Landscapes

Coastal processes produce landforms

Learning objective – to study the landforms of the coastal area and the processes that occur there.

Learning outcomes
- To know the characteristics of destructive and constructive waves.
- To understand the impact of weathering, erosion and mass movement on the coast.
- To be able to describe and explain the formation of cliffs and wave-cut platforms, headlands and bays, caves, arches, stacks and stumps.
- To recognise the impact of longshore drift on the coastline.
- To be able to describe and explain the formation of beaches, spits and bars.

Figure 1 Aerial photo of Swanage facing North

What types of waves are there?

Destructive waves

Destructive waves are mainly responsible for coastal erosion and for taking sediment away from coastlines. They have a number of characteristics:

- The backwash is much stronger than the swash and is therefore able to carry sand and pebbles away from the shore.
- They break frequently; there are between ten and fifteen every minute.
- They are high in proportion to their length.
- They are generally found on steep beaches.

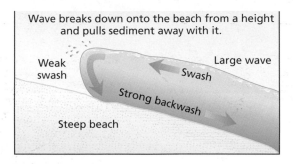

Wave breaks down onto the beach from a height and pulls sediment away with it.

Weak swash · Large wave · Swash · Strong backwash · Steep beach

Figure 2a A destructive wave

Constructive waves

Constructive waves are responsible for deposition in coastal areas. They have a number of characteristics:

- The swash is more powerful than the backwash and therefore deposits sediment on beaches.
- They break infrequently at a rate of ten or fewer per minute.
- They are long in relation to their height.
- They are usually found on gently sloping beaches.

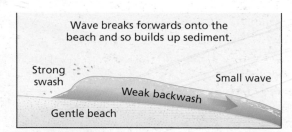

Wave breaks forwards onto the beach and so builds up sediment.

Strong swash · Small wave · Weak backwash · Gentle beach

Figure 2b A constructive wave

How are coasts eroded?

The coast is a narrow strip between land and sea. It is under continual attack from waves at the base of the cliff and other processes on the cliff face such as weathering and mass movement. (You should always refer to these processes when answering a question on landform formation.) The theory box below should be referred to throughout this chapter to understand the processes of erosion.

These processes are the main ways in which the sea erodes the base of a cliff.

The processes of coastal erosion:
Hydraulic action – this is the pressure of the water being thrown against the cliffs by the wave. It also includes the compression of air in cracks: as the water gets into cracks in the rock face, it compresses the air in the cracks; this puts even more pressure on the cracks and pieces of rock may break off.
Corrasion – sand and pebbles carried within waves are thrown against the cliff face with considerable force. These particles break off more rocks which, in turn, are thrown against the cliff by the breaking wave.
Corrosion (solution) – this is a chemical reaction between certain rock types and the salt and other acids in seawater. This is particularly evident on limestone and chalk cliffs where the water is a milky blue at the bottom of the cliffs due to the dissolved lime.
Attrition – this is a slightly different process that involves the wearing away of the rocks which are in the sea. As the boulders in the sea continually roll around, they chip away at each other until smooth pebbles or sand are formed.

What are the main types of weathering?

There are three main forms of weathering: physical, chemical and biological. Not all of them occur on every coastline, but combinations of them are usually evident.

Physical weathering – Freeze-thaw weathering or frost action is when water gets into cracks in rocks. When the temperature falls below freezing, the water will expand as it turns into ice. This expansion puts pressure on the rock around it and fragments of rock may break off. This type of weathering is common in highland areas where the temperature is above freezing during the day and below freezing during the night.

Chemical weathering – Rainwater contains weak acids that can react with certain rock types. The carbonates in limestone are dissolved by these weak acids and this causes the rock to break up or disintegrate. This can be seen on limestone statues or limestone pavements.

Biological weathering – This is the action of plants and animals on the land. Seeds that fall into cracks in rocks will start to grow when moisture is present. The roots the young plant puts out force their way into cracks and, in time, can break up rocks (see Figure 3). Burrowing animals, such as rabbits, can also be responsible for the further break-up of rocks.

Figure 3 Biological weathering in (a) Zanzibar, and (b) South Africa

What is mass movement?

Mass movement is when material moves down a slope due to the pull of gravity. There are many types of mass movement, but for the purposes of this chapter, only soil creep and slumping will be discussed.

Soil creep

This is the slowest downhill movement of soil. Gravity will pull the water that is contained in the soil down a slope. The soil will move downhill with the water. As this happens very slowly, it's not possible to see it happening, although it does move more quickly after heavy rainfall. The slope may appear rippled (like sheep paths around the hill). These ripples are known as terracettes (see Figure 4).

Figure 4 Soil creep in the Cuckmere Valley, East Sussex

Slumping

This is common on the coast. Also known as rotational slipping, it involves a large area of land moving down a slope. Due to the nature of the slip, it leaves behind a curved surface. This is very common on clay cliffs. During dry weather the clay contracts and cracks; when it rains, the water runs into the cracks and is absorbed until the rock becomes saturated (see Figure 5). This weakens the rock and, due to the pull of gravity, it slips down the slope on its slip plane.

Figure 5 Slumping east of Bowleaze Cove, Weymouth

What landforms are created by coastal erosion?

Distinctive and dynamic landforms are formed by destructive waves. These include headlands and bays; cliffs and wave-cut platforms; caves, arches, stacks and stumps.

Headlands and bays

On coastlines where rocks of varying resistance lie at right angles to the sea, the bays are the softer rock and are indentations in the land. The headlands are the more resistant rock and protrude into the sea (see Figure 6). As the bays are made from a less-resistant rock type, the erosion rates are greatest at first. In time, as the sea cuts the bays back, the waves reaching the coast are less powerful because they have to travel over a longer expanse of beach. At this point the headlands, which are further out to sea, start to experience the more powerful waves and are eroded at a faster rate than before.

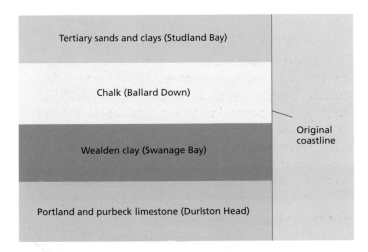

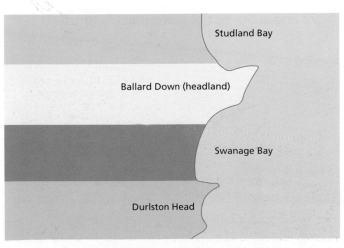

Figure 6 The formation of headlands and bays

Cliffs and wave-cut platforms

Headlands are usually formed from cliffs. When the sea moves against the base of the cliff using corrasion and hydraulic action (and if the rock type is limestone or chalk, corrosion), it undercuts the cliff and forms a wave-cut notch. Above this notch, an overhang will form; in time, it will fall into the sea as a result of the pressure of its own weight and the pull of gravity.

The sea will then continue to attack the cliff and form another notch. In this way, the cliff will retreat, becoming higher and steeper (see Figure 7). The remains of the cliff rock, now below the sea at high tide, form a rocky, wave-cut platform. As a result of erosion and weathering, some boulders will have fallen from the cliff onto the platform. As the width of the platform increases, so the power of the waves decreases, as they have further to travel to reach the cliff.

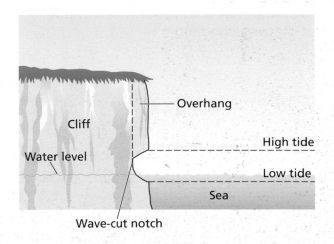

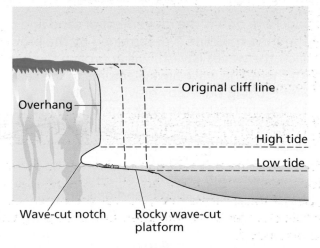

Figure 7 The formation of cliffs and wave-cut platforms

Caves, arches, stacks and stumps

These are formed in rocks that have a fault or line of weakness. The action of the sea will exploit the fault, through erosional processes such as hydraulic action. In time the fault will widen to form a cave. If the fault is in a headland, caves are likely to form on both sides. When the backs of the caves meet, an arch is formed. The sea will continue to erode the bottom of the arch. Weathering will also take place on the bare rock faces. As the sea undercuts the bottom of the arch, a wave-cut notch will form. It will collapse in time, as it is pulled down by the pressure of its own weight and gravity. This leaves behind a column of rock not attached to the cliff, known as a stack. Continued erosion and weathering will lead to the formation of a stump that is visible only at low tide (see Figures 8 and 9).

Figure 8 Photo of the coast east of Durdle Door in Dorset to show erosional features

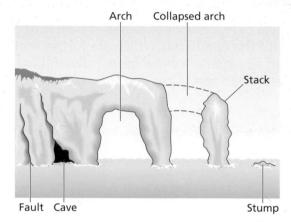

Figure 9 The formation of caves, arches, stacks and stumps

The process and impact of longshore drift on the coastline

Longshore drift is the movement of sand and pebbles down a coastline. The direction of the waves hitting the coastline is determined by the prevailing wind. If the wind is blowing at an angle to the beach, the waves (swash) will approach the beach at this angle, transporting the sand and pebbles with them. The wave always returns to the sea in a straight line at 90° to the coast (backwash). As the water is being pulled by gravity, it will take the shortest route back down the beach. In this way, material is moved along the beach until it meets an obstruction (see Figure 10).

Longshore drift creates landforms on a coastline such as spits and bars. It is also a problem in river estuaries due to the deposition of sediment. Some estuaries which are used to harbour boats have to be constantly dredged because of longshore drift depositing material.

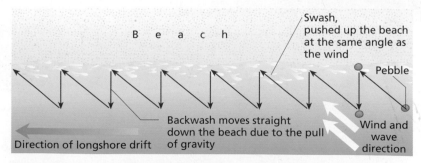

Figure 10 Diagram of longshore drift

What landforms are created by coastal deposition?

The other type of wave which operates in coastal areas is a constructive wave (see Figure 2 on page 43). As its name suggests, this wave builds rather than destroys the coastal environment. It deposits sand and pebbles that form beaches. Constructive waves form a number of landforms in coastal areas. These include beaches, spits and bars.

Beaches

Beaches are perhaps the most easily recognised and named coastal feature around the British coast. A beach is an area of land between the low tide and storm tide marks and is made up of sand, pebbles and, in some places, mud and silt. They are formed by constructive waves, often in bays where the waves have less energy due to the gently sloping land and, as a result, deposit material. They can also be found along straight stretches of coastline where longshore drift occurs. Seaside resorts often build groynes to keep beaches in place and to reduce the effects of longshore drift.

Spits

A spit is a long, narrow stretch of pebbles and sand which is attached to the land at one end, with the other end tapering into the sea. It forms when longshore drift occurs on a coastline. When the coastline ends, the sea deposits the material it is transporting because the change in depth affects its ability to transport the material further (see Figure 11).

If there is a river estuary, then the meeting of the waves and the river causes a change in speed which results in both the waves and the river dropping their sediment. In time, the material builds up to form a ridge of shingle and sand known as a spit. On the land side, silt and alluvium are deposited and salt marshes form. The wind and sea currents may curve the end of the spit around. Spits are very dynamic, which means that their shape and form continually change. If spits are present on a coastline, it should be possible to determine the direction of longshore drift (see Figure 12).

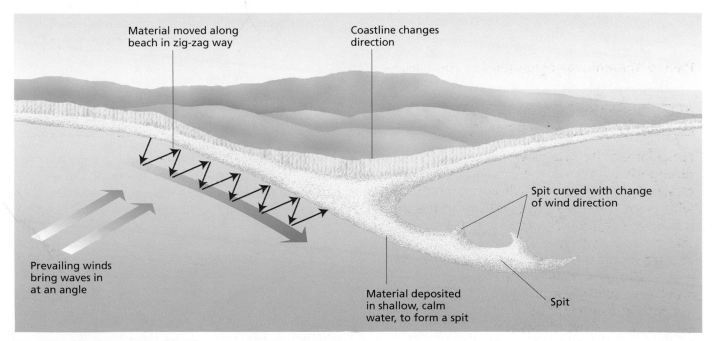

Material moved along beach in zig-zag way

Coastline changes direction

Spit curved with change of wind direction

Prevailing winds bring waves in at an angle

Material deposited in shallow, calm water, to form a spit

Spit

Figure 11 The formation of a spit

Figure 12 Hurst Castle spit, Hampshire

Bars

If a spit develops in a bay, it may build across it, linking two headlands to form a bar. This is only possible if there is a gently sloping beach and no river entering the sea. In this way, bars can straighten coastlines.

An example is Slapton Ley in Devon which also has the characteristic lagoon formed behind the bar where any run-off water is trapped and slowly seeps through the bar to the sea.

ACTIVITIES

Higher

1 Draw a field sketch of Figure 1 on page 42. Include the following on the sketch:

   a four landforms created by erosion,

   b two landforms created by deposition,

   c two processes which occur on this coast.

   d name the rock types (see Figure 6 on page 45).

2 What is the difference between corrasion and corrosion?

3 List three differences between constructive and destructive waves.

4 Using only an annotated diagram, explain how wave-cut platforms are formed.

5 Explain the process of longshore drift.

Foundation

1 Match the term with its correct definition.

Term	Definition
A Corrasion	1 The wearing away of rocks which are in the sea.
B Corrosion	2 The wearing away of cliff by the rocks in the sea.
C Attrition	3 A chemical reaction between certain rock types on seawater.

2 Longshore drift is the process used to transport material along the coast. How does it work?

3 List three differences between constructive and destructive waves.

4 Draw a field sketch of Figure 1 on page 42. Include the following on the sketch:

   a landforms: headlands, bays, stack, wave-cut platform, spit.

   b processes: slumping, longshore drift.

Review

By the end of this section you should be able to:

• describe the characteristics of destructive and constructive waves

• understand the impact of weathering, erosion and mass movement on the coast

• describe and explain the formation of cliffs and wave-cut platforms, headlands and bays, caves, arches, stacks and stumps

• recognise the impact of longshore drift on the coastline

• describe and explain the formation of beaches, spits and bars.

Coastal landforms are subject to change

> **Learning objective** – to study the way that coastal landforms can be changed by nature or by people.
>
> **Learning outcomes**
> - To understand that the rate of cliff recession is influenced by a number of factors.
> - To recognise the effects that coastal recession has on people who live by the coast.
> - To understand the ways that people can predict and prevent coastal flooding.
> - To know the main types of soft and hard engineering around the UK coastline; their advantages and disadvantages.

What affects the rate of coastal erosion?

Waves are the main agents of erosion on coasts. Their power is determined by two main factors: wind speed and the distance over which the wind blows over open water, known as the fetch. The longer the fetch, the stronger the wind and the more powerful the wave. The south-west coast of England experiences south-west winds that may have blown for several thousand kilometres (see Figure 13).

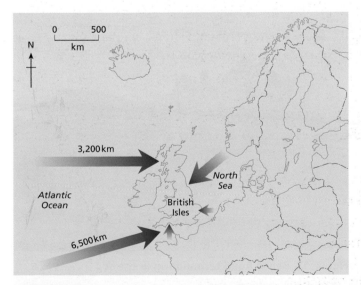

Figure 13 Diagram showing the fetch of waves around the British coast

Waves are created by a transfer of energy from the wind to the sea. As the wave approaches the coast, it begins to lose energy due to friction with the beach. The more gentle the beach's incline, the more energy the sea will lose. On steep beaches, however, the wave retains much of its energy until it reaches the beach and consequently forms a destructive wave.

The type of rock on a coastline also affects the rate of erosion. If the cliffs are made from resistant rock, like granite, they will erode more slowly than cliffs made from less resistant rock, such as clay. The rock's structure can also have an effect on the rate of erosion. Rocks that are well jointed or with many faults, such as limestone, will erode more quickly as the waves exploit these lines of weakness. Cliffs that are gentle and well vegetated will be more resistant to mass movement and weathering than cliffs of bare rock. This will also affect the rate at which they can be eroded by the sea.

What are the effects of coastal recession on people and the environment?

Coastal recession is having an effect on the coastline of the UK. The amount of effect is determined by the land use. If the area suffering from cliff recession is used for settlement, the effect is greater than if the cliff recession is affecting farmland, which is seen to be less important as it is not worth as much money. The effects of coastal recession can be seen all around the coast of the UK.

Coastal recession on the North Norfolk coast

The North Norfolk coast's new Shoreline Management Plan which adapts a managed retreat rather than 'hold the line' policy will mean that nearly 1,000 homes, 1,400 caravan and chalet parks, six hotels and guest houses, seven historic buildings, 3.5 km of road, seven golf course holes and three community halls will be lost to the sea over the next 100 years. The government will save £41 million by not building coastal defences but the human and environmental costs will be great. The estimated economic cost is £100 million with another £357 million lost in tourist income.

There are three golf courses which are suffering from the effects of coastal recession. These are Mundesley, Brancaster and Sheringham. Figure 14 shows how close the cliff edge now is to the fifth and sixth holes at Sheringham golf course. There is no coastal protection in this area and no plans to build any.

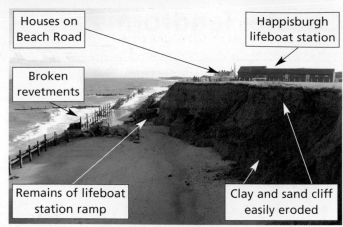

Houses on Beach Road

Happisburgh lifeboat station

Broken revetments

Remains of lifeboat station ramp

Clay and sand cliff easily eroded

Figure 15 The lifeboat station and ramp, Happisburgh

Figure 14 The fifth and sixth holes at Sheringham golf course

One village under threat from this policy is the village of Happisburgh which has a population of approximately 850. It is one of the fastest eroding areas in the world. The area was defended in1958 with revetments which reduced the amount of erosion to about 50 cm a year. In 1995 the council stopped repairing the coastal defences which caused the rate of erosion to accelerate. Since this time, 25 properties and the village's lifeboat launching station have been washed away (see Figure 15). The main area of concern is Beach Road which terminates in the sea. The houses were worth £80,000 when the coast was defended but are now valued at £1, even though their sea view improves each year (see Figure 17).

The government has refused to protect Happisburgh because it is not cost effective. In other words, the village is less valuable than the cost of the defences to protect it even though it contains 18 listed buildings including a Grade 1 listed church which is only 60 m from the cliff and estimated to be in the sea by 2020. The cost of sea defences is approximately £4 million for 500 m. However, the district council did defend the area in 2007 with 5,000 tonnes of granite rip-rap at a cost of £200,000; the local villagers raised a

Figure 16 The landward end of Beach Road

further £40,000 on a website which bought another 1,000 tonnes of rock. This is slowing down the rate of erosion but there is no hope for the residents of Beach Road whose homes will soon be in the sea.

Figure 17 Beach Road terminating in the sea

Local resident of Beach Road
I went to a meeting organised by the council – all I was offered was a form about homelessness. I cannot insure my property against coastal erosion so I presume when the sea takes it I will be homeless.

Local resident of Happisburgh village
We are climate change migrants – we're the first wave and we get no assistance whatsoever. The government is creating third-world conditions around the edge of this country.

Coastal Concern Action Group (CCAG) coordinator
Victims of coastal erosion in Germany, France and Holland get 100 per cent compensation from government insurance or 'solidarity' funds; in Britain it's zero. The government should take urgent action to protect Happisburgh or compensate those whose homes are at risk.

Happisburgh Post Office owner
Erosion of the coastline is a worry because it's constantly on your mind but we have still got a shop, a pub and a primary school, and a lot of villages have lost those services.

A local resident who moved to the village two years ago
Everyone is so worked up about the erosion, but there are worse places. I didn't have a problem with getting a mortgage.

Resident of Beach Road
I remember when we first moved here – we'd hang over the fence and say: 'Wouldn't it be nice if all those bungalows weren't in the way so we had a clear view of the sea…'
Well, be careful what you wish for. There's one fence pole left, then a little bit of meadow, then us. Everything else has fallen in. The first thing I do each morning is look at the view – but more to see what's gone than what's still there.
We went on holiday five years ago for two weeks – when we came back six bungalows and the road had gone and we were next.

A Defra spokesman
Spending on flood and coastal erosion risk is at record levels. We have plans agreed with local communities to protect the coast where that is practical. However, we must ensure taxpayers' money is used wisely.

Local GP
My surgery is full of people from all around (not just Beach Road) reporting erosion-related stress, sleeplessness and depression.

Figure 18 Happisburgh – the views of interested parties

Coastal recession at Walton-on-the-Naze

The cliffs at Walton-on-the-Naze are receding and the town is getting closer to the cliff edge. This is illustrated by the pill boxes on the beach 55 m from the cliff which in 1945 were on top of the cliff (see Figure 19). The reasons for this are shown in Figure 21. It is due to less resistant rocks found in this area which are easily eroded by the sea.

Due to the value of the properties at risk the cliff was protected. However, the northern section of the coastline was not protected due to the nature of the land use. The land use of this area is recreational which is not seen as valuable. The cliffs here continue to erode at a rate of approximately 1.5 m a year. The famous Tower and houses such as Haven House are now at risk because the coastline has not been protected.

Figure 19 A pill box on Walton beach

Figure 20 Warning notice on Walton cliffs

Figure 21 Unprotected cliff at Walton

Coastal recession at Barton on Sea

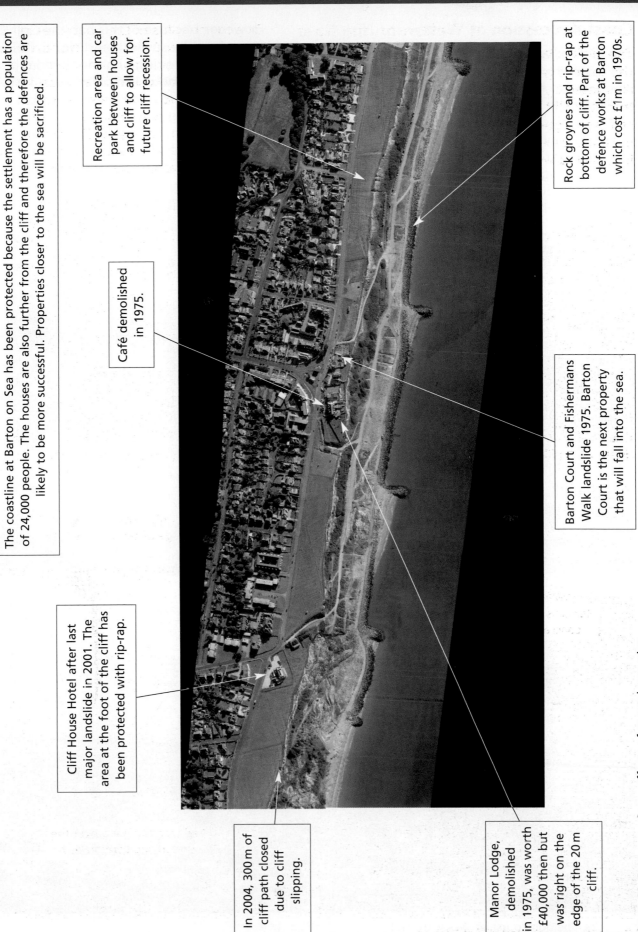

The coastline at Barton on Sea has been protected because the settlement has a population of 24,000 people. The houses are also further from the cliff and therefore the defences are likely to be more successful. Properties closer to the sea will be sacrificed.

Recreation area and car park between houses and cliff to allow for future cliff recession.

Rock groynes and rip-rap at bottom of cliff. Part of the defence works at Barton which cost £1m in 1970s.

Café demolished in 1975.

Barton Court and Fishermans Walk landslide 1975. Barton Court is the next property that will fall into the sea.

Cliff House Hotel after last major landslide in 2001. The area at the foot of the cliff has been protected with rip-rap.

In 2004, 300 m of cliff path closed due to cliff slipping.

Manor Lodge, demolished in 1975, was worth £40,000 then but was right on the edge of the 20 m cliff.

Figure 22 Barton on Sea – effects of coastal recession

Coastal recession at Westward Ho!

The Royal North Devon Golf Club near Westward Ho! is suffering from coastal erosion. The problem with erosion has been happening for many years. However, the club used to ask local people twice a year to replace by hand the stones that had been washed away. They have been ordered by Natural England to stop doing this process of 'potwalloping'. A spokesman for Natural England said: 'Our view is that recharging the ridge is interfering with the natural processes of the sea in the Northam Burrows SSSI.'

However, because of this ban the Golf Club is likely to lose the seventh and eighth holes next year because the ridge has not been replaced. Up until this year about 1 m of land was lost a year but last year 30 m of coastline were lost. Natural England have agreed that the club can resume the process of 'potwalloping', but in the medium to long term the holes will have to be moved. The sea will be allowed to erode the land and take its natural course.

Figure 23 The golf course at Westward Ho!

Coastal recession at Dawlish

The main railway line into the south-west to Penzance runs along the coast at Dawlish. When the sea is rough the trains have to be cancelled or delayed. On one occasion 160 passengers were stranded for four hours when their train's electrics were affected by seawater which washed over the track. The train was eventually pulled into the station at Dawlish. The railway line is protected by a seawall that was built in the 1800s; the wall has no wave-refracting curve and is in need of constant repair. The annual rebuilding and repair bill is £400,000 but Network Rail, at present, have no plans to re-route the railway. In the light of global warming causing sea level rises and more frequent storms, the effect on the line will only increase. If the line is washed away the main rail link into the south-west of England will be lost, which will have a major effect on the economy of the area.

Figure 24 Train caught by wave at Dawlish

Figure 25 The railway line at Dawlish

Prediction and prevention of the effects of coastal flooding by forecasting, building design, planning and education

In England 2.1 million properties are at risk from flooding. Nearly 50 per cent of these properties are at risk from flooding from the sea.

There are a number of ways that the effects of flooding can be reduced. Householders can be warned about a flood so that they can take precautions. This is done in the UK through a chain of events. The Met Office predicts the likelihood of a coastal flood and gives information to the public through weather forecasts and news broadcasts on the television. These advise householders to be proactive and either ring a flood hotline number or go onto the Environment Agency website to check the likelihood of a flood in their area.

On the Environment Agency website there will be information on the likelihood of a flood. This will be identified by a system of warning codes: flood watch, flood warning, severe flood warning and all clear. These warning codes give people information on what to expect and how to react (see Figure 27). In this way the government is helping to prevent the effects of floods by providing an effective warning system.

There are also a number of websites which are run by the government to give advice to the public who live in areas which are prone to flooding, for example, www.direct.gov.uk. There is general advice given about how to protect homes from flooding and advice on what to do if a flood actually happens and specific information about coastal flooding.

DEFRA (The Department for Environment, Food and Rural Affairs) has the responsibility for deciding which areas of the coastline are going to be defended against the risk of flooding. The Environment Agency then organises for the defences to be built and maintained. DEFRA provides the money for most of the work that is completed.

As well as the monitoring which is being done by the Met Office, the Environment Agency also monitors sea conditions over a 24-hour period, 365 days a year. The Storm Tide Forecasting Service provides the Environment Agency with forecasts of coastal flooding which the Environment Agency communicates to the public via their website or phone line.

Other ways that the effects of flooding can be reduced is by building design and control. Before houses can be built the local authority has to give planning permission. This is not granted in flood risk areas unless a flood risk assessment has been carried out. However, some building does still take place in areas where it is not really advisable to build houses. By 2010 the government has indicated that planning laws will change so that all new housing in flood risk areas must be flood resistant or resilient.

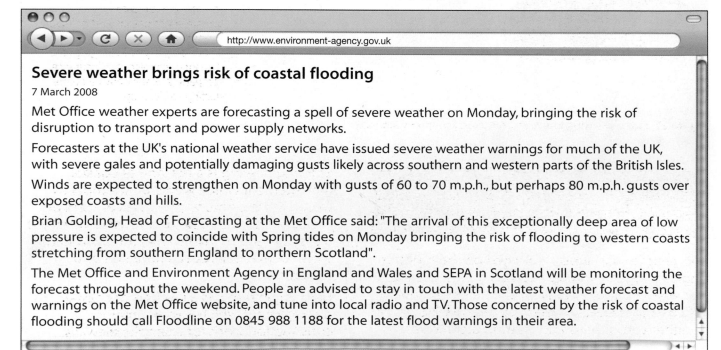

http://www.environment-agency.gov.uk

Severe weather brings risk of coastal flooding

7 March 2008

Met Office weather experts are forecasting a spell of severe weather on Monday, bringing the risk of disruption to transport and power supply networks.

Forecasters at the UK's national weather service have issued severe weather warnings for much of the UK, with severe gales and potentially damaging gusts likely across southern and western parts of the British Isles.

Winds are expected to strengthen on Monday with gusts of 60 to 70 m.p.h., but perhaps 80 m.p.h. gusts over exposed coasts and hills.

Brian Golding, Head of Forecasting at the Met Office said: "The arrival of this exceptionally deep area of low pressure is expected to coincide with Spring tides on Monday bringing the risk of flooding to western coasts stretching from southern England to northern Scotland".

The Met Office and Environment Agency in England and Wales and SEPA in Scotland will be monitoring the forecast throughout the weekend. People are advised to stay in touch with the latest weather forecast and warnings on the Met Office website, and tune into local radio and TV. Those concerned by the risk of coastal flooding should call Floodline on 0845 988 1188 for the latest flood warnings in their area.

Figure 26 Weather warning about the possibility of severe flooding, The Met Office

	What it means	What to do
Flood Watch Flood Watch ⚠	Flooding of low lying land and roads is expected. Be aware, be prepared, watch out.	• Monitor local news and weather forecasts. • Be aware of water levels near you. • Be prepared to act on your flood plan. • Check on the safety of pets and livestock. • Charge your mobile phone.
Flood Warning Flood Warning ⚠	Flooding of homes and businesses is expected. Act now!	• Move cars, pets, food, valuables and important documents to safety. • Get flood protection equipment in place. • Turn off gas, electricity and water supplies if safe to do so. • Be prepared to evacuate your home. • Protect yourself, your family and help others. • Act on your flood plan.
Severe Flood Warning Severe Flood Warning ⚠	Severe flooding is expected. There is extreme danger to life and property. Act now!	• Collect things you need for evacuation. • Turn off gas, electricity and water supplies if safe to do so. • Stay in a high place with a means of escape. • Avoid electricity sources. • Avoid walking or driving through flood water. • In danger call 999 immediately. • Listen to emergency services. • Act on your flood plan.
All Clear All Clear	Flood watches or warnings are no longer in force for this area.	• Keep listening to weather reports. • Only return to evacuated buildings if you are told it is safe. • Beware sharp objects and pollution in flood water. • If your property or belongings are damaged, contact your insurance company. Ask their advice before starting to clean up.

Figure 27 Flood warning codes from the Environment Agency

What are the main types of soft and hard engineering used on the coastline of the UK?

This chapter has already touched on the types of engineering techniques used on the UK coastline but what are the options for the defence of the UK coastline? Coastal defences can be classified as either soft or hard engineering techniques.

- Soft engineering is a method of coastal management which works, or attempts to work, with the natural processes at work on the coastline and to be unobtrusive visually. It does not tend to involve major construction work, for example, beach nourishment/replenishment.
- Hard engineering is a method of coastal management which involves major construction work, for example, seawalls.

Figure 28a Types of hard engineering techniques

Hard engineering	Description	Advantages	Disadvantages
Rip-rap  Rip-rap and seawall to protect the sand dunes.	Large rocks placed in front of the cliff. COST – £300 per metre	• Dissipates wave energy. • Can be very cheap, depending on rock type. • Effective for many years.	• Can make the beach. inaccessible to tourists. • Unattractive. • Not effective in storm conditions.
Recurved seawall  Seawall to protect the base of the sand dunes.	Walls usually made of concrete. The modern ones have a recurved face. COST – £3,000 per linear metre	• Reflects and absorbs wave energy. • Very visible – makes residents feel safe. • Effective for many years.	• Ugly – puts tourists off. • Expensive to build. • Can cause wave scouring if not positioned correctly.
Groynes  Seawall providing extra protection. Rip-rap – protects the caravan site which is of lower value than the buildings / hotel. Groynes building up the sediment on the beach.	Usually made of wood. Stretches from the coastline into the sea. COST – £5,000 each	• Prevents longshore drift (LSD) – sand builds up on one side of the groyne. • Keeps beach in place for tourist industry. • Effective for many years.	• Unattractive – difficult to walk along the beach. • Disrupt the natural processes working on the beach such as LSD.
Gabions  Gabions	Wire cages filled with stone used to reduce erosion. COST – £11 per m	• Cheaper than other forms of coastal defence. • Rock cages absorb wave energy.	• Wire cages can break, they need to be securely tied down. • Not as efficient as other forms of coastal defence.
Offshore reef  The beach is being eroded between the offshore reefs. Offshore reef – the beach behind the reef is well developed.	Enormous concrete blocks and natural boulders are sunk offshore to alter wave direction and to dissipate the energy of waves and tides. COST – £1,950 per m	• The waves break further offshore and therefore reduce their erosive power. • They allow the build up of sand due to the reduction in wave energy.	• May be removed by heavy storms. • Difficult to install the reefs.

Figure 28b Types of soft engineering techniques

Soft engineering	Description	Advantages	Disadvantages
Beach replenishment  Steps leading onto sand are evidence that the beach has been replenished. Old seawall, now buried in sand. New groynes sunk deep into replenished beach.	The placing of sand and pebbles on a beach. COST – £5,000 per 100 m	• Looks natural. • Provides beach for tourists. • A beach is the best form of natural defence because it dissipates wave energy. • Cheap.	• May affect plant and animal life in the area. • The scheme requires constant maintenance; it can all be washed away very quickly in as little as one year. • Disruption for home-owners; large noisy lorries full of sand regularly replenish the beach.
Cliff regrading	The cliff is cut back and given a new gentle slope to stop it slumping.	• May be covered in ecomatting to encourage vegetation growth. • Very natural – will encourage wildlife in the area.	• Not effective alone – needs other defences at the cliff foot. • Some homes on the cliff may have to be demolished.
Managed retreat	Allowing the sea to gradually flood land or erode cliffs. COST – Depends on the coastal area	• Creates new habitats for plants and birds. • Cheap.	• Upsetting for landowners who lose land. • Difficult to estimate the extent of sea movement especially with rising sea levels.

ACTIVITIES

Higher

1 Explain the factors that cause cliffs to recede.
2 Why are settlements defended while agricultural land is left to the actions of the sea?
3 Some people are for coastal protection schemes and others are against. Explain these different opinions.
4 How does the public find out about the possibility of coastal flooding?
5 What is a flood warning code?
6 What should residents do if they are in a zone with a severe flood warning?
7 Happisburgh has not been protected from coastal recession whereas Barton on Sea has been protected. Explain why.

Foundation

1 Cliffs made of soft rock recede more quickly than cliffs made of hard rock. Why?
2 Which of the following land uses in coastal areas do you think should be protected? Give a reason for your answer: farmland, housing, industry, golf courses, parks.
3 Would each group of people named below agree or disagree with coastal defences?
  a home-owners on a cliff
  b home-owners inland
  c environmentalists
  d coastal defence construction firms.
4 How does the public find out about the possibility of coastal flooding?
5 What is a flood warning code?
6 What should residents do if they are in a zone with a severe flood warning?
7 Happisburgh has not been protected from coastal recession whereas Barton on Sea has been protected. Give one developed reason why not.

Coastal management

Learning objective – to study how the coast is managed in a named location.

Learning outcome
- To be able to describe and explain how the coast is managed at Walton-on-the-Naze.

Walton-on-the-Naze is a coastal town in Essex. It suffers from coastal erosion due to the types of rock which make up the cliff. The rock types are London Clay and Red Crag and both of these rock types are easily eroded by the sea. The cliffs also suffer from slumping which makes the defence of the area even more complex. Longshore drift moves sand along the coastline from south to north. All of these factors must be considered when deciding the type of management that will be effective in an area.

Walton can be split into two distinct areas. The northern end of the coastline has not been protected because the Environment Agency does not consider the buildings there worth saving. The only buildings there are a Grade II listed Tower and several houses on Old Hall Lane. The southern part of the coastline has been protected because of the coastal town of Walton with its population of 12,000.

The management of coastal recession at Walton-on-the-Naze

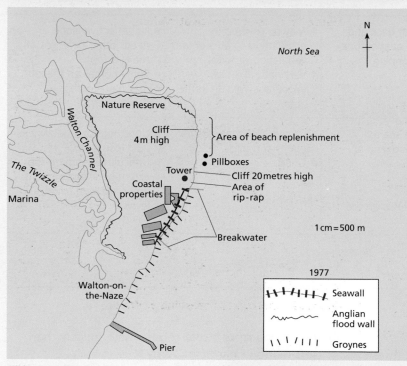

Figure 29 Map of Walton-on-the-Naze

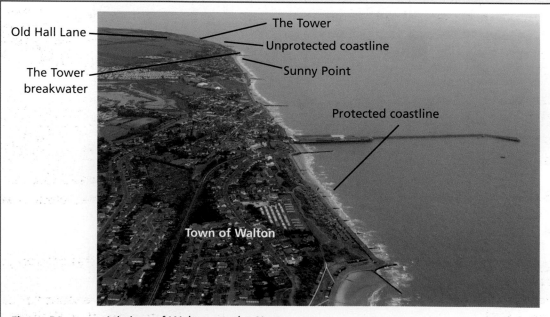

Figure 30 An aerial view of Walton-on-the-Naze

In 1977 a major project was completed on the southern part of the coastline. It consisted of a seawall, breakwaters and groynes and the cliff was regraded. This was to protect the properties on the cliff such as Sunny Point road where the average house price is £400,000. It must be considered why these particular techniques were used at Walton.

Groynes were used because longshore drift was occurring along the coastline from the south to the north. The groynes would help to stop longshore drift and keep the beach in place. Breakwaters, which are large groynes, were also placed at regular intervals because of the power of the longshore drift on this particular coastline. The cliff was regraded to produce a gentler slope and drainage channels were installed to allow water to flow underground through special tunnels and out onto the beach through holes in the seawall: The regraded cliff was planted with a variety of shrubs and trees which included gorse and nettles at the side of the path to stop people from scrambling on the cliff. At the bottom of the cliff there is a seawall: this is to protect the London clay there which is very easily eroded by the sea.

In 1998 the council paid £167,000 for 300 tonnes of Leicester granite to be placed around the Tower breakwater. This rip-rap has slowed down erosion in this area but has not stopped it. The beach in front of the cliffs at the northern part of the coastline was replenished in 1999 with sand and gravel which had been dredged from Harwich Harbour. However, the majority of this material had been removed by 2003 illustrating the power of longshore drift along this stretch of coastline.

Figure 31 Coastal defence at Walton

Figure 32 Unprotected coastline at Walton

Figure 33 View of the protected coastline from the Tower

ACTIVITIES

1 Why are the cliffs at Walton receding so quickly?
2 The protected cliff has vegetation growing on it and the unprotected cliff does not. Explain why.
3 Give two reasons why groynes were constructed on Walton beach.
4 Explain why the cliff was regraded and a seawall was built at the bottom of the cliff.

Extension
Find out more information about Walton. The following website will help: www.stacey.peak-media.co.uk.

Review
By the end of this section you should be able to:
* explain the reasons for coastal management at Walton-on-the-Naze.

Sample Examination Questions

Higher tier

1 Study the photograph in Figure 8 on page 46.

   a Draw a sketch of the photograph. Include on it: a stack, arch, cave, stump. **(2 marks)**

   b Was this photograph taken at high or low tide? **(1 mark)**

   c Give one reason for your answer. **(1 mark)**

   d There is a white area shown on the beach. What is it made of and how did it get there? **(3 marks)**

2 a Name three causes of cliff recession. **(3 marks)**

   b How do groynes protect cliffs from erosion by the sea? **(3 marks)**

   c Explain the soft engineering techniques which are now being used to protect coastlines. **(3 marks)**

3 How are householders prepared for a likely coastal flood event? **(3 marks)**

4 Describe and explain the effects of coastal recession on the people and the environment. Use examples in your answer. **(6 marks)**

Total 25 marks

Foundation tier

1 Look at the photograph in Figure 8 on page 46.

   a Complete the table below to show if the features are present on the photograph. **(4 marks)**

Feature	True	False
Arch		
Spit		
Cave		
Stump		

   b Was this taken at high or low tide? **(1 mark)**

   c Give one reason for your answer. **(2 marks)**

   d There is a white area shown on the beach. What is it made of and how did it get there? **(3 marks)**

2 a Which two of the following are causes of cliff recession? Circle the correct answers. **(2 marks)**

   Weathering Corrasion Eutrophication Attrition

   b What is a groyne and how does it protect the coastline? **(3 marks)**

   c The following are soft engineering techniques used to manage coastlines. Draw a line between the correct soft engineering technique and its description. **(2 marks)**

Soft engineering techniques	Description
Beach replenishment	The sea is allowed to flood areas which were once defended.
Managed retreat	The land by the sea is made into a gentle slope instead of a steep one.
Cliff regrading	The coastline is built up with sand and pebbles from elsewhere.

   d Choose one soft engineering technique. State one advantage and one disadvantage of this technique. **(2 marks)**

3 Describe and explain the effects of coastal recession on the people and the environment. Use examples in your answer. **(6 marks)**

Total 25 marks

River processes produce distinctive landforms

Learning objective – to study drainage basin terms, river processes, characteristics and landforms.

Learning outcomes
- To be able to define and recognise watershed, confluence, tributary, source and mouth.
- To understand the impact of weathering, erosion and mass movement on river landscapes.
- To know the changes in the characteristics of a river and its valley between source and mouth.
- To be able to describe and explain the formation of interlocking spurs, waterfalls, meanders, river cliffs, ox-bow lakes, floodplains and levees.

What is a drainage basin?

Rivers begin in upland areas and make their way downhill to the sea. A river starts at its source and meets the sea at its mouth. As it makes its way to the sea, the river channel (the area in which a river flows) and its valley experience a number of changes. The river becomes wider and deeper as it is joined by other, smaller rivers (called tributaries); the point at which rivers meet is known as a confluence. The river valley also changes: the sides become less steep, the gradient decreases and the shape of the valley changes from a V to a broader shape, almost like a flat-bottomed U.

   The land that is drained by a river system is called a drainage basin; the boundary of the drainage basin, usually made up of highland, is called the watershed.

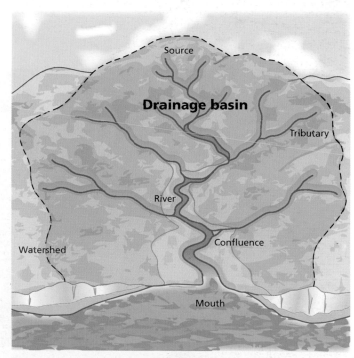

Figure 1 Features of a drainage basin

How do rivers erode?

The banks and bed of a river are under continual attack from the water within the river channel and other processes such as weathering and mass movement. (You should always refer to these processes when answering a question on landform formation.)

The processes of river erosion

Hydraulic action – this is the pressure of the water being pushed against the banks and bed of the river. It also includes the compression of air in cracks: as the water gets into cracks in the rock, it compresses the air in the cracks; this puts even more pressure on the cracks and pieces of rock may break off.

Corrasion – particles (the load) carried along the river are thrown against the river banks with considerable force.

Corrosion (solution) – this is a chemical reaction between certain rock types and the river water. This is particularly evident on limestone where the river often eats through the rock and flows underground.

Attrition – this is a slightly different process that involves the wearing away of the rocks which are in the river. In the upper course of a river rocks continually roll around and knock into each other. They chip away at each other until smooth pebbles or sand are formed.

What are the main types of weathering?

There are three main forms of weathering: physical, chemical and biological.

Physical weathering

Freeze-thaw weathering or frost action is when water gets into cracks in rocks. When the temperature falls below freezing, the water will expand as it turns into ice. This expansion puts pressure on the rock around it and fragments of rock may break off. This type of weathering is common in highland areas where the temperature is above freezing during the day and below freezing during the night (see Figure 1 in Chapter 5 Glaciated Landscapes, page 83).

Chemical weathering

Rainwater contains weak acids that can react with certain rock types. The carbonates in limestone are dissolved by these weak acids and this causes the rock to break up or disintegrate. This can be seen on limestone statues or limestone pavements, for example at Malham (see Unit 3 Chapter 14).

Biological weathering

This is the action of plants and animals on the land. Seeds that fall into cracks in rocks will start to grow when moisture is present. The roots the young plant puts out force their way into cracks and, in time, can break up rocks. Burrowing animals, such as rabbits, can also be responsible for the further break-up of rocks.

Figure 2 Biological weathering to the land, by the Yangtze River

What is mass movement?

Mass movement is when material moves down a slope due to the pull of gravity. There are many types of mass movement, but for the purposes of this chapter, only soil creep and slumping will be discussed.

Soil creep

This is the slowest downhill movement of soil. Gravity will pull the water that is contained in the soil down a slope. The soil will move downhill with the water. As this happens very slowly, it's not possible to see it happening, although it does move more quickly after heavy rainfall. The slope may appear rippled (like sheep paths around the hill). These ripples are known as terracettes.

Slumping

This is common on the banks of rivers. Also known as rotational slipping, it involves a large area of land moving down a slope. Due to the nature of the slip, it leaves behind a curved surface. This is very common on clay riverbanks. During dry weather the clay contracts and cracks; when it rains, the water runs into the cracks and is absorbed until the rock becomes saturated. This weakens the rock and, due to the pull of gravity, it slips down the slope on its slip plane.

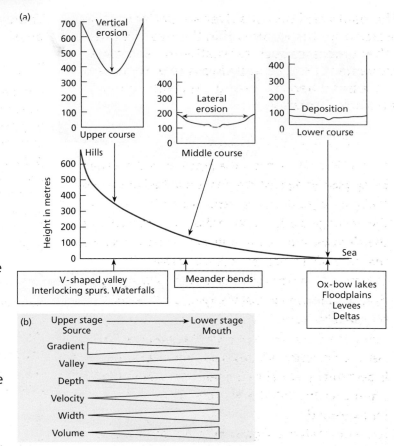

Figure 5 The features of a river's course

Figure 3 Terracettes in South Wales

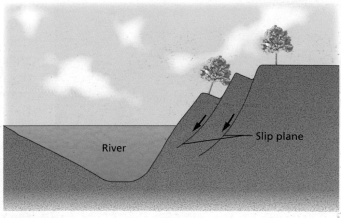

Figure 4 Slumping of a riverbank

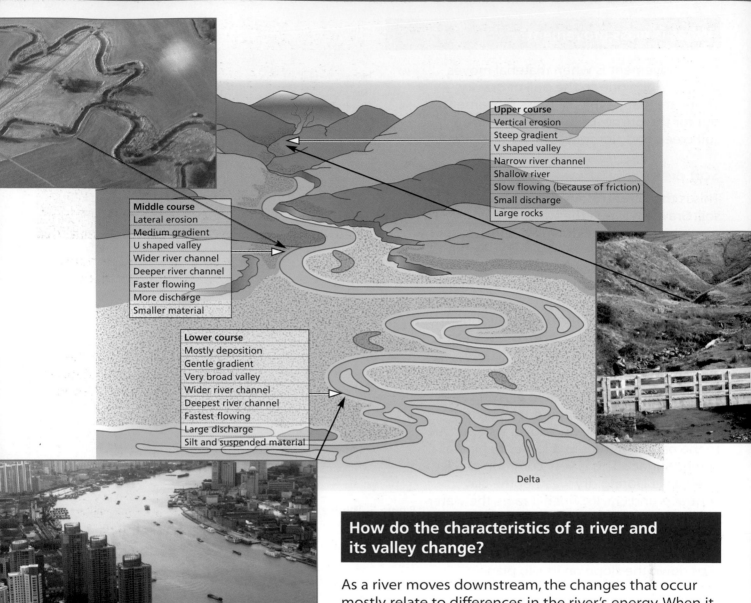

Upper course
Vertical erosion
Steep gradient
V shaped valley
Narrow river channel
Shallow river
Slow flowing (because of friction)
Small discharge
Large rocks

Middle course
Lateral erosion
Medium gradient
U shaped valley
Wider river channel
Deeper river channel
Faster flowing
More discharge
Smaller material

Lower course
Mostly deposition
Gentle gradient
Very broad valley
Wider river channel
Deepest river channel
Fastest flowing
Large discharge
Silt and suspended material

Delta

Figure 6 Characteristics of a river and its valley

How do the characteristics of a river and its valley change?

As a river moves downstream, the changes that occur mostly relate to differences in the river's energy. When it is in an upland area, a river has the power to erode downwards, as it is way above sea level, and it forms a V-shaped valley. As the gradient (slope) of the valley decreases, the river uses its energy to transport the material it has eroded. Due to the lack of gradient, it begins to erode sideways (laterally). As the river moves closer to sea level, the gradient decreases further. Although the river is still eroding sideways at this point, deposition is the most important process and the valley becomes wider and flatter. This change from erosion to deposition helps to explain the change in landforms and the shape of the river valley as the river moves towards the sea (see Figure 5).

The long profile of a river shows the steep gradient at the source gradually becoming more gentle until the river reaches sea level. These changes usually show a river to be split into three sections, known as the upper, middle and lower courses (see Figure 6).

As a river moves downstream, its discharge also changes. Discharge is the amount of water passing a specific point at a given time and is measured in cubic metres (m^3) per second. The discharge depends on the river's velocity and volume. The volume is the amount of water in the river and the velocity is the speed of the river. The velocity × the volume is the river's discharge. As a river moves towards the sea, its discharge will increase because of the increased volume as more tributaries join the river. The velocity of the river is determined by the amount of water which is touching the river's bed and banks. If the river is deeper, there will be less contact between the river and its banks and bed, therefore less friction will occur and the river velocity will be greater.

ACTIVITIES

Activities for Figures 7 and 8

1 Using Figure 7 to help you, describe the course of the river's channel and its valley shown on the map extract.
2 The photograph was taken at grid reference 752 843; in which direction was the camera pointing?

What landforms can be found in river valleys?

A river's course can be split into three sections: the upper course, the middle course and the lower course.

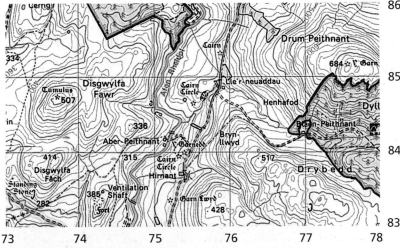

Figure 7 Map extract of upper course of river Rheidol

Figure 8 River Rheidol's upper course

Upper course

In the upland area at the start of the river, there is the upper course. Features of the upper course include V-shaped valleys, interlocking spurs and waterfalls.

V-shaped valleys and interlocking spurs

In the upper course, the river is small and because most of its water is in contact with its bed and the banks, there is a lot of friction. Ninety-five per cent of the river's energy is used to overcome this friction. A result of this is that the river flows more slowly here than in the lowlands. The rest of the river's energy is used to erode downwards, hence the characteristic V-shape of the valley. As the river winds its way down between barriers of more resistant rock, spurs which interlock down the valley are formed (see Figures 9 and 10).

Waterfalls

A waterfall forms when a river crosses a band of less resistant rock, after flowing over relatively hard, resistant rock (see Figure 11). The sudden drop in the river's course that results is known as

Figure 9 Interlocking spurs

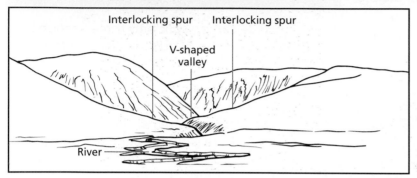

Figure 10 Field sketch of Figure 10

a waterfall. The softer rock is cut back more quickly, leaving an overhang of harder rock. In time, due to the pull of gravity, the harder rock becomes too heavy and falls into the river below. As the water splashes back from the plunge pool, hydraulic action against the back wall of the waterfall also erodes the softer rock. Over time the waterfall moves back or retreats up the valley, often forming a gorge.

The deep pool below the waterfall is known as a plunge pool. It is deeper than the rest of the river because of the power of the water falling

into it (the Hardraw Force waterfall (Figure 12) has a drop of 60 m and a 9 m plunge pool). It contains large boulders that have fallen from the overhang and smaller rocks that have been eroded off the back wall of the waterfall. The river erodes these rocks by the process of corrasion.

Middle course

In the middle course, the river is deeper as a result of being joined by a number of tributaries. Less water is in contact with the channel which means that there is less friction and the river has more power to erode. The river erodes laterally (sideways), rather than vertically (downwards), as there is less of a gradient in this part of a river's course because the valley is flatter with more gentle slopes. A meander bend is one feature of the middle course which is caused by this increase in lateral erosion (see Figures 13 and 14).

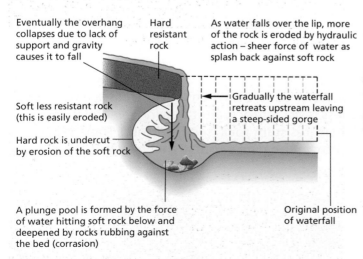

Eventually the overhang collapses due to lack of support and gravity causes it to fall

Hard resistant rock

As water falls over the lip, more of the rock is eroded by hydraulic action – sheer force of water as splash back against soft rock

Soft less resistant rock (this is easily eroded)

Gradually the waterfall retreats upstream leaving a steep-sided gorge

Hard rock is undercut by erosion of the soft rock

A plunge pool is formed by the force of water hitting soft rock below and deepened by rocks rubbing against the bed (corrasion)

Original position of waterfall

Figure 11 Formation of a waterfall

Figure 12 Hardraw Force waterfall, Yorkshire

Figure 13 Meander bend, Ardèche river, France

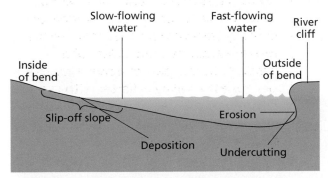

Figure 14 A cross-section of a meander bend

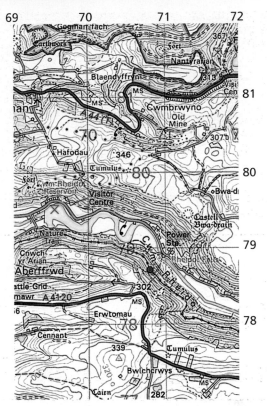

Figure 15 Map extract of middle course of river Rheidol

Meanders

The outside of a meander bend has the deepest water because this is where the greatest erosion takes place and forms a river cliff. The water is moving fastest at this point and therefore erodes the bank using corrasion. The water moves more quickly on the outside due to the lack of friction because of the river's depth and consequent lack of contact with the bed and banks. A slip-off slope forms on the inside of the meander bend because of deposition. Deposition occurs on the inside because the water is moving more slowly and is shallower. As a result, there is more friction here and the river is less powerful. The river is therefore unable to carry its load and deposition takes place. An underwater current takes some of the eroded material from the river cliff across the river and deposits it on the slip-off slope (see Figure 14).

Lower course

In the lower course of the river, the channel is wide and deep and is surrounded by a wide valley floor. The velocity of the river is greater as there is less friction with the channel. The slopes of the valley and the gradient of the river channel are

Figure 16 River Rheidol in middle stage

ACTIVITIES

Activities for Figures 15 and 16
1 Describe the course of the river shown on the map extract.
2 The river becomes much wider at this point. Why?
3 Draw a field sketch of the photograph in Figure 16 to show the main features of a river in its middle course.

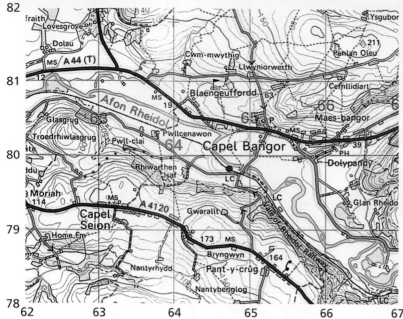

Figure 17 Map extract of lower course of river Rheidol

Figure 18 Lower course of river Rheidol

ACTIVITIES

Activities for Figures 17 and 18
1 Measure the width of the floodplain.
2 What evidence is there to show that the river channel has changed course? Use diagrams to help your answer.
3 Describe and explain the route of the A roads.

very gentle. The river's main process has now become deposition as a result of the large load of eroded material (such as sand and silt) that it is carrying. However, there is still some lateral erosion taking place. A number of features, such as ox-bow lakes, floodplains, levees and deltas, can be found in the lower course.

Ox-bow lakes

In the lower course of the river, meander bends become very large. With continual erosion on the outside of the banks and deposition on the inside, the ends of the meander bend become closer (see Figures 19 and 20). When flooding occurs, the river is able to cut through the gap and, in time, forms a new straight channel. Continued deposition of alluvium at times of low flow, results in the old bend of the river becoming cut off. This is called an ox-bow lake.

Figure 19 Meander bend, almost an ox-bow lake

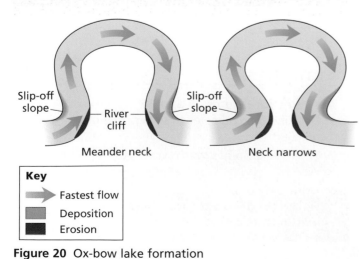

Figure 20 Ox-bow lake formation

Floodplains and levees

A floodplain is the low, flat area of land on either side of a river. It can be found in the middle course of a river, but is more usually found in the lower course. When the river contains too much water to stay within its channel, it floods the surrounding land. As it moves away from its channel, it becomes shallower and friction increases. The river has less energy and, therefore, must drop some of the load it is carrying. It drops the largest amount of material close to the river channel. After a number of floods, this builds up to form levees (see Figure 21). The river water drops the heaviest material first.

Another contributing factor to the formation of the floodplain is the migration of meanders downstream. Meanders are formed by lateral erosion which causes the bend to move across and down the valley in the direction of the river's flow. The outside of the bend, where erosion is greatest, moves the bend in that direction and the inside bend fills in the floodplain with the deposition that occurs there.

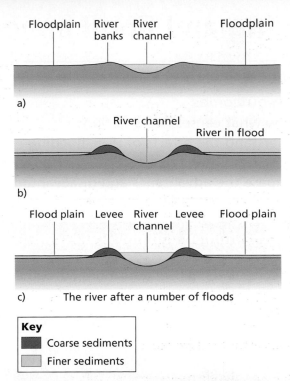

Figure 21 Levee and floodplain formation

ACTIVITIES

1 Look at the diagram showing the formation of a waterfall (Figure 11). Draw your own series of annotated diagrams to show how a waterfall is formed.

2 Look at Figure 13 which shows a meander bend on the Ardèche river in France. Draw a labelled field sketch of the photograph and explain how this bend has formed.

3 The photograph in Figure 19 shows a meander bend. What is likely to happen to this bend in the future?

Review

By the end of this section you should be able to:

- define and recognise watershed, confluence, tributary, source and mouth
- understand the impact of weathering, erosion and mass movement on river landscapes
- know that characteristics of a river and its valley change between source and mouth
- describe and explain the formation of interlocking spurs, waterfalls, meanders, river cliffs, ox-bow lakes, floodplains and levees.

Flooding and flood prevention

> **Learning objective** – to understand the causes, effects and management of river flooding.
>
> **Learning outcomes**
> - To know what causes rivers to flood.
> - To understand the effects of river flooding.
> - To understand how the effects of river flooding can be predicted and prevented.
> - To compare the advantages and disadvantages of river defence techniques.

What are the human and physical causes of river flooding?

Flooding occurs when a river gets more water than its channel can hold. There are both human and physical causes of flooding.

Dams may burst which will cause excess water in river channels and flooding of large areas.

Ploughing up and down slopes rather than around them channels the rainwater to the river faster.

If vegetation has been removed, then there is less interception and water will move to the river more quickly.

Similarly, if there is a town on a floodplain, storm drains will allow water to move into the river at a greater speed and so make flooding more likely.

Figure 22 Human causes of flooding

Impermeable rocks mean that rainwater cannot soak into the rocks and it therefore flows more quickly to the river either through the soil or over the surface.

If there is a sudden rise in temperature, a rapid thaw can happen. Rivers are unable to cope with the amount of water and flood.

A long period of hot dry weather makes the soil very hard so that water cannot soak in when it rains. Therefore it runs off the surface into the river.

River beds that have become silted up make the channel smaller and more likely to flood.

Steep valley slopes make rainwater run off rapidly into the river channel.

If there are large amounts of rain day after day, the water will saturate the ground and flow more quickly into the river.

During a cloudburst in a thunderstorm, the rain droplets are so large and fall so quickly that there is no time for the water to sink into the ground. Water runs very quickly into the river and causes flooding.

Figure 23 Physical causes of flooding

What are the effects of flooding on people and the environment?

When a river floods it can affect the environment and the people who live in the flooded area. The effects of flooding depend upon the area of the flood and where the flood happens. Obviously the effects will be greater in a densely populated area.

USA 2006
200,000 people were evacuated from their homes in north-eastern Pennsylvania because of rising waters on the **Susquehanna River**.
  A state of emergency was declared across large parts of New Jersey, New York and Pennsylvania states.
  The largest evacuation effort
took place in Wilkes-Barre, in Pennsylvania. A group of children were ferried out of a tennis camp by raft in Philadelphia as flooding closed many roads in and around the city.
  The National Weather Service reported nine fatalities across the eastern USA. Two truckers were killed on Interstate 88 in Sidney, New York, after part of the motorway was washed away by flood waters. A motorist died as he swerved to avoid a washed-out road in Holmesville, New York.

Mexico 2007
The state of Tabasco's Governor, Andres Granier, said more than half of the state's 2.1 million residents were affected by the flooding of the **Grijava River**. 70 per cent of the state was under water and 100 per cent of the crops were destroyed.
  Tabasco's capital, Villahermosa, was turned into a brown lake with only treetops and roofs visible. 300,000 people were trapped in their homes. Sandbags were placed around several giant heads carved by the Olmecs, an ancient pre-Columbian people, at Tabasco's La Venta archaeological site.

Bolivia 2007
Unusually heavy seasonal rains caused rivers to burst their banks. At least 19 people died as a result of flooding of the **Rio Grande, a tributary of the Amazon**. 340,000 people were estimated to have been affected. About 100,000 people were left homeless. Roads in the worst-hit departments of Santa Cruz and Beni were blocked by mudslides.

Susquehanna River

Amazon River

Grijava River

Rio Grande

River

Figure 24 Some major floods in 2006–2008

Serbia, Romania and Bulgaria 2006
As the waters of the Danube flooded, hundreds of houses in the area were under water.

In Bulgaria the flooding affected 2 million people and claimed the lives of at least 20, while 10,000 have lost their homes. A tent city with space for 1,200 was put up near Vidin.

The damage to the economy is estimated to be one billion leva ($625 million; £346 million) with huge amounts of farmland and vital infrastructure destroyed.

The railway system was severely damaged, causing the Bulgarian national railway company to lose hundreds of thousands of leva every day.

In the Serbian capital Belgrade some streets were under water for several days, forcing evacuations. Hundreds of people were taken to safety in Smederevo, 40 km east of Belgrade.

Nepal 2008
The flooding began when a dam burst on the **Saptakoshi River** in Nepal. Nearly 1,000 houses were completely destroyed, and power supplies and transport were severely affected.

Hundreds of people were hit by illnesses such as diarrhoea and pneumonia, and an estimated 50,000 were homeless, more than 40,000 of them were forced to live in government run camps.

The cost to the economy was estimated at one billion Nepalese rupees ($14.25 million).

India 2008
The **Kosi River** is known to Indians as the 'River of Sorrow' because of its flooding during the monsoon season, which lasts from June to September.

The river flows into the Ganges river.

More than 2.7 million people in 1,600 villages were affected, thousands of people were still stranded on rooftops and trees or marooned on thin strips of dry land, more than two weeks after the floods started: 55 people were killed.

The flooding submerged roads and railway tracks, and cut off electricity. The road linking Saharsa village to the rest of the hard-hit Saharsa district was completely washed away.

Flood water flowed so forcefully that it actually changed the course of the river, which now flows 120 km east of its original course.

Sudan 2007
Three-and-a-half million people were at risk from water-borne diseases such as cholera as the **River Nile** flooded in Sudan: 89 people were killed and 73,000 homes were destroyed.

Somalia and Kenya 2007
The **Shabelle, Tana and Juba Rivers** flooded their banks, affecting towns and villages in Somalia and Kenya. The town of Garissa was underwater, with houses near the river Tana submerged. The floods destroyed bridges and made roads impassable, meaning aid drops by plane were the only way to deliver food to the starving population. One Somali refugee in Kenya told the BBC he and others were living in trees and were attacked by wild animals.

River Danube
Kosi R.
Saptakoshi R.
Shabelle R.
Tana R.
Juba R.

Prediction and prevention of the effects of river flooding by forecasting, building design, planning and education

Forecasting and education

In England 2.1 million properties are at risk from flooding. Over 50 per cent of these properties are at risk from flooding by rivers.

There are a number of ways that the effects of flooding can be reduced. Householders can be warned about a flood so that they can take precautions. This is done in the UK through a chain of events. The Met Office predicts the likelihood of a river flooding and gives information to the public through weather forecasts and news broadcasts on the television. If there is a likelihood of flooding the Met Office advises householders to be proactive and either ring a flood hotline number or go onto the Environment Agency website to check the likelihood of a flood in their area.

On the Environment Agency website there will be information on the likelihood of a flood. This will be identified by a system of warning codes; they are flood watch, flood warning, severe flood warning and all clear. These warning codes give people information on what to expect and how to react (see Figure 27 on page 57). In this way the government is helping to prevent the effects of floods by providing an effective warning system.

There are also a number of websites which are run by the government to give advice to the public who live in areas which are prone to flooding, for example, www.direct.gov.uk. There is general advice given about how to protect homes from flooding and advice on what to do if a flood actually happens, and specific information about river flooding.

DEFRA (The Department for Environment, Food and Rural Affairs) has the responsibility for deciding which areas of the coastline are going to be defended against the risk of flooding. The Environment Agency then organises for the defences to be built and maintained. DEFRA provides the money for most of the work that is completed.

Planning and building design

Before houses can be built the local authority has to give planning permission. This is not granted in flood risk areas unless a flood risk assessment has been carried out. However, some building does still take place in areas where it is not really advisable to build houses. By 2010 the government has indicated that planning laws will change so that all new housing in flood risk areas must be flood resistant or resilient.

If houses are built in flood risk areas or were built there many years ago there are a number of ways that the houses can be protected against the effects of flooding. It can cost anything from £3,000 to £10,000 to protect a house from the effects of flooding. This cost is much less if it is done after a major flood event when the house has been damaged. The type of measures that should be used depend on the flood risk of the property. They vary from protecting existing houses by moving electrical sockets higher up the walls to building houses with special foundations which are above the surface (see Figure 25 below):

- Moving electricity sockets higher up the walls.
- Replacing doors with ones that are lightweight and can be moved upstairs if necessary.
- Concrete floors instead of wooden ones so they do not rot if they are wet.
- Using yacht varnish on wooden skirting boards to protect them from water.
- Waterproof MDF can also be used instead of wood as a door frame.
- Buildings on stilts.

Figure 25 River and Rowing Museum in Henley on Thames

There was severe flooding in the UK in August 2008. Doncaster Council in association with St Leger homes implemented a series of flood resilient repairs to 138 council properties:

- Waterproof plaster and wall covering
- Chemical waterproofing of concrete floors
- Waterproof medium density fibreboard used instead of wood for skirting boards.

These implementations will not stop flooding but will mean that the houses will become habitable much quicker if they are affected by flooding in the future.

Hard and soft engineering techniques

- Hard engineering is a method of river flood management which involves major construction work.
- Soft engineering is a method of river flood management which works or attempts to work with natural river processes. It does not tend to involve major construction work, e.g. floodplain zoning.

Figure 26 Advantages and disadvantages of hard engineering

Hard engineering technique	Description	Advantages	Disadvantages
Embankments	These are raised banks along the river.	<ul><li>Can be used as a path for pedestrians beside the river.</li><li>Concrete embankments are effective at stopping bank erosion.</li><li>Earth embankments provide habitat for plants and animals.</li></ul>	<ul><li>The banks are often not built high enough.</li><li>Concrete embankments are ugly and spoil the view.</li></ul>
Channelisation	The river channel may be widened or deepened allowing it to carry more water. A river channel may be straightened so that water can travel faster along the course.	<ul><li>Effectively protects immediate area because water is moved away quickly.</li><li>Long lasting.</li></ul>	<ul><li>Altering the river channel may lead to a greater risk of flooding downstream, as the water is carried there faster.</li><li>Unnatural and visually intrusive.</li></ul>
Flood relief channels	The channel course of the river can also be altered, diverting floodwaters away from settlements.	<ul><li>Makes the people who live close to the main river safer as the flood water is diverted into the relief channel.</li><li>Can be used for water sports.</li></ul>	<ul><li>They require a large amount of land which might be difficult to purchase particularly if it is productive farmland.</li><li>Extremely expensive.</li></ul>
Dams	Dams are often built along the course of a river in order to control the amount of discharge. Water is held back by the dam and released in a controlled way.	<ul><li>Water is usually stored in a reservoir behind the dam. This water can then be used to generate hydroelectric power or for recreation purposes.</li></ul>	<ul><li>Building a dam can be very expensive.</li><li>Sediment is often trapped behind the wall of the dam, leading to erosion further downstream.</li><li>Settlements and agricultural land may be lost when the river valley is flooded to form a reservoir.</li></ul>

Figure 26 Advantages and disadvantages of hard engineering continued

Hard engineering technique	Description	Advantages	Disadvantages
Flood walls 	A vertical barrier usually made from prefabricated concrete.	• Can be used in areas where space is limited. • Easily and quickly erected in pre-constructed sections.	• They have to be assembled very well so that water doesn't get through joints.
Storage areas 	A large depression close to the river that will fill with water if the river overflows and therefore protecting the surrounding land.	• Natural looking. • Does not damage the environment.	• Need a large area of land that is not being used. • Only come into use when the river has flooded.

Figure 27 Advantages and disadvantages of soft engineering

Soft engineering technique	Description	Advantages	Disadvantages
Floodplain zoning	Local authorities and the national government introduce policies to control urban development close to or on the floodplain.	• A very cheap way of reducing the risk of damage to property. • It is sustainable because it reduces the impact of flooding and building damage is limited. • Also because the floodplain has not been built on, surface runoff is less likely to cause flooding.	• There can be resistance to restricting developments in areas where there is a shortage of housing. • Enforcing planning regulations and controls may be harder in LICs.
Washlands 	The river is allowed to flood naturally in wasteland areas, to prevent flooding in other areas, for example, near settlements.	• Very cost effective as nothing is built. • Provides potential wetland sites for birds and plants. • The deposited silt may enrich the soil, subsequently turning the area into agricultural land.	• Large areas of land are taken over and cannot be built on. • Productive land can be turned into marshland.

Figure 27 Advantages and disadvantages of soft engineering continued

Soft engineering technique	Description	Advantages	Disadvantages
Warning systems	A network of sirens which give people early warning of possible flooding. The Environment agency uses TV, radio, email, fax, text and phone messages to keep people informed.	• A very cheap system. • Electronic communication is a very effective way of informing people. • Because the people have warning of floods they can move valuable belongings to a safer place.	• The sirens could be vandalised, so they are tested annually. • There might not be enough time for residents to prepare.
Afforestation	Trees are planted in the catchment area of the river to intercept the rainfall and slow down the flow of water to the river.	• This is a relatively low cost option. • It improves the quality of the environment. • Soil erosion is avoided as trees prevent rapid run off after heavy rainfall. • Very sustainable.	• It is often conifers that are planted which can make the soil acidic. • Dense tree plantations spoil the natural look of the landscape. • It increases fire risks because of leisure activities in the forest.

Review

By the end of this section you should be able to:

• know what causes rivers to flood
• understand the effects of river flooding
• understand how the effects of river flooding can be predicted and prevented
• compare the advantages and disadvantages of river defence techniques.

ACTIVITIES

Higher

1 Explain the physical factors that cause rivers to flood.

2 Draw two spider diagrams, one for hard engineering schemes, the other for soft engineering schemes. Include their advantages and disadvantages.

3 People have different opinions about flood management. Choose either the argument for or against hard engineering schemes and write a letter to *The Times* newspaper stating your case.

Foundation

1 Describe three climatic factors that can cause flooding.

2 Complete the table below to show the advantages and disadvantages of the different engineering techniques.

Type of technique	Advantages	Disadvantages
Hard: embankments		
Hard: channelisation		
Hard: dams		
Soft: washlands		
Soft: land use zoning		
Soft: afforestation		

River management

Learning objective – to study the management of a riverine area.

Learning outcomes
- To describe the management techniques used on the River Nene.
- To explain the management techniques used on the River Nene.

Introduction
The River Nene used to flood frequently at Northampton. Heavy rain on 9 April 1998 caused the River Nene and Grand Union Canal to overflow, flooding parts of the town and leading to two people's deaths. It was decided to manage the River Nene to protect Northampton against the possibility of future flooding. By 2002 The Environment Agency had completed a £6.8 million project to protect areas of Northampton hardest hit by past flooding. In 2003 and 2007 further defence works were carried out in the town.

In 2002 a 450 m clay flood embankment was built in Weedon across the river valley upstream of Northampton. This raised the level of the land by 6.8 m. This will create a flood storage area behind the embankment. It cost £2 million. In times of flood, water can be stored here, preventing flooding downstream in Northampton. The river flow is regulated by a culvert through the embankment. The embankment has been landscaped to minimise visual impact and the storage area has been developed as a habitat for aquatic flora and fauna.

A new housing estate called Upton Square has been built just above the level of the floodplain. This housing has become possible due to the management of the area which has made the area safe from flooding.

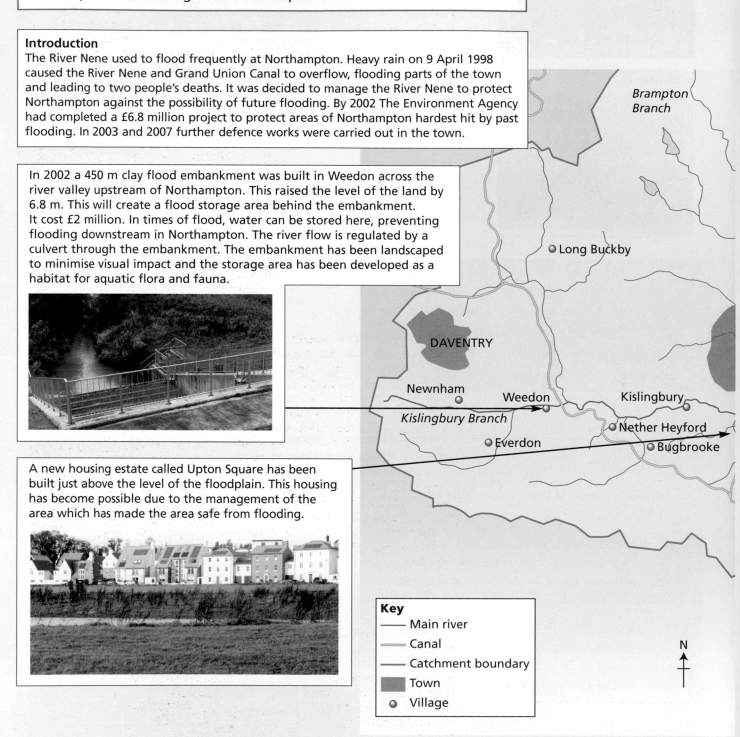

Key
- —— Main river
- ══ Canal
- —— Catchment boundary
- ▨ Town
- ⦿ Village

Brampton Branch

Long Buckby

DAVENTRY

Newnham
Weedon
Kislingbury
Kislingbury Branch
Nether Heyford
Everdon
Bugbrooke

N

Figure 28 The management of the River Nene

In 2003 the warning system was upgraded. The areas at risk of flooding are covered by the environment agency Flood Warning service where they aim to give two hours' notice of the possible onset of flooding. Testing in the Far Cotton and St James areas and a Flood Season Awareness Campaign was put into operation.

A flood retention reservoir has been built at Billing, near the aquadrome.

At Foot Meadow close to the railway station 4 m high floodwalls have been installed to protect housing, industry and the Castle Inn. This has created an open area of land which the river can flood onto giving protection to the railway station which is on the other side of the river. Debris was cleared from here so the river velocity would increase and rainwater would be taken away more quickly. Gabion boxes were also added which protect the river banks from erosion giving added security to the new housing beside the river.

In 2007 work began to build defences around Upton, near Sixfields. These defences cost £8 million. The aim of the works is to create an area, called a washland, where water can be diverted from the River Nene in a controlled manner in order to reduce the risk of flooding downstream.

Major roads in this area such as Upton Way (A45) are on embankments up to 6 m high. The embankments join up with specially built floodgates to create an area of open land where up to 1.2 million cubic metres of flood water can be stored during times of heavy rain. The water can be held harmlessly in open grassland. When the rain has passed, the gates will be opened to allow the water to flow steadily back into the River Nene.

The road is also protected by a 2 m high floodwall which is made of concrete sections.

The river channel capacity at Upton was increased by building earth embankments set back 10 m from the river which have footpaths along the tops. The area has been visually improved by planting trees.

Brixworth

Pitsford Reservoir

NORTHAMPTON

Billing Aquadrome

R. Nene

Northampton Washlands

Wootton

Hackleton

Wootton Brook

Horton

0   5   10 km

Review

By the end of this case study you should be able to:

- describe the management techniques used on the River Nene
- explain the management techniques used on the River Nene.

Sample Examination Questions

Higher tier

1 a   Study Figure 2 on page 64. Draw a sketch of Figure 2 and annotate it to explain the process of biological weathering.   (4 marks)

   b   Name two types of mass movement.   (2 marks)

2   Study Figures 7, 15 and 17 on pages 67, 69 and 70. How does human use of the valleys in the map extracts change as you move from the upper to the lower stage of the Rheidol river?   (3 marks)

3   Study Figure 14 on page 69. Describe and explain why the speed of the river varies across a meander.   (4 marks)

4   Choose one soft and one hard engineering technique. Describe and explain the advantages and disadvantages of each technique.   (6 marks)

5   For a river management scheme that you have studied, describe and explain the management techniques that have been used.   (6 marks)

Total 25 marks

Foundation tier

1 a   Complete the following sentences by putting in the missing words. Use some of the words in the box.

physical biological chemical moisture seawater
animals sun wind rocks meander waterfall

.... weathering is the action of plants and .... on the land. Seeds that fall into cracks in rocks will start to grow when .... is present. The roots put out by the young plant force their way into cracks and, in time, can break up the ....   (4 marks)

   b   Name two types of mass movement.   (2 marks)

2 a   Study Figure 15 on page 69. Name two ways that people use the valley.   (2 marks)

   b   Give one piece of map evidence to say why this river is in the middle stage.   (1 mark)

3   Complete the paragraph to explain why the speed of the river varies across a meander. Use some of the words in the box.

fastest gravity deposition shallowest deepest
friction erosion transportation slowest cleanest

The outside of a meander bend has the .... water because this is where the greatest erosion takes place and forms a river cliff. The water is moving .... at this point and therefore erodes the bank using corrasion. The water moves more quickly on the outside due to the lack of .... because of the river's depth and consequent lack of contact with the bed and banks. .... occurs on the inside because the water is moving more slowly and is shallower.   (4 marks)

4 a   What does the term 'afforestation' mean?   (2 marks)

   b   Choose one hard river engineering technique. Describe the advantages and disadvantages of this technique.   (4 marks)

5   For a river management scheme that you have studied, describe and explain the management techniques that have been used.   (6 marks)

Total 25 marks

The impact of glaciation on river valleys

Learning objective – to study the impact of glaciation on river valleys.

Learning outcomes
- To understand the processes of glacial erosion.
- To understand the process of freeze-thaw and how it provides material for abrasion and moraine formation.
- To be able to describe and explain the formation of corries, arêtes, pyramidal peaks, corrie lakes, U-shaped valleys, truncated spurs, hanging valleys and ribbon lakes.
- To be able to describe and explain landforms of glacial deposition: moraines, drumlins and erratics.

What are the processes of glacial erosion?

Glaciers erode by two main processes:

As a glacier moves down a valley, it puts pressure on the valley sides and bottom. This pressure creates heat. (If you push your hands together, they will become warm because of the pressure you are using.) The heat causes a small amount of ice to melt, the water runs into cracks in the valley sides or bottom and almost immediately refreezes because of the cold temperatures. As the glacier moves, it then pulls away some of the rock face. This process is known as plucking.

The rocks that have been removed from the hillsides by plucking (and freeze-thaw weathering) are carried in the ice of the glacier. As they move down the valley, they wear away (erode) the valley sides and bottom causing more rock to be broken off. This process is known as abrasion.

How does freeze-thaw provide material for abrasion and the formation of moraines?

Freeze-thaw can only work where daytime temperatures allow ice to melt, and it is cold enough at night for the water to freeze again. During the day, while the sun is shining, cracks, hollows and other weaknesses get wet or filled with water as glacial ice melts and soaks the rocks. At night the temperatures become colder and the

water in the cracks freezes. When the water freezes it expands, puts pressure on the rock and causes the cracks to widen. The next time the temperature is warm enough for the ice to melt, the water thaws and contracts. This cycle continues, each time widening or enlarging the cracks by a tiny amount. Eventually this continuous process causes rocks to break up. The broken rock material is then used by the glacier to erode through abrasion or is deposited as moraine.

 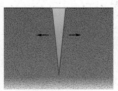 

A small crack in a rock fills with water during the daytime. As the water begins to freeze at night, it starts at the top, sealing the crack.

As the water freezes completely, its 9% growth exerts an outward force on the sides of the crack, increasing the size of the crack by a maximum of 9%.

If the ice thaws the next day the resulting water will not fill the crack, which is now both wider and deeper because of its 9% expansion. Dew or rainfall on the rock surface can refill the crack.

 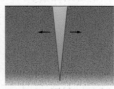

The process begins again, this time with a larger initial crack.

Again the crack expands by as much as 9%. Continued freezing and thawing, particularly with the daily addition of the water to keep the crack full, eventually leads to significant fracturing of the rock.

Figure 1 The process of freeze-thaw

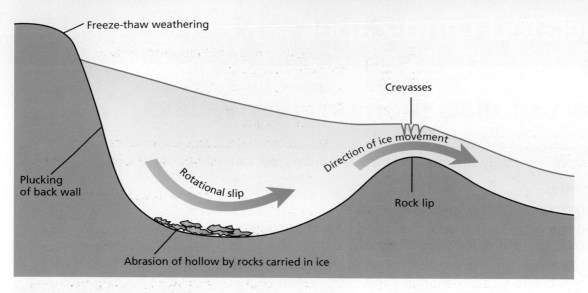

Figure 2 The formation of a corrie

Labels on figure: Freeze-thaw weathering · Crevasses · Direction of ice movement · Plucking of back wall · Rotational slip · Rock lip · Abrasion of hollow by rocks carried in ice

What landforms can be found in glaciated uplands?

As a glacier moves down a valley, it carves out a number of distinctive landforms: **corries**, pyramidal peaks, arêtes, truncated spurs, hanging valleys, ribbon lakes and U-shaped valleys. Eroded material, known as moraine, is also deposited on the valley sides and bottom.

Corries and corrie lakes

Corries or cirques are armchair-shaped hollows. Corries have a steep, rocky back wall, often up to 200 m high in the UK but much higher in the Alps. The corrie is fringed by sharp ridges, known as arêtes. Corries begin to form when the snow that accumulates on high mountain slopes is compacted into ice. After a time, the ice starts to move due to the pull of gravity and as it moves, it carves out a corrie, usually in an area that already has a small depression (see Figure 2). The ice erodes by plucking and forms the steep back wall; the hollow is formed by abrasion. After glaciation, the corrie can be filled by a small lake known as a corrie lake or tarn.

The rotational movement of the ice causes greater pressure at the bottom of the steep back wall and in the base of the hollow than it does at the front where the ice leaves the corrie. Because there is less pressure, erosion rates at the front of the hollow are slower. A rock lip forms here which can be increased in size by deposition of moraine. This works as a dam after glaciation, and a corrie lake or tarn forms behind it. Freeze-thaw weathering occurs at the top of the steep back wall and adds rocks to the ice. These become embedded and are used in the process of abrasion.

Arêtes and pyramidal peaks

If two corries form next to each other on a mountainside, their sides will be both steep and rocky. The piece of land between them will be a sharp ridge of rock (arête) that is continually attacked by freeze-thaw weathering and plucking. If corries form on at least three sides of the mountain, the top of the mountain will become a sharp peak of jagged rock known as a pyramidal peak (see Figure 3). This is continually sharpened by frost action and plucking.

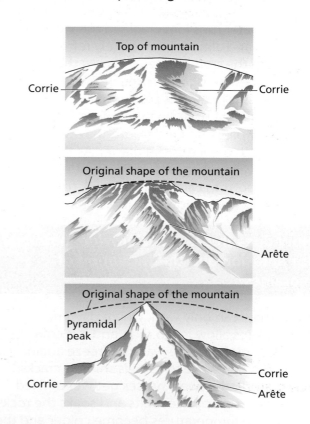

Figure 3 Arête and pyramidal peak formation

Figure 4 Corrie, arête and pyramidal peak

ACTIVITIES

Use Figures 5 and 6 to help you to answer the following questions.

1 Name two corrie lakes.
2 Name a ribbon lake.
3 Name one arête.
4 Work out the difference in height between:
   a the spot height at Blea Water and the pyramidal peak
   b the spot height at Haweswater Reservoir and Blea Water
   c What is the total difference in height?
5 a Study the aerial photo of the Blea Water area.
   b Find Blea Water and draw a sketch of this area of the photo. In your sketch, include two arêtes, a pyramidal peak, the steep back wall of the corrie, the corrie lip and Blea Water.

Figure 5 Blea Water aerial photo

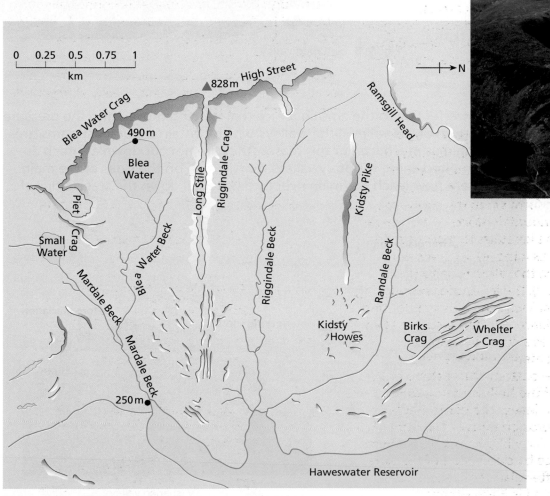

Figure 6 Blea Water map

U-shaped valleys and truncated spurs

A U-shaped valley is formed by a valley glacier.

A valley glacier will completely fill a valley in an upland area. By doing this, it has far more power to erode the whole valley than the original river which only flowed across the valley floor, winding its way around crops of more resistant rocks to form interlocking spurs.

As a glacier moves down a valley, its immense power erodes any rock in its path. It does not need to go around outcrops of harder rock but simply removes them. In this way, interlocking spurs are cut back to produce truncated spurs (see Figure 7). The valley, which used to be V-shaped with a river in the bottom, now has steep walls of bare rock for its sides and a flat bottom and it is also straighter than it was before glaciation. These are the characteristics of a U-shaped glaciated valley.

Figure 8 U-shaped valley

Hanging valleys

The main valley glacier is very powerful due to the amount of ice that is being moved and the pressure that it exerts on the sides and bottom of the valley. Other valleys, which contain tributary streams, are smaller and therefore do not contain as much ice. For this reason, they are not cut down as much as the main valley. After the ice has melted, these tributary valleys remain high on the sides of the main valley. The streams that flow in them now reach the main river by a waterfall down the steep sides of the main valley (see Figure 7).

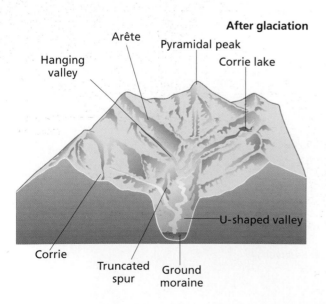

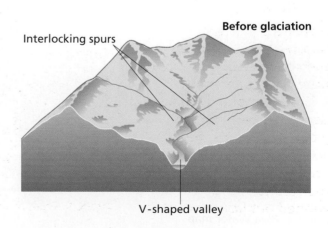

Figure 7 U-shaped valley formation

Ribbon lakes

These are long, narrow lakes that can be left in a valley after glaciation. They are formed when the glacier meets a band of softer rock that it can erode more quickly. This leaves a groove in the valley bottom which, after glaciation, becomes filled with water. An example of a ribbon lake is Wastwater in the Lake District.

The processes of deposition including ablation and lodgement

Glacial material deposited directly by a glacier, can be classified as either lodgement till or ablation till.

Lodgement till is where material beneath the glacier has become lodged in the bed as the glacier is advancing or retreating, for example, where a glacier is so full of debris that it spreads it onto the valley floor. An increase in ice thickness can also increase friction beneath the ice, causing lodgement.

Ablation till is where material is deposited as the ice around it melts away. This may be because of solar radiation causing melting along the margins of a glacier, or it may be due to the changing seasons. A glacier will expand and retreat with changes in temperature. As a glacier retreats due to ablation at the snout, material is left behind.

What landforms are created by glacial deposition?

Moraines

Moraine is material transported by a glacier and then deposited. There are four main types of moraine.

Ground moraine is material deposited beneath the glacier and forms the flat valley floor. It is made up of unsorted, irregular shaped rocks, sand and clay. It may be washed out from under the

glacier by meltwater streams, or left in situ when the glacier melts and retreats.

Lateral moraine forms along the edges of the glacier. Material from the valley walls is broken up by freeze-thaw and falls onto the ice surface. It is then carried along the sides of the glacier. When the ice melts it forms a ridge of material along the valley side.

Medial moraine is formed from two lateral moraines. When two glaciers join, the two edges that meet form the centre line of the new glacier. In consequence, two lateral moraines find themselves in the middle of the glacier forming a line of material on the glacier surface. When the ice melts it forms a ridge of material along the valley centre.

Terminal moraine forms at the end (snout) of the glacier. It marks the furthest point that the ice reaches down the valley. It is a large mound of material that forms across the valley floor and can be hundreds of metres high.

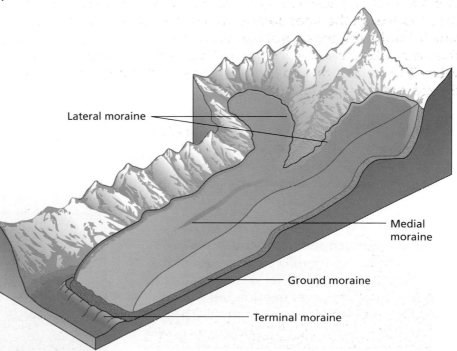

Lateral moraine

Medial moraine

Ground moraine

Terminal moraine

Figure 9 Types of moraine

Drumlins

Drumlins are formed by moraine material deposited by ice sheets in lowland areas. They are elongated features that can reach a kilometre or more in length, 500 m or so in width and over 50 m in height. One end is quite steep, while the other end tapers away to ground level. The stoss end is the steeper of the two ends and faced into the direction of ice flow. The lee slope is the more gentle slope. This means that the highest point will always be at the top of the stoss end of the drumlin. It is common to find several drumlins grouped together. The collection of drumlins is called a swarm. Areas with swarms of drumlins are sometimes referred to as 'basket of eggs' topography because of the rounded bumps that remind people of a box containing eggs.

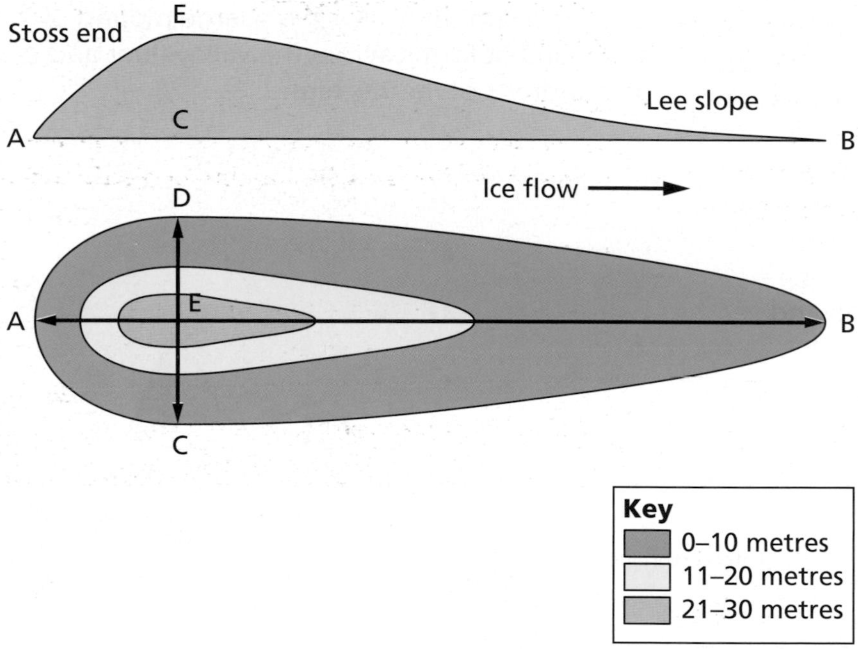

Figure 10 Plan and profile diagrams of a typical drumlin

Drumlins were formed when the ice had collected too much sediment and could no longer transport it. Therefore the power of the glacier was reduced, material was deposited, in the same way that a river overloaded with sediment deposits the excess material. The glacier may have experienced a reduction in its power for several reasons, including melting of the ice and changes in velocity. If there is a small obstacle on the ground, this may cause material to build up around it. As the ice continued to move it formed the drumlin into its characteristic shape. It may also have been reshaped by further ice movements after it was deposited.

In Figure 10, the ice was flowing from left to right. The long axis of the drumlin is the line A–B, the point of maximum width is the line C–D, and the highest point on the landform is at E. Not all drumlins will show such a distinct difference in slope angle between the stoss end and lee slope, but the stoss end will always be the steeper of the two.

Erratics

Erratics are large boulders that have been transported by glaciers or ice sheets, and often deposited a considerable distance from their origin. Therefore they will be made of a different rock type from the rock that they are deposited on. For example, there are granite erratics in the county of Norfolk (UK) that originated in Norway more than 600 km away.

By knowing where the erratic originated, it is possible to determine the direction of ice flow that brought it to its present location. This helps glaciologists to monitor and plot past ice movements across large areas.

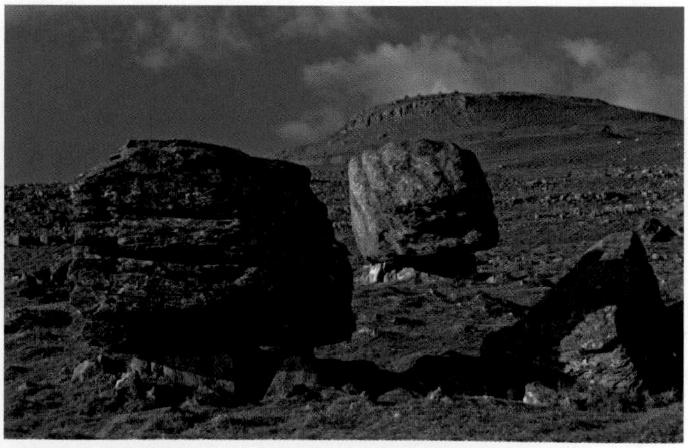

Figure 11 Erratics

ACTIVITIES

Higher

1 Study Figure 8 on page 86.

  a Describe the valley.

  b Draw a sketch of the photograph and label:

   i   a hanging valley

   ii a truncated spur

   iii a corrie

   iv an arête

   v   a pyramidal peak.

2 How was this valley formed?

3 How is moraine used to erode a valley?

Foundation

1 Study Figure 8 on page 86.

  a Describe the valley.

  b Draw a sketch of the photograph and label:

   i   a hanging valley

   ii a truncated spur

   iii a corrie

   iv an arête

   v   a pyramidal peak.

2 How was the valley in Figure 8 formed?

Complete the paragraph below.

Use some of the words in the box.

abrasion	interlocking	plucking	gravity
attrition	U	V	deposition

One way a glacier erodes is by .... This is where the glacier freezes on to rock and pulls it away as the glacier moves downhill by the force of .... The second way a glacier erodes is by .... This is where the material in the glacier acts like sandpaper. As the glacier moves down the valley it cuts through the .... spurs and changes the original .... shape of the valley.

3 Look at the table below. It shows features of glacial deposition and their description. Draw lines to match the feature with the correct description.

Feature	Description of glacial feature
Drumlin	Material carried by a glacier
Erratic	A hill made of glacial deposits
Moraine	A boulder deposited on a different rock base

Review

By the end of this section you should be able to:

- understand the processes of glacial erosion
- know how corries form
- understand the process of freeze-thaw and how it provides material for abrasion and moraine formation
- be able to describe and explain the formation of corries, arêtes, pyramidal peaks, corrie lakes, U-shaped valleys, truncated spurs, hanging valleys and ribbon lakes
- be able to describe and explain landforms of glacial deposition: moraines, drumlins and erratics.

How people use glaciated landscapes

Learning objective – to study how people use glaciated valleys.

Learning outcome
- To know the ways in which people use glacial and glaciated landscapes.

How do people use glaciated landscapes?

There are several uses for glaciated landscapes.

1 Glaciers provide water for drinking and irrigating crops

People living in Peru and Bolivia rely on water from melting glaciers and ice caps to provide water during dry spells. Global warming is causing the ice to melt for a longer period each year. While this means more plentiful water at the moment, if the melting continues the glaciers will retreat. This may lead to the loss of the water altogether.

India, Afghanistan and Pakistan rely on glacial meltwater for both drinking and irrigation during the dry season. Although they experience very heavy rainfall during the monsoon season, it is not a reliable source for year round supplies so glacial meltwater is essential for the huge and ever growing population in these areas.

In Switzerland's Rhone Valley, farmers have irrigated their crops for hundreds of years by channelling meltwater from glaciers to their fields. The Rhine and Rhone rivers in Europe start as glacial meltwater. If global warming continues and the Alpine glaciers melt, these rivers will possibly dry up, leaving parts of Europe lacking sufficient water supplies.

2 Glaciers can generate hydroelectric power

In many countries in the world, such as Norway, Canada, New Zealand and France, glacial waters are used to generate electricity by channelling it through hydroelectric turbines. In Norway 99 per cent of its energy is produced by hydroelectric power (HEP). In Svartissen, Norway, engineers combined a scheme to drain a dangerously high glacial lake with a hydroelectric scheme, making the glacier safer and producing cheap electricity at the same time.

Previously glaciated areas contain ribbon lakes such as Loch Tummel and Loch Rannoch which are ideal as natural reservoirs that can be dammed and used to generate electricity.

Figure 12 Irrigation in the Rhône Valley

Pump storage systems use corries high up in the hills to store water, which flows down to the power station via turbines. This generates electricity during the day. At night, where there is surplus energy, water is pumped back up to the reservoir. The Dinorwig Power Station in Wales was built in 1984 and generates 1.7 gigawatts (GW) of power. Ten miles of underground tunnels buried beneath Elidir mountain carry water down from the corrie lake, Marchlyn Mawr, to the six 288 megawatt (MW) turbine generators situated in Europe's largest man-made cavern. During construction 12 million tonnes of material was excavated and 1 million tonnes of concrete and 4,500 tonnes of steel used.

Industry, and therefore jobs, can be attracted to remote areas to harness the cheap energy produced by HEP. The power generated by the Lochaber hydroelectric turbine is used to produce aluminium at Fort William in Scotland.

3 Glaciated areas are used for leisure and tourism

In areas where glaciers are accessible, such as in the European Alps, glaciers attract tourists. Glaciers are used by ice climbers, hikers and for tourists who are simply curious to get up close to one and see what a 'river of ice' looks like.

Previously glaciated landscapes attract hill walkers, climbers, mountaineers, mountain bikers, photographers and other outdoor enthusiasts. Fast-flowing waters are used by canoeists and anglers. The English Lake District and the Cairngorms in Scotland are good examples of formerly glaciated landscapes that are now National Parks preserved for their natural beauty. In winter, parts of Scotland become skiing destinations as the glaciated hills take on a covering of snow. Aviemore, for example, survives on its winter tourist income.

Snowdonia, another National Park, has spectacular glaciated landscapes. Tourism provides much needed income to this economically poor area:

- 5,000 people are employed in the leisure and tourism industry
- £180 million is made by tourism
- £22 is the average amount spent by day tourists
- £80 is the average spent by overnight tourists.

In Europe and North America many glaciated areas acquire a thick layer of snow and become popular ski runs. Skiing has increased in popularity steadily since the 1960s.

Figure 13 Hydroelectric power station

Figure 14 Skiing in the Alps

4 Agriculture in glaciated areas

Hill sheep farming is usually the main type of agriculture on upland slopes in Snowdonia where it is cold and the soils are poor. Steep-sided valleys make access difficult and the cool temperatures and poor soils make growing crops almost impossible. If the slopes are used for growing crops they are most likely to be planted with coniferous trees which can survive on the northern slopes of valleys. The trees grow fast and can be sold for timber and paper making.

Lowland glacial deposits are often very good areas for agriculture. Being lowland, the temperatures are more suitable for crops and the glacial deposits are very fertile. Such soils are often poorly drained and need additional drainage before they become really good.

5 Communications

In highland areas, the steep valley sides make it difficult to run roads up and down the hills, so communication routes usually follow the valley floors. In Scotland railways were often built along the edges of valleys, and in the English Lake District many roads follow the lake shores. In Alpine areas the valley floor will often have a motorway and railway side by side. This can lead to long journeys between places that are close together, but separated by mountains.

ACTIVITIES

Extension work

1 Locate a glaciated upland area in the UK.
   a List all the leisure activities that take place there.
   b Look at the photograph of a hydroelectric power station in Figure 13 on page 91. Draw a sketch diagram and annotate it to explain how it works.

Review

By the end of this section you should be able to:
* understand the ways that people use glacial and glaciated valleys.

Avalanches and their management

> **Learning objective** – to study avalanches and their management.
>
> **Learning outcomes**
> - To know the causes and effects of a named avalanche.
> - To understand how avalanches can be predicted and the ways that avalanches can be prevented.

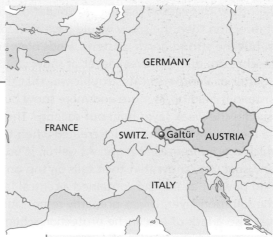

Figure 15 Map showing location of Galtür

Introduction

Galtür is a small village (population 900) in the Tyrol region of Austria. In the winter it is a popular ski resort. Avalanches happen frequently, in fact in most years there is a small avalanche which follows the same route, but trickles out safely long before the village. It even has a name: the Wasser-Leiter, or water ladder. The avalanche had never hit the village before because Galtür is more than 200 m away from the base of the mountain. Historical records had never reported the avalanche to be a problem. Despite this, to be absolutely safe, the Wasser-Leiter had influenced the building zones of the village. No houses are built in the red area which is vulnerable to avalanches. In the yellow zone buildings must be reinforced to make them avalanche-proof. Only in the green zone are there no building restrictions at all. It was here, in the safe zone, that the avalanche caused the most damage.

On 23 February 1999 at 8 a.m. a huge chunk of ice broke away from the mountain starting a massive avalanche and it raced down the slope at around 290 km/h. As it travelled down the mountain, the avalanche picked up twice the amount of the initial snow volume. The avalanche was estimated to contain around 300,000 tonnes of snow. It had a height of around 100 m and took only 50 seconds to reach the village. At 8.01 it rushed into Galtür passing through the red zone and into the yellow zone. Within seconds many of the reinforced buildings were buried by the snow. It then continued into the green zone where buildings did not stand a chance. At 8.02 the avalanche finally died out.

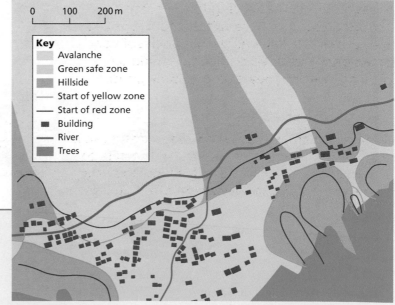

Figure 16 Map of zones and area affected by avalanches

What caused the avalanche?

A complex weather system led to the avalanche. On 20 January 1999, an Atlantic storm formed 4,000 km away. Warm tropical air which was heavily saturated with moisture was heading north. As it moved north it cooled forming a system of fronts with towering clouds. The system then swung back towards Europe. What made this frontal system exceptional was that it produced a relentless series of storms rather than a single storm. During February, 4 m of snow fell in the Galtür area breaking all records.

Another problem was the wind. Galtür had almost three weeks of very strong winds up to 100 km/h. Within an hour these winds can move 20 tonnes of snow from one side of a ridge to the other. This caused massive accumulations of snow. If the wind had come from a different direction then the snow would have drifted onto the slopes facing away from the village, but the strong north-westerly winds blew towards Galtür.

All avalanches are due to a weak layer of snow which tumbles down the slope. What made the Galtür avalanche so catastrophic was that the weak layer didn't collapse soon enough. Instead it held on as more and more snow built up on top before it finally gave way. So why did the weak layer hold out so long? The weak layer was a special type known as a melt crust. Melt crusts are created when the upper snow layers thaw during the day which then refreezes at night. At Galtür, it bonded with ice and hence lasted longer than usual. Any snow that then falls on top only binds partially to the snow below. The resulting powder avalanche contained a central layer scientists did not know existed. This was the saltation layer; it was primarily responsible for the destruction of buildings.

There was also a lack of avalanche protection schemes in Galtür. Snow fences had been built on many slopes elsewhere in the valley as a protection against dangerous avalanches, but they weren't thought necessary in the Wasser-Leiter area.

Arrows show main avalanche flow.

Area of village engulfed also marked.

Figure 17 Aerial view of Galtür

What were the human effects of the avalanche?

People

- Soon after the avalanche rescuers began to look for survivors; in 24 hours the rescuers saved 26 people. A rescue sniffer dog named Heiko saved many lives.
- 31 people died in the avalanche, the last body (a little German girl) was found four days after the event on 27 February.
- The people who died were 26 tourists from Germany, Denmark and the Netherlands, and five local Austrians.
- 11 people were severely injured. Six of the wounded required intensive care and were taken immediately to the hospital near Landeck, 25 miles from Galtür.
- 25 people sustained minor injuries.
- A memorial service was held in Innsbruck, the capital of Austria, in remembrance of those who died in the avalanche.

Economy/infrastructure

Roads into the mountainous area were blocked and an international rescue team of Austrian, German, Swiss and US helicopters ferried people stranded in Galtür to safety. Some 30,000 people were evacuated from the area, most of them in US Black Hawks and other helicopters landing on a blocked-off section of the autobahn (motorway) outside Landeck and at Pontlatz Kaserne, a training base for the Austrian army.

- The first roads did not open until 27 February.
- Tour operators cancelled bookings in the Austrian villages of Galtür and at Valzur.
- The risk of new avalanches closed ski resorts in the region. The Paznaun Valley, where disaster struck, lost £5 million a day for as long as the tourists stayed away.

Figure 18 Rescue workers and volunteers searching for survivors

Property

- 4 local houses were completely destroyed, one of which had its roof chopped off by a slab of ice.
- 12 buildings were severely damaged.
- 40 other buildings were buried beneath the snow but remained intact.
- Rescue equipment was buried at the fire station of Galtür. It took two days to dig it out.
- 100 cars were smashed.
- There was approximately £7.5 million damage done to property.
- Both Galtür and Valzur, the next door village also affected, were evacuated except for rescue crews and locals wishing to stay. But 1,000 tourists refused to leave, either waiting for roads to reopen or determined not to quit their holidays.
- 25 February – helicopters took in supplies of fresh fruit and vegetables.

Figure 19 Devastation caused by the avalanche

What were the physical effects of the avalanche?

Only a little damage was done to the environment as the path of the avalanche was mostly over open terrain. Some trees were destroyed which had a minor effect on animal habitats.

It was decided to build a barrier wall directly in the centre of the village. This barrier wall is the basis of the Alpinarium project.

The Alpinarium project allows Galtür to continue its philosophy of promoting gentle tourism and developing awareness for the Alpine environment among all its visitors.

A day later, a second avalanche in Valzur, Austria, just 6 miles away from Galtür, caused more devastation. The sliding snow destroyed eleven homes and two farms in its path and killed seven people.

Figure 20 The Alpinarium

Can avalanches be predicted?

In order to reduce deaths and to protect villages and roads, people attempt to predict and prevent avalanches. Accurate avalanche prediction requires an experienced avalanche forecaster who often works both on the snow covered mountain to gather snowpack information and in the office with sophisticated equipment such as remotely accessed weather data, detailed historical weather and avalanche databases, weather models and avalanche-forecasting models. Avalanche forecasters combine their historical knowledge of past conditions with their knowledge of the mountainside, current weather and current snowpack conditions to predict when and where avalanches are most likely to occur. Such forecasting work typically takes place along mountain highways next to potentially affected villages, at ski areas, and on slopes heavily used for skiing and snowboarding. By using this information ski resorts prepare avalanche warnings. The risk of avalanche is assessed on a five-level scale. In the resort there will be a board showing the predicted avalanche risk for that day. The resort will also signal the avalanche risk using flags and other fixed signs. These are usually located at the top of major ski lifts. Yellow signifies a low to medium risk of 1–2, a chequered flag a high risk of 3–4 and black a very high risk of 5.

Figure 21 Avalanche risk sign in the Alps

Can the effects of avalanches be prevented?

Prevention by planning and education

Sometimes avalanche control experts create smaller, controlled avalanches to break up heavy masses of snow and prevent larger, uncontrolled avalanches. Percussion guns, explosives, and even artillery have been used to produce these controlled avalanches. In Canada, the Canadian army patrols between towns each winter, armed with 105 mm howitzer cannons. They use an average of 423 rounds of ammunition to guard the 150 km stretch of the Trans-Canada Highway, breaking up snow before it can avalanche and cover the road.

In the USA ski rangers and patrol teams test ski runs and hiking areas before opening them to the public. These rangers often work in pairs, one testing the snow while the other watches from a safe spot. The tester will zigzag back and forth across a slope, bouncing up and down, always looking for signs of instability. Obviously, these patrollers have very dangerous occupations. Both people will carry electronic transceivers to keep in touch, as well as anchor themselves to a tree or boulder before venturing into untested territory.

Skiers are continually told of the risks of causing avalanches if they venture into unprepared areas in ski resorts. Some resorts have sensitive areas fenced off to restrict entry by skiers. Land use zoning exists in most mountainous areas susceptible to avalanches. People will not be allowed to build in high risk areas.

Figure 22 Ski patrol team

Prevention by defences

Trees are the best natural defence against avalanches. Forests in the Alps are being killed by acid rain, insect damage and disease. Cold, windy winters can also leave nothing but bare rocky surfaces, which then become permanent avalanche paths. The reforestation of slopes with trees helps to prevent avalanches. An area of trees can keep a layer of snow from slipping and triggering an avalanche. However, once a snow slide starts, the largest trees cannot stand against hundreds of thousands of tonnes of snow and ice that move downhill at 200 miles an hour.

Snow shed or avalanche shed is a structure that provides avalanche protection for roads and railway tracks. Depending on the threat level and size of area to be protected, they are built of wood or reinforced concrete.

Snow fences are built to stabilise snow. They usually have gaps between the beams and are built perpendicular to the slope, with reinforcing beams on the downhill side. These barriers are often considered unsightly, especially when many rows must be built. They are also expensive and vulnerable to damage from falling rocks.

Diversion structures such as dams or wedges are used at the base of the slope to stop, split, or deflect the snow in an avalanche. Though expensive, these defensive measures are common throughout the Alps.

Prevention by building design

All new buildings in avalanche threat zones must be avalanche-proof. This involves building with reinforced concrete walls and no windows on the avalanche side.

Figure 23 Snow shed at Val Thorens

Figure 24 Snow fences in the Pyrenees

Review

By the end of this section you should be able to:
- know the causes and effects of a named avalanche
- understand how avalanches can be predicted and the ways that avalanches can be prevented.

Sample Examination Questions

Higher tier

1 There are two main processes by which a glacier erodes its valley.

    a   Name the two processes.   (2 marks)

    b   Explain how one of these processes operates.   (3 marks)

2 Draw a sketch of Figure 4 on page 85. Annotate the sketch to explain the formation of a corrie.   (5 marks)

3 With the aid of a diagram describe the difference between lateral and medial moraines.   (3 marks)

4 How are glaciated landscapes used for leisure and recreation? Use examples in your answer.   (4 marks)

5 The effects of avalanches can be prevented in building design. Describe one building design that can prevent the effects of avalanches.   (2 marks)

6 For a named avalanche, describe and explain its effects.   (6 marks)

> Total 25 marks

Foundation tier

1 The statements in the table explain the process of plucking. They are not in the correct order.

    a   Number them in the correct order. The first one has been done for you.

Statement	Correct order
The water runs into cracks in the valley sides and refreezes.	
As a glacier moves down a valley, it puts pressure on the valley sides and bottom.	1
As the glacier moves, it then pulls away some of the rock face.	
The heat causes a small amount of ice to melt.	
This pressure creates heat.	
This process is known as plucking.	

(5 marks)

    b   Name another process of glacial erosion.   (1 mark)

2 Study the diagram below which shows a glaciated area.

On the diagram label:

    a   a corrie

    b   an arête

    c   a pyramidal peak

    d   lateral moraine

    e   medial moraine.   (5 marks)

3 Complete the sentences below. Use some of the words in the box.

hiking	poor	work	sleeping	swimming
cow	sheep	crop	good	recreation

Glaciated landscapes can be used for leisure and .... Two examples of this are skiing and ....

The most common type of farming in glaciated landscapes is hill .... farming.
This is because the soil is ....   (4 marks)

4 Describe two ways that the effects of avalanches can be predicted or prevented.

Way 1 _____

_____

Way 2 _____

_____

(4 marks)

5 For a named avalanche describe and explain its effects.   (6 marks)

> Total 25 marks

Location and characteristics of tectonic activity

Learning objective – to study the location and characteristics of tectonic activity.

Learning outcomes

- To be able to describe the global distribution of volcanoes and earthquakes.
- To understand how the movement of plates leads to earthquakes and volcanic activity.
- To know the characteristic features of convergent, divergent and conservative plate boundaries.
- To recognise the different ways that an earthquake can be measured.

The world's distribution of earthquakes and volcanoes

The distribution of the world's main earthquakes and active volcanoes is shown in Figures 1 and 2. If you compare Figures 1, 2 and 3, you will see a clear pattern emerging between the distribution of volcanoes, earthquakes and the world's plate boundaries. Earthquakes occur in long narrow bands on all three types of plate boundary, both on the land and in the sea. The largest belt runs around the Pacific Ocean. Other major belts travel along the middle of the Atlantic Ocean and through the continents of Europe and Asia from the Atlantic Ocean to the Pacific Ocean.

Volcanoes also occur in long narrow bands. The largest band, called the Pacific Ring of Fire, goes around the entire Pacific Ocean. They are found at constructive and destructive plate boundaries, occurring both on the land and in the sea. They are sometimes found away from plate boundaries at 'hot spots' where the crust is particularly thin.

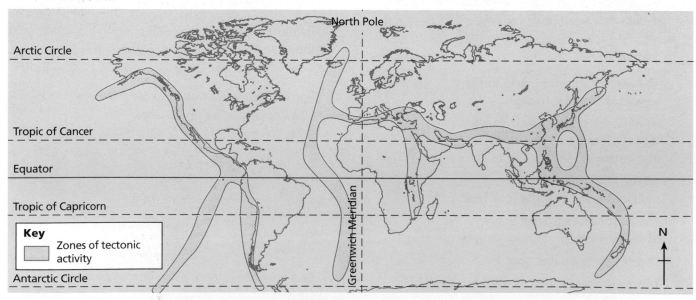

Figure 1 The world's distribution of earthquakes and volcanoes

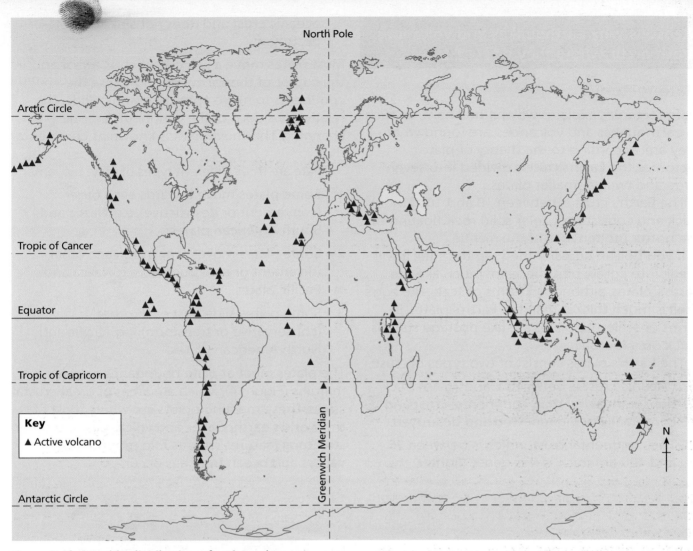

Figure 2 The world's distribution of active volcanoes

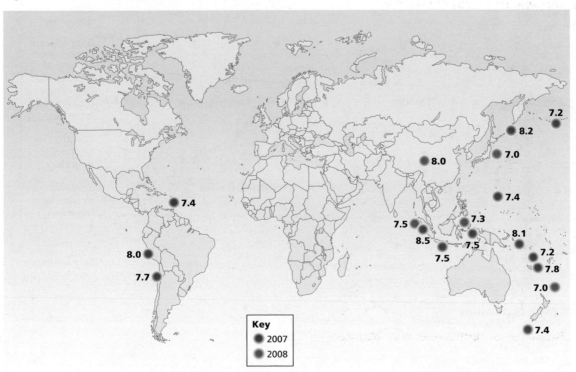

Figure 3 Major earthquakes for the years 2007 and 2008

Reasons why earthquakes and volcanoes both occur where they do

Plate tectonics

Plate tectonics explains why natural hazards, such as earthquakes and volcanoes, are found where they are. According to the theory of plate tectonics, the Earth's crust is divided into seven large and twelve smaller plates.

The Earth's crust is between 10 and 100 km thick and consists of cooler solid rock 'floating' on the hotter molten rock of the mantle.

If you boil an egg and then tap the shell it will break into jigsaw bits. These are much like the Earth's plates, although in terms of scale, the egg's shell is much thicker than the Earth's plates. In terms of scale, the plates are like postage stamps stuck on a football.

The Earth's plates consist of two types of crust:

1 Oceanic crust is between 5 and 10 km thick, denser (heavier) than continental crust and continually being renewed and destroyed.

2 The continental crust, which is between 25 and 100 km thick, is less dense (lighter) than oceanic crust and does not sink. It is not destroyed.

Most plates move a few centimetres a year and, in the course of the Earth's history, cause the continents to move, split apart and collide. The relative positions of the continents are still changing. This movement is known as continental drift.

There are three different types of plate movement:

1 Some plates move towards each other (convergent or destructive), e.g. Nazca and South American plates.

2 Some plates move away from each other (divergent or constructive), e.g. Nazca and Pacific plates.

3 Some plates slide past each other (conservative or transform), e.g. Pacific and North American plates.

The plates meet at plate boundaries or plate margins (Figure 4), which are areas of great crustal stress. These meeting points are where most of the world's earthquakes and volcanoes, and other structural features such as fold mountains, rift valleys and ocean trenches occur.

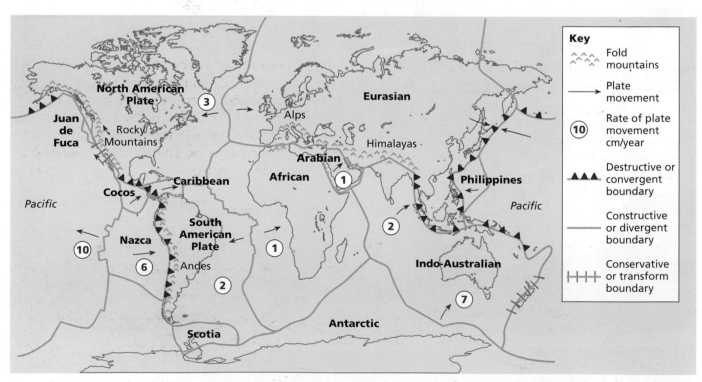

Figure 4 World map of plate boundaries

What are hotspots?

Why do some volcanoes not occur on plate boundaries? Island chains such as Samoa and Hawaii are known as hotspots, where magma from the mantle erupts through the crust. This creates volcanoes that often rise above the ocean surface to form islands. The Samoa chain formed as the Pacific crustal plate moved over the stationary source of magma or hotspot.

This can be confirmed because the lava has been radiometric age dated on all the islands and Savai'l

has been dated at 5 million years old, whereas Vailulu'u is a new island that is presently being formed. The volcano, recently named Vailulu'u by local students, is located about 40 km east of Ta'u Island and rises more than 5,000 m from the seafloor to within 600 m of the ocean surface.

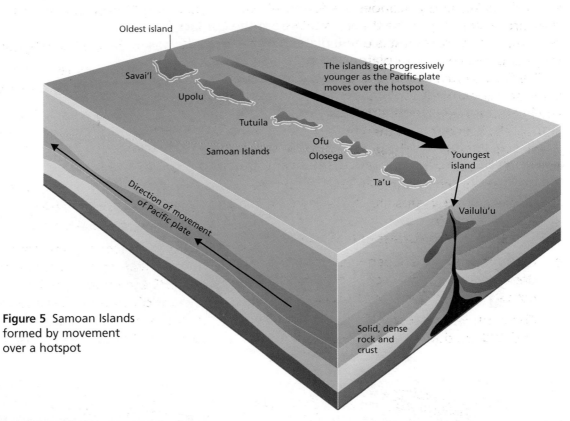

Figure 5 Samoan Islands formed by movement over a hotspot

Characteristics of plate boundaries

1 Convergent or destructive boundaries

At a destructive plate boundary, two plates move towards one another. Where they meet, one plate is subducted (slides) below the other. The cause of this subduction is the difference in density between the two plates, with the heavier one being subducted below the lighter one.

Three types of destructive plate boundary have been identified:

a Ocean-to-ocean boundaries

The Ryuku Islands, just to the south of the Japanese island of Kyushu, are a direct result of destructive plate activity in the western Pacific. The Philippine plate to the east is subducting beneath the Eurasian plate to the west (see Figure 6). As it subducts, the tremendous pressures that are released cause earthquakes. At about

100 km below the surface, the subducting plate begins to melt and magma escapes to the surface to form volcanoes. After several eruptions, these volcanoes break the ocean surface to form islands. When several of these islands form together they are called an island arc. The Ryuku Islands are an example.

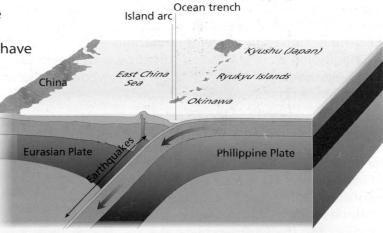

Figure 6 Ocean-to-ocean convergent plate boundary

b Ocean-to-continent boundary

Figure 7 shows the Nazca plate being subducted below the South American plate. As the oceanic plate is being subducted, a deep oceanic trench forms. These oceanic trenches are the deepest part of the ocean. If it were possible to drop Mount Everest into the Marianas Trench, part of the Pacific Ocean close to the Philippines, it would be completely covered.

The heat from the mantle and friction from the contact between the two plates causes the oceanic plate to be destroyed.

At the same time, this friction and pressure causes earthquakes to occur along the subduction zone. The melting plate creates liquid magma that rises towards the surface to form volcanoes such as Aconcagua, the highest peak in the Andes (6,960 m).

The collision of the plates also causes severe folding and uplift of the rocks. This process has contributed to the growth of the Andes.

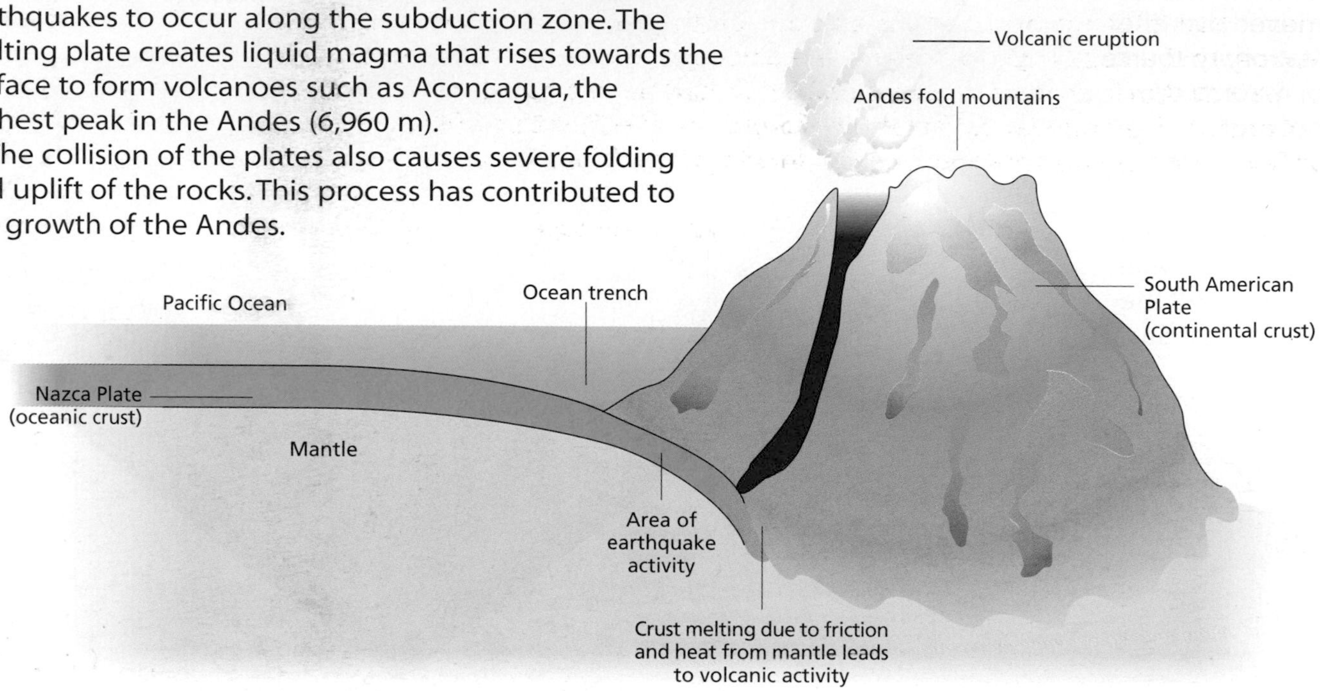

Figure 7 Convergent plate boundary of Nazca and South American plates

c Continental-to-continental boundary

Continental crust is less dense than oceanic crust and so, when two continents meet at a destructive plate boundary, a slow collision rather than any marked subduction takes place. This results in intense folding, faulting and uplift and leads to the formation of mountains. As there is very little, if any, subduction at this plate boundary, there are few earthquakes and no volcanoes.

Figure 8 shows the movement of India. About 100 million years ago the Indian plate started to converge with the Eurasian plate. Gradually, the ocean between them narrowed until the two continental land masses collided. The thick layers of sediments between the two continents were carried into the sea by rivers which had eroded them from the land. As the plates collided, these sediments were squeezed and folded to form the Himalayas. The process continues today, with the Indian plate grinding into the Eurasian plate at a rate of 5 cm a year.

Figure 8 The formation of the Himalayas

2 Divergent or constructive boundaries

Constructive boundaries occur where two plates move away from each other and create a new crust. This occurs most commonly in the middle of oceans. Figure 9 shows how the North American plate is moving apart from the Eurasian plate, causing the Atlantic Ocean to widen by about 3 cm a year. The convection currents that are causing this movement are creating a gap called a mid-oceanic ridge. Magma rises to fill the gap, thus forming new land.

Where the magma builds up above the surface of the ocean, volcanic islands form. Iceland, which is a volcanic island, did not exist 2 million years ago when Britain entered its last Ice Age. Iceland's location on the Mid-Atlantic ridge means that it is a major site of volcanic and earthquake activity. The island of Surtsey to the south-west of Iceland was a volcano under the sea that erupted in 1963. Within four years an island of 2.8 km^2 had been created.

Constructive boundaries can also be found on land. The East African Rift Valley is opening up and new land is being formed in the bottom of the valley.

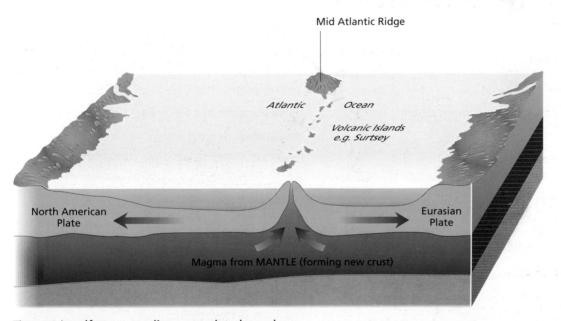

Figure 9 Landforms at a divergent plate boundary

3 Conservative or transform boundaries

Conservative boundaries are where plates move alongside each other. No new crust is created nor is any destroyed and no new landforms appear. However, these can be sites for violent earthquakes. The San Andreas Fault in California marks the junction of the North American and Pacific plates (see Figure 11). Both plates are moving north-west but at different speeds. Instead of slipping smoothly past each other, they tend to 'stick'. The pressure builds up until suddenly the plates jerk forward, sending shock waves to the surface and triggering a sudden earthquake. There is no volcanic action because the crust is not being destroyed at conservative boundaries.

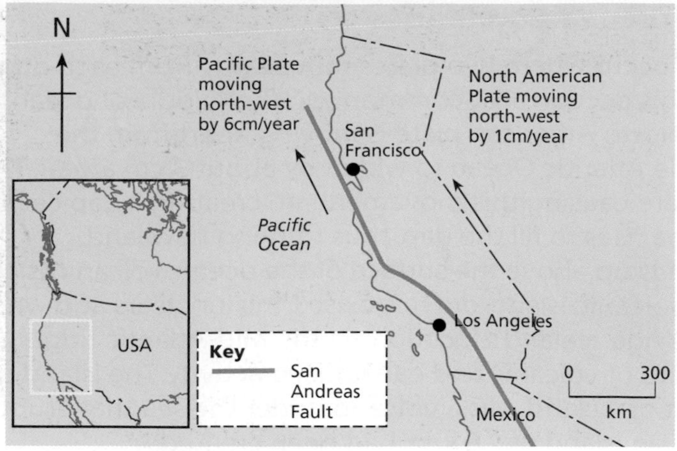

N

Pacific Plate
moving
north-west
by 6cm/year

North American
Plate moving
north-west
by 1cm/year

San
Francisco

Pacific
Ocean

USA

Los Angeles

Key

San
Andreas
Fault

Mexico

0   300

km

Figure 11 The San Andreas Fault

ACTIVITIES

Higher

1   a   What are plates?

   b   What are the differences between oceanic and
       continental crusts?

2   Draw simple annotated diagrams to show the
    main features of:

   a   convergent

   b   divergent

   c   conservative plate boundaries.

3   Describe the distribution of earthquake activity.
    Use specific place names.

4   Explain why no volcanoes exist along conservative
    plate boundaries.

Foundation

1   Name two plates that:

   a   move away from each other

   b   move towards each other

   c   move alongside each other.

2   Name three differences between oceanic and
    continental crusts.

3   a   Make a copy of Figure 12 (below). Add the
        following labels in the correct place:

        continental crust, oceanic crust, ocean trench,
        fold mountains, volcano, area of earthquakes,
        crust being destroyed.

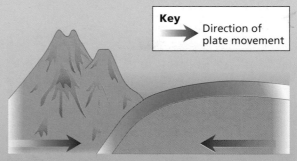

Key

Direction of
plate movement

Figure 12 Plate boundary

   b   What type of plate boundary is this?

   c   Draw and label a similar diagram for a
       divergent (constructive) boundary.

How are earthquakes measured?

Two main methods are used to measure earthquakes. The Mercalli scale gives an indication of the intensity of an earthquake while the Richter scale refers to its magnitude.

The Mercalli scale

The intensity of an earthquake is a measure of the violence of earth motion produced by the earthquake. The Mercalli scale is determined by the effects the earthquake has on humans, buildings and the local landscape. The magnitude has a unique value for a particular earthquake. The magnitude of an earthquake at a place depends on the distance of that place from the epicentre and the depth of the focus.

Many places, including Hong Kong, have adopted the Mercalli scale which classifies earthquake effects into twelve grades. Figure 13 shows the typical effects that can be witnessed for each level of intensity.

The problem with the Mercalli scale is that it is an arbitrary set of definitions based upon what people in the area feel, and their observations of damage to buildings around them. While this scale is fine if you happen to experience an earthquake in an inhabited area of a developed country, it is of no use at all in the middle of a desert or in any other place without people and buildings. Descriptions such as 'Similar to vibrations caused by heavy traffic' depend very much on the observer having felt heavy traffic in the past. Even then, what one person in a small town considers being 'heavy' will be different from what a person living in major city close to an urban motorway would describe as 'heavy'.

IV/V

VI/VII

IX

XII

Intensity	Effects
I	Detected only by seismographs.
II	Noticed only by sensitive people.
III	Similar to vibrations caused by heavy traffic.
IV	Felt by people walking. Free standing objects will gently rock.
V	People will be woken up if asleep. Church bells will shake causing them to ring.
VI	Trees sway and there will be some damage from overturning and falling objects.
VII	There is general alarm. Walls will show signs of cracking.
VIII	Chimneys fall and there is some general damage to buildings.
IX	The ground begins to crack. Underground pipes break and houses begin to collapse.
X	Ground badly cracked and many buildings are destroyed. There are some landslides.
XI	Few buildings remain standing. Bridges and railways are destroyed. Water, gas, electricity and telephones are put out of action.
XII	Total destruction. Large objects such as cars are thrown into the air. There is considerable earth movement.

Figure 13 Earthquake intensities

The Richter scale

The Richter scale is designed to allow easier comparison of earthquake magnitudes. Using this scale it is much easier to compare the power of two earthquakes regardless of their location. C.F. Richter was a geologist living and working in California, USA, an area which gets hundreds of earthquakes every year. He took the existing Mercalli scale and tried to add a scientific scale based on accurate measurements that could be recorded by seismographs (instruments used to measure vibrations).

By measuring the violence of the ground when it suddenly moves, he devised a scale that reflected the magnitude of the shock.

The Richter scale for earthquake measurements is logarithmic. This means that each whole number represents a ten-fold increase in power. Thus, a magnitude 7 earthquake is 10 times larger than a 6, 100 times larger than a magnitude 5 and 1,000 times larger than a 4. This is an open ended scale since it is based on measurements not descriptions, although very few earthquakes occur which are in excess of 8.

What is the focus and epicentre of an earthquake?

An earthquake is a violent shaking of the Earth's crust. They are caused by the sudden release of enormous stresses and lead to the crust snapping. The point at which the snapping occurs is called the focus (see Figure 14) and is below the surface of the earth and may be many kilometres deep. The point on the ground surface immediately above the focus is called the epicentre and this is where the greatest damage usually occurs.

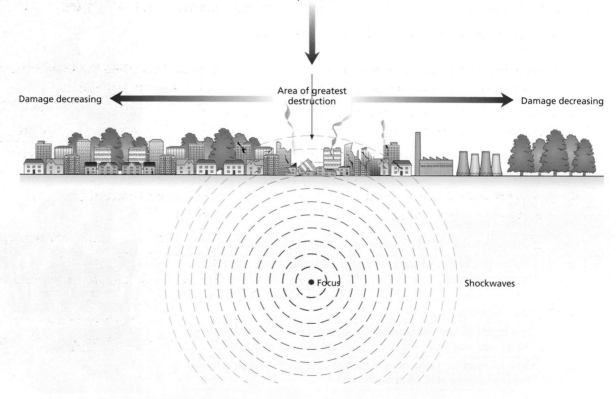

Figure 14 Earthquake destruction

Review

By the end of this section you should be able to:

- describe the global distribution of volcanoes and earthquakes
- understand how the movement of plates leads to earthquakes and volcanic action
- know the characteristic features found at plate boundaries
- recognise the different ways that earthquakes can be measured.

ACTIVITIES

Higher

1 Study the table in Figure 15 (below).

Foundation

1 Study the table in Figure 15 (below).

**Number of Earthquakes Worldwide for 2000–2008
Located by the US Geological Survey National Earthquake Information Center**

Magnitude	2000	2001	2002	2003	2004	2005	2006	2007	2008
8.0 to 9.9	1	1	0	1	2	1	2	4	0
7.0 to 7.9	14	15	13	14	14	10	9	14	9
6.0 to 6.9	146	121	127	140	141	140	142	178	111
5.0 to 5.9	1,344	1,224	1,201	1,203	1,514	1,693	1,712	2,074	864
4.0 to 4.9	8,008	7,991	8,541	8,462	10,888	13,919	12,838	12,078	7,481
Estimated Deaths	231	21,357	1,685	33,819	228,802	82,364	6,605	712	87,746

Figure 15 Number of earthquakes worldwide for 2000–2008

a What is the relationship between the magnitude of an earthquake and frequency?

b Draw a scatter graph showing the number of deaths and the number of earthquakes.

c Is there a relationship between the number of earthquakes and the number of deaths?

d There were many more deaths in 2004 than in 2007. Suggest reasons why?

a Copy and complete the following sentences. Use the words in the box.

no	two	2005	2004
less	more	most	least

The .... frequent the earthquake the .... its magnitude.

The year which had the .... deaths was 2004.

There were .... earthquakes over 8.0 in 2002 and 2008.

The year with the most earthquakes was ....

b In some years there were many more deaths than in other years. Suggest two reasons for this.

Management of the effects of tectonic activity

Learning objective – to study the management of tectonic activity.

Learning outcomes
- To understand the reasons why people continue to live in active tectonic zones.
- To know the causes and effects of a named volcanic eruption or earthquake.
- To recognise the different ways that volcanic activity and earthquakes can be predicted and prevented.

Why do people continue to live in areas of volcanic and earthquake activity?

Why do people continue to live in areas of:	Economic reasons	Social reasons	Environmental reasons
Volcanic activity	Volcanic soils are especially fertile. The region around Naples, Italy, is a huge wine growing area sited on volcanic ash from nearby Vesuvius. The lower slopes of Mount Mayon, Philippines, are covered with rice fields, coconut plantations, tomatoes and other vegetables. Mayon's eruption in 1993 killed 75 people – all of them tomato farmers in the Bonga Valley, one of the areas declared off-limits by the government. Today nearly 20,000 locals live and farm within Mayon's Permanent Danger Zone. The world's best coffee is grown on volcanic soil in Colombia.	A lot of poor people, particularly in low-income countries (LICs) don't move because they can't afford to. Their livelihood is based on the life and jobs they have in that area. People do not want to leave families and friends.	Some volcanoes are popular tourist areas. Mount Etna in Sicily attracts thousands of tourists who travel up to the crater by cable car and four-wheel drive vehicles. A whole range of tourist facilities give the local population many jobs.
	Minerals such as tin, silver, gold, copper and diamonds can be found in volcanic rocks. The money that can be made by mining these precious minerals often outweighs the risk of volcanic activity.	Many people who live close to Mount Merapi in Indonesia worship ancient spirits and they believe that the spirits watch over the peak and will warn them of an eruption. Often at full moon locals climb to the volcano crater and throw in rice, jewellery and live animals to calm the volcano's spirits.	
	In Iceland the volcanoes provide very cheap geothermal energy. The energy is so inexpensive that in the wintertime, some pavements in Reykjavík, the capital, are heated. In 2008, 28 per cent of electricity generation in Iceland came from geothermal energy.	People believe that the chance of the volcano erupting is very low. Volcanoes can remain dormant for hundreds of years so locals think it is worth the risk.	

Figure 16 The reasons why people continue to live in areas of volcanic and earthquake activity

Figure 16 The reasons why people continue to live in areas of volcanic and earthquake activity continued

Earthquake activity	Some earthquake areas like Turkey and Iceland are popular tourist areas and provide many jobs for the locals.	People in middle-income countries (MICs) feel safe in earthquake zones because of the advances that have been made in earthquake proof buildings. Since 1981 all new buildings in Japan have had to be earthquake proof. It is also common to have disaster plans to tell people what to do in an emergency.	Some places are known for their beauty and some individuals buy houses in exclusive areas despite potential earthquake risks, e.g. Malibu, California.
	Landslides, triggered by earthquake tremors, have caused loss of lives at numerous mining sites around the world. In 2007 an earthquake measuring 7.7 hit an area of many large copper mines in Chile, killing two people and injuring 117. In August 2008 a moderate tremor at a coalmine in the north-eastern province of Liaoning, China killed six workers and injured one other worker. The people consider the risk is acceptable as they can make a good living from mining.	People believe that the chance of them being affected by an earthquake is very low.	People feel safer as buildings can now be built to be earthquake proof.

Figure 17 Mount Etna attracts many tourists each year

Figure 18 Geothermal energy in Reykjavik, Iceland

What caused the earthquake?

On 17 August 1999 at 3.02 a.m. a magnitude 7.4 earthquake hit Turkey. The epicentre of the earthquake was near the industrial city of Izmit, about 88 km east of Istanbul. Turkey sits close to the boundary of three tectonic plates of Eurasia, Africa and Arabia, which are pushing into one another. The Turkish landmass is a small tectonic plate, which is being squeezed between these plates. This plate movement has created several faults throughout Turkey and the east Mediterranean. The Arabian plate is pushing the small Turkish microplate westwards causing earthquakes on the North Anatolian fault as the tectonic plates slide past each other. Izmit lies on the North Anatolian fault, which is one of the most active fault lines in the world. The length of the fault is 860 km, from Yalova on the west side to Sapanca on the east. The North Anatolian fault represents a conservative margin, which slipped between 2 and 5 m causing the earthquake in 1999. Making matters worse is that the ground in the area around Izmit mostly consists of very thick soft clay or loose sand layers which move much more than solid rock.

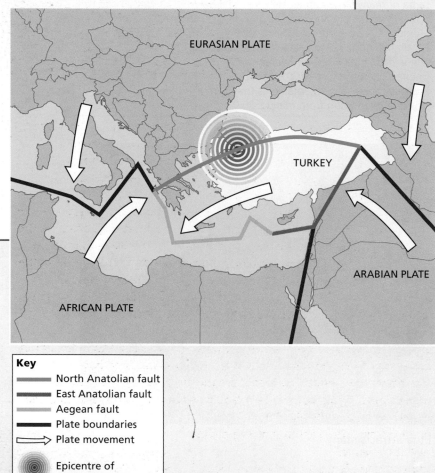

Key
- ── North Anatolian fault
- ── East Anatolian fault
- ── Aegean fault
- ── Plate boundaries
- ⇒ Plate movement
- ◉ Epicentre of earthquake

Figure 19 The cause of the 1999 earthquake in Turkey

Effects on the people

The damage from the initial tremor was particularly intense because of the unusually shallow depth of the earthquake's focus, just 10 km below the surface. This means the shock waves are felt much more strongly at the surface than for a deeper earthquake. Its effects were devastating, an estimated 18,000 people died and 300,000 were left homeless. In Yalova alone 65,000 buildings were destroyed. Almost all of the deaths occurred due to the collapse of buildings. The most common type of housing in Turkey is two- to five-storey buildings which were not constructed well enough to withstand the tremors.

Figure 20 Collapsed buildings in Izmit

- Destruction occurred over a wide area. Buildings were destroyed in Turkey's largest city, Istanbul, 80 km north-west of Izmit.
- Parts of the motorway between Ankara and Istanbul buckled, causing cars to crash into each other.
- Hospitals in the city of Gebze ran out of beds causing more suffering for the injured.
- In Golchuk there was a solid jam of vehicles along the main road as people evacuated the area. This caused problems for rescue workers trying to get to the devastated zone. The job of keeping lanes open for the rescue services had been given to vigilantes who used sticks and in some cases guns to threaten people.
- The earthquake also caused a tidal surge. A tidal wave swept into the coastal areas of Izmit Bay on the Sea of Marmara smashing boats, marooning a passenger ferry in the middle of an amusement park and drowning Turkish tourists. The wave that struck the seaside resort of Degirmendere was 6 m high. All but one of the sculptures in the town park were destroyed. Survivors of the wave said that subsequent waves repeatedly struck the shore at intervals, an effect known as a seiche. When the wave reached one end of Izmit Bay, it rebounded and hit the other end until it finally calmed down.
- Two years after the earthquake more than 20,000 people were still living in temporary accommodation, some of them in tents, most of them in prefabricated huts.
- Memories of the earthquake remained long after the event, and psychological problems have multiplied. Some people have trouble sleeping, others have become withdrawn. In 2007 when a relatively minor tremor shook Istanbul during the night, thousands of people fled into the streets in panic.

The worst hit region around the eastern end of the Sea of Marmara is part of Turkey's industrial heartland. Big businesses have recovered well, and there has been less disruption in many industries than was initially anticipated. Small companies and entrepreneurs have suffered badly, however. Many shopkeepers were unable to reopen for business, as thousands of their former customers migrated away from the earthquake zone, and returned to other parts of the country. This meant they either had to close down or suffer large losses. It was estimated that rebuilding the region cost about $10 billion.

Figure 21 A tented village in the affected area

Environmental effects of the earthquake

Turkey's largest oil refinery at Tupras with 700,000 tonnes of oil was set on fire. The fire burnt itself out, but by then it had poured out large quantities of pollution into the air, the water and onto land. The smoke caused health problems for local people who suffered from breathing illnesses like asthma. The oil was dispersed over a wide area but could have caused considerably more environmental damage if it had not been for a UK-based Oil Spill Response company using booms and absorbent materials for containing and clearing up the oil.

Tupras oil refinery on fire

The oil refinery at Korfez was also affected. For days after the earthquake struck it was burning out of control causing considerable damage to the local ecosystems.

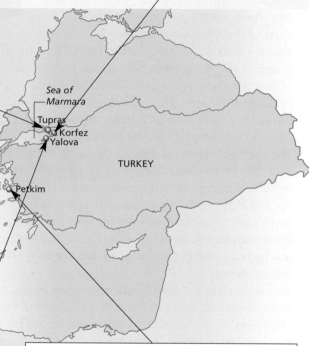

In Yalova next door to a chlorine plant, was a factory producing synthetic fibres, where there was some chemical leakage, though it was brought under control quickly.

The toxic waste dump at Petkim was cracked, exposing the waste which had been dumped there for years. There was also damage to the nearby PVC factory and to the waste treatment plant causing raw sewage to contaminate rivers killing fish.

The earthquake actually caused massive land movements on the coast of the Sea of Marmara causing some land to be reclaimed from the sea.

Throughout the area people suffered from diarrhoea due to lack of clean water and spillages of untreated sewage. There were concerns that diseases such as cholera could infect the area.

Figure 22 Environmental effects of the earthquake

Eyewitness reports

The quake struck Istanbul pretty hard. My house was quite vigorously shaken up and moved around, but nothing was broken.

As I am typing this e-mail I can feel the aftershock tremors shaking the building. It is very frightening. I have never been in an earthquake before. It was so powerful that when it first started I was thrown out of my bed.

The electricity went off. I threw myself onto the bed. My room was shaking and there were some crunchy noises coming from the walls. It lasted about 20–25 seconds.

I arrived in Adapadzari a week after the earthquake and saw buildings slumped down on their foundations, balconies buckled, walls lurching at insane angles.

Figure 23 Eyewitness accounts

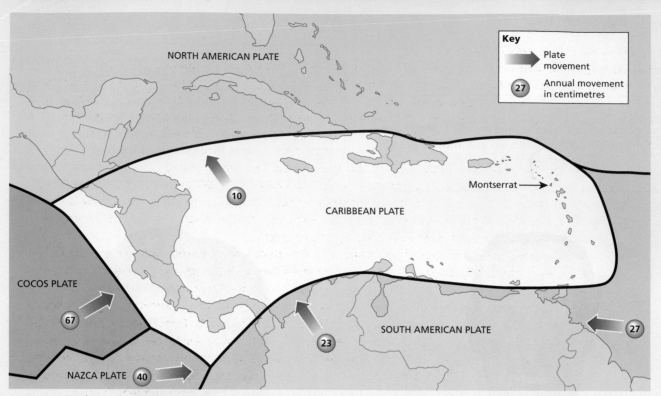

Figure 24 The causes of the Montserrat eruption

The causes of the Montserrat eruption

The volcanic island of Montserrat is situated on a destructive plate boundary. A plate boundary occurs when two of the plates that make up the surface of the earth meet. The North American plate is slowly being forced under (subducted) the Caribbean plate. This happens because the oceanic North American plate is denser than the Caribbean continental plate. Convection currents pull the dense North American plate into the mantle where intense heat and friction causes the rock to melt. This molten rock is lighter than the surrounding rock, forcing it to rise through cracks in the rock towards the Earth's surface forming the volcanic island of Montserrat.

On 25 June 1997, at about 1 p.m., Chances Peak Volcano on the island of Montserrat erupted catastrophically. What made the eruption so catastrophic was that the volcano produced thick sticky lava called andesite. The lava is so thick that it builds up at the top of the volcano in a dome until it becomes too heavy and the dome collapses. As the dome collapsed, a huge ash cloud was formed. The ash cloud rose rapidly to a height of about 10 km. Strong winds blew the clouds of ash westwards over the island. Some parts of Montserrat suffered blackout conditions as the sun was obstructed by the ash cloud. As the ash cooled it fell back on to some parts of the island depositing ash 2–3 mm thick. Also when the dome collapsed hot rocks, gases and ash were ejected from the volcano causing pyroclastic flows. These are extremely fast moving and can destroy everything in their path.

Effects of the eruption

The eruption on 25 June 1997 affected Montserrat in a number of ways. For the first time an eruption on the island killed and injured people. Villages were destroyed and land previously used for farming was covered in rock and ash deposits.

Effects on the people

The eruption of the volcano should not have had a major impact on the people of Montserrat as the areas affected were in the Exclusion Zones. This zone had been set up after an eruption in 1995. Most of the people had been evacuated to the north of the island in 1995 and were living in makeshift shelters.

On 25 June 1997 some authorised people were in the Exclusion Zone to carry out essential tasks and monitor the volcanic activity. When an eruption looked likely all these people were able to evacuate safely by responding to the emergency sirens. Some unauthorised people were also in the Exclusion Zone. They were too far away to hear the sirens but thought they would receive audible warning from the volcano if it was going to erupt.

Unfortunately this didn't happen and many people were caught unawares. Nineteen people were killed by the pyroclastic flows. All the people who were killed or injured by the pyroclastic flows and surges were in the Exclusion Zone. Seven people were killed by the surge in the Streatham and Windy Hill area. Six of the victims were found outside houses where they had been attempting to seek shelter. Two other bodies were recovered from the pyroclastic flow deposits near Trant. The remaining missing persons are thought to have been in the village of Farm, which was buried by deposits several metres thick, and were never recovered. Common injuries were severe burns to the feet as a result of walking on ash deposits. Other survivors suffered burns to various parts of their bodies, including burns to the nose and mouth due to breathing in the hot gases.

Of the 11,000 people who lived on Montserrat when the volcano first erupted in 1995, 7,000 had been evacuated. Almost 3,000 went to the neighbouring island of Antigua. The UK received nearly 4,000 evacuees and the rest went to the USA.

Effects on transport

Montserrat was cut off from air travel in 1995 when the volcano destroyed Bramble airport. It was not until the new Gerald's Airport was reopened in July 2005 that international travel could resume. WinAir currently has four daily flights from Montserrat to Antigua and two daily flights to St Maarten. The tourist industry is still suffering with few visitors except for cruise ships looking at the volcano. Although the capital, Plymouth, was no longer occupied the port was still in use. The port was not destroyed by this eruption; however an emergency jetty was built in the north of Montserrat. Some people in the Exclusion Zone tried to escape using their vehicles but the ash was so thick that it was impossible to see the road. The intense heat also burned the tyres of the cars.

Effects on buildings

Numerous villages were affected by deposits: Dyer, Streatham, Riley's Yard, Farrell's Yard, Windy Hill, Harris, Bramble, Bethel, Spanish Point, Farm and Trant were all affected.

The villages of Farm and Trant were completely buried by ash flow deposits. The eruption on 25 June 1997 destroyed 100–150 houses. Houses were partially buried or burned by the intense heat. Aluminium window shutters were melted and twisted. Everything made from wood was burned.

Other houses were destroyed by direct impact of rocks, up to 5 m in size. The houses destroyed were in the Exclusion Zone and should have been empty but an estimated 15 people were living and sleeping in the Exclusion Zone. These were mostly farmers. The farmers were producing crops to feed evacuees and believed that they were helping their country in crisis. Most land suitable for farming was in the south of the island, close to the volcano.

Figure 25 Ruined court house after the eruption

Environmental effects of the eruption

Figure 26 shows the environmental effects of the eruption.

The pyroclastic flows broke and flattened thousands of trees. In some areas there was no vegetation left at all. Vegetable beds were bare of plants and the soil was baked hard.

Many rivers were blocked causing flooding.

A total of 4 square kilometres of land was covered by the deposits.

Flow deposits completely filled Pea Ghaut and formed a thick, broad fan emerging north-west from Paradise River just north of Bethel. Houses up to 200 metres from the edge of the fan were completely buried by deposits.

The pyroclastic surges spread out and flattened trees on the ridges surrounding Farrell's Yard.

Some of the rocks deposited in Bethel were up to 5 metres in size. This caused widespread destruction.

The pyroclastic flows extended westwards travelling as far as the last bend in the valley before Cork Hill causing the Belham River to flood.

During the eruption 5 million cubic metres of rock and ash was deposited.

The main part of the flow in Mosquito Ghaut caused intense scouring to the top of the steep valley walls ripping off all the vegetation. Pyroclastic flow deposits nearly filled this valley.

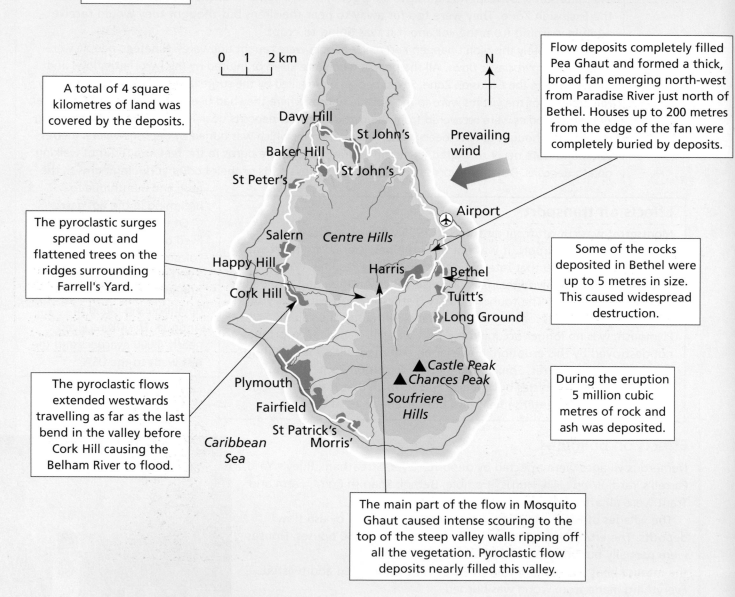

Figure 26 Environmental effects of the eruption

Eyewitness reports of the eruption

Figure 27 describes some eyewitness accounts of the eruption.

We were going to leave in just a few weeks. Before this we had checked around in the north and there was absolutely no place to go. There was no place to rent. That is why we were still here.

Ash come up on the school field and cover the whole of Harris. There was one grey and black mighty cloud. Started to feel hot, hot, hot, like I was in an oven. The whole place turned black for about 20 minutes. The houses on the side of the road next to the ghaut were burnt.

My house in Streatham is burned. The house is burned flat, everything I had is gone. You can see here I don't get no burns (on his legs) I have long pants (trousers) on but I didn't have nothing on my foot. So from that I get damaged – if I had on my shoes I wouldn't have got damaged. I lose me toes and spend six months in hospital.

Went to Dyers almost 2 hours after the eruption. Had to stop the car because of ash on the road. I got out the vehicle and took a small stick and pushed it through the material on the road - it burned immediately where it went in about 3 inches. I went up further and pushed it into the flow. It did not come back out and it burned completely.

When I reach Dyer's corner rain shelter, me feel heat and see black stuff running down the road. Me feel the heat all over, me say "see how me foot burn down", me feel like me been in a fire meself. Got a lot of ash, shirt was full of ash, couldn't see the colour of the red shirt.

Figure 27 Eyewitness accounts of the eruption

ACTIVITIES

1 The movement of which plates were responsible for:
   a the Turkish earthquake?
   b the Monserrat volcano?
2 Draw annotated pictures to show the environmental effects of the Montserrat volcano or the Turkish earthquake.
3 Were short- or long-term effects more damaging in the worst affected areas in Turkey?

Prediction and prevention of the effects of volcanic eruptions and earthquakes

Can earthquakes and volcanic eruptions be predicted?

A variety of methods are being used by scientists to predict these hazards but they are not completely accurate. Despite sophisticated monitoring equipment it still remains very difficult to pinpoint exactly when an eruption or an earthquake will happen. High risk areas are now constantly monitored.

As magma nears the surface of a volcano its pressure decreases and gases escape. Sulphur dioxide is one of the main volcanic gases and changes in the amount of this gas can give an indication of an eruption. The area surrounding Mount Pinatubo was evacuated because of gas monitoring undertaken by the Philippine Institute of Volcanology and Seismology.

Pressure from rising magma deforms the volcano. The ground can change shape by rising up, subsiding, tilting, or forming bulges as at Mount St Helens in New York State, USA, in 1997. The newest and most accurate system of measuring ground deformation is the Global Positioning System (GPS). This involves using a number of satellites and radio waves. A receiver is set up close to the volcano then data can be transmitted between satellites orbiting the earth and the receiver. Data is obtained in just a few minutes and is extremely accurate.

Before an eruption, magma moves into the area beneath the volcano and collects in a magma chamber, or reservoir. The movement of magma produces small earthquakes and vibrations. This is called seismic activity. A seismometer is an instrument that measures ground vibrations caused by earthquakes. In Montserrat, 14 seismometers close to the volcano record ground movements which are converted to radio signals. These signals are transmitted to computers that record the earthquakes 24 hours a day.

Tiltmeters measure tiny changes in the slope angle or 'tilt' of the ground. Five electronic tiltmeters record ground movement on the slopes of the Soufrière Hills volcano on Montserrat.

What can be done to limit (prevent) the effects of volcanic eruptions and earthquakes?

Education

In Japan, 1 September is Disaster Prevention Day. On this day emergency drills organised by local governments are held throughout the country. Some of these drills consist of ducking under desks to escape falling objects and evacuating from buildings. At many elementary and middle schools, 1 September is the first day of school after the summer holiday. So a lot of schools carry out an evacuation drill as part of the back-to-school routine.

In the USA, The Federal Emergency Management Agency (FEMA) gives information on how to prepare for an earthquake. It states six ways to plan ahead. These are:

1   Check for hazards in the home.
2   Identify safe places indoors and outdoors.
3   Educate yourself and family members.
4   Have disaster supplies on hand.
5   Develop an emergency communication plan.
6   Help your community get ready.

More information on these can be found on the FEMA website.

Figure 28 Earthquake drill in Japan

Building design

Many buildings in earthquake zones in high-income countries (HICs) are now built to earthquake-proof regulations. Figure 29 shows a range of techniques that are currently being used.

Some famous earthquake proof structures

At the Tamaki building in Auckland, the two wings of the main building block have been split by a movement joint, a gap of approximately 10 cm right across the building on all levels. The building is designed to allow a controlled, even movement that will dissipate the earthquake's force before it causes structural damage.

Yokohama Landmark Tower (Figure 30) is the tallest building in Japan. It has a flexible structure to absorb the force of earthquakes.

The San Francisco International Airport (Figure 31) uses many advanced building technologies to help it withstand earthquakes. One of these technologies involves giant ball bearings.

The 267 columns that support the weight of the airport each ride on a steel ball bearing 1.5 m in diameter. The ball rests in a concave base that is

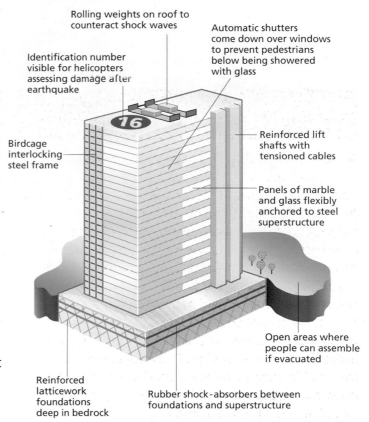

Rolling weights on roof to counteract shock waves

Automatic shutters come down over windows to prevent pedestrians below being showered with glass

Identification number visible for helicopters assessing damage after earthquake

Birdcage interlocking steel frame

Reinforced lift shafts with tensioned cables

Panels of marble and glass flexibly anchored to steel superstructure

Open areas where people can assemble if evacuated

Reinforced latticework foundations deep in bedrock

Rubber shock-absorbers between foundations and superstructure

Figure 29 Earthquake proof buildings

Figure 30 Yokohama Landmark Tower

Figure 31 San Francisco International Airport

connected to the ground. In the event of an earthquake, the ground can move 50 cm in any direction. The columns that rest on the balls move a lot less than this as they roll around in their bases, which reduces the movement of the ground. When the earthquake is over, gravity pulls the columns back to the centre of their bases. Go to http://science. howstuffworks.com/bearing4.htm for a demonstration of how this works.

Defences

There are three ways that have been used to stop or divert lava flows.

1   Detonating explosives can disrupt lava flow. In 1996, the Italian army detonated 7,000 kg of mining explosives to successfully block a lava flow leading from Mount Etna and threatening villages below.

2   Construction of earth walls can deflect lava. During the 1955 eruption of Kilauea (Hawaii), barriers temporarily diverted flows from two different plantations. Diversion structures have been constructed in Hawaii to protect the Mauna Loa Observatory from future lava flows. Mount Etna has also used earth walls to deflect flows. During the July 2001 eruption on the southern slopes, three fissures spewed out lava flows that

caused damage and threatened to cause much more extensive destruction in the area of the Rifugio Sapienza and the Etna cable car, where there are numerous tourist facilities (hotels, restaurants and souvenir shops). In order to limit destruction to a minimum, earth barriers were erected and ditches were dug. Two major lava flows, on 26 and 30–31 July, rapidly spilled down the steep slope and were largely confined by the barriers and artificial ditches.

3   Spraying large volumes of water can cool an advancing flow. One of the lava flows from Etna went to within 50 m of the departure station of the cable car, another nearly reached a building of the Provincial Tourism Agency, but both were relatively small and were cooled by spraying water onto the lava. Lava flows erupting in Heimaey, Iceland were also stopped by spraying the advancing fronts with millions of gallons of seawater.

Review

By the end of this section you should be able to:

* understand the reasons why people continue to live in active tectonic zones

* know the causes and effects of a named volcanic eruption or earthquake

* recognise the different ways that volcanic activity and earthquakes can be predicted and prevented.

ACTIVITIES

Extension work

1   Research designs for earthquake-proof buildings. Design your own building to withstand an earthquake.

Sample Examination Questions

Higher tier

1 Study Figure 3 on page 101 which shows major earthquakes in 2007 and 2008.

   a Which continent did not have any earthquakes? **(1 mark)**

   b Describe the distribution of the earthquakes. **(3 marks)**

   c Explain why there was earthquake activity on the west coast of South America. **(4 marks)**

   d Outline the attempts that have been made to predict earthquakes and say how successful these attempts have been. **(5 marks)**

2 Read the following passage.

   Mount Etna in Italy has a long history of frequent eruptions, yet more than 1 million people live on its slopes. This is because of fertile soils, rich orchards, vineyards and orange groves. There is also a thriving tourist industry, including skiing, which is a source of employment for many inhabitants. When the volcano erupts the lava has been diverted away from villages by digging channels and erecting dams.

   Give three reasons why so many people choose to live close to Etna. **(3 marks)**

3 What is the difference in the way earthquakes are measured using the Mercalli and Richter scales? **(3 marks)**

4 Earthquakes occur in many parts of the world. Evaluate the impact that the earthquake that you have studied has had on the community and the environment. **(6 marks)**

Total 25 marks

Foundation tier

1 Look at Figure 3 on page 101. It shows the distribution of large earthquakes in 2007 and 2008.

   a In which year – 2007 or 2008 – were there more large earthquakes? **(1 mark)**

   b Which continent did not have any earthquakes?

   Circle the correct answer from the list below.

   South America   Asia   Africa
   North America **(1 mark)**

   c Describe the distribution of earthquakes. **(3 marks)**

   d Earthquakes commonly occur at plate boundaries. Explain why. **(4 marks)**

   e Give two ways that scientists try to predict earthquakes. **(2 marks)**

   f How successful are scientists at predicting when earthquakes will happen? **(3 marks)**

2 Read the following passage.

   Mount Etna in Italy has a long history of frequent eruptions, yet more than 1 million people live on its slopes. This is because of fertile soils, rich orchards, vineyards and orange groves. There is also a thriving tourist industry, including skiing, which is a source of employment for many inhabitants. When the volcano erupts the lava has been diverted away from villages by digging channels and erecting dams.

   Give three reasons why so many people choose to live close to Etna. **(3 marks)**

3 Earthquakes can be measured using the Mercalli and Richter scales What differences are there between the two scales? **(2 marks)**

4 Earthquakes and volcanoes happen in many parts of the world. For an earthquake or a volcano that you have studied say:

   a what effect it had on the local people **(3 marks)**

   b how it affected the environment. **(3 marks)**

Total 25 marks

Types of waste and its production

Learning objective – to study the different types of waste and its production.

Learning outcomes
- To recognise the differences between low-income countries' and high-income countries' waste production
- To explain why high-income countries' amount of waste is increasing.
- To categorise different types of waste produced.

What types of waste are there?

Waste can be categorised in many different ways. It can be biodegradable and non-biodegradable, domestic and industrial, hazardous or non-hazardous, solid or liquid. These are some of the main ways to categorise waste but whichever way we categorise it there is a lot of waste about and the amount of it continues to grow.

What are the differences between HIC and LIC waste production?

The production of waste is not evenly spread globally. Compared with their population sizes high-income countries (HICs) produce far more waste than low-income countries (LICs). This is due to the consumer society. They have the ability to buy more products and therefore generate more waste. Globally, 20 per cent of the world's people who live in HICs account for 86 per cent of consumption of the world's products. The poorest 20 per cent consume only 1.3 per cent of the world's products. Figure 1 breaks these facts down further.

Commodities	HIC (% usage)	LIC (% usage)
Protein foods	45	5
Energy	58	4
Telephone lines	74	1.5
Paper	84	1.1
Motor vehicles	87	1

Figure 1 Consumption of the world's products

The mass consumption of so many of the world's products inevitably leads to the HICs producing a greater amount of waste. This can be illustrated by the fact that the city of Los Angeles, USA, produces around 1,256 kg of rubbish per person each year, due to the wealth of the people who live there who consume vast amounts of products and therefore have a lot of waste. The people in Abidjan, on the Ivory Coast, Africa, only generate 200 kg of rubbish a year! These are poor people without the means to buy many consumer products.

Figure 3 shows the amount of municipal waste generated per country in 2002. Municipal waste is the waste collected from homes, schools and businesses. This waste includes packaging, paper, organic waste and bulky waste such as fridges and mattresses. The size of the country indicates the amount of waste generated. The most waste is produced by China which has the highest population; the most waste per person is generated in Russia. The map in Figure 3 shows clearly that little waste is produced by the poorer African nations.

Country	Waste generated in 2002; kilograms per person per year	Population in 2002	Stage of development
Angola	32	15,900,000	MIC
Australia	677	20,100,000	HIC
Bangladesh	17	140,000,000	LIC
Brazil	330	186,400,000	MIC
Cameroon	114	16,300,000	LIC
Canada	347	32,300,000	HIC
China	149	1,300,000,000	MIC
Congo	10	4,000,000	LIC
Ethiopia	4	77,400,000	LIC
France	538	60,500,000	HIC
Germany	593	82,700,000	HIC
Haiti	34	8,500,000	LIC
Iceland	697	295,000	HIC
India	81	1,100,000,000	MIC
Indonesia	217	222,800,000	MIC
Iraq	171	28,800,000	MIC
Kenya	87	34,300,000	LIC
Kuwait	584	2,600,000	HIC
New Zealand	406	4,000,000	HIC
Pakistan	62	157,900,000	LIC
Poland	272	38,500,000	MIC
Russian Federation	1439	143,200,000	MIC
Singapore	1048	4,300,000	HIC
Slovenia	431	1,900,000	HIC
Spain	642	43,000,000	HIC
United Kingdom	590	59,700,000	HIC
United States	715	298,200,000	HIC
Venezuela	328	26,800,000	MIC

Figure 2 Statistical comparison of waste produced by different countries

The average daily output of solid waste alone from Asia's largest cities today has been estimated to be 760,000 tonnes, and it is expected to increase to 1.8 million tonnes per day by 2025 as Asia becomes more of a consumer society.

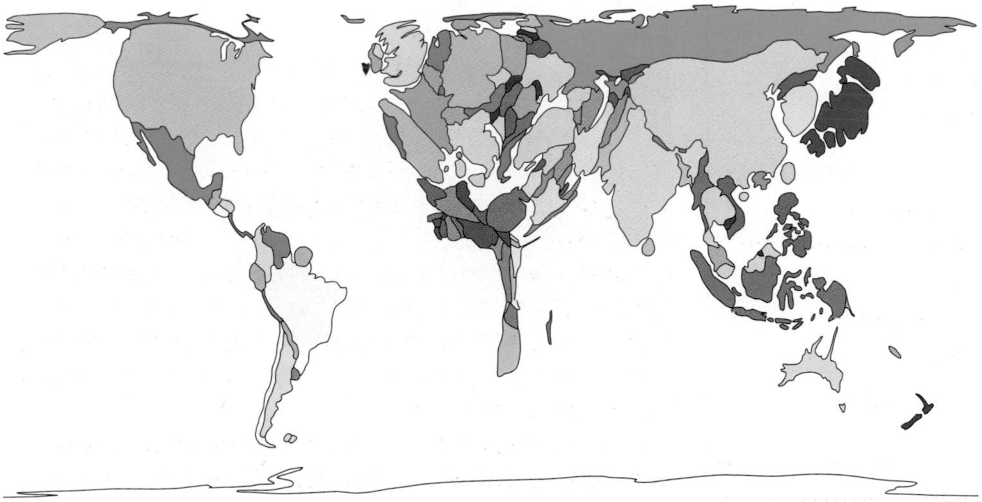

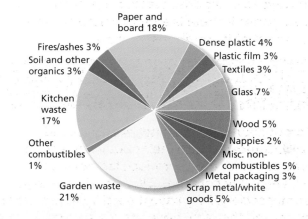

Figure 3 The amount of waste collected from homes, schools and businesses

What types of domestic waste are produced by HICs?

Domestic waste refers to the waste that is produced by the average household. During the period 2003/04 it is estimated that 30 million tonnes of household waste was collected in the UK – that's half a tonne of rubbish per person per year.

What is this waste made up of?

Figure 4 shows the different types of waste that the average household produces. If you add together the paper and board, glass, metal packaging, dense plastic and plastic film it shows that 35 per cent of household waste, or more than one-third of the waste, is from packaging or old newspapers alone. Many of these products can be recycled.

Over time the types of waste will have changed. Fifty years ago the percentage for fires/ashes would have been much higher and the percentage for nappies would not have existed. The other type of waste which is growing considerably, three times faster than any other type of waste, is e-waste. E-waste is any product which contains electrical parts. While some of these goods are disposed of when they are broken, others are simply discarded when they still work but are no longer the newest model.

Mobile phones should last for seven years but most people change their mobile after just eleven months. In the USA approximately half of the computers which are thrown away still work but people want newer versions. The United Nations Environment Programme estimates that up to 50 million tonnes of e-waste is generated every year. More than half of the goods are still in good working order. All of these products keep adding to the problem of e-waste – the biggest one being that the products are made up of many different parts and therefore have to be dismantled and the different parts separated before they can be reused. This is a difficult and expensive process. Some e-waste also contains toxic metals such as mercury which have to be disposed of with great care.

Figure 4 Types of domestic waste

Paper and board 18%
Fires/ashes 3%
Soil and other organics 3%
Kitchen waste 17%
Other combustibles 1%
Garden waste 21%
Dense plastic 4%
Plastic film 3%
Textiles 3%
Glass 7%
Wood 5%
Nappies 2%
Misc. non-combustibles 5%
Metal packaging 3%
Scrap metal/white goods 5%

Review

By the end of this section you should be able to:

- recognise the differences between low-income countries' and high-income countries' waste production
- explain why high-income countries' amount of waste is increasing
- categorise different types of domestic waste produced in HICs.

Recycling and disposal of waste

Learning objective – to study the different ways that waste is disposed of.

Learning outcomes
- To learn how waste is recycled and reused by Reading, Wokingham and Bracknell Forest councils.
- To investigate how Germany disposes of different types of waste.

What happens to all of this waste?

In the UK, for the period 2003/04, 72 per cent went to landfill sites, 9 per cent was incinerated and 19 per cent was recycled. By 2007, 31 per cent of waste in the UK was being recycled. This is a good sign for the environment as less was being sent to landfill or being incinerated which produces greenhouse gases. There is, however, a great difference between local authorities. Figure 5 shows the best and worst performing local authorities for the period 2006/07.

Type of waste disposal	Best performing local authority	Lowest performing local authority
Rubbish	449 kilograms per person	180 kilograms per person
Recycling	55.5%	11.8%
Landfill	7%	93%

Figure 5 The best and worst performing local authorities for waste disposal 2006/07

How is waste recycled at a local level?

Bracknell Forest Council in Berkshire works with Reading and Wokingham council for the disposal of waste. It has created re3 which is a waste management partnership.

There are two household waste recycling centres, one at Smallmead, Island Road, Reading and one at Longshot Lane, Bracknell which is replacing the old facility on this site. Both of these sites will have a one-way system and will have excellent signage making the disposal and recycling of rubbish as easy as possible. There are 150 recycle sites around the three authorities located at convenient sites

Figure 6 Recycling facilities at a supermarket in Reading

such as large supermarkets (Figure 6). There are clear directions on each local authority's website as to what can be recycled at the sites and where the sites are located.

House collections

Bracknell Forest Council operates an alternate waste collection scheme to encourage residents to recycle and compost more of their products (Figure 7). The brown garden bin, the blue plastic bottle and tins bin and the green paper box are collected one week. On the alternate week the green general waste bin is collected. Many other types of rubbish can be taken to the household waste recycling centres such as shoes, foil and e-waste.

General domestic waste   Garden waste

Plastic bottles and cans   Newspapers and magazine

Figure 7 Types of domestic waste collection, Bracknell Forest Council

How is the recycled material reused?

re3, the waste management partnership, have agreements with many different companies to recycle the waste that they collect. Here is how four of the products which are recycled by the residents are turned into usable products.

Paper and cardboard

The paper and cardboard which is collected from the kerbside and taken to the household recycling plants is taken to the Severnside recycling facility in Maidenhead which is the recycling division of St Regis Paper company (Figure 8). The material is sorted and small contaminates such as ink are separated out. The paper which is by now in a pulp form is baled and sent to the St Regis paper mill in Kent. Here the pulp is rolled and layered to make large reels of paper. The final stage of the production also carried out on this site is to turn the paper into new packaging material.

Figure 8 The Severnside paper recycling facility in Maidenhead

Glass

The glass is sorted into three different colours at the recycling points by residents as they recycle, which means that the glass can be more effectively recycled into new glass bottles and jars. Mixed glass is mainly used by the aggregate industry. The glass is collected for reprocessing by Berryman's from Dagenham. The glass is collected into large loads from different local authorities and then taken to be reprocessed in Yorkshire. The glass is washed and crushed to make a product called 'cullet', which is mixed with raw materials such as sand, limestone and soda ash to make new glass containers. During the process as much recycled glass is used as possible because then they do not have to heat the mixture to such high temperatures, therefore saving energy.

Cans

Cans which are recycled are sent to a Biffa Waste Management facility in Southampton where they are baled. They are then transferred to a reprocessing facility in Leicester. Before this can occur the cans have to be sorted into aluminium and steel.

Steel is easy to sort from aluminium because it is magnetic. Once the steel cans have been sorted and baled, they are processed by European Metals Recycling Ltd. Cans are sent into a furnace where they are mixed with molten iron. The liquid metal that is produced is poured into a mould to make large slabs. These slabs are rolled into coils which are then used to make new products such as bikes, cars and bridges or even a new can!

Aluminium cans are shredded to the size of a 10 pence piece. These shreds are then passed through a magnetic drum which removes any last shreds of steel. The shreds are then melted down and any gases or contaminants are removed. The molten aluminium is then pumped into moulds and chilled with cool water until it solidifies. It can then be used for any aluminium product including cans!

Plastics

Plastic bottles are recycled by Baylis Recycling at their plant in Keynsham near Bristol. On arrival the bottles are sorted by polymer type and/or by colour. The plastic is then either melted down and formed into a new shape or is flaked and then melted down depending upon the polymer type. A wide range of products can be made from used plastic such as garden furniture, water butts, fleece jackets and, yes, new plastic bottles.

How do HICs dispose of different types of waste?

There are many different types of waste. HICs dispose of this waste in a number of different ways. This section will deal with how Germany deals with some of its municipal and industrial waste.

Municipal waste

Germany is known as the recycling capital of Europe; it produces 14 million tonnes of municipal waste a year (municipal waste is the waste from homes and small businesses) of which 60 per cent is recycled. The amount of industrial waste which is recycled is 65 per cent although this varies between the different industrial sectors. Waste is a big business in Germany with 250,000 people employed in waste management – from engineers to refuse collectors to civil servants. There are also a number of colleges which offer courses in waste management.

In the early 1970s every urban area in Germany had its own landfill site. There were approximately

Figure 10 An incinerator in Germany

50,000 across the country. By 2008 there were only 160 landfill sites for domestic waste and since 2005 all waste has had to be treated before it is allowed to be put into landfill. One of these treatment plants is owned by The Group and is sited in Luebeck in Germany (Figure 9). It can treat 200,000 tonnes of domestic waste annually. The waste is sorted and incinerated. The final product is a low emission material which is ready for landfill sites as it has already been composted or fermented.

Another way that municipal waste is disposed of in Germany is through incineration. At present there are 68 incinerators with an annual capacity of 68 million tonnes. For example, the incinerator at Darmstadt (Figure 10) deals with 212,000 tonnes a year. There are also numerous mini power plants which operate on a local level on refuse driven fuel. The owners of these plants receive money to incinerate the waste and income from the heat it gives off. The plants are also exempt from carbon emission rules. They are free to release carbon dioxide gas because they do not use up fossil fuel. There are plans to build another 100 incinerators around the country. This could lead to a shortage of waste to feed the incinerators. Germany has already been approached to dispose of the waste of other countries. Italy, in particular Naples, now sends 160,000 tonnes of waste annually to be incinerated in Germany. Other countries such as the Netherlands also send Germany their waste totalling 6 million tonnes in 2007. However, some German cities that are close to the border send their waste to other countries to be incinerated if the incinerator is closer than a German one. In 2007, 1.8 million tonnes of waste was exported.

Figure 9 A waste disposal site in Germany

Figure 11 The Grune Punkt emblem

But what happens to the recyclable rubbish in Germany? All products that can be recycled have the 'Grune Punkt' emblem (Figure 11). This is a small, round, green symbol – two arrows in an endless spiral. Buying these recyclable products costs the average family between £100 and £200 a year which has been added to their cost by the producer to pay for the recycling. The producers of the products have to contribute towards the DSD (Duales System Deutschlands). Their contribution pays the firms who collect and divide the rubbish. Other companies then recycle plastic, glass, paper and cardboard and re-sell them. There are a number of problems with the system:

- Firms did not pay their conscriptions and it is very difficult to enforce this by law.
- Recycling produces heavy toxic gas emissions which damage the environment.
- Germany has problems recycling all of their products due to the large amounts and their lack of capacity at recycling facilities.

Figure 12 Sellafield Nuclear Reprocessing Plant in Cumbria which receives nuclear waste from Germany to be reprocessed

- They have had to export their recyclables to other European and Asian countries which is costly. For example, plastic shampoo bottles from Oggersheim are turned into sandals in Indonesia.

Nuclear waste

Germany does not have any reprocessing sites for nuclear waste therefore it can either store its waste without reprocessing or send it to another country to be reprocessed. Germany has contracts with the UK and France until 2009 to send them nuclear waste to be recycled (Figure 12). The Germans have been trying to get out of these contracts since 2000 because they are very expensive but also because the movement of nuclear waste is very dangerous (Figure 13). Germany also sends nuclear waste to be stored in Siberia. In Germany low level waste will, in the future (approximately 2013) be stored at Konrad. This is 95 per cent of the total of nuclear waste but only 1 per cent of the radioactivity. The site at Gorleben will from 2025 be able to take the high level waste which is about 5 per cent of total waste but with 99 per cent of the radioactivity. At present, low level waste is stored around the country at about 50 locations and high level waste is exported. After these dates all nuclear waste will be contained within Germany and other countries will be able to return reprocessed waste to be stored in Germany.

Other toxic waste products

Germany disposes of its toxic waste in a number of different ways. The majority of it is exported for disposal. Between 1990 and 1995 shiploads of German toxic waste have turned up in Poland, Estonia, Egypt and the Black Sea. One famous case which made the headlines in the world media involved the shipment of toxic waste to Albania. During 1991 and 1992, 480 tonnes of toxic waste was sent to Albania by the German company Schmidt-Cretan. The shipment was labelled 'humanitarian aid for use in agriculture'. It contained pesticides made in the former East Germany that were either banned or past their sell-by date. The idea was that the pesticides would help to revive the farming industry in Albania. However, one of the chemicals was toxaphene, one litre of which released into a water system can contaminate 2 million cubic metres of

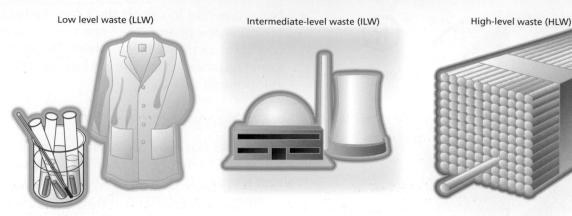

Low level waste (LLW)   Intermediate-level waste (ILW)   High-level waste (HLW)

Figure 13 Types of nuclear waste

water, killing all the fish. The 480 tonnes sent to Albania contained 6,000 litres of toxaphene. In Germany it would have cost the company $5,500 per tonne to dispose of the pesticides due to the nature of the materials involved. The Albanian government did accept the shipment but when they realised what it was they asked the Germans to take it back. However, the shipment remained in Albania for a number of years until the Germans were forced to take it back. The shipment was located in Albania at Bajza, where the pesticides were seeping into Lake Shkodra and the port of Durres. Other shipments are unaccounted for. It was reported that local people were emptying the barrels and using them to store water and food.

While Germany has an excellent record on its handling of rubbish at home, its reputation abroad is very poor. In 2007 Germany exported approximately 2 million tonnes of authorised waste of which 75 per cent was recycled and the rest was incinerated.

In 2007 Germany imported approximately 6 million tonnes of authorised waste from its neighbouring countries such as France, Belgium and Italy. The waste which is imported into Germany is recycled 45 per cent, incinerated 35 per cent or stored in landfills (20 per cent).

For other waste which does not have to be authorised, such as glass, plastics and paper, exports were approximately 19 million tonnes and imports 14 million tonnes. The Netherlands is the main partner in this trade.

Review

By the end of these case studies you should know:

- how waste is recycled and reused by Reading, Wokingham and Bracknell Forest councils
- how Germany disposes of different types of waste.

ACTIVITIES

Higher

1 How can waste be categorised?

2 How much more waste was recycled in 2007 than in 2004?

3 Study Figure 4 on page 125. How much domestic waste is from packaging or old newspapers?

4 State one way that Bracknell reuses its waste products.

Foundation

1 What types of waste are there?

2 a How much waste was recycled in 2004?

   b How much waste was recycled in 2007?

3 Study Figure 4 on page 125. What percentage of domestic waste is from gardens. How much domestic waste is from gardens?

4 Study Figure 7 on page 126. State what goes in the different Bracknell waste bins. Choose one product and describe how it can be reused.

Sources and uses of energy

Learning objective – to study the sources and uses of energy.

Learning outcomes
- To describe the advantages and disadvantages of renewable and non-renewable fuels.
- To recognise energy surplus and energy deficit on a global scale.

Types of fuels

In the world today there is an ever-increasing demand for energy. Energy is produced by burning different types of fuels. These fuels can be split into renewable and non-renewable fuels.

Non-renewable fuels are ones that once they have been used can never be used again, they are known as finite resources.

Renewable fuels are ones which can be reused and therefore will not run out, they are known as infinite resources. They can be used to produce energy in a way that does not contribute to climate change and after the initial set-up cost are more cost effective than non-renewable fuels. Figures 16, 17, 18 and 19 show a range of renewable fuels, while Figure 15 shows a global energy surplus and energy deficit maps.

Type of fuel	Where does it come from?	Advantage	Disadvantage
Coal **Non-renewable – fossil fuel**	This is formed from fossilised plants. It can be found in seams either close to the surface or it has to be mined from deep under the ground. It has to be burnt to produce energy.	It is relatively cheap to mine. It is relatively easy to convert it into energy by simply burning it. Coal supplies should last for another 250 years.	When burnt it gives off greenhouse gases, for example, carbon dioxide.
Oil **Non-renewable – fossil fuel**	This is formed from fossilised animals. Lakes of oil are found under the land or sea, trapped between seams of rock. Pipes are put down through the ground and the liquid is pumped to the surface. It is burnt to provide energy.	It is relatively cheap to mine. It is relatively easy to convert it into energy by simply burning it. Oil supplies should last for another 50 years.	When burnt it gives off greenhouse gases, for example, carbon dioxide.
Natural gas **Non-renewable – fossil fuel**	Methane gases are trapped between seams of rock under the Earth's surface. Pipes are put down through the ground and the gas is pumped to the surface. It is burnt to provide energy.	It is relatively cheap to mine. It is relatively easy to convert it into energy by simply burning it. It is a cleaner fuel than oil or coal giving off fewer greenhouse gases. Gas supplies should last for another 70 years.	When burnt it gives off greenhouse gases, for example, carbon dioxide.
Nuclear **Non-renewable**	This is produced from uranium which is obtained by mining. Energy is produced when the atoms are split or joined together in nuclear reactors.	A small amount of uranium gives off a lot of energy. Raw materials will last a long time. It does not give off greenhouse gases.	Nuclear reactors are expensive to build and run. Nuclear waste is radioactive and highly toxic. It has to be stored for 100s/1,000s of years which is very expensive. If there is a leak it is extremely dangerous for people and the environment.

Figure 14 Types of non-renewable fuels

Figure 14 Types of non-renewable fuels continued

Type of fuel	Where does it come from?	Advantage	Disadvantage
Biomass Non-renewable or renewable if the plants are regrown	This is decaying plant or animal matter. It is an organic matter which can be used to provide energy. One example is oil seed rape. This is the fields of yellow flowers which can be seen in the UK in the summer. After being treated with chemicals it can be used to fuel diesel engines.	It is a cheap and readily available energy source. If plants are regrown it is renewable.	When burnt it gives off greenhouse gases, for example, carbon dioxide. If large areas of land are taken to produce energy crops there may be food shortages.
Wood Non-renewable or renewable if trees are re-grown	This is obtained from felling trees. The trees are burnt to provide energy.	It is a cheap and readily available energy source. If trees are re-grown it is renewable.	When burnt it gives off greenhouse gases, for example, carbon dioxide.

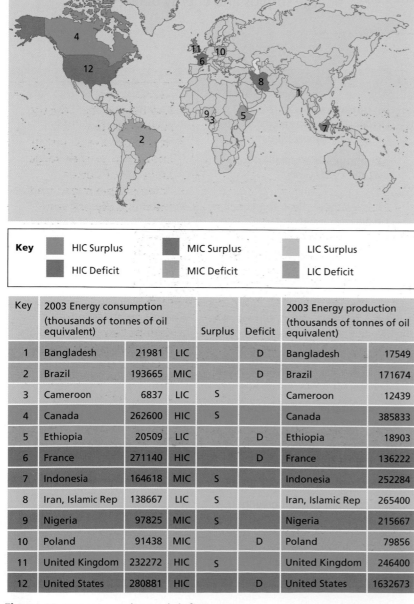

Key						
	HIC Surplus		MIC Surplus		LIC Surplus	
	HIC Deficit		MIC Deficit		LIC Deficit	

Key	2003 Energy consumption (thousands of tonnes of oil equivalent)			Surplus	Deficit	2003 Energy production (thousands of tonnes of oil equivalent)	
1	Bangladesh	21981	LIC		D	Bangladesh	17549
2	Brazil	193665	MIC		D	Brazil	171674
3	Cameroon	6837	LIC	S		Cameroon	12439
4	Canada	262600	HIC	S		Canada	385833
5	Ethiopia	20509	LIC		D	Ethiopia	18903
6	France	271140	HIC		D	France	136222
7	Indonesia	164618	MIC	S		Indonesia	252284
8	Iran, Islamic Rep	138667	LIC	S		Iran, Islamic Rep	265400
9	Nigeria	97825	MIC	S		Nigeria	215667
10	Poland	91438	MIC		D	Poland	79856
11	United Kingdom	232272	HIC	S		United Kingdom	246400
12	United States	280881	HIC		D	United States	1632673

Figure 15 Energy surplus and deficit maps

Advantages
- A ground source system can cut energy costs by up to 70%.
- It costs approximately £12,000 to install.
- It does not give off greenhouse gases.
- Cheap once built as it is an infinite resource.

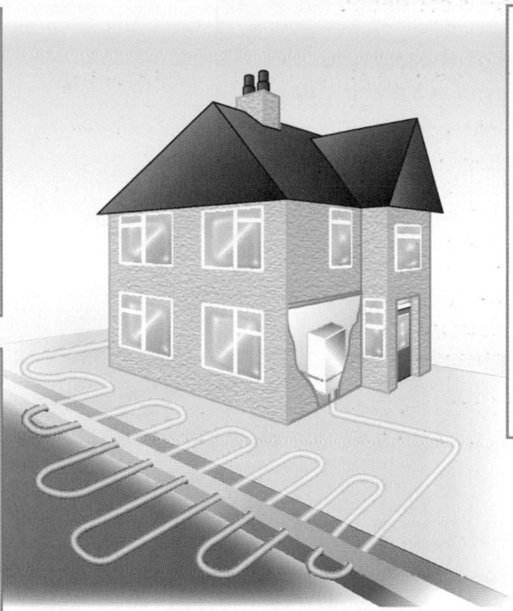

Disadvantages
- Enough space in the garden to install the pipework.
- It is expensive to build.
- Some of the water has minerals in it which are corrosive which damages the machinery and pipework.

How does it work?
Ground source – Ground source heat pumps take heat from the ground into the house via lengths of pipe filled with a mixture of water and antifreeze. These supply radiators or an under-floor heating system with warmth. The lengths of pipe are buried in the ground either straight down or under an area of, for example, lawn.

Figure 16 Ground source heating

Advantages
- Costs approximately £12,000 for each home.
- Is fitted onto buildings and therefore does not take up extra land space.
- Energy which is not used can be sold to the National Grid.

Disadvantages
- Can be used by industry such as tertiary.
- It is expensive to install enough to provide large amounts of power.
- Some people might find them visually polluting.

How does it work?
Photovoltaic cells – these are panels or tiles which produce energy (electricity) from light, preferably sunlight.

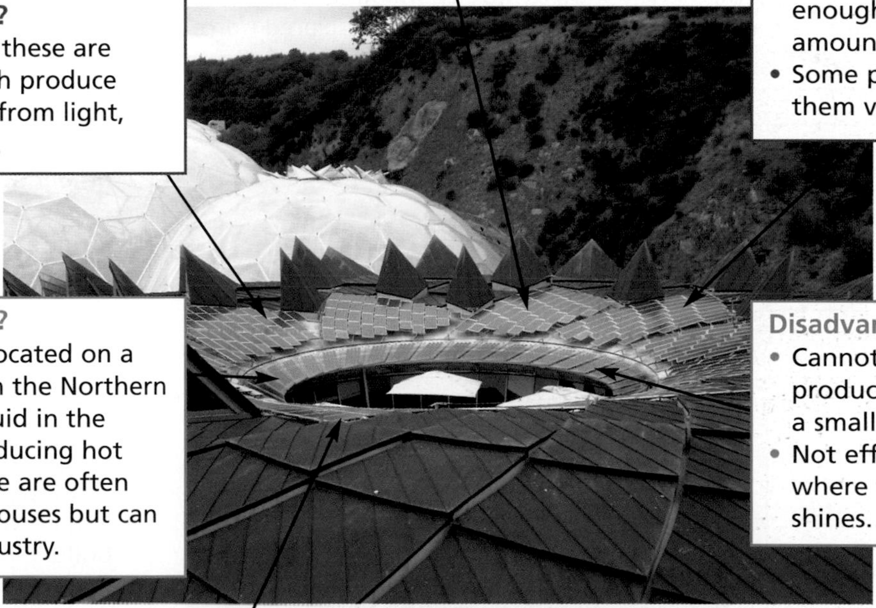

How does it work?
Solar panels – are located on a south facing roof in the Northern hemisphere. The fluid in the panel heats up producing hot water for use. These are often put on individual houses but can also be used by industry.

Disadvantages
- Cannot be mass produced; is best used on a small scale.
- Not efficient in countries where the sun rarely shines.

Advantages
- Can provide up to 35% of a house's hot water.
- There are no running costs.
- Fairly cheap to set up; approximately £4,000 per home.
- It does not give off greenhouse gases.
- Is fitted onto buildings and therefore does not take up extra land space.

Figure 17 Power from the sun

How does it work?
Turbines which rely on the force of the wind to power aerodynamic blades to generate electricity.

Advantages
- New wind turbines are quiet and efficient. Costs £1,500 for 1kW.
- Wind turbines can be on land or sea.
- The turbines do not give off any emissions and can save up to 30% of the average household's energy bill of about £400–£500.

Disadvantages
- There needs to be an annual local wind speed of more than 6 m per second.
- They can have a life expectancy of 20 years, but require regular servicing.
- They can be unsightly/visually intrusive.
- Offshore turbines may disturb migration patterns of birds.

Figure 18 Power from the wind

How does it work?
Hydroelectricity is power from water. Hydroelectric power stations are normally built in highland areas. Rivers are dammed and the flow of water is controlled. The water passes through a tunnel from the top of the dam. The water turns a turbine which generates hydroelectricity.

Disadvantages
- Can only be built in certain areas due to the site requirements of the dam.
- They alter the water flow of rivers affecting ecology.
- They can cause a build-up of sediments behind the dam which can release methane, a greenhouse gas.
- Dams have enormous impacts on people. Already 40–80 million people globally have been displaced (forced to move) by dam construction.

How does it work?
Tidal energy – the movement of seawater drives turbines which produce electricity.

Advantages
- It does not give off greenhouse gases.
- Cheap once built as it is an infinite resource.
- Can produce large bodies of water for leisure purposes.

Advantages
- It does not give off greenhouse gases.
- Cheap once built as it is an infinite resource.
- Tidal barrages can also be used as bridges.

Disadvantages
- Can be a problem for shipping if built across an estuary.
- Can be very expensive to build.
- Can negatively affect wildlife.
- May impede the flow of treated sewage out to sea.

Figure 19 Power from water

Review
By the end of this section you should be able to:
- describe the advantages and disadvantages of renewable and non-renewable fuels
- recognise energy surplus and energy deficit on a global scale.

Management of energy usage and waste

> **Learning objective** – to study the management of energy usage and waste.
>
> **Learning outcomes**
> - To learn the ways in which energy is being wasted.
> - To calculate the carbon footprints for countries at different levels of development.
> - To look at the solutions to energy wastage at a domestic, local and national scale.

How energy is being wasted – the domestic situation

The amount of energy that is used in the UK increases every year, in fact during the twentieth century energy usage doubled every 20 years. For example, we used twice as much in 1980 as we did in 1960.

This vast increase has slowed down but we still use more energy every year. Much of the energy that goes through our meters is wasted due to many different factors. Most households could save up to £350 a year if they were more energy efficient.

Energy in the home is wasted in many ways. There are many adverts in the media about ways to save energy because of energy wasted through not having the correct insulation or leaving lights on in empty rooms, but much energy is wasted almost invisibly through leaving electrical appliances on standby or mobile phone chargers plugged in. In this way £740 million worth of energy is wasted every year. The breakdown is as follows:

- Stereo systems: £290 million
- Video recorders: £175 million
- Televisions: £88 million
- Games consoles: £70 million
- Computer monitors: £41 million
- DVD players: £19 million
- Set-top boxes: £11 million
- Mobile phone chargers: £47 million

This is enough energy to supply 66,000 homes.

Energy wasted is not only costing the nation a lot of money, it is also harmful to the environment. Energy used in homes accounts for 48 per cent of Britain's greenhouse gas emissions. Industry has greatly reduced its total energy use by being more efficient. Domestic consumption continues to rise because although more people are insulating their homes they are also buying more electrical products and living in larger houses which demand more energy.

Heating systems are the largest consumer of energy in the home followed by cooling appliances and dishwashers. It is much more efficient for a house to develop its own energy producing systems than it is to take energy from the National Grid where 70 per cent is lost in production and distribution. However, it is the inefficiency of the housing stock that also causes a lot of the energy produced to be wasted in the UK. Figure 20 shows the ways that energy is lost from homes.

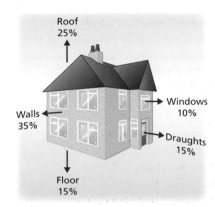

Figure 20 Energy lost from poorly built houses

How energy is being wasted – in industry

British industry wastes £12.7 billion on energy every year. It is estimated that the amount of energy wasted over the ten-day Christmas shutdown is enough to roast 4.4 million turkeys. This is mainly through office devices being left running – the cost of this to industry is estimated to be £8.66 million. In offices, the worst energy-wasters are computers and printers which are left on; other wasteful machines are fax machines and other office equipment.

Other British industries, for example the iron and steel industry – the fourth largest in Europe – uses more energy to produce a tonne of steel than the other steel industries in Europe. Approximately £1 in every £12 spent on fuel is being wasted by the UK steel industry.

On the other hand, the UK paper industry uses half the EU average of energy consumption, and the rate at which it improved its energy use was the third fastest in Europe. Other energy-intensive sectors, including chemicals, glass, ceramics and cement, are all consistently better in energy performance than the EU average.

In research carried out by the Building Research Establishment (BRE), it was found that the manufacturing sector's annual energy bill of £1.8 billion could be cut by 12 per cent if it introduced efficiency measures, while the service sector could make a 19 per cent saving on its yearly expenditure of £1.6 billion.

A study for the Carbon Trust says that the 'staggering' £570 million wastage of energy every year by industry in the UK will result in more than 8 million tonnes of carbon dioxide (CO_2) being released unnecessarily into the atmosphere.

Countries have carbon footprints of differing sizes

A carbon footprint is a measure of the impact that human activities have on the environment in terms of the number of greenhouse gases they produce. There are a large number of websites which enable individuals to work out their carbon footprint, for example, www.carbonfootprint.com. On the websites you are asked a series of questions about your lifestyle and you are then informed how much carbon you are producing. There are also sites which offer this facility for businesses. Countries can also be calculated. A country's carbon footprint tends to be linked to its stage of development. As a country develops its carbon footprint tends to increase, therefore the least developed, low income countries will have the lowest carbon footprints; the most developed, high income countries the highest. This is illustrated in Figure 21 which is ranked with the highest carbon emission country in 2004 at the top.

The countries are also categorised according to the World Bank list of economies in 2006 to show if they are a high-income (HIC), middle-income (MIC) or low-income country (LIC). The table does show some anomalies such as Trinidad and Tobago, and at the other end of the spectrum, Angola.

ACTIVITIES

Higher

1 Choose one renewable and one non-renewable fuel. Compare their advantages and disadvantages.
2 How is energy wasted from homes?

Foundation

1 Choose one renewable and one non-renewable fuel. State their advantages and disadvantages.
2 Draw a sketch of a house and label on it all the ways that energy is wasted.

ACTIVITIES

Learn to use the Human Development Report figures and interactive maps.
1 Look up the figures for carbon footprint for this year. Go to the following website: http://hdr.undp.org/en/climatechange/
2 This website is totally interactive. Explore the following links:
   ● inequalities in carbon footprinting – some people walk more lightly than others
   ● unequal carbon footprints: shares of emissions and population
   ● indicators world map

Country	HIC, MIC, LIC	GDP per capita ppp output divided by population	Carbon emissions metric tonnes of carbon dioxide per capita
Qatar	HIC	60,000	69
Kuwait	HIC	39,000	38
United Arab Emirates	HIC	37,000	38
Trinidad and Tobago	Upper MIC	12,000	24
Netherlands	HIC	29,000	22
United States	HIC	36,000	20
Australia	HIC	28,000	16
Japan	HIC	27,000	10
United Kingdom	HIC	26,000	10
New Zealand	HIC	21,700	8
Sweden	HIC	26,000	6
China	Lower MIC	4,600	4
Thailand	Lower MIC	7,000	4
Turkey	Upper MIC	6,300	3
Tunisia	Lower MIC	6,700	2
Brazil	Lower MIC	7,800	1.8
India	LIC	2,700	1.2
Republic of Congo	LIC	600	1
Angola	Lower MIC	2,200	0.5
Chad	LIC	1,000	0.1

Figure 21 The carbon footprint of selected countries

How energy is being saved

Much of the energy that is produced in the UK is wasted. We must become more energy conscious and start to save energy if we are to cut our carbon footprint. It will, of course, also save a lot of money on fuel bills. The solutions to energy wastage have been initiated from a national to a local level. Many companies have also been set up to produce energy saving gadgets, two of which are described in Figure 22.

Figure 22 Energy saving on a domestic scale

Solutions to energy wastage at a national scale

In March 2008 the government announced that the £10 million support for householders going green will be extended until June 2010 for new applications. A grant of £2,500 is available per household for green technologies from the Low Carbon Buildings Programme. There is now no need for planning permission to install wind turbines, solar panels, ground and water source heat pumps and biomass systems.

There are also grants of up to £1 million for public buildings such as schools and hospitals where the government will pay up to 50 per cent of the start-up costs. More than 200 schools have already applied to install green technologies. For example, Howe Dell Primary School in Hatfield, which among other sustainable ideas, has a wind turbine, solar panels and recycles its rainwater (Figure 23).

The UK had its first e-day on 7 April 2008 when people were asked to think about their energy usage and switch off at least one light bulb that was not needed. It was calculated that if every one of the 22 million households in the UK switched off one 100 watt bulb on the same day, 4,500 megawatt of electricity would be saved.

Solutions to energy wastage at a local and domestic scale

A number of councils have opted for community energy schemes where a communal boiler produces the energy for everyone in the scheme. Approximately 1,300 sites in the UK with community energy programmes use CHP. CHP is a combined heat and power system which recovers the heat which is lost through the production of electricity and distributes it as hot water to heat houses and public buildings. The system is up to 90 per cent efficient, whereas some parts of the national systems are only 22 per cent efficient. Normally gas is used as the fuel but it can be easily replaced by biofuel should the need arise.

British Gas is also working with 16 local councils, including Reading Borough Council, to improve energy efficiency. If households implement energy efficiency measures such as loft insulation they will receive £100 off their council tax bill.

Over the past five years there has been an increase in the number of wind turbines which can be seen around the UK. Large numbers of them feed into the National Grid. Others provide for more local electricity demands. The turbine at Green Park in Reading has been providing energy since 2005 for 1,500 homes and businesses.

Figure 23 Howe Dell Primary School in Hatfield

Aberdeen County Council

Many local authorities are trying to save energy use by both householders and industry. In Aberdeen the local council adopted a strategy in 1999 to save energy through upgrading their housing stock, mainly by improving the heating systems and insulation.

The council own 23,500 dwellings; some are low rise but 4600 are high rise as shown in Figure 24. The work started on four high rise dwellings containing 288 flats in the Stockethill area of the city; a new CHP (combined heat and power) scheme would be installed in a facility close to one of the blocks. These properties were chosen because they were close together and therefore the cost of distribution of the energy would be lower. Also, their existing electric storage systems were inefficient as they had been installed in the 1970s and were due for an upgrade, and what's more, 70 per cent of the residents were estimated to be in fuel poverty. The tenure of the buildings was 98 per cent council tenants and 2 per cent owner occupied. The dwellings' energy efficiency ratio was very low at 3.3. When the CHP system had been installed this would improve to 6.0 and energy bills would be reduced by 40 per cent. There would also be no maintenance costs for individual heating systems.

The tenants were asked how they would like to pay for the heating system. It was decided to pay for it weekly, the cost in 2003 when the scheme started being £4.75 a week; everyone paid the same due to there being no metering. It was felt that this would make people more energy efficient. This was below the price that the tenants paid at that time for their heating. The system is run from a central boiler facility which provides electricity and a heating system. The hot water for the heating system then travels along well insulated pipes into each household where it warms the properties through radiators.

Figure 24 Stockethill housing and CHP facility

Oldham City Council

Oldham is helping its residents to save energy by upgrading their social priority housing and giving ideas on their website on how to save energy. The following list gives four of the ways the council will be upgrading their housing stock:

- installing cavity wall insulation
- fitting UPVC double glazed windows and doors
- installing 270 mm of loft insulation
- fitting hot water cylinder insulation.

The council's website also gives tips on how to reduce energy use and explains where to obtain free advice.

Lighting accounts for 10–15 per cent of the average household's energy bill; using one energy saving bulb can save £5 a year in energy costs. The council are giving away two energy saving light bulbs to each household.

Penwith Housing Association, Penzance, Cornwall

This project was completed in 2004. It was the first of its kind because it involved supplying 14 bungalows with ground source heat pumps. This provided the householders with heating via radiators and hot water. There is no mains gas in this area and, therefore, although the houses were well insulated their bills were high due to having to use solid fuel heating systems. The cost of the project was £200,000, much of which was obtained through grants. Due to the success of this scheme there are now 700 schemes across the country which are either running or being installed.

Woking Borough Council

Woking Borough Council started to explore energy efficient systems during the 1990s. It set up a company called Thameswey in order to be able to work with private companies on this project.

The council has put in its own electricity cables so that it does not have to pay to be part of the National Grid and also to save on distribution losses. The council installed a CHP system. The system powers six buildings in the town centre and excess electricity is used by sheltered housing residents and other council buildings which are close by.

The CHP system is to be extended with a new power plant being installed at Woking Leisure Centre which will be linked to the Leisure Lagoon Pool at Woking Park and which will supply the pool and 136 homes close by with power. A further 770 dwellings will benefit from lower cost surplus electricity. The annual fuel saving per household is shown in Figure 25.

	Large House (£)			Medium sized house (£)			Apartment (£)		
	Gas	Electricity	Total	Gas	Electricity	Total	Gas	Electricity	Total
National energy company	650	450	1100	350	250	600	180	150	330
Thameswey Energy	580	420	1000	320	220	540	160	140	300

Figure 25 Annual fuel saving per household

Woking council has also made moves towards being more sustainable in other areas. By 2011 it wants to provide 20 per cent of its energy through renewable sources. It has the largest concentration of photovoltaic cells in the country. Many of the clusters of cells produce too much energy which is then fed into other systems such as the ones at Vyne Community Centre and Knaphill surgery. The ones at Woking Park are used to help provide the electricity for the leisure centre. The council also has cells on street lights and signs.

Figure 26 Woking Park Leisure Centre.

Figure 27 Vyne Community Centre and Knaphill Surgery, Woking.

ACTIVITIES

Higher

1   What is meant by the term carbon footprint?
2   Which countries have the largest carbon footprints? Suggest reasons why.
3   a   Draw a scattergraph of the information in the table in Figure 21 on page 136.
    b   Describe and explain the trends that are shown by your scattergraph.
4   Choose two examples of how energy is saved on a local or domestic scale. Describe the methods used to save energy.

Foundation

1   What is meant by the term carbon footprint?
2   Which countries have the largest carbon footprints? Suggest reasons why.
3   Choose two examples of how energy is saved on a local or domestic scale. Describe the methods used to save energy.

Solutions to energy wastage at a domestic scale

There are many ways that energy can be saved at a domestic scale. These are shown in Figure 28, which illustrates how energy can be saved in the home. This is besides all the ways that energy can be generated in a more eco-friendly way

Review

By the end of this section you should be able to:

- explain how energy is wasted
- calculate the carbon footprints for countries at different levels of development
- describe and explain the solutions to energy wastage at a domestic, local and national scale.

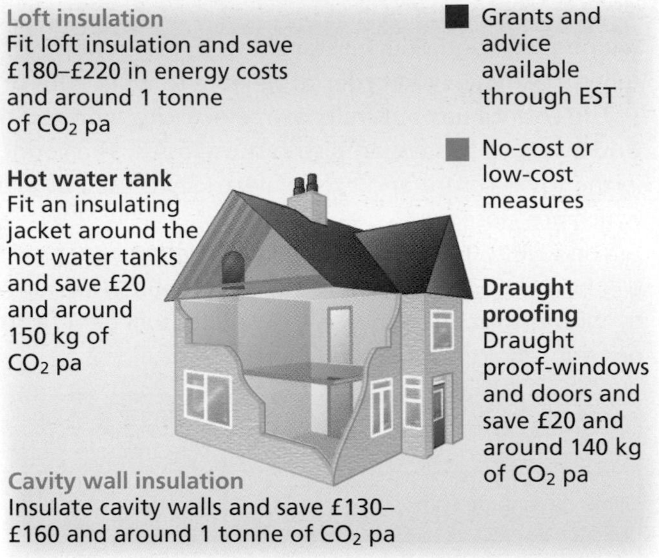

Loft insulation
Fit loft insulation and save £180–£220 in energy costs and around 1 tonne of CO_2 pa

Hot water tank
Fit an insulating jacket around the hot water tanks and save £20 and around 150 kg of CO_2 pa

Cavity wall insulation
Insulate cavity walls and save £130–£160 and around 1 tonne of CO_2 pa

■ Grants and advice available through EST

■ No-cost or low-cost measures

Draught proofing
Draught proof-windows and doors and save £20 and around 140 kg of CO_2 pa

Figure 28 How energy can be saved in the home

Sample Examination Questions

Higher tier

1   Study Figure 3 on page 125. It shows the amount of waste collected from homes, schools and business. The size of the country signifies the percentage of the world's municipal waste generated by that country. Describe the distribution of waste collection.   **(3 marks)**

2   Study Figure 4 on page 125. It shows types of domestic waste in the UK.

   a   Name the top three producers of domestic waste.   **(1 mark)**

   b   The type of waste growing the fastest in the UK is e-waste.

      i   What is e-waste?   **(1 mark)**

      ii   Why is there such a large increase in this form of waste?   **(4 marks)**

3   Fuels can be either renewable or non-renewable.

   a   Choose one type of renewable fuel.
      Chosen fuel ....

   b   Describe how it works.   **(2 marks)**

   c   What are its advantages and disadvantages?   **(4 marks)**

Foundation tier

1   Study Figure 3 on page 125. It shows the amount of waste collected from homes, schools and business. The size of the country signifies the percentage of the world's municipal waste generated by that country.

   Complete the sentences below to describe the distribution of waste collection.

   Use the words in the box.   **(3 marks)**

large	biggest	China
numbers	decline	Canada
small	Australia	density

   The USA produces a .... percentage of the world's waste. There seems to be a link between population .... and waste collected. Countries with large populations like .... have a large percentage of the world's waste.

▶

Sample Examination Questions

Higher tier (cont.)

4 Study Figure 22 on page 137. It shows ways in which energy can be saved.

   a Explain how Bye-Bye Standby works. **(1 mark)**

   b Explain one way that energy can be saved on a local level. Use an example you have studied in your answer. **(3 marks)**

5 Choose a study you have made of how waste is recycled on a local scale.

   Chosen study of local scale recycling

   ....

   Describe how the rubbish to be recycled is collected and the ways in which the recycled rubbish is reused. **(6 marks)**

   Total 25 marks

Foundation tier (cont.)

2 Study Figure 4 on page 125. It shows types of domestic waste in the UK.

   a Which type of waste produces the highest amount? **(1 mark)**

   b The type of waste growing the fastest in the UK is e-waste.

      i What is e-waste? Tick the correct answer ✓

      e-waste stands for waste from electrical goods. ☐

      e-waste stands for expensive waste. ☐

      (1 mark)

      ii Why is there such a large increase in this form of waste? **(3 marks)**

3 Fuels can be either renewable or non-renewable.

   a Name one type of renewable fuel. **(1 mark)**

   b Describe how it works. **(2 marks)**

   c State two advantages of this fuel in producing energy. **(2 marks)**

   d State two disadvantages of this fuel in producing energy. **(2 marks)**

4 Study Figure 22 on page 137. It shows ways in which energy can be saved.

   a Describe how Bye-Bye Standby works. **(2 marks)**

   b Describe one way that energy can be saved on a local level. **(2 marks)**

5 Choose a study you have made of how waste is recycled on a local scale.

   Chosen study of local scale recycling

   ....

   Describe how the rubbish to be recycled is collected and the ways in which the recycled rubbish is reused. **(6 marks)**

   Total 25 marks

Water consumption and sources

Learning objective – to study the consumption and sources of water.

Learning outcomes
- To recognise the differences in water consumption between low-income countries and high-income countries.
- To understand that greater wealth and increasing levels of development contribute to increasing water consumption.
- To know how we obtain our water.
- To relate global rainfall patterns to water surplus and deficit.

What are the differences between LICs and HICs in water consumption?

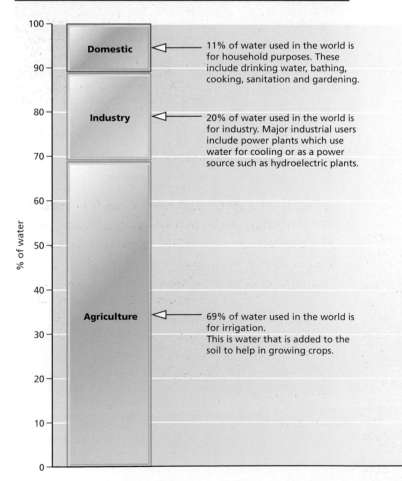

Figure 1 Water consumption

Water consumption can be measured by comparing how much water is being used at home (domestically), in farming (agriculture) and in industry.

The global averages shown in Figure 1 vary a great deal between regions. In Africa, for instance, agriculture uses 85 per cent of all the water, while domestic use accounts for 8 per cent and 7 per cent for industry. In Europe, most water is used in industry (54 per cent), while agriculture uses 33 per cent and domestic use is 13 per cent. In the USA, industry is the biggest user with 45 per cent, followed by agriculture with 41 per cent and 14 per cent domestic.

Figure 2 shows the staggering difference in the amount of water used per person per day in different parts of the world.

Region	Water used daily
USA	600 litres
Europe	300 litres
United Nations recommended minimum	50 litres
Sub-Saharan Africa	25 litres

Figure 2 Amount of water used per person per day around the world

Why should there be these differences?

Domestic usage

Why do high income countries (HICs) use more water than low income countries (LICs)?

HICs use water for a wide range of domestic practices which include personal hygiene (bathing and showering), kitchen appliances such as dishwashers and washing machines, gardening (using hosepipes) and other luxury uses such as washing cars and filling swimming pools (Figure 3).

Flush
From 6 to 12 litres

Bath
From 120 to 200 litres

Shower
From 60 to 80 litres

Washing machine
From 70 to 120 litres

Figure 3 Water usage in the homes of high-income countries

In many LICs a high percentage of people do not have piped water coming to their houses and have to rely, usually, on the women and children walking to their nearest water source (Figure 4). In LICs it is common for water collectors to have to walk several kilometres every day to fetch water. Once filled, pots and jerry cans weigh as much as 20 kg.

Because of the difficulty in getting water it has to be used very sparingly. Washing up is done by hand and the same water will often be used for personal hygiene. If they are lucky enough to live close to a river or lake they will do their washing at source (Figure 5).

Figure 5 Cleaning in the river, Sri Lanka

The following is a true story from Ghana.

I get up at 3 a.m. every day to collect water from a river 5 km walk away which is the main water source for my village. The earliest I returned was 10 a.m. which meant I was often late for work. I always go alone so that my children can go to school. Sometimes they have water to wash with and prepare breakfast. Sadly, sometimes they do not. In my village women are expected to provide water every morning for their husbands. The lack of water often results in quarrels, wife beating or even divorce. Girls are also expected to carry water and so very few go to school.

Source: WaterAid

Figure 4 Collecting water

Agricultural usage

HICs use a much greater amount of water to irrigate their crops. The main reason is the type of irrigation methods used. Figures 6 and 7 show a hand worked system in China and a modern automated spray system in the UK. The hand worked bucket in China can produce 2 litres of water a second, so long as there is somebody to operate it. The automated spray system can operate at 75 litres of water per second just with the press of a button.

Figure 6 Irrigation in Guilin, China

Figure 7 Irrigation in Norfolk, England

Industrial usage

Industry in HICs is mostly large scale with factories that use millions of litres of water in the production of various items. Industry in LICs is often very small scale with businesses being run from homes or self-built units. These cottage industries will often use very little or no water. Because large multi-national companies are moving their factories to many LICs and MICs the amount of water that will be used in industry in these countries is going to grow rapidly. In India Coca-Cola alone uses 1 million litres of water a day. Figures 8 and 9 show a small-scale industry in an LIC and a large-scale industry in an HIC.

Figure 8 Cottage industry, Gambia

Figure 9 Steel factory, Port Talbot

How does greater wealth lead to increasing water consumption?

As a country's economy becomes stronger, then the wealth of the individual increases and there is more money available for luxuries. There has been an incredible growth in labour saving devices that use a considerable amount of water. The graph in Figure 10 shows the trend in the number of households in the UK that have washing machines and dishwashers. As the average dishwasher uses 3,000 litres of water a year then obviously there has been a continual increase in domestic water usage.

There has also been a change in personal hygiene. Before the 1950s it was quite common for there to be a weekly bath night. Many houses did not have fitted bathrooms so the bathwater was heated in the kitchen, brought into the living room, and poured into a metal bath in front of the fire. Quite often all members of the family would, in turn, use the water. Now, of course, people bath or shower several times a week. Bathing and showering is still unusual in rural areas of many LICs.

With greater wealth there has been a boom in the number of holidays and short breaks taken by people in HICs. The growth of the leisure and tourism industry has seen huge demands on the use of water. Golf in Sweden is very popular and has seen a 92 per cent increase in the number of golf courses built since 1990 (Figure 11). Between 1990 and 2004 there have been 603 new golf courses built in the UK, all of which need large amounts of water to make the grass grow. They cannot rely on rain alone. Although the number of new courses is now declining there have been many technological improvements in watering systems which automatically water the course at selected times each day, dramatically increasing the amount used. Many new golf courses have artificial lakes included as part of their design. The water level in these lakes has to be constantly topped up.

In countries such as Spain which are very dry in the summer, so much water is used on golf courses and swimming pools that local communities often suffer water shortages. The authorities consider that it is more important to keep the interests of the tourist industry running, which provides money for the economy, rather than allowing the locals their water.

Figure 11 Golf course lake, Sweden

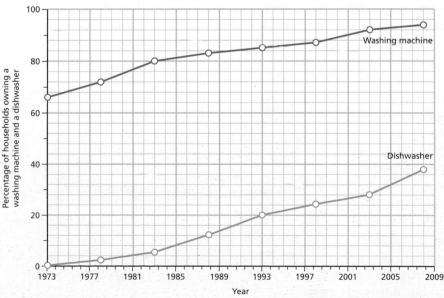

Percentage of households in the UK owning a washing machine and a dishwasher 1973–2008

Figure 10 The number of households in the UK that have washing machines and dishwashers

ACTIVITIES

Higher

1 Use the percentage figures for water usage in agriculture to draw a bar graph for Africa, Europe and USA. Give reasons for the differences.

2 Look at the photographs in Figures 6 and 7 on page 144. Explain why HICs use more water in agriculture than LICs.

3 Compare the amount of water used in industry between HICs and LICs.

4 Using examples explain why HICs use more water than LICs

Foundation

1 Use the percentage figures for water usage in homes, industry and agriculture to draw divided bar graphs for Africa, Europe and USA. Give reasons for the varying percentages.

2 Study Figure 3 on page 143.

   a How many showers can you have to use the same water as one bath?

   b How much water will you use in a week if you go to the toilet five times a day?

3 What problems do women have in Ghana when they collect water? You will need a map of Africa showing the country outlines.

4 Look at the photographs in Figures 6 and 7 on page 144.

   a What is irrigation?

   b Describe the two methods of irrigation shown in the photographs.

   c Why do HICs use more water in agriculture than LICs?

5 Name three examples of where HICs use more water than LICs.

Where does the water we use come from?

Aquifers

In some places water soaks into the ground and settles in large areas of porous rock such as chalk or sandstone. These are like giant sponges that fill up with water. They are called aquifers. The highest level of water in an aquifer is known as the water table. The level of this varies according to whether there is a lot or a little rainfall and also if temperatures are high this can lead to water being sucked from the ground and lowering the water table. To extract water from an aquifer a hole is drilled down to below the water table and pressure will cause water to flow up the pipe to the surface where it is stored in tanks and then transferred to areas of need by pipeline. The London Basin (Figure 12) is an aquifer.

The extraction of water from aquifers can lead to problems. Mexico City is built on an aquifer. It has a population of 20 million and to provide water for the growing population the aquifer is being drained quicker than it can be replenished. Areas of the city are sinking. Pavements and roads

are cracked and the walls of buildings are buckled. The monument celebrating Mexico's independence from Spain had to have 23 new steps added to reach its base as the city had sunk around it. A water pipe built into the ground in 1934 is now 6 m above ground. The city has stopped pumping water in the city centre, instead getting it from wells at the periphery. In recent years, this has slowed the sinking of the city centre to about 2 cm a year, but some suburbs with many wells continue to sink 45–60 cm each year.

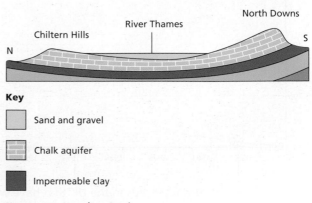

Key

   Sand and gravel

   Chalk aquifer

   Impermeable clay

Figure 12 London Basin

Reservoirs

A reservoir is an artificial lake of water held behind a dam to store water for irrigation, drinking, recreation, power, or other use. The best place for a reservoir is a river valley in an upland area with steep sided slopes which act as natural walls. The rock underneath needs to be impermeable so that the stored water does not leak away.

There are two main types of reservoir:

1   Direct supply reservoirs store water and supply it straight to a water treatment works.

2   River regulating reservoirs store water during rainy periods so that the river can be topped up during dry spells. They release extra water into the river so that it can be taken out further downstream for treatment and supply.

Some reservoirs are entirely underground. In the UK, Thames Water has many underground reservoirs beneath London built in the 1800s by the Victorians, most of which are lined with thick layers of brick. Honor Oak Service reservoir, which was completed in 1909, is the largest of this type in Europe. The roof is supported using large brick pillars and arches and the outside surface is used as a golf course.

Kielder Water

Kielder Water is a river regulating reservoir. It is owned by Northumbrian Water, one of the ten water companies in England and Wales, and holds 200 billion litres, making it the largest reservoir in the UK. It was constructed between 1975 and 1981 and was opened by the Queen in 1982. It took two years for the valley of the North Tyne river to fill with water completely once construction was completed. The reservoir releases water into the North Tyne river, which joins the Tyne near Hexham. The water can also be transferred into three of the region's other rivers. Huge pumps take water from the Tyne at Riding Mill and transfer it through a tunnel to the River Derwent near the Derwent reservoir, then to the River Wear at Frosterley and then to the River Tees at Eggleston. In this way water treatment works at Horsley on the Tyne, at Mosswood near Consett on the Derwent, at Lumley near Chester-le-Street on the Wear and at Broken Scar near Darlington on the Tees, can all be supplied with water from Kielder. The main conurbations served by the reservoir are Tyneside, Wearside and Teesside.

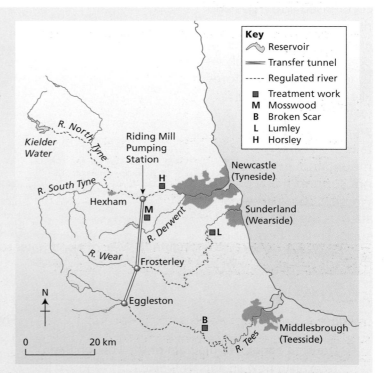

Figure 13 Map showing water transfers from Kielder Water

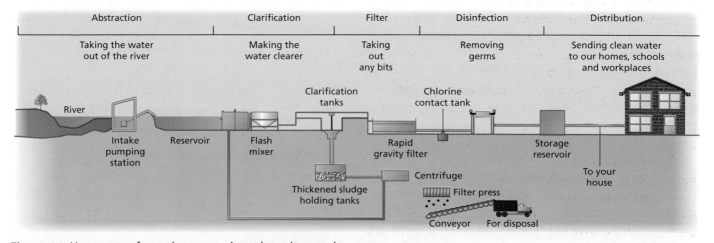

Figure 14 How water from the reservoir ends up in your home

Why do water supplies vary?

Water supply is uneven. The distribution of rainfall varies from region to region and country to country. Some places in the world have a surplus of water and some have a deficit. The main reason for this is the amount of rainfall a place receives. Another reason is that some areas with a reasonable amount of rainfall have very high evapotranspiration rates. This is where the temperature is high and rainfall is quickly condensed into a gas and rises back into the atmosphere. The water does not have enough time to enter water stores like groundwater. The wettest places in the world such as the rainforests and mountainous areas do not support many people, whereas some dry areas such as the Nile valley support high populations.

Figure 15 shows the areas with little or no scarcity. They are nearly all HICs although there are some MICs in South America. The countries that are suffering a scarcity of water, with the exception of Australia, are all MICs or LICs. They are split between countries with a physical scarcity because they are very arid and very poor countries who cannot afford to access the water.

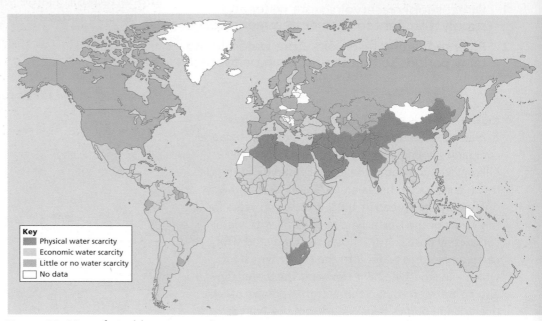

Figure 15 Map of world water scarcity

Key
- Physical water scarcity
- Economic water scarcity
- Little or no water scarcity
- No data

ACTIVITIES

Higher

1 Draw an annotated diagram of the London Basin to explain how an aquifer works.
2 You will need a map of Africa showing the country outlines. Complete a choropleth map of Africa showing the percentage of the population with access to safe drinking water in 2005. The following countries should be added:

Foundation

1 What is an aquifer?
2 Complete a choropleth map of Africa showing the percentage of the population with access to safe drinking water in 2005.
  Your map should have three colours:
  Yellow = less than 40%, Orange = 41%–65%
  Red = over 66%

Country	%	Country	%	Country	%	Country	%
Angola	38	Botswana	95	Zimbabwe	78	Namibia	77
Uganda	52	Chad	27	Togo	54	Ghana	73
Nigeria	62	Ethiopia	24	Uganda	52	Angola	(–)38
Lesotho	78	South Africa	86	Senegal	78		

a Describe the pattern shown on your map.
b Explain why there should be such wide variations between the countries.
3 Study Figure 15 (above). Describe the pattern of water scarcity.

The following countries should be added:
Describe the pattern shown on your map.

3 Study Figure 15 (above). Describe the pattern of water scarcity.

Water supply problems

Learning objective – to study water supply problems in high-income and low-income countries.

Learning outcomes

- To recognise that HICs and LICs have water supply problems.
- To understand the different water supply problems in HICs and LICs.

What are the problems associated with water supply in HICs?

Rainfall and population imbalance

The population and the rainfall of the UK is unevenly distributed (see Figures 16 and 17). One-third of the UK's population live in south-east England but this is also the driest part of the UK with average annual rainfall of less than 800 mm. The least populated areas of the UK are in the mountain areas of Scotland, Wales and north-west England, but it is here that the most rain falls: over 2,000 mm.

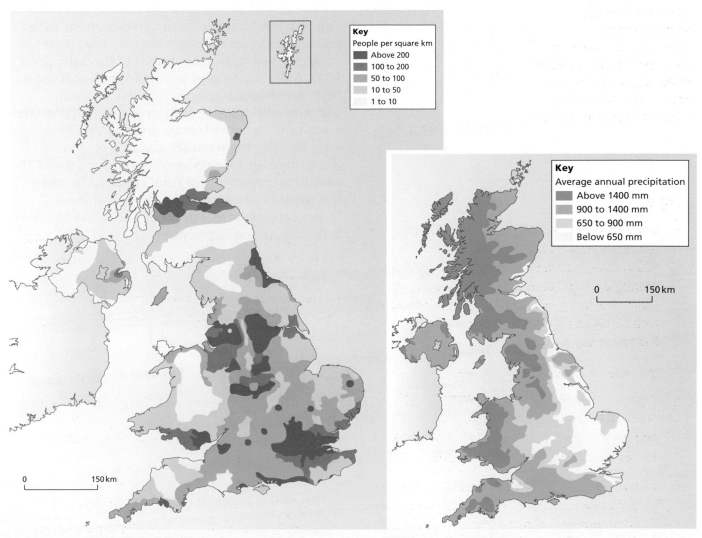

Key
People per square km
- Above 200
- 100 to 200
- 50 to 100
- 10 to 50
- 1 to 10

Key
Average annual precipitation
- Above 1400 mm
- 900 to 1400 mm
- 650 to 900 mm
- Below 650 mm

0   150 km

0   150 km

Figure 16 Population density in the UK

Figure 17 UK rainfall

Leakage

In London, more than half of the water mains are more than 100 years old, and around a third are more than 150 years old. The ageing pipes do not seem to affect the quality of water, but the problem is that they leak. Thirty per cent of the water supply is lost through leaks and cracks. More than 3.5 billion litres of water were lost daily through broken and leaking pipes in England and Wales in 2006. That's more than a fifth of the 15 billion litres supplied by the UK water system each day and is more than the entire amount of bottled water drunk by Britons in a year. This water that leaks daily through broken pipes is a loss to the economy of between £1,512,000 and £3,600,000 because this is how much it will cost to re-treat the water to make it drinkable.

There will always be water leaks, because the pipes wear out and suffer damage from the environment, for example, from freezing weather and the impact of traffic on the roads. However, water companies have also been very slow in repairing and replacing the pipes.

Seasonal rain imbalance

There is a problem with the seasonal supply of water in many of the Mediterranean holiday areas. These places, like the Costa del Sol in Spain, receive most of their rainfall in the winter months and very little in the summer months. In the six months of May to October, Malaga receives only 70 mm compared with 385 mm in the other six months. Unfortunately it is in the summer months when they require the greatest amount of water for the influx of tourists who want full swimming pools and well-watered golf courses. They also need food which means crops need to be heavily irrigated.

In 2008 there were many problems in southern Spain. Murcia has undergone a resort-building boom in recent years. Farmers are fighting developers over water rights. They are fighting one another over who gets to water their crops. And as a sign of their mounting desperation, they are buying and selling water like gold on a rapidly growing black market, mostly from illegal wells. The Spanish Ministry for the Environment called on residents and holidaymakers to save water as Spain started its worst summer of drought since 1947. A dry winter and spring left national water reserves almost 50 per cent down on total capacity with no expectation of rain in the driest areas until October. Murcia and the Valencia regions were the most critical with reservoirs on the Segura and Júcar rivers running at 29 and 16 per cent respectively of total capacity. To make the situation worse it was a dry hot summer. Temperatures were 2 degrees above average for July, August and September.

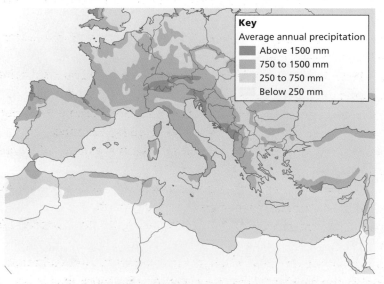

Figure 18 Map of the Mediterranean with rainfall figures

Variability

Because rainfall in an area cannot be relied upon there are often times of deficit. The graph of UK rainfall in Figure 19 shows that in 2005 and 2006 there were long periods where the rainfall was below average. This would lead to problems such as reservoir levels dropping and water restrictions, for example, hosepipe bans. By contrast 2007 saw a long wet period in the summer which lead to reservoirs and aquifers being replenished.

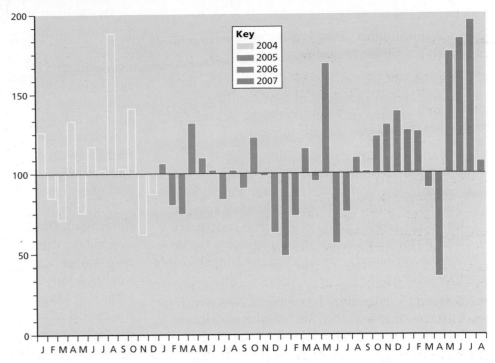

Figure 19 Rainfall variability in the UK, 2004–2007

What are the problems associated with water supply in LICs?

The greatest problem in the LICs is the high proportion of the population that do not have access to clean piped water. This leads to a range of diseases which can be caused by resource exploitation.

Fact file: Water supply in LICs

- 1.1 billion people in the world do not have access to safe water – this is roughly one-sixth of the world's population.
- 2.6 billion people in the world do not have access to adequate sanitation – this is roughly two-fifths of the world's population.
- 1.8 million children die every year as a result of diseases caused by unclean water and poor sanitation. This amounts to around 5,000 deaths a day.
- At any given time, almost half the population of the developing world is suffering from one or more of the main diseases associated with inadequate provision of water and sanitation.
- Around 90 per cent of incidences of water-related diseases are due to unsafe water supply, sanitation and hygiene and are mostly concentrated in children in developing countries.
- At any one time, half of the developing world's hospital beds are occupied by patients suffering from water-related diseases.
- Intestinal worms infect about 10 per cent of the population of the developing world. Intestinal parasitic infections can lead to malnutrition, anaemia and stunted growth.
- One gram of human faeces can contain 10,000,000 viruses, 1,000,000 bacteria, 1,000 parasite cysts, 100 parasite eggs.
- India spends eight times more on military budgets than on water and sanitation. Pakistan spends 47 times more. Diarrhoea claims some 450,000 lives every year in India, more than in any other country.

Water-related diseases

Dirty contaminated water is responsible for a range of health problems including:

- Dysentery – an infectious disease of the large intestine. Symptoms of dysentery include diarrhoea, often containing blood, sickness and stomach cramp.

- Malaria – caused by a parasite which is transmitted via the bites of infected mosquitoes. Symptoms of malaria include fever, headache and vomiting, and usually appear between 10 and 15 days after the mosquito bite. If not treated, malaria can quickly become life-threatening by disrupting the blood supply to vital organs.

- Bilharzia – caused by parasitic worms which get into the blood system and can cause kidney failure.

- Trachoma – caused by parasites in contaminated water and will lead to blindness if untreated.

Pollution of water courses through resource exploitation

Many of the indigenous tribes in the Amazon region have suffered from water contamination due to mining operations and oil exploitation. This contamination has led to increased risks of cancer, abortion, dermatitis, fungal infection, headaches, and nausea. Their drinking, bathing and fishing water contain levels of toxins much higher than the safety limits set by the US Environmental Protection Agency. Unlined waste pits (Figure 20) provide a major source of pollution in the Oriente region of Ecuador. Over the years, the toxic contents of the waste pits have leeched into the rivers, contaminating the larger ecosystem and sending toxins downstream into Peru. Since there are no other options for obtaining water, local people now depend on these contaminated sources for drinking water and are slowly poisoning themselves. Childhood leukemia rates are four times higher in this area than in other parts of Ecuador; children as young as a few months of age have died of leukemia.

The Achuar people (Figure 21), who have lived for thousands of years in the rainforest of Peru, allege that the Occidental Petroleum company contaminated their territory during more than 30 years of oil drilling. The water contains high concentrations of hydrocarbons and heavy metals, like lead, cadmium, mercury and arsenic. It is widely acknowledged that high levels of heavy metals, hydrocarbons and chlorides can cause serious physical and mental health problems, including cancer and genetic deformities.

The Achuar people say this pollution is destroying the fragile ecosystem in which they live, killing the fish and wildlife, contaminating their water source and seriously damaging their health. A survey carried out by Peru's Ministry of Health in May 2008 found that cadmium levels in the blood of more than 98 per cent of the Achuar exceeded safe levels. More than 66 per cent of children had levels of lead in their blood which exceeded the maximum safe amount.

Figure 20 Contaminated waste water pit

Figure 21 The Achuar tribe

ACTIVITIES

Higher

1 Study Figures 16 and 17 on page 149.

   a Name two areas of the UK that have a high population density and a low rainfall.

   b What problems does this cause for these areas?

   c Is it true to say that all areas with a high population in the UK have a low rainfall?

2 Variability of rainfall causes problems. Discuss.

3 Study the climate figures below which are for a town on the Costa del Sol.

   a Where is the Costa del Sol?

   b Explain why the Costa del Sol suffers from a seasonal rain imbalance.

Foundation

1 Study Figures 16 and 17 on page 149.

   a Name two areas of the UK that have high population density.

   b Name two areas of the UK that have high rainfall.

   c Is it true to say that areas with high population in the UK have high rainfall?

2 Differences in the amount of rain that falls in winter and summer can cause problems for an area. State three problems that can be caused by seasonal variations.

3 Study the climate figures below which are for a town on the Costa del Sol.

	Jan	Feb	Mar	Apr	May	Jun	Jul	Aug	Sep	Oct	Nov	Dec
mm	70.0	61.1	64.1	52.4	36.8	14.9	1.2	4.6	17.5	57.3	77.8	76.4
°C	10.7	11.9	14.0	16.1	19.6	23.4	26.7	26.7	24.3	19.5	14.5	11.2

4 How does resource exploitation lead to pollution of water courses?

5 The table below shows residential water usage in California in 2006.

Landscape	58%
Clothes washers	9%
Showers	7%
Toilets	11%
Dishwashers	1%
Baths	1%
Faucets (taps)	6%
Other	7%

   a Use the figures to construct a pie graph.

   b Comment on the water usage that your graph shows.

   c What might be included in Other?

   d How would the water usage in an LIC be different?

   a Where is the Costa del Sol?

   b Which months had less than 15 mm rainfall?

   c Which months had temperatures greater than 20°C?

   d Explain why the Costa del Sol suffers from a seasonal rain imbalance.

4 a Name three waterborne diseases.

   b How have the Achuar been affected by polluted water?

5 Study Figure 19 on page 151 and use it to answer the following questions.

   a How many months in 2004–2007 was the UK's rainfall above average?

   b When did rainfall stay below average for four months in a row?

   c There was a lot of rain in May 2006. However a hosepipe ban was in operation in August. Why did this happen?

Management of water usage and resources

Learning objective – to study the management of water usage and resources.

Learning outcomes

* To recognise that water usage is managed differently in HICs and LICs.
* To categorise ways to manage water.
* To understand that disputes occur over water transfers.
* To explain why a water management scheme was necessary and its effects.

How is water usage being managed in HICs?

Domestic

Water can be used more efficiently in the house. Figure 22 and Figure 23 show a variety of ways to reduce water usage at home.

Efficient	Non-efficient
Shower: 60 litres	Bath: 120 litres
Short flush toilet: 3 litres	Normal flush: 11 litres
Water butt: rainwater	Hosepipe: 50 litres
Water meter: controls usage	No water meter: no control
Turn off taps	Running tap: 10 litres a minute
Fix dripping taps	Dripping tap: 2,000 litres a month
Economy setting on dishwasher and washing machine	Full cycle on dishwasher and washing machine

Figure 22 Ways to reduce water usage at home

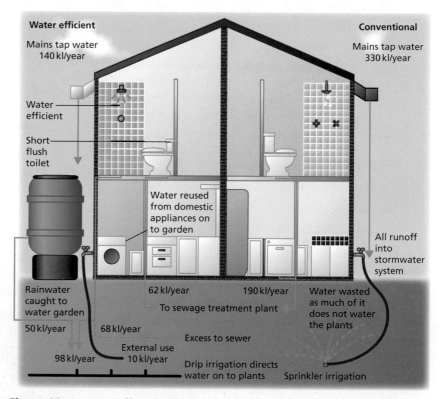

Figure 23 A water efficient house

Industrial

Industry has come to realise that it needs to use water more sensibly. In many cases this requires the particular company to be more aware of how much water they are using and indeed wasting. Many companies have taken advice from 'Envirowise' a free government website which is running an initiative called 'The ripple effect'. This outlines how businesses can become water efficient. Companies had to register their interest by September 2008 and then would be given advice on ways in which they can cut water usage such as reusing waste water, and, how to implement a plan on saving water.

Case study – Walkers Crisps in Leicester

Walkers Crisps has reduced its use of water by 50 per cent. This has saved 700 million litres of water a year. They have achieved this saving by taking the following steps.

1 They installed 30 water meters at their production plants. This allowed them to see where they were using most water.
2 They then implemented engineering solutions such as recycling water from the starch recovery programme for use in another part of the production process.
3 They also re-educated their staff about the use of water in the sanitation facilities. Water usage is now monitored per shift. 'Leak busters' and 'water champions' are assigned to each shift. The best performing teams over a period of time are rewarded by the company for their contribution towards sustainability.

Overall, the strategy has led to water consumption falling at both of their sites in Leicester. In Bursom it has dropped from 17.67 litres to 9.24 litres per kilogram of potatoes processed, and in Leycroft, 13.65 litres to 6.38 litres per kilogram.

Fact file: Ways that industries are saving water

- Tap restrictors – valuable for providing equal flow at a number of taps in a washroom. This reduces water flow by 15 per cent.
- Push taps – ideal for public areas where taps may be left running. For a tap dripping at 3.5 l/h, this saves 31 m³ of water a year.
- Shower regulators – valuable for providing equal flow at a number of outlets. This reduces water flow in showers by 20 per cent.
- Push-button showers – ideal for public areas where showers may be left running. This saves 5–15 per cent per shower depending on the location.
- Urinal flush controls – several systems are available from different manufacturers. Typical saving of 10 per cent per toilet.
- Toilet water dams. Adequate flushing needs to be ensured to maintain hygiene standards. Typical savings of 20 per cent per toilet.

Figure 24 Walkers Crisps factory, Leicester

Case study – Cadbury Trebor Bassett in Birmingham
Cadbury Trebor Bassett is committed to saving water. This has been achieved by reusing waste water. The company has installed an onsite wastewater treatment plant, at a cost of £2 million, to clean water that has been through the production process. This water can then be reused in a variety of different ways, for example in the cooling towers. As a result of its investment, Cadbury Trebor Bassett has been able to reduce demand for water usage at the site by about 15 per cent per year resulting in a saving in water costs of around £10,000 per annum and water usage of 17 million litres per year.

Agricultural

Water can be used more efficiently in agriculture. For crop irrigation, optimal water efficiency means minimising losses due to evaporation or run-off. Flood irrigation is the most common type of irrigation, but it gives a very uneven distribution, as parts of a field may receive excess water in order to deliver sufficient quantities to other parts. Overhead irrigation sprinklers give a much more equal and controlled distribution pattern, but in extremely dry conditions, much of the water may evaporate before it reaches the ground. Drip irrigation is the most expensive and least-used type, but it is the most efficient as it delivers water straight to the plant roots with minimal losses (Figure 25). As changing irrigation systems can be a costly undertaking for farmers, conservation efforts often concentrate on maximising the efficiency of the existing system. This may include loosening compacted soils, creating **furrows** to prevent run-off, and using soil moisture and rainfall sensors so that crops are only watered when it is needed.

Figure 25 Drip irrigation

How is water usage being managed in LICs?

A range of schemes are now in place to develop and make use of local water supplies. Technology appropriate to an area is being used. Money for these schemes comes from charity organisations such as WaterAid, Oxfam and Christian Aid.

1 Hand-dug wells

Hand-dug wells are the most common method of getting water in LICs. However, traditional hand-dug wells often dry out as they are too shallow and also become polluted as the sides are not lined and the top is uncovered. Without proper drainage, pools of water can form around the wells and these can act as breeding grounds for disease-carrying insects like mosquitoes. New technology uses the traditional hand-dug methods, with additional features to prevent these problems. Hand-dug wells are usually 1.2 m in diameter to allow sufficient digging space. Depths vary, from shallow wells at 5 m to deep wells over 20 m, but all are deep enough to ensure the water table can still be reached during the dry season. They are lined with concrete to prevent pollution and make them more stable.

2 Rainwater harvesting

Falling rainwater is some of the cleanest naturally occurring water available and where it falls regularly there is scope to collect it, before evaporation takes place and before it becomes contaminated. This is called rainwater harvesting. Water is generally collected from cleaned roofs, where it runs down a gutter into a storage tank.

3 Gravity-fed schemes

In hilly areas, water can be piped down to communities from higher water sources through gravity-fed schemes. The spring or small unpolluted stream is dammed and protected at its source before being piped down to storage tanks in villages. Distribution pipes then feed protected tapstands allowing people to draw water close to their homes. This method avoids the potential mechanical problems of pumps, but still needs careful maintenance to keep the water clean.

4 Tubewells and boreholes

Tubewells are small diameter holes drilled by hand-power. Although hand-dug wells can retain more water, tubewells can be built quickly and cheaply, require less maintenance, can reach greater depths and are safer to construct. Handpumps can be used to draw water from tubewells. Where there are harder rocks and the water table is very low, engine powered drills are necessary to cut through the earth to depths of 100 m or more. These are called boreholes and the water then has to be pumped to the surface using diesel or electric engines. The water is then usually stored in large tanks before being piped to tapstands in surrounding villages. The diesel or electric pumps needed are expensive to maintain.

Figure 26 Digging a well in Mali

Figure 27 Tubewell, India

5 Recycling

In India great emphasis is being put on recycling water rather than continually trying to find new sources for the rapidly growing population. Bangaloreans will get to drink a mixture of recycled water and rainwater in future as plans have been announced to supply 600 million litres of recycled water for drinking purposes. In Bangalore they are also treating sewage to make it drinkable. A factory with the capacity to treat 425 million litres of sewage from Koramangala valley to make about 400 million litres of recycled water is proposed to be built at Samethanahalli, and the recycled water from this plant would be pumped to the Hessarghatta reservoir. In many Indian cities it has now become compulsory for new housing developments to use recycled water. Kolkata has used the services of Unitech Water Technologies Ltd to recycle sewage water into drinking water. The Mumbai Municipal Corporation intends to reduce water supply from 140 to 90 litres per person per day.

ACTIVITIES

Higher

1   How is industry managing the conservation of water?

2   Explain how a house can be made more water efficient.

3   Describe and explain a scheme that is in place in an LIC to develop and make use of local water supplies.

4   What is the difference between a tubewell and a borehole?

5   On a base map of India mark all the recycling cities named in the text. Add information on the map to describe the recycling schemes.

Foundation

1   State three ways that water is being conserved in industry.

2   List the ways that you could make your house more water efficient.

3   Draw a sketch of the well in Figure 26 on page 157. Add labels to explain how it works.

Extension

Read the following extract from a UN Development Programme (UNDP) report.

> The main conflicts in Africa during the next 25 years could be over that most precious of commodities, water, as countries fight for access to scarce resources. Potential 'water wars' are likely in areas where rivers and lakes are shared by more than one country.

Research on the internet.

a   Do you agree with the extract? Explain your answer fully using appropriate examples.

b   Name another area in the world where water conflicts are happening.

How water transfers can cause conflicts

The Tigris–Euphrates River System is an example where differing national interests and withdrawal rights for water have been in conflict. The main problem is that both rivers have their source in Turkey and then flow through Syria and Iraq. Turkey has created several dams which are restricting the flow of water into Syria and Iraq.

The Southeastern Anatolia Project (GAP) is a massive $32 billion project to harness the power and potential of the upper reaches of the Tigris and Euphrates rivers and to irrigate the fertile plains that lie between them. When completed in 2010, 21 dams and 17 hydroelectric power plants will produce approximately 22 per cent of Turkey's projected electricity requirements.

The Ataturk Dam, the sixth largest rock filled dam in the world, is the key structure for the development of the Lower Euphrates River region. Completed in 1993, it presently generates 8.9 billion kWh in electricity and is responsible for opening more than 180,000 acres of farmland to irrigation in the Harran plain.

Turkey argues that GAP is beneficial to Syria and Iraq, as the flow of the rivers is now more constant. However, this has not happened. After GAP the waters of the Euphrates will decrease from 30 billion m^3 a year (BCM/a) at the Syrian boarder to 16 BCM/a, and at the Iraqi boarder from 16 BCM/a to 5 BCM/a.

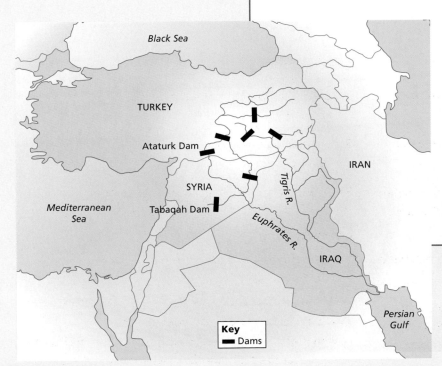

Figure 28 Water conflict in the Middle East

Some of the water used in Turkey will find its way back into the rivers, and this water can of course be reused by the downstream countries. The problem is the water quality will decrease as the used water will carry greater quantities of salt and chemicals caused by fertilisers and pesticides. This is especially a problem for Iraq, as it is the lowest downstream country on the Euphrates and the Tigris. Already 74 per cent of the irrigated areas in Iraq suffer from salinity.

In Syria the Tabaqah Dam forms a reservoir, Lake Assad, that is used for irrigating cotton. Syria has dammed its two tributaries and is in the process of constructing another dam. The scarcity of water in the Middle East leaves Iraq in constant fear that Syria and Turkey will use up most of the water before it reaches Iraq.

Conflict in this area has been ongoing since the 1940s. In 1974 Iraq put troops on the Syrian border and threatened to destroy Syria's Al-Thawra dam on the Euphrates.

The potential for war over these waters is the subject of much diplomacy. Animosity was very great towards Turkey during the conference on international law over shared water resources in the Arab region, held at Sharm el Sheik in May 2000. Since only a minimal part of the GAP irrigation project has been realised, tensions are likely to increase as more water is used by these projects.

Figure 29 Ataturk Dam

Introduction

The Three Gorges Dam (Figure 30) is a hydroelectric dam that spans the Yangtze river in Sandouping, Hubei province, China. It is the largest hydroelectric power station in the world. The total electric generating capacity of the dam will reach 22,500 megawatts.

Reasons for the scheme

The reasons for the building of the Three Gorges Dam were to produce clean electricity, to control flooding and to improve shipping along the Yangtze.

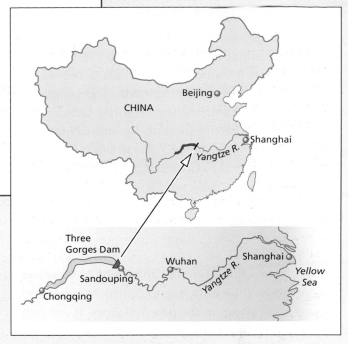

Figure 30 The location of the Three Gorges Dam

What are the negative effects of the Three Gorges Dam?

Resettlement

Around 1.4 million people have had to move because their villages and towns have been lost beneath the rising waters. Gaoyang was the last town to be evacuated in July 2008 as it would be submerged by the giant Three Gorges Dam, making way for water levels in the reservoir to rise to their final height of 175 m above sea level. The displaced people have had to move to new settlements (Figure 31).

Landslides

One of the most worrying consequences of the project has been the sharp increase in landslides around the dam. These landslides are being caused by the huge weight of water behind the dam and fluctuations in the water level. The reservoir has already collapsed in 91 places and a total of 36 km have caved in. Landslides have produced waves as high as 50 m. In July 2007 a hillside collapsed, dragging 13 farmers to their deaths and drowning 11 fishermen. A big mudslide hit a village in the Gaoyang area in April 2008, sweeping into the local school's playground and part of the village. In July 2008, a landslide in Badong County in Hubei Province, beside the reservoir, killed more than 30 people after burying a bus.

Environment

Of the 3,000 to 4,000 remaining Siberian Crane, a large number currently spend the winter in wetlands that have been destroyed by the Three Gorges Dam. The dam also contributed to the extinction of the Yangtze river dolphin. In addition, populations of the Yangtze sturgeon are guaranteed to be 'negatively affected' by the dam. There are high levels of pollution currently in the Yangtze. More than 1 billion tonnes of wastewater are released annually into the river. The water quality of the Yangtze's tributaries is deteriorating rapidly, as the dammed river is less able to disperse pollutants effectively. The incidence of algae blooms has risen steadily since the reservoir was completed in 2006.

Figure 31 New settlements

What benefits will the Three Gorges Dam Project bring to the people?

Economic growth

The new navigable waterways along the Yangtze will provide mass transit of raw materials to the area allowing massive economic growth. This combined with the significantly reduced transportation costs provides an attractive location for industry seeking a cheap labour force. A new railway, linking the area with the rest of the north-east, will be built alongside a new highway linking with Shanghai. Also a new airport will open up the region for industrial development.

Figure 32 The hydro dam

Flood control

It will have a flood control capacity of 22.15 billion m³, which will be sufficient to control the greatest flood experienced in the past 100 years. It will protect 1,500,000 hectares of farmland and the lives and property of 15 million people.

Power generation

The amount of energy produced by the hydroelectric turbines is 84.6 billion kilowatt hours which is the equivalent of 18 nuclear power stations (Figure 32).

Navigation

It has allowed container shipping to reach all the way up the Yangtze river from Shanghai to Chongqing, the biggest city of south-west China. The river transport will be improved from 10 million to 50 million tonnes per year and the costs reduced by 35 per cent. Navigation on the Yangtze river will become much easier in the drier season when water levels used to be low (Figure 33).

Tourism

Yichang City in Hubei Province, where the Three Gorges Dam is located, plans to spend 3 billion yuan to improve tourism in the dam area. To develop tourism, the China Three Gorges Dam Project Corporation built the Tanziling to enable visitors to see the panorama of Three Gorges from the highest point. More than 800,000 tourists visited the Three Gorges Dam area in 2007, with tourism revenue of US$15.6 million.

Cruising along the river is very popular and many tourist sites are being developed along with thousands of jobs. Ex-farmers are now being used in the tourist industry, for example, the Tujia, a local ethnic minority now cater for tourists by dragging small boats by rope along the Shennong stream, to allow the tourists access to beautiful scenery (Figure 34).

Figure 33 Container on the Yangtze River

Figure 34 Boats along the Shennong stream

Review

By the end of this section you should be able to:

- recognise that water usage is managed in different ways
- understand that when water is transferred disputes occur
- explain why water management schemes are necessary.

Sample Examination Questions

Higher tier

1   Study the photographs in Figures 5 and 7 on pages 143 and 144. They show how water can be used.

   a   State how the water is being used in the figures.

   (2 marks)

   i   Why is the water being used in this way in Figure 5? (1 mark)

   b   Explain how drinking water can be polluted in LICs. (4 marks)

2   Study Figure 35 below. It shows the amount of water used in two continents.

   a   Complete the pie graph for Europe using the figures in the table in Figure 36. (2 marks)

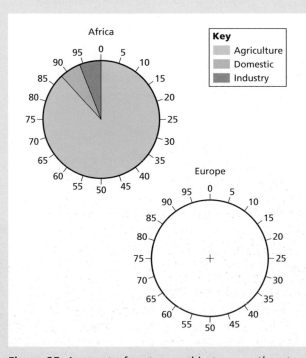

Figure 35 Amount of water used in two continents

Foundation tier

1   Study the photographs in Figures 5 and 7 on pages 143 and 144. They show how water can be used.

   a   Complete the table below. Tick (✓) the correct box

	Domestic	Industrial	Agricultural
Figure 5			
Figure 7			

   (2 marks)

   b   Suggest ways that cause water to be unsafe to drink. (3 marks)

2   Study Figure 35. It shows the amount of water used in two continents.

   a   Complete the pie graph for Europe. Use the figures in the table in Figure 36. (2 marks)

   b   Complete the following sentences about how water is used in the two continents.

   Choose from the words in the box:

88%	15%	less	86%	more	30%

   In Africa ....of water is used on farming.

   In Europe only ....is used on farming.

   This shows that the HICs use..... water on farming than LICs. (3 marks)

   c   There are many ways that water is being saved in homes in HICs. Name and describe two ways that water is being saved in homes in HICs.

   Way one ....

   Description .... (2 marks)

Sample Examination Questions

Higher tier (cont.)

Type of water usage	Amount of water used %
Farming	30
Domestic	15
Industry	55

Figure 36 Water usage in Europe

b The percentage of water used domestically is much higher for Europe than Africa. Why?

(2 marks)

c There are many ways that water is being saved in homes in HICs. Explain how water is being saved in homes in HICs. (4 marks)

3 Study Figure 37. It is a diagram showing an aquifer.

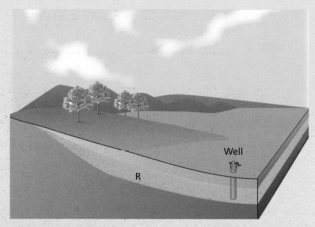

Well

R

Figure 37 An aquifer

a Is rock layer R permeable or impermeable?

(1 mark)

b Explain how water can be obtained from an aquifer. (3 marks)

4 Many water management schemes have been built around the world. Choose a study you have made about a water management scheme.

Chosen water management scheme

....

Describe the scheme and explain the effects, both positive and negative, on the area it serves. (6 marks)

Total 25 marks

Foundation tier (cont.)

Way two ....

Description .... (2 marks)

3 Study Figure 37. It is a diagram showing an aquifer.

a Is rock layer R permeable or impermeable?

(1 mark)

b The sentences in the box below explain one way that we obtain water. They are in the wrong order. Rewrite the sentences in the correct order.

The rainwater flows through the rock due to gravity.

Rain falls at area V.

If a well is built, water can be pumped to the surface.

The water is stored in the rock.

(4 marks)

4 Many water management schemes have been built around the world. Choose a study you have made about a water management scheme.

Chosen water management scheme

....

Describe the effects of the scheme and explain how it has brought benefits to the area it serves.

(6 marks)

Total 25 marks

UNIT 3
The Human Environment

This unit is about human geography and people issues. There are six chapters in this unit.

- **Chapter 9 Economic Change:** the changes in economic structure and location of industry.

- **Chapter 10 Farming and the Countryside:** the changes to the UK countryside and countryside management.

- **Chapter 11 Settlement Change:** settlement site and shape, changes to land use in urban areas.

- **Chapter 12 Population Change:** the growth, density, distribution and structure of population.

- **Chapter 13 A Moving World:** the different movements made by people around the world and the reasons for these movements.

- **Chapter 14 A Tourist's World:** the changing shape of the tourist industry and the impact of tourists around the world.

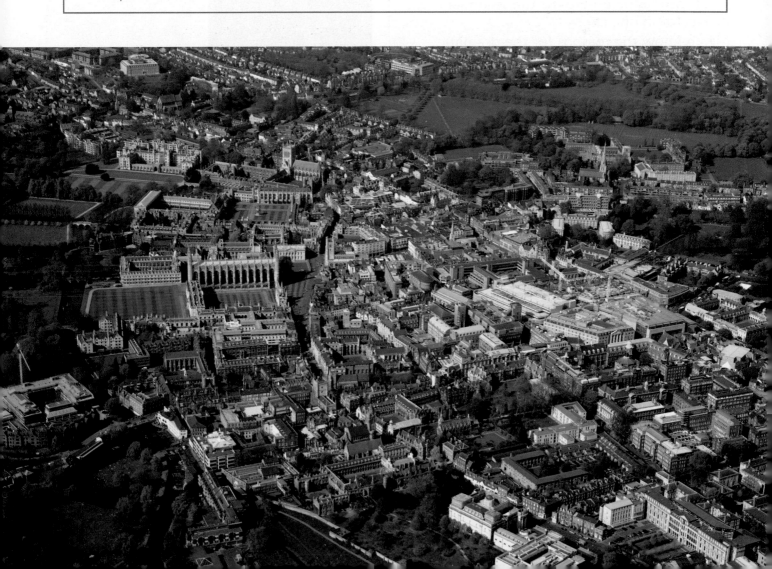

Changes to different economic sectors

Learning objective – to study changes to different economic sectors.

Learning outcomes

- To recognise the relative importance of primary, secondary and tertiary sectors in countries at different levels of development.
- To understand that these sectors change over space and through time.
- To know the reasons for the decline in numbers employed in the primary sector in the UK.
- To know the reasons for the decline in the secondary sector.
- To study the growth of the secondary sector in one LIC.
- To know the reasons for the dramatic growth of the tertiary sector since 1970.

Figure 2 Different jobs

Figure 1 Jobs advertised in a local newspaper

What are the sectors of industry?

Look at Figure 1 which shows advertisements for jobs offered in a local newspaper.

If you looked in your local newspaper, many of the jobs shown would be similar. In another country, the jobs on offer might be very different. Although there are hundreds of different jobs or occupations, they can all be classified into three categories.

- Primary industry is the extraction of raw materials from the ground or the sea. It includes farming, fishing, forestry and mining.
- Secondary industry is the manufacturing of goods using the raw materials from primary industry.
- Tertiary industry does not produce anything, but often involves the provision of different services. Teachers, solicitors, sales assistants and cleaners are all tertiary occupations.

It is usual to divide industry into these three sectors, but they are often linked together as one job relies on another. Figure 3 on page 167 shows the stages in the production of a book. The raw material for the book comes from coniferous forests. The growing and cutting down of the trees is a primary industry. The wood is formed into pulp and turned into paper in a paper mill, which is a secondary industry. The paper is then used by an author to write the book, a tertiary sector job. The book is then printed, another secondary industry. Finally the book will be transported to shops where it will be sold, both processes being tertiary industries.

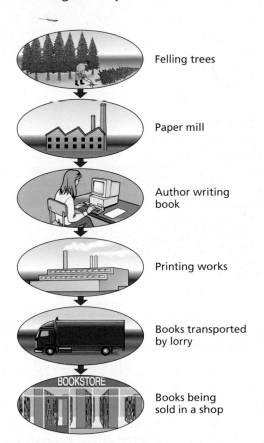

Felling trees

Paper mill

Author writing book

Printing works

Books transported by lorry

Books being sold in a shop

Figure 3 Stages in the production of a book

How do employment patterns differ between countries?

The relative importance of primary, secondary and tertiary industries can be used to compare the levels of development between countries.

Figure 4 shows divided bar charts for Mali, Taiwan and Germany. The bar chart for Mali shows that a high proportion of the population works in primary industries. This is a very common situation in an LIC. The poorest LICs are in a similar position to that of the UK 150 years ago. They are in the early stages of economic development with most of their population still working on the land as farmers. In contrast, a high proportion of the workforce of an HIC like Germany is involved in the tertiary sector. Up to 70 per cent of the workforce in some HICs with mature economies are in tertiary occupations.

Taiwan is a newly industrialised country (NIC) and has a strong manufacturing sector. Many transnational companies have factories in countries like Taiwan so that they can take advantage of cheaper labour and land. Up to 40 per cent of the workforce in NICs are involved in manufacturing.

Figure 5 shows the employment patterns for selected countries. This information has been plotted onto a triangular graph in Figure 6. You will see that LICs and HICs form separate clusters. Construction lines have been drawn on Figure 6 to show how Mali and Germany have been plotted.

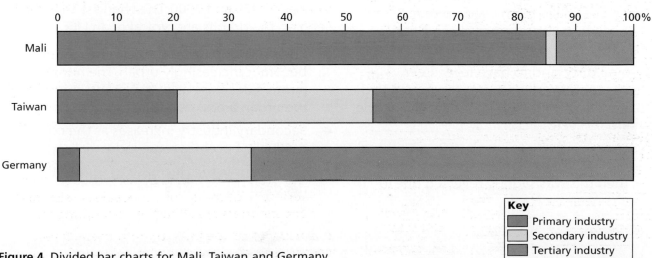

Figure 4 Divided bar charts for Mali, Taiwan and Germany

Country	Number on graph	Percentage of people in each sector		
		Primary	Secondary	Tertiary
Brazil	1	25	35	40
Bangladesh	2	57	10	33
Germany	3	4	30	66
Mali	4	85	2	13
Nepal	5	93	1	7
North Korea	6	18	32	50
Romania	7	31	44	25
Taiwan	8	21	34	45
UK	9	3	24	73
USA	10	3	21	76
India	11	62	11	27
Mexico	12	23	29	48
China	13	73	14	13

Figure 5 Table of employment patterns for selected countries

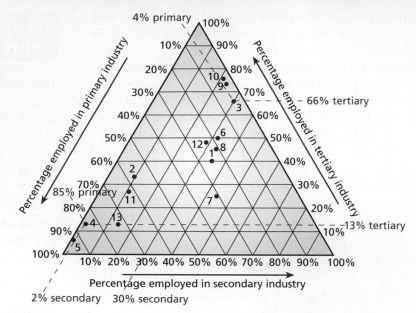

Figure 6 Triangular graph of employment patterns

How do employment patterns change over time?

All countries undergo changes in their economic systems. The graph in Figure 7a shows how the relative importance of the different economic activities in the UK has changed over the last 150 years. Three trends are apparent:

1 A steady decrease in the primary sector has been caused by:

   a Improvements in technology led to increased mechanisation which has reduced the need for agricultural workers in particular.

   b Many raw materials, for example iron ore and coal, have been used up or are cheaper to import from abroad.

   c Jobs in primary industries are often seen to be 'dirty' and to have few career prospects. Workers prefer the better paid and less physically demanding jobs in the tertiary sector.

2 An increase in tertiary employment. This was gradual but steady until the Second World War, then this was slightly reversed due to increased manufacturing as part of the war effort. The growth in the tertiary sector increased rapidly in the last decades of the twentieth century. Most of this was in the new hi-tech industries such as micro-electronics and in associated fields like research and development.

3 The manufacturing industries were steady until a decline in the 1990s which mirrored the growth of the tertiary sector. The decline was due to the cheaper labour in LICs which encouraged manufacturing industries to locate there.

Employment patterns have also changed in LICs. The pie graphs in Figure 7b show how the three sectors of industry have changed in China between 1960 and 2000. The changes that can be seen on the graphs are typical of an LIC:

● Primary industry decreases as the country becomes increasingly urban. The number of farmers decrease as rural workers migrate to the urban areas.

● Secondary industry increases as the country gradually becomes more industrialised.

● Tertiary industries increase to service the needs of the growing cities.

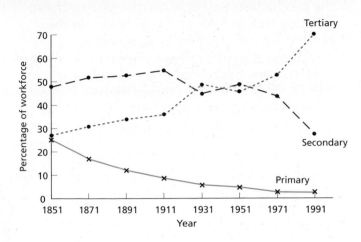

Figure 7a Graph showing changes in UK employment sectors

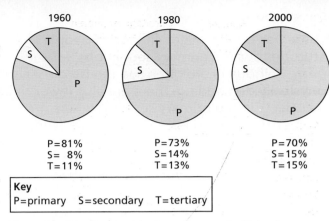

P=81%
S= 8%
T=11%

P=73%
S=14%
T=13%

P=70%
S=15%
T=15%

Key
P=primary   S=secondary   T=tertiary

Figure 7b Pie charts showing changes in China's employment structure

The reasons for the decline in numbers employed in the primary sector in the UK

The numbers employed in the primary industry have shown a steady decline since the 1850s and this is shown in Figure 8.

Key
= 5%   = 1%

Figure 8 The numbers employed in the primary sector in the UK

The reasons for this decline are:

Depletion of resources

One primary industry is the mining industry. This industry has declined because many raw materials which used to be mined in the UK have been used up. For example, production of coal in the UK peaked in 1913 at 287 million tonnes. In 2007 this had decreased to only 17 million tonnes. This is reflected in the workforce. In 1913 more than 1 million people were employed in the coal mines; now there are only 5,500. There are still underground supplies of coal in the UK but they are inaccessible and difficult to mine which makes it very costly.

Cheap imports

It has become cheaper to import raw materials from abroad. This is due to the raw materials which are left in the UK being inaccessible and difficult to mine as they are deep underground. For example, the Port Talbot steel works in South Wales gets its iron ore from Norway and its coal from Russia. Both of these raw materials used to be mined locally in South Wales.

Mechanisation

Improvements in technology have led to increased mechanisation which has had a serious impact on the numbers of people employed in the primary sector. Mechanisation has reduced the need for agricultural workers. In modern times, powered machinery has replaced many jobs formerly carried out by men or animals such as oxen and horses. Agricultural machinery has got progressively larger over the last 30 years. It is now possible for one man to plough 10 hectares in a day. In 1996 the majority of all tractors sold were above the 100 horsepower bracket.

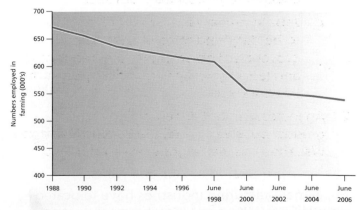

Figure 9 Numbers employed in farming between 1988 and 2006 in the UK

Social change

There has been a major change in people's attitude towards primary sector jobs. Jobs in primary industry are often seen to be 'dirty' and physically demanding. There are also fewer career prospects in the primary sector. Workers prefer the better paid and less physically demanding jobs in the tertiary sector. Tertiary sector jobs also tend to have more regular hours and be situated in urban areas where facilities are better.

What are the reasons for the decline in the secondary sector in the UK?

The industries that have declined are the traditional ones such as textiles, tobacco and car manufacturing. Not all secondary industries have suffered from decline in the UK: there has been a growth in several areas including office machinery, electrical goods and pharmaceutical products, shown in Figure 10. There has also been a considerable decline in the percentage of people employed in the secondary industry as shown in Figure 11. The reasons for this decline are:

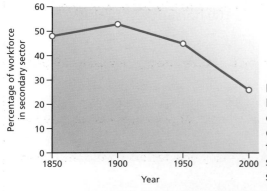

Figure 10 Change in employment in selected secondary industries in the UK

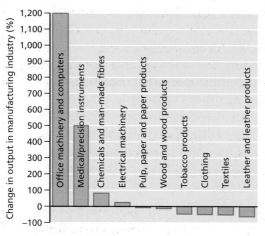

Figure 11 Percentage of workforce employed in the secondary sector

Cheaper production in LICs and MICs

Many manufacturing industries have relocated from HICs to MICs and LICs where production costs of manufacturing are less. The reasons why the production costs are less are due to cheap labour, a lack of rules and regulations in the productive process and, in some cases, government grants to help the establishment of industry. The loss of manufacturing industry in certain areas of the UK caused high unemployment rates, especially in the 1980s when the UK had an unemployment rate of 10.8 per cent. For example, in the 1980s, 40 per cent of the population of Birmingham worked in manufacturing whereas in 2007 only 20 per cent were employed in manufacturing.

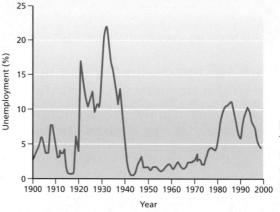

Figure 12 The unemployment rate in the UK 1900–1999

Globalisation

The factor that has enabled companies to move their manufacturing base to other cheaper locations is globalisation. This is the growing economic interdependency of countries worldwide which has been brought about by technological advancements. Firms can now have branch plants all over the world or outsource their manufacturing because they can keep in contact with the producers easily and quickly using the internet. There have also been developments in transport technology which means that goods can be moved around the world easily and quickly. This is not only the development in aircraft and containers but also the efficient motorway networks which cross Europe. This is obvious on the motorways of the UK where European lorries are very visible as they deliver goods which have been made in countries in eastern Europe such as Poland where manufacturing costs are less. Many Marks and Spencer (M&S) products are made in Portugal where land and labour costs are less and therefore goods can be produced more cheaply and then transported to the UK by lorry using the European motorway system. M&S also has established manufacturing bases in Sri Lanka, Portugal, Morocco, the Far East and Middle East.

Reasons for the growth of the secondary sector in China

The economic development of China is a recent phenomenon. In 1995 China's GNP per capita was $620 but by 2005 this had risen to $1,700, nearly a threefold increase. Over the last 20 years it has become the world's fourth largest economy and second largest manufacturer of goods. This growth has been aided by both physical and human factors. These factors have had a number of effects on the country.

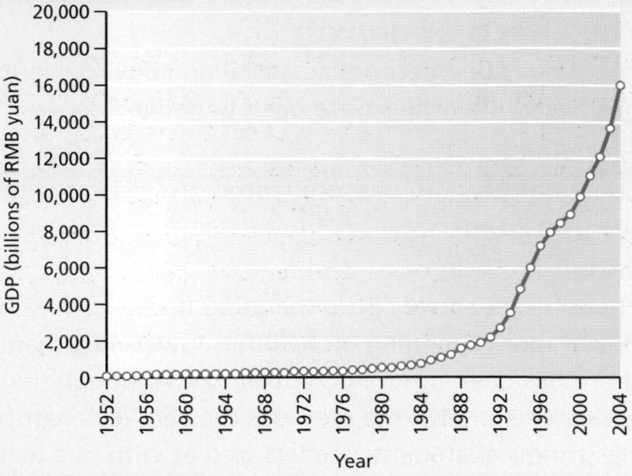

Figure 13 China's Gross Domestic Product (GDP) 1952 to 2004

Physical factors

Raw materials

China has a great wealth of natural resources having vast reserves of coal, oil and natural gas. These are being used to fuel the industrial development of the country.

Location

China's geographical position in the world is also beneficial for its development as it has developing markets all around it in South Korea, Taiwan and India. It is also on major trade routes.

Human factors

There are a number of human factors which have enabled China to grow so phenomenally.

Workforce

There is a plentiful supply of workers in China with a steady stream of people moving from the rural areas to the urban areas in search of work due to the modernisation of agriculture. It is estimated that 500,000 million people will leave the Chinese countryside in search of work over the next two decades. It is estimated that the unemployment rate in China is 25 per cent. This has resulted in Chinese workers being the lowest paid in the world because there are plenty of other people to take their jobs if they demand more pay; they earn about 40p an hour. Other Asian workers earn ten times as much. This has meant that factory owners can invest money in the business rather than pay their workers a fair wage.

Government policy

There has been a change in government policies, for example, laws which used to stop people investing in China have been abolished. Many companies from foreign countries now have factories in China. For example, in Xiamen City the Taiwanese company EUPA have a factory making coffee machines which employs 23,000 workers.

Education

Literacy levels in China have risen dramatically over the past 20 years and now stand at 90 per cent. This has also fuelled the economic development of the country. Therefore, China has both large numbers of unskilled workers and a growing number of highly skilled workers; for example, China trains 600,000 new engineers every year.

Private enterprise

For many years all manufacturing in China was state owned (owned by the government); nowadays 20 per cent of firms are privately owned and this figure is increasing.

Energy

Since the 1990s China has also been developing its energy base, with new hydroelectric and nuclear power stations.

Infrastructure improvements

The government has built many new roads and allowed the building of many new factories which have also fuelled the growth of the economy.

Globalisation

The shrinking of the world by the process known as globalisation has enabled companies in HICs to have goods assembled in LICs at a fraction of the price of the manufacturing process in the HIC. Goods can be transported easily around the world from where they are produced to where they are sold. China has a large workforce which can be employed cheaply.

The effects of growth

There have been economic, social and environmental effects of this growth. Some of these effects have been positive while others have been negative.

Economic

There has been an unprecedented growth in the Chinese economy over the past 20 years.

Social

There has been very little spending on social infrastructure. For example, government spending on health is lower now than in the 1980s although there has been input into education. Although the schools produce well-educated students the methods are very different from western classrooms as students are lectured at with one teacher speaking to up to 80 students in one room.

Figure 14 Xian city wall, China

There are also few laws to protect the workers, particularly the millions of migrant labourers. Despite recent reforms, they are excluded from the health care system and state education, live in appalling, overcrowded conditions and are routinely exposed to some of the most exploitative working conditions. They are forced to work long stretches of time under hazardous conditions for very low wages. Many managers withhold pay for two to three months to ensure that they hold onto their workforce which is in short supply due to the amount of jobs which are available in this rapidly industrialising country.

Environmental

The rapid industrial growth in China has had a major impact on the environment not only locally but also national and globally. One of the main problems is that 75 per cent of China's energy is still produced from coal. Many research projects have been carried out but most of them agree that 16 of the world's 20 most polluted cities are in China.

The most polluted city in the world is Linfen in China's inland Shanxi province. The hills around Linfen are dotted with coal mines, legal and illegal, and the air is filled with smoke from burning coal. The local residents do not bother to hang out their washing because it turns black before it is dry. There is also arsenic in their water supply. Potentially 3 million people are being affected by this pollution.

In the whole country there are 760,000 recorded deaths a year from air and water pollution. China is already the world leader in the production of carbon dioxide and by 2025 it is estimated that it will surpass the USA in the production of greenhouse gases. Although this will not be the case if the calculation is done per head of population in which case it will still be below countries such as USA and UK. In China 80 per cent of rivers are below the standard for fishing and 90 per cent of underground water in urban areas is polluted.

The government has recognised the problems and has set itself targets:

- 10 per cent of energy generated will be renewable by 2010
- 16 per cent of energy generated will be renewable by 2016
- Reduce energy consumption by 20 per cent.

The government has also spent considerable amounts of money over the last ten years to cope with the problems, for example:

- $172 billion on environmental protection
- $37 billion for desulphurisation
- $25 billion on industrial waste water treatment
- $22 billion on municipal waste water treatment.

Figure 15 Shanghai industrial development

What are the reasons for the growth of the tertiary sector in the UK since 1970?

The tertiary sector employed 76 per cent of the workforce in 2005, making it the largest sector of industry in the UK economy. The biggest area of expansion in the tertiary sector in the UK has been in financial and business services. In the 20 years between 1984 and 2004 there was an 80 per cent increase in the number of workers in this industry. According to government statistics in 1980 one in ten people employed in the UK worked in this industry; now this is one in five.

Computing and ICT (information and communication technologies), consultancy (offering advice to businesses) and research and development (R&D) (research, particularly in scientific fields), sometimes called the quaternary sector, have also seen dramatic increases, particularly in the last 20 years. The reasons for this dramatic increase are:

A rise in demand of services linked to disposable incomes

Households are on average getting richer. Their disposable income is steadily increasing. Disposable income is the amount of money which an individual has available to spend on non-essential items after essential bills have been met. The average amount that households had to spend on non-essential items doubled between 1987 and 2006. This meant that there was a rise in luxury services such as beauticians and health clubs to meet the perceived needs of the growing 'middle classes'. Gym membership has increased every year since the initial boom of the early 1980s. In 2000, 4 million people were members of fitness centres. This has continued to increase by 12 per cent a year.

The development of new technologies

There have been incredible developments in new technologies, particularly in the computing and telecommunications sector. This has lead to large numbers of people being employed in this sector. Most high streets now have a number of shops which sell mobile phones. This is due to the high demand for these products as people tend to update mobiles yearly. This is caused by the companies giving yearly contracts and incentives

to keep people in their contract. There is also the development of communications such as the internet. Many people now shop and bank on the internet. This has caused the development of many jobs to service the websites. Large numbers of people are employed at call centres which answer calls from numbers given on internet sites. In 2000, there were 350,000 people working in call centres; this had increased to 950,000 by 2008. Over the past five years there has been a shift to move these centres to cheaper location such as Bangladesh, notably by the high street banks, but the numbers employed in call centres in the UK continues to increase.

Decrease in employment in the primary and secondary sector

The reasons for this decrease were discussed previously. However, if people are not employed in the primary and secondary sectors they must be employed in the tertiary sector and hence the large increase in this sector.

Demographic changes

The fact that people are marrying later and having fewer children means that they have more time and indeed money to spend on services provided by the tertiary sector. There is a growing number of people in their twenties who spend a high proportion of their income on entertainment, socialising and beautification services. This fact has been recognised by the high street and there are a growing number of

Figure 16 Advert for a health spa

coffee shops and bars which are frequented by the young who have no ties and plenty of disposable income to spend.

The ageing population has led to an increasing number of wealthy retired people. They have both the money and time to spend on leisure and tourism. Saga, which started as a small holiday firm for pensioners, has been instrumental in attracting the 'grey pound'. Saga looked at the fact that people are living longer and have disposable income and has invested in garden centres. Plants are one of the more predictable ways in which older people will spend their money, since the British have always loved their gardens. But 'seniors' are becoming increasingly adventurous. Saga's holidaymakers are travelling as far afield as Madagascar and Mongolia and Saga claims to be the largest tour operator to Cuba, South Africa and Nepal. It doesn't stop there. 'Silver surfers' are the next target market, as many over 65s become extremely competent at using the internet. Saga has even launched the 'Saga Zone' social networking website, its version of MySpace but for the over fifties.

Figure 17 Young people socialising

Review

By the end of this section you should be able to:

- recognise the relative importance of primary, secondary and tertiary sectors in countries at different levels of development
- understand that these sectors change over space and through time
- explain the reasons for the decline in numbers employed in the primary sector in the UK
- explain the reasons for the decline in the secondary sector
- explain the reasons for and the effects of the growth of the secondary sector in one LIC
- explain the reasons for the dramatic growth of the tertiary sector since 1970.

ACTIVITIES

Higher

1 Study Figure 1 on page 166. Decide which sector of industry is represented by each advertisement. Tabulate your results and say why Figure 1 comes from a newspaper in an HIC.

2 Use the figures in the table on page 175 to construct divided bar graphs for the three countries. Describe and explain the differences between the graphs.

Foundation

1 Look at the photographs in Figure 2 on page 166. Decide whether each of them is a primary, secondary or tertiary job.

2 a Look at Figure 1 on page 166. Decide whether each job is primary, secondary or tertiary. Add up how many are in each sector. Construct a table of your results and draw a bar graph to show your results.

b Explain what your graph shows.

ACTIVITIES

Country	Primary	Secondary	Tertiary
UK	3	24	73
Nepal	92	1	7
Mexico	23	29	48

3 Look at Figure 7a on page 169.

  a When did the percentage of people working in secondary industries become greater than those in tertiary industries?

  b For how many years did the percentage of people employed in secondary industry remain higher than the percentage employed in tertiary industries?

  c Why was the percentage employed in secondary industries high during this period?

  d Draw pie charts for 1851, 1931 and 2001.

  e Briefly describe what your pie charts show.

4 Why is the number employed in primary sector declining in the UK?

5 Study Figure 11 on page 170.

  a Name 2 industries which have increased their output between 1978 and 2002.

  b Name 2 industries which have decreased their output.

6 Study Figure 12 on page 170. It shows unemployment rates between 1900 and 1999. Describe the changes since 1920. Use data in your answer.

7 Define the term globalisation.

8 Study Figure 13 on page 171. It shows a large increase in manufacturing industry in China. Explain why there has been this large increase.

9 Explain 3 reasons for the growth of the secondary sector since 1970.

3 The following is a list of jobs involved in the manufacture of a motor car:
- mining iron ore
- turning iron ore into steel at an integrated steel works
- transporting the steel sheets to a car assembly plant
- manufacturing a car at the factory
- selling the car.

Draw a series of diagrams to illustrate these jobs and say which sector of industry each diagram represents.

4 The number of people employed in the primary sector is declining in the UK.

Which of the sentences below confirm this sentence?

  There are more raw materials being found in the UK.

  Farmers are using more machinery on their farms.

  There are bigger tractors.

  People do not want to work in jobs they perceive as 'dirty'.

5 Study Figure 11 on page 170.

  a Name 2 industries which have increased their output between 1978 and 2002.

  b Name 2 industries which have decreased their output.

6 Complete the following sentences. Use Figure 12 on page 170 to help you.

The unemployment rate rises at the beginning of the 1920s to .... then falls.

It rises again to .... in 1935.

The rate is steady from the late 1940s until the ....

It then fluctuates between 6 and 11 per cent over the next .... years.

7 What is globalisation?

8 There are many reasons why China's secondary industry has grown rapidly. State 4 of these reasons.

9 Since 1970 the tertiary industry has grown. Give 3 reasons for this.

Economic locations

Learning objective – to study the location of different types of economic activity.

Learning outcomes
- To understand the factors affecting the location of primary, secondary and tertiary activities.
- To be able to explain the benefits and costs of deindustrialisation in rural areas.

Figure 18 A china clay quarry near St Austell, Cornwall

The factors that affect economic locations

The location of primary, secondary and tertiary industries is influenced by different factors. However the following factors are important to all types of industry.

- Labour supply – the number of people who live in the area. The industry may need them to have specific skills.
- Accessibility – how easily can the site be reached by road and rail links?
- Raw materials – does the site have the necessary materials to make the product?
- Distance to market – is the market for the product close by or are there good transport links to the market?
- Government incentives – are there any grants or other incentives available from the government or local councils to persuade a company to move to an area?
- Power supply – is there an adequate supply of energy to produce the goods?

What factors affect the location of primary industry?

Primary industry involves the extraction of raw materials from the land or sea. Therefore the most important factor affecting the location of primary industry will be the availability of raw materials. If the primary industry is to succeed then the other factors affecting its location will be important, for example, market and accessibility.

An example of a successful primary industry is china clay extraction in Cornwall. More than 120 million tonnes of china clay has been extracted from the area and reserves should last another 100 years. Kaolin, as china clay is also known, is used to make porcelain and by many other industries including the paper industry.

But what made the industry so successful in this area?

- The most important factor is that kaolin is only found in the south-west of England.
- There was a demand for kaolin for the production of porcelain. The pottery manufacturer Josiah Wedgwood based in Stoke-on-Trent formed the Cornish Clay company. This ensured the success of the industry as the mined kaolin had a definite market. By 1860, 65,000 tonnes was being mined each year, much of it for the Wedgwood factory at Stoke-on-Trent.
- There was also a way of transporting the raw material to the factory where it was made into the finished product. The china clay was moved by tramway and train to the ports of Charlestown, Pentewan and Par on the south coast of Cornwall. The ships then took the raw material to Liverpool where it was then transported by barge along the Trent and Mersey canal to Winsford in Cheshire and then by packhorse the final 30 miles to Stoke-on-Trent to be made into porcelain.

By 1910 the industry was producing a million tonnes a year. Most of the production was now used by the paper industry and 75 per cent was exported. Nowadays, 80 per cent of the china clay extracted is used by the paper industry, 12 per cent by the ceramics industry and the rest in products such as toothpaste and paint. The raw material is still transported by train and 50 per cent of the production is moved by rail to the ports of Par and Fowey which handle 2 million tonnes of china clay a year.

What factors affect the location of secondary industry?

Secondary industries have a number of factors that affect their location. The most important factor will vary with the particular secondary industry. For some industries raw material will be the most important factor, such as aluminium smelting. For other secondary industries market will be the most important factor, for example, the soft drink industry. The car manufacturing industry has a number of important factors which have affected its location including government policy, as can be seen in Figure 19.

Large area of flat land giving room for expansion: 280 hectares.

The area has a tradition in car manufacturing. There are many suppliers of component parts and engineering components.

Location on the edge of the city. Greenfield site with ample room for expansion.

The Peak District National Park, which is close by, has many opportunities for leisure activities.

Derbyshire County Council offered to buy a £20 million stake in the company. It also pledged to improve the transport infrastructure by upgrading the A50 to a dual carriageway.

Excellent transport routes. On the junction of two main trunk roads – the A50 and A38. The A50 and A38 are dual carriageways and link to the M1 and M6. This allows easy transportation of parts and the finished product throughout the UK.

Attractive village location such as Findern for managerial workers.

Figure 19 Why did Toyota locate at Burnaston, near Derby?

What factors affect the location of tertiary industry?

These types of industries are less dependent on factors that tie them to a specific geographical location. Unlike manufacturing industries, tertiary or services companies do not have to be near a source of raw materials but, given good transport, energy and communications, can locate themselves virtually anywhere in the world. Examples are computer software development, health clubs and call centres.

What factors lead to David Lloyd Health Club locating on Hatfield Business Park?

There were a number of reasons why David Lloyd Health Club located in Hatfield (see Figure 20).

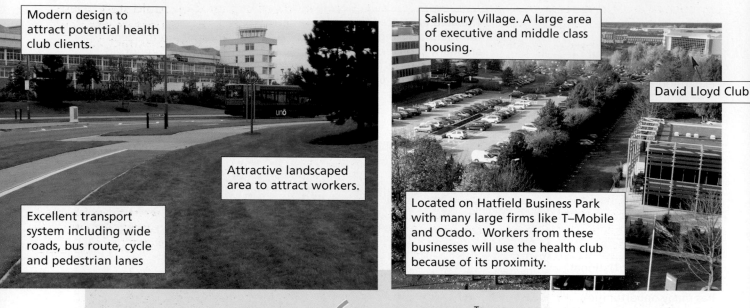

Modern design to attract potential health club clients.

Attractive landscaped area to attract workers.

Excellent transport system including wide roads, bus route, cycle and pedestrian lanes

Salisbury Village. A large area of executive and middle class housing.

David Lloyd Club

Located on Hatfield Business Park with many large firms like T–Mobile and Ocado. Workers from these businesses will use the health club because of its proximity.

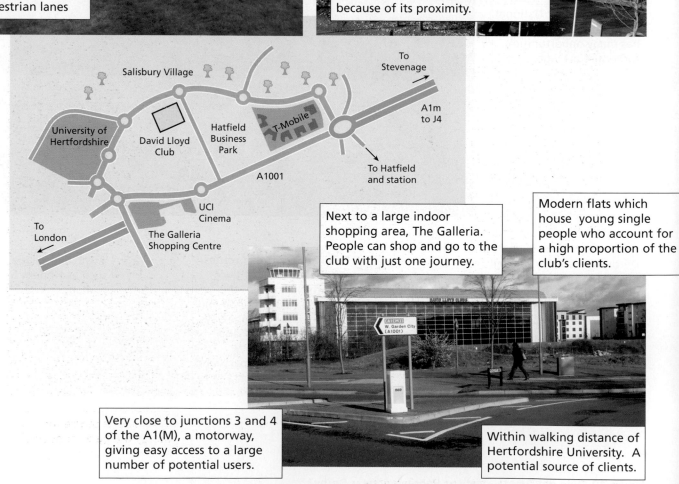

Next to a large indoor shopping area, The Galleria. People can shop and go to the club with just one journey.

Modern flats which house young single people who account for a high proportion of the club's clients.

Very close to junctions 3 and 4 of the A1(M), a motorway, giving easy access to a large number of potential users.

Within walking distance of Hertfordshire University. A potential source of clients.

Figure 20 The reasons for the location of David Lloyd Health Club

The benefits and costs of deindustrialisation in rural areas

Many rural areas have suffered from deindustrialisation. This means that they are no longer used for industrial purposes. This deindustrialisation can have many costs and benefits for an area. The benefits include cleaning up the site to use for recreation purposes, agriculture and urban growth. There can be a number of costs of deindustrialisation which can include problems with toxic waste.

Many areas of the UK have been used for the extraction of raw materials which have left the land scarred. The extraction of coal in South Wales left the area with many waste heaps which were potentially dangerous. This was illustrated in 1966 with the Aberfan disaster when a landslide occurred from a coal waste heap after heavy rainfall and tonnes of material fell onto the village school killing 144 people, 116 of them children. After this disaster, coal waste heaps have been made safer by regrading and landscaping them. Many of them are now being used as agricultural land and visitors to the area would be unaware of its industrial past.

Other rural areas have been used for open-cast mining. In 1957 the National Coal Board bought Bays Leap Farm, Town House and Heddon Mill in Northumberland so that they could start open-cast mining in the area. The 25 hectare site was excavated to a depth of 70 m to extract 2.5 million tonnes of coal. The mining stopped in 1965 and the land was returned to farm land.

The extraction of sand and gravel around Reading in Berkshire left many dangerous water filled quarries. These are now being used in a number of different ways, as is shown in Figure 21.

Copthorne Hotel, next to 10 acre lake. The hotel has many sporting facilities including water sports.

Green Park, which is a science park covering 70 hectares and employing 7,000 people.

Madejski stadium, built on waste tip which was an old gravel quarry. The land cost £1.

Quarry still in use.

Former gravel quarry now agricultural land.

Watersports centre for use by the general public.

Figure 21 Deindustrialisation in the Reading area

Another area which has benefited from being redeveloped after mineral extraction is an old china clay pit in Cornwall which is now known as the Eden Project. The pit is 60 m deep and covers an area equivalent to 35 football pitches. The pit has been totally transformed into a tourist attraction with landscaped walks, a huge diversity of plants and two enormous pods. The pods provide a very different experience: one is an Equatorial rainforest which has a wide variety of plants from the Equatorial biome and the other is the Mediterranean biome. The whole of the project is run in a sustainable way and there are many information boards which inform about sustainable development. There is also a building which is called The Core which teaches people in a user-friendly way how to be more aware of the damage we are causing to the planet. Much of the energy for the Eden Project is produced by sustainable means.

Figure 22 The Eden Project near St Austell

Figure 23 A reclaimed waste heap at Swadlincote

ACTIVITIES

Higher

1 Explain two factors that affect the location of industry.

2 What is the most important factor to consider when locating a primary industry?

3 Draw a table to show three factors affecting the location of Toyota at Burnaston.

Factor	Reason for location

4 Figure 20 on page 178 shows the reasons for the location of David Lloyd Health Club in Hatfield. For a Health Club or other tertiary industry in your area, explain the factors affecting its location.

5 There are many benefits to rural areas of de-industrialisation. What are the costs?

Foundation

1 Describe two factors that affect the location of industry.

2 What is the most important factor to consider when locating a primary industry?

3 Complete the table below to show the factors affecting the location of Toyota at Burnaston. Match the correct factor and reason.

Accessibility   Site   Location

Large area of flat land giving room for expansion: 280 hectares.

Excellent transport routes. On the junction of two main trunk roads – the A50 and A38. The A50 and A38 are dual carriageways and link to the M1 and M6. This allows easy transportation of parts and the finished product throughout the UK.

Attractive village location such as Findern for managerial workers. Location on the edge of the city Greenfield site with ample room for expansion.

Factor	Reason for location

4 Figure 20 on page 178 shows the reasons for the location of David Lloyd Health Club in Hatfield. For a health club or other tertiary industry in your area, explain the factors affecting its location.

5 There are many benefits to rural areas of deindustrialisation. What are the costs?

Extension

Research the Eden Project in Cornwall. Find out about its previous use and explain its present use.

Review

By the end of this section you should be able to:
- understand the factors affecting the location of primary, secondary and tertiary activities
- explain the benefits and costs of deindustrialisation in rural areas.

Sample Examination Questions

Higher tier

1   Define the term secondary industry. Use an example in your answer.   **(2 marks)**

2   There has been a change in HICs from many people employed in primary industry to many people employed in tertiary industry. Why? **(3 marks)**

3   Study Figure 8 on page 168. By what percentage did the number of primary workers decline between 1850 and 2000?   **(1 mark)**

4   Study Figure 11 on page 170. It shows changes in the percentage of the workforce employed in the secondary sector. Describe these changes. Use data in your answer.   **(3 marks)**

5   Give reasons for the decline in secondary industry.   **(3 marks)**

6   Study Figure 13 on page 171. In 1992 China's GDP rose significantly. This was due to a rise in the secondary sector. Explain the reasons for this increase in the secondary sector.   **(4 marks)**

7   There are many factors which affect the location of tertiary industry. Explain these factors. Refer to an example you have studied in your answer.   **(3 marks)**

8   There are many benefits of deindustrialisation to rural areas. Choose a rural area you have studied. Explain the benefits of deindustrialisation. **(6 marks)**

> **Total 25 marks**

Foundation tier

1   The term secondary industry means:

   a   extraction of raw materials from the ground or the sea

   b   the manufacturing of goods using the raw materials

   c   the provision of different services such as teachers, solicitors, sales assistants and cleaners.   **(1 mark)**

2   HICs have moved from the majority of people being employed in the primary industry to the majority of people being employed in the tertiary industry. Give three reasons why.   **(3 marks)**

3   Study Figure 8 on page 168. By what percentage did the number of primary workers decline between 1850 and 2000?   **(1 mark)**

4   Study Figure 11 on page 170. Complete the sentences below to shows the changes in the percentage of the workforce employed in the secondary sector.

   In 1850 .... of the population was employed in the secondary sector. By 1900 this had .... It then decreased to .... in 1950. The percentage continued to decrease by .... in 2000.   **(4 marks)**

5   List two factors which affect the location of secondary industry.   **(2 marks)**

6   Study Figure 20 on page 178. Explain the location of David Lloyd Health Club in Hatfield.   **(4 marks)**

7   Study Figure 13 on page 171. In 1992 China's GDP rose significantly. This was due to a rise in the secondary sector. Describe the reasons for this increase in the secondary sector.   **(4 marks)**

8   There are many benefits of deindustrialisation to rural areas. Choose a rural area you have studied. Describe the benefits of deindustrialisation. **(6 marks)**

> **Total 25 marks**

Changes to the UK countryside

> **Learning objective** – to study changes to the UK countryside.
>
> **Learning outcomes**
> - To recognise the reasons for the changes to the UK countryside.
> - To be able to explain the consequences of the changes to the UK countryside.
> - To study a UK farm that has diversified.
> - To recognise the changes that have happened to UK farming practices.

What changes are occurring in the UK countryside and what are the consequences of these changes?

The decline in primary employment

In the UK there has been a decline in the numbers of people employed in the primary industry over the last 60 years. The decline has hit some areas of the UK which are more reliant on primary employment than others. Primary employment is mainly made up of agriculture, fishing, mining and forestry and all of these industries have seen a decline in employment. The decline has been more in some types of primary industry than in others. However, the decline in agriculture has been much less than the decline in other primary industry; for example, the number of people in coal mining fell from nearly 600,000 in 1960 to 10,000 in 1995. There are now only a few deep shaft mines left whereas in 1960 there were 700.

In 2007 the UK farming industry contributed approximately £6 billion to the economy. It uses about three-quarters of the country's land area and employs 500,000 people. It is supported by policies agreed in Brussels which provide about £3 billion to UK agriculture every year in the form of grants. The number of people employed in farming has decreased steadily over the past 60 years as can be seen in Figure 1. This is partly due to a reduction in the need for farm workers due to increased mechanisation on farms and also due to the nature of the work which involves long hours for little pay which puts people off.

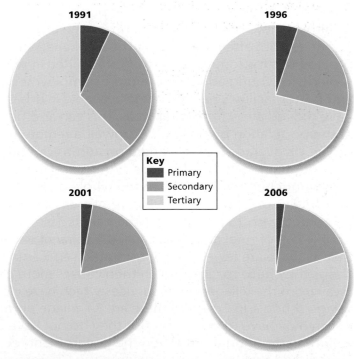

Figure 1 Employment in rural areas

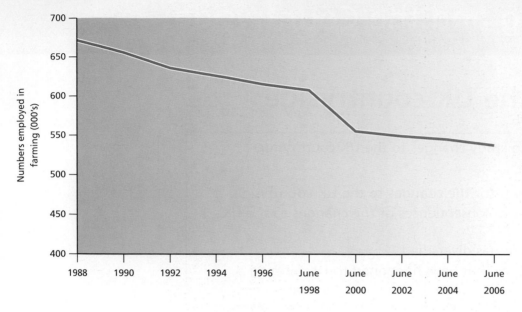

Figure 2 Numbers employed in farming between 1988 and 2006

The depopulation of rural areas causing a loss of service provision and a spiral of decline

This decline in employment opportunities in rural areas has lead to outmigration especially of 16–34 year olds. This is the movement out of rural areas by people either looking for better employment opportunities or for a better provision of facilities. This is backed up by figures from the 2001 Census which state that only 24 per cent of the in-migrants to rural areas are aged 16–29 compared with 33 per cent of the out-migrants. As the population has become wealthier there has been a demand for the provision of leisure activities both after work and at the weekend. While rural areas can provide this for some people they are limited in what they can provide for young adults. Therefore, as employment has declined and better facilities have become available in urban areas, people have moved away from rural areas. This can also be seen by looking at the population pyramid for Cornwall, a remote rural area (Figure 4). The UK average is also marked on and, as can be seen, there are far more people in the older age groups and far fewer people in the younger age groups. When the whole of the UK is considered 18 per cent of people who live in rural areas are aged 65 or over, compared with 15 per cent in urban areas. This movement of people out of rural areas has caused a spiral of decline. This means that as there are fewer people using the services such as village shops they have to close which then causes more people to move away from the village. Other services which have closed have been village schools. In Cornwall there are 34 village primary schools which may have to close because they do not have enough children attending them. When the government recently announced that many Post Offices in the UK were to be closed 50 of them were in Cornwall, in some cases due to only 16 people using them in a week.

The Post Office in Week St Mary near Bude in Cornwall is run as part of the local shop which sells groceries to the local people who do not have cars and find it difficult to shop in the local towns due to there being limited public transport provision.

If the Post Office closes, the shop will have to close also because it will not have enough business. This will mean a seven mile journey to Bude to visit a Post Office or to get some bread or milk.

The bus does not come to the village unless passengers inform the company that they want to travel. It will only then come once a day diverting from its normal route to collect them in the morning. Passengers will then have to stay in Bude until the afternoon when the bus returns.

A number of the older villagers will have to move to the local town if the Post Office closes because they will not be able to buy food or collect their pensions within walking distance.

Figure 3 An example of the spiral of decline

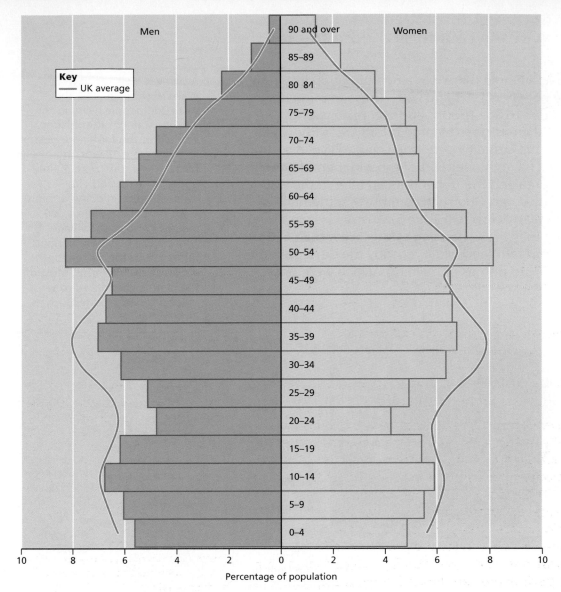

Figure 4 A population pyramid for Cornwall and the Scilly Isles

The trend for retired people to move to the countryside causing an ageing population structure

Some people when they retire want to move away from the noise and stress of living in an urban area and move to a more tranquil location. This might be in a small rural village or in a town in a more rural area. A large number of people have moved to the south-west of England which has a slower pace of life and milder climate than the south-east where many of them have moved from. This can be seen in the population pyramid (see Figure 4). There are a lot more people over the age of 50 than the UK average. (This is dealt with in more detail in Unit 3 Chapter 13, A Moving World.)

The development of commuter settlements leading to the suburbanisation of the countryside close to urban areas

If rural areas are taken as a whole there was a net migration into rural areas of 33,000 people between 1991 and 2001. These in-migrants are in the over 30 or under 16 age groups and comprise young families moving into rural areas close to large urban areas, known as commuter settlements. This is due to people wishing to live in a rural environment and yet still have the benefits of the wider employment choice of a large urban area and the benefits it can offer in the way of entertainment, education, etc. One such commuter settlement is the village of Austrey in Warwickshire (Figure 5). Austrey began to grow in the 1970s when many new housing estates were built in the village, usually on adjacent farmland. More recently the development has been the conversion into homes of buildings which were once used for farming.

Austrey is a village in North Warwickshire. In 1961 there were 300 people living in the village. Many of the villagers worked in the farming industry as there were 18 working farms. The farms were mainly under 80 acres and concentrated on dairy farming.

By 2001 there were 1,000 people living in the village. There were only two working farms left in the village; both are large arable farms. Most of the people commuted to work in local towns or cities such as Birmingham.

1970s' infilling, village pub in background.

St Nicholas Close and Elms Drive were the first estates to be built in the 1960s. They comprised of 25 new houses on each estate. These houses were all built on the sites of farmsteads. The next estate called Orchard Close was built in the 1970s with another 20 houses.

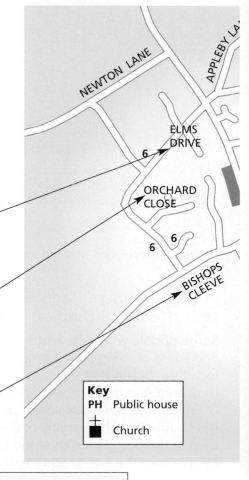

Key
PH   Public house
✝   Church

Bishops Cleeve estate was built in the 1980s on farmland and the site of the working men's club, meaning that the village also lost a social gathering place.

Figure 5 Austrey – a commuter settlement

Key
1 Site of old school
2 Site of new school
3 Site of old village store, now a house
4 Site of new village store and Post Office
5 Site of Methodist Chapel, now a house
6 Farm houses and buildings which have been converted into houses
7 Site of old Post Office

1970s' infilling

Restored farmhouse and converted barns.

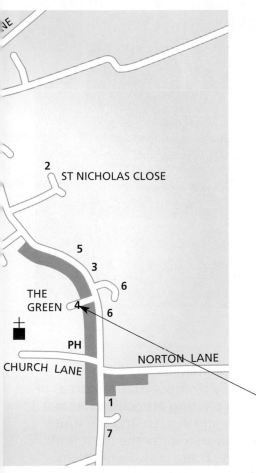

The village school in 1961 had 16 children on roll between the ages of 5 and 11. By the 1970s a new school had been built in the centre of the village. The new school started with 100 children on roll. It now has approximately 150 children and its own nursery on the site, whereas in the 1960s there was no nursery provision. In the 1970s there was only a private nursery run in the Methodist Chapel.

Village store opened in 1970s. 1970s infilling in the background.

The diversification of farming into other profit-making activities

One other major change in the UK countryside has been the diversification of farming. British farmers have had to diversify their buildings and land in order to survive. In 2005 farmers earned 23 per cent less for the food they produced than in 1988. Many of them recognised the need to diversify. This diversification has taken many forms, some of them quite ingenious. The farmer in Figure 6 has turned his sheds into commercial units providing space and security for small firms. Other farmers have used their original business but have developed into manufacturing their own products and selling them to supermarkets. For example, the Keebles who were pig farmers in Yorkshire with 350 sows. In 1999 they were faced with going out of business due to cheap pork imports. But then they started to make their own bacon and sausages; they stressed the personal touch in their marketing and now have a turnover of £2 million.

Figure 6 Elms Farm commercial units

The development of the leisure, recreation and tourism industry causing many rural villages to turn into tourist honeypots

The countryside has also seen the development of the leisure and recreation industry. This is possibly the most obvious change as the countryside has diversified to survive.

In 1997 rural tourism generated £12 billion in consumer spending and supported either directly or indirectly 380,000 jobs. Recreation and tourism in rural areas is now a larger employer and generates more income than farming. These benefits are not equally distributed. Some areas of the country, although offering attractions, are not so well known. It is the north-west and the south-west which benefit but also suffer the most from recreation and tourism. There is also a problem with seasonality and there is a need to develop out of season attractions. One village that has benefited and lost from tourism is Malham in Yorkshire. There is very little left of the original farming village. All of the services are geared towards tourism and most of the villagers are employed in the tourist industry (see Figure 5).

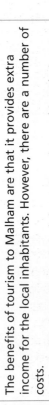

The benefits of tourism to Malham are that it provides extra income for the local inhabitants. However, there are a number of costs.

- The main street is congested due to tourists parking their cars.
- Farmers have put up signs to instruct tourists about the country code.
- There are many billboards in the village which cause visual pollution.

This is the main street in Malham. It has many attractions for tourists including gift shops, hotels, restaurants, cafes and pony trekking.

The local farmers have diversified and are using their fields as campsites.

Figure 6 Malham – a tourist honeypot

ACTIVITIES

Higher

1 Study Figure 1 on page 183.

   a By how much has primary industry declined between 1991 and 2006? Give reasons for this decline.

   b Which sector has increased the most?

   c Why has this sector increased?

2 Figure 2 on page 184 shows that the number employed in farming has decreased. Give reasons why.

3 What does rural depopulation mean?

4 What is a commuter settlement?

5 Austrey is a commuter settlement. Draw a timeline of the changes that have occurred to the village.

6 What is the link between rural depopulation and loss of service provision in countryside areas?

7 Many farms are diversifying into other business. Explain the reasons why. You should use the internet to find more examples.

Foundation

1 Study Figure 1 on page 183. It shows changes in employment in rural areas.

   a By how much has primary industry declined between 1991 and 2006?

   b Give one reason for the decline in primary industry.

   c Which sector of industry has increased?

   d Give one reason for this increase.

2 Farming is a type of primary industry. The number of people working on farms has decreased between 1988 and 2006. Why?

3 What does rural depopulation mean?

4 What are the characteristics of a commuter settlement?

   Choose two statements from the list below

   The population varies during the summer.

   The population numbers are highest in the morning and low at night.

   The population goes down in the morning but goes up in the evening.

   A lot of people live in family groups.

5 Figure 5 on pages 186–187 shows a commuter settlement. Make a list of the changes that have occurred to the village. Arrange them in order of the date they occurred.

6 Many rural areas have lost services such as Post Offices. Give reasons why.

7 State two ways that farmers have diversified their farms.

   Extension

   Choose one of the changes to the UK countryside such as the development of commuter settlements or the diversification of farming. Research your own case study on the internet. For example it might be a village near your school which has grown due to suburbanisation.

A study of Home Farm in the West Midlands

One farmer who has diversified is Nigel Redfern of Home Farm in Hampton in Arden, close to the Birmingham conurbation.

Mr Redfern has had to diversify due to a fall in profits from farming activities. His farm is a mixed farm on which livestock are reared and a varity of crops are grown. He used to have a dairy herd; however, the EU has gradually reduced the subsidies on milk. This means that Mr Redfern has decided that there is no point in putting in the hours looking after cows for very poor return (milk costs approximately 60p a litre in shops, of which farmers receive approximately 16p a litre). The farm's milk quota has been sold as has the herd of cows. The only animals left on the farm are the young bulls, which are being raised for meat, and a flock of 300 sheep.

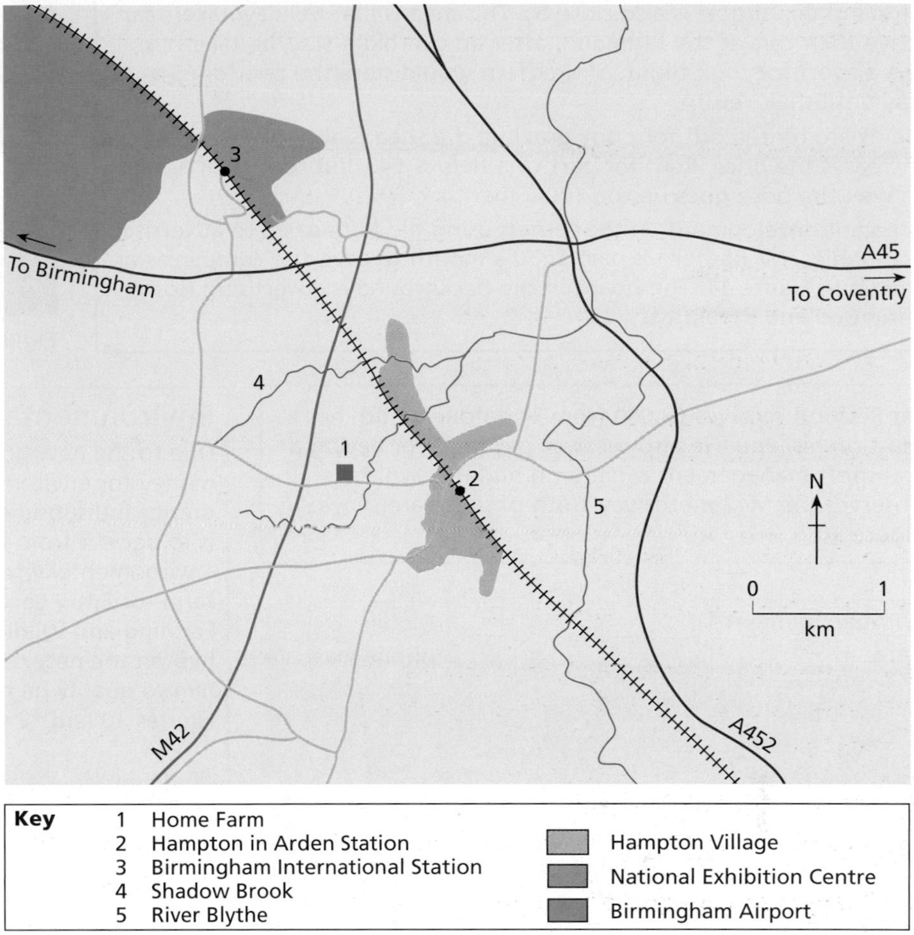

During the last ten years, Mr Redfern has begun to diversify his farm. This is due to the decrease in subsidies for arable crops, which meant that his income from the crops decreased by £40,000 between 1998 and 1999, with a further decrease in 2000. The farm has made a profit on its arable crops in only two of the last six years. Due to this decrease in profit for arable crops Mr Redfern has turned to other means of making a profit. He has diversified his farm which means turning his land and buildings to other uses rather than farming in order for him to make a living.

Key

1	Home Farm
2	Hampton in Arden Station
3	Birmingham International Station
4	Shadow Brook
5	River Blythe

Hampton Village
National Exhibition Centre
Birmingham Airport

Figure 8 Map showing the location of Home Farm

Diversification techniques on Home Farm

The old cow sheds and outbuildings have been converted into accommodation for bed-and-breakfast visitors (Figure 9). These are either people who wish to holiday on a farm or people who are attending conferences at the NEC (National Exhibition Centre) which is only two miles away (see Figure 8). The cost of overnight accommodation is £55 for a single room and £65 for a double room.

There is now an area on the farm on which caravans are stored. For this to occur, planning permission had to be granted by the local council. It was delayed because of opposition from the Hampton Society, a local voluntary organisation which tries to oppose changes to the area. Up to 20 caravans can be stored at an income of £300 per caravan per year. This is very popular as many people who live nearby in Solihull need somewhere to store their caravans.

Home Farm farmhouse

Bed-and-breakfast accommodation in old cow sheds

Figure 9 Accommodation on Home Farm

Birmingham airport is also close by. This means that holidaymakers can leave their cars at the farm and, after an overnight stay, be taken to the airport for their flight. Mr Redfern would store the cars for £5 a day until their return.

Fields are rented out for pony grazing; if a shed is also rented, this increases the price. Rent for part of a field is £40, but for use of a shed as well the price goes up to £100 a month.

A recent development on the farm is using old lorry bases to advertise companies. Mr Redfern is paid £250 a month to advertise companies as shown in Figure 11. The board in the background is advertising Home Farm Bed and Breakfast.

Figure 11 Advertising boards

Mr Redfern receives £3,000 from Vodafone, which has a mast on his land. He also receives payment for having a transport management camera on his land, which observes the M42 motorway. Both of these are shown in Figure 10.

Environmental stewardship policies

Due to the new government policies Mr Redfern gets money for environmentally friendly farming. All other grants and subsidies are being phased out. If Mr Redfern is to benefit from the new payments for environmentally friendly farming he must register his farm for Entry Level Stewardship. He has employed the Farming and Wildlife Advisory Group (FWAG) to advise him on the new payments that are available. In order for him to qualify he must register 30 points a hectare. Figures 10 and 12 show how the points can be acquired.

Traffic management camera

Mobile phone mast

Two trees in an arable field are worth 12 points each

Figure 10 Vodafone phone mast

Hedgerow management earns 22 points for every 100 m and ditch management earns 24 points per 100 m.

Figure 12 Hedgerow management

ACTIVITIES

1 The government has introduced new environmental policies for farmers and stopped giving them subsidies to produce crops. Why has the government made these changes? What does the word subsidy mean?

2 Why has Mr Redfern decided to diversify his farm?

3 Name the ways in which Mr Redfern has diversified his farm.

4 Home Farm is on the edge of the Birmingham conurbation. Draw up a list of the advantages and disadvantages of this position. Clues: communication links, urban fringe problems including crime.

5 What other diversification schemes might Mr Redfern introduce? The following websites may help you in your answer: www.nfuonline.com or www.defra.gov.uk.

What changes have there been to UK farming practice in the twenty-first century?

The shift to more environmentally friendly forms of farming

For many years farming in the UK has been managed by the EU. Farmers were paid subsidies if their crops did not achieve a guaranteed price and they worked to quotas on other types of production such as milk. These initiatives tended to encourage farmers to use greater amounts of chemical fertilisers and pesticides and to cultivate as much land as possible. In the 1990s the EU introduced the Countryside Stewardship Scheme which gave farmers grants to protect certain areas of their farm for wildlife. This was taken a step further seven years ago with the introduction of a new way of giving farmers subsidies. Farmers only receive money now if they are farming in an environmentally friendly way.

The scheme is called the Environmental Stewardship Scheme. Farmers enter into a five-year agreement to protect a certain amount of their land. There is a range of 50 options they can choose from. Each of the options earns the farmer points. The options include hedgerow management (22 points per 100 m), beetle banks (580 points per hectare), stone wall management (15 points per 100 m) and buffer strips (300 points per hectare). Farmers must register 30 points a hectare for their farm, then they will receive £30 a hectare for each year of the scheme. Farmers have to submit a plan of what they are going to do which is then checked annually by DEFRA. Many farmers turn to the voluntary group FWAG (The Farming and Wildlife Advisory Group, www.fwag.org.uk) for help and advice.

Other voluntary groups such as LEAF (Linking Environment and Farming, www.leafuk.org/leaf[/) provide a checklist which farmers can use to help them to identify how they can farm in a more environmentally friendly way. There are now more than 4 million hectares of land being farmed in the scheme in a more environmentally friendly way.

There are many advantages to farming in a more environmentally friendly way and some of them are covered in the section on organic farming. For the schemes mentioned above, the main advantage is the increase in wildlife in countryside areas. For example, in Devon the numbers of hedgerow birds have increased. The number of pairs of Cirl Buntings had decreased to only 118 pairs in 1989; 450 pairs were recorded in 2007. Farmers in the scheme have the advantage of receiving money for working with nature rather than against it, but do have the drawback of filling in lots of paper work and the inconvenience of having people inspect their efforts. Another disadvantage is that farmers do not feel that they are really farming because they are not using the land to its maximum potential.

Figure 13 A beetle bank in Leicestershire

Figure 14 A buffer zone on the edge of a field in Berkshire

The rise of organic farming

Over the past 60 years, British farmers have intensified their use of chemicals to increase their profits. The British public demanded an alternative to crops that were produced using chemical fertilisers, and the alternative was organic farming. The amount of land farmed organically in the UK grew steadily until the late 1990s when the rate of growth then speeded up between 1998 and 2002. In recent years the growth of land farmed organically has decreased whereas the number of producers continues to increase. The value of the organic produce market is also still growing. During 2006 the sales from box schemes, farmers' markets and farm shop sales grew by 54 per cent and is now worth approximately £150 million. Sales in supermarkets also rose 21 per cent in the same time period. So although the land area being farmed organically has become slightly smaller the market has continued to grow. There are a number of reasons for this including:

● Organic food is no longer bought by just the middle classes – more than 50 per cent of people in lower income groups are now buying organic produce and this is where the market increase has come from.

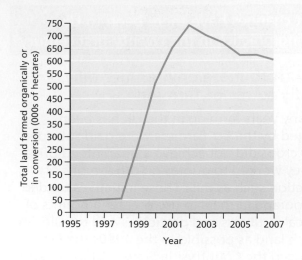

Figure 15 The amount of land farmed organically in the UK

● Three-quarters of parents now buy organic baby food.

● Many school dinners are now being sourced from organic farms.

● More farmers' markets are being organised.

● Box schemes are taking off due to the internet.

The consumers in the UK seem to be convinced that organic produce is better for them. This is shown by the increasing value of the organic retail market. However, the debate about the advantages and disadvantages of organic farming continues in the media and is discussed in Figure 16. It must also be remembered that although the percentage of the market continues to grow it is still only 1 per cent of the food sold in Britain. This is obvious from the amount of space given to organic produce in the major supermarkets.

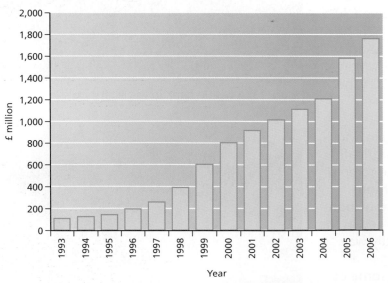

Figure 16 The organic retail market

Advantages

Produce is pesticide and insecticide free which makes it healthier. It contains more vitamin C and essential minerals such as calcium and iron.

Better for animal welfare because animals are kept in free range conditions.

30 per cent more wild species of plants and animals are found on organic farms.

Organic farming provides more than 30 per cent more jobs than non-organic.

There is a 36 per cent lower incidence of eczema in children who have organic dairy products than children who have non-organic.

Disadvantages

Crop yields are lower, therefore more land is needed for the same output.

Organically reared cattle burp twice as much methane as conventionally reared cattle.

According to some sources a litre of organic milk requires 80 per cent more land than conventional milk to produce, and contributes 20 per cent more to global warming.

A hectare of non-organic farmed land produces 2.5 times more potatoes than organic.

Organic produce costs more.

Figure 17 The advantages and disadvantages of organic farming

Figure 18 An organic farm box scheme

Figure 19 A farmers' market

The retailing of locally sourced and labelled products

The Countryside Agency, now known as Natural England, ran a campaign between 2000 and 2006 with the slogan 'Eat the View'. The campaign tried to promote the sourcing of foods locally. It has to some extent been successful which is confirmed by the number of products in supermarkets that are from the local or regional area and even have the name of the farmer on the labels. The strawberries being grown in the photograph in Figure 20 are collected from the farm and taken straight to the local stores. The containers are labelled with the farmer's name and when they were picked. The strawberries are grown under the covers to give them a longer growing season.

Many people are now aware of the impact of importing food from other countries due to the carbon emissions this causes and are willing to pay a little extra to buy food that has been produced

locally. A number of large companies are beginning to source their products locally and this is shown in Figure 21.

Figure 20 Strawberries being grown in Derbyshire for Tesco

Tesco has employed regional buyers who try to source local foods to be sold in their supermarkets in that area and sometimes throughout the country. In East Anglia, for instance, shoppers can buy a number of local products ranging from Adnams beer, which is brewed in Southwold in Suffolk, to Lincolnshire Plum Loaf, which is made in Horncastle. Tesco also has regional road shows where small local suppliers can meet with the Tesco buyers to talk to them about the products they produce. The first of these took place in Padstow in Cornwall in 2006 and resulted in 50 new Cornish products appearing in Tesco stores. In Tesco stores at present 90 per cent of the fresh chicken, 95 per cent of the beef, 92 per cent of pork, 80 per cent lamb and 100 per cent of eggs and milk come from British farms.

Other companies are starting to source their products locally. Booker, a supplier to the food industry, encourages its branch managers to source their products locally. During 2006, Booker in Plymouth and four other Cornish branches of the company launched the first range of locally sourced products with products such as beef, ice-cream, pies and biscuits all coming from the local area.

Asda has a dedicated team of people for sourcing local foods. It has 500 local suppliers many of whom have fewer than 20 employees. It is Asda policy now to sell more products from the local area. Therefore, there are more Cornish products in the stores in Cornwall and more Welsh products in their Welsh stores.

Somerfield in the south-west of England sources all of its beef locally and has contracts with farmers to supply a set number of cattle every week. For example, one farmer from Dorset supplies three cattle every week of the year. There are 1,500 members of the Southern Counties producers' club who provide the meat for 140 Somerfield shops in the south-west of England.

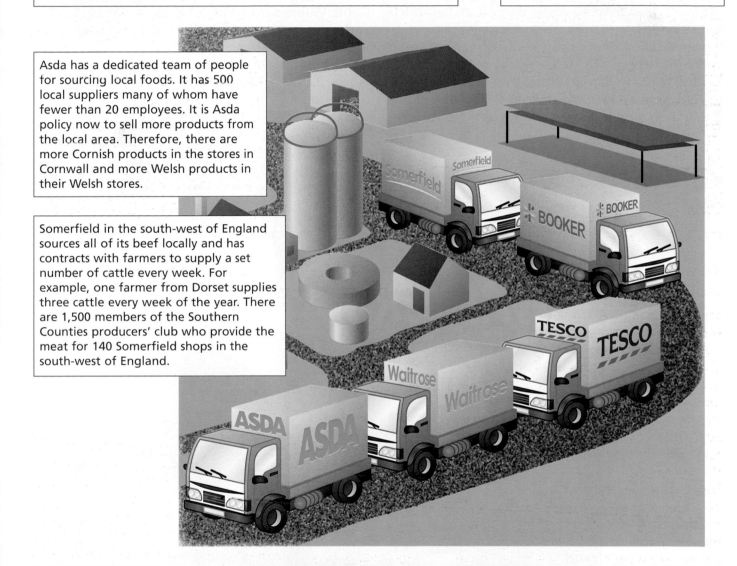

During 2008 Waitrose opened the first of 100 new food stores which are to be known as 'Market Town' food stores. As the name suggests they will be opened in medium-sized towns across the country. The first was opened in St Neots in Cambridgeshire. The shops will be individual and hope to sell 200 per cent more locally sourced food than the larger Waitrose stores. The stores will therefore cut the carbon footprint of the products and that of the consumers as they will have to travel shorter distances to do their shopping.

Figure 21 Locally sourced produce from large supermarkets

Large public sector organisations such as hospitals and schools are also looking to source their produce locally and if possible to use organic produce. The Royal Brompton hospital in London wanted to buy organic milk as locally as possible. The hospital's main supplier is Medina Food Service. After a number of months of trying to source the milk locally they found a farmer in Bedfordshire who produced milk organically and could supply the hospital and two other hospitals close by.

The Carbon Trust have developed a label which shows consumers the carbon footprint of a product, called the Carbon Reduction Label. The Carbon Trust is a private company which is funded (£100 million in 2007) by a number of government agencies including DEFRA. It has researched a method of working out the carbon footprint of products. The figure measures the total emissions of greenhouse gases during the production, distribution, storage and use of the products. For example, organic potatoes generate 160 g of CO_2 emissions per unit, the same as conventionally grown King Edwards potatoes.

Tesco has started putting the label on a number of its products showing the carbon footprint of that product – including tomatoes, potatoes, orange juice, light bulbs and washing powder. The Carbon Trust is also working with Boots, Walkers Crisps and Innocent drinks on carbon footprints and carbon labelling projects. Walkers Crisps are now displaying the label on 13 varieties of their 34.5 g and 50 g bags (see Figure 22), and 150 other companies have also expressed an interest in displaying the label on their products.

Carbon footprint information which states that 'this product is 80g per pack'.

Figure 22 A Walkers crisp packet with carbon footprint label

The growth of biofuel crops

These are crops which are grown to produce energy. Some are grown to produce electricity and generate heat.

They include:

- short rotation coppice of willow and poplar which can be harvested after three years
- micanthus (elephant grass) which is a grass from Asia. Once planted it can grow up to 3.5 m high and can be harvested annually for 15 years.

Others are grown for the production of transport fuels:

- cereals – crops such as wheat can be converted into bioethanol
- sugar beet and fodder beet – like wheat, sugar beet can be converted to bioethanol
- oilseeds – these are refined to produce biodiesel.

The government wants to encourage the growth of biofuels as it sees them as the way to cut greenhouse gas emissions and meet the requirements of the Kyoto Protocol. They have introduced a new Energy Crops Scheme and given it greater funding.

There has also been a development of the plants which process the crops into fuel for transport. A £250 million plant is to be built on Teesside to produce environmentally friendly fuel. The plant at Wilton, Teesside will use 1 million tonnes of wheat sourced from Europe, including the UK, to make 410 million litres of bioethanol a year, which can be mixed with petrol. Other plants are already in operation across the country.

Another British company, Greenergy Fuels Limited, have a number of plants around the country which produce bioethanol. Their Wissington ethanol refinery now uses sustainable sugarbeet supplies from the UK whenever possible. Tesco owns a 25 per cent share of Greenergy and has been selling biodiesel blends since 2003; since 2006 it has been selling biodiesel blends in half of its filling stations. Tesco now runs 72 of its 2,000 trucks and vans on 50 per cent biodiesel blend. Other companies who trade with Greenergy are BAA, Sainsbury and Shell.

There are also a number of power stations planned that will use biofuels to produce electricity. The first of these is to be built at Beckton in London and will be subsidised by the government through its Renewable Obligation. It will be followed by seven similar plants around the country. The company Blue NG wishes to introduce 43 plants around the country which would consume 2.4 million litres of vegetable oil a day.

Figure 23 A field of elephant grass (micanthus) in Derbyshire

Biofuels – the pros and cons

Advantages

- Biodegradable
- Non-toxic
- Renewable
- Performs just as well as the normal diesel fuel
- Contains no sulphur – the element responsible for acid rain
- Engines last longer when using it
- Saves drivers money due to government initiatives
- Could help the UK reach its target under the Kyoto Protocol to reduce its greenhouse gas emissions by 12.5 per cent below 1990 levels by 2008–2012
- On average it produces 78 per cent less carbon dioxide than fossil fuels
- Biodiesel can be used alone or mixed in any ratio with petroleum diesel fuel. The most common blend, however, is a mix of 20 per cent biodiesel with 80 per cent petroleum diesel, or 'B20'.

Disadvantages

- The grain required to fill the petrol tank of a Range Rover with ethanol is sufficient to feed one person per year
- Rapeseed – some research shows the crop generates copious amounts of nitrous oxide, an even more powerful global warming gas than CO_2
- A land area twice the size of Britain is needed to grow enough biofuel crops to halve our greenhouse gas emissions
- 37 countries across the world are facing food shortages
- The global food price index rose 40 per cent this year to the highest level on record
- Scrapping of set-aside for growth of biofuels will cause problems for birds, insects and biodiversity
- Many people want a moratorium on biofuel – 10 per cent by 2010 – because of problems caused.

ACTIVITIES

1 Complete the table with the advantages and disadvantages of UK farming practices in the twenty-first century.

21st-century farming practice	Advantages	Disadvantages
Environmentally friendly farming		
Organic farming		
Retailing of locally sourced products		
Biofuels		

2 Take each of the changes and explain the reasons why that change has occurred.

Extension

Group work.

Each group could research a different item. For example, find out more about biofuels by using the biofuelwatch website www.biofuelwatch.org.uk to research where new plants are going to be introduced and what they are going to produce.

Energy crops scheme 2007–2013

The energy crops scheme before 2007 led to the planting of 4,500 hectares of energy crops and a further 8,600 were approved in 2006 for planting in 2007. Under the new scheme £47 million is available to support the establishment of 60,000 hectares of energy crops. For short rotation coppice (SRC) and miscanthus a grant will be paid amounting to 40 per cent of the establishment costs. Farmers must get estimates from contractors and identify those parts of the planting process they are going to do themselves. An independent verifier will then check the costings. If there is disagreement, written justification will be needed. Receipt invoices and actual costings will then be required after planting for the grant to be paid. Crops should only be moved a maximum of 25 miles before being processed into their end use.

Review

By the end of this section you should be able to:

- describe the changes that have occurred to the UK countryside
- understand the consequences of these changes
- describe and explain the diversification schemes that have occurred on Home Farm
- recognise the changes that have happened to UK farming practices in the twenty-first century.

Management of the UK countryside

Learning objective – to study how the UK countryside is managed.

Learning outcomes

- To study the reasons for the designation and the different ways of managing the UK countryside.
- To recognise the pressures and conflicts in one UK National Park.
- To understand the management objectives in one UK National Park.

World heritage sites

The UK countryside is under pressure. Many different groups want to use the countryside and unless it is protected it will deteriorate. There are many different bodies that have a say in the management of the countryside; the UK countryside has been designated in a number of ways to protect it from its many users. These designations include World Heritage Sites, National Parks, National Nature Reserves (NNRs), Country Parks, Areas of Outstanding Natural Beauty (AONB), Environmentally Sensitive Areas (ESA) and wildlife reserves.

Reasons for designation

World heritage sites are areas of 'outstanding universal value'. They are unique areas of cultural or natural value which could deteriorate or even disappear if they are not protected. The World Heritage Committee run by UNESCO is responsible for the designation of world heritage sites. There are guidelines which were written by the World Heritage Convention in 1972 which the World Heritage Committee must adhere to when it is designated a site. The committee is made up of representatives from a number of different countries. The members of the World Heritage Committee are allowed one nomination per year. The UK's current nomination is The Pontcysyllte Aqueduct, which will go before the committee in June 2009. The UK at present has responsibility for 28 world heritage sites – these are listed on Figure 24.

There are two different lists which are determined by the following criteria:

- To be included on the cultural list a property or group of properties must meet criteria such as being an outstanding example of a type of building or bearing a unique testimony to a cultural tradition or civilisation which is living or has disappeared.

- To be included on the natural list a feature or group of features must meet criteria such as being an outstanding physical or biological feature which has outstanding universal value from an aesthetic or scientific point of view or they may be the habitat of an endangered species.

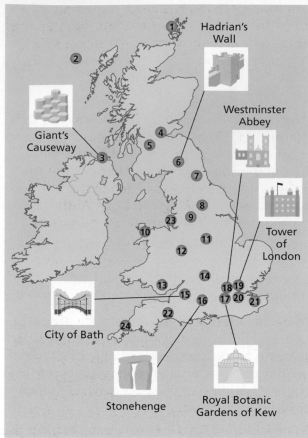

Figure 24 The World Heritage Sites in the UK

Key
1 Heart of Neolithic Orkney
2 St Kilda
3 Giant's Causeway and Causeway Coast
4 Edinburgh Old and New Towns
5 New Lanark
6 Hadrian's Wall
7 Durham Castle and Cathedral
8 Studley Royal Park and ruins of Fountains Abbey
9 Saltaire
10 Castles and Town Walls of King Edward in Gwynedd
11 Derwent Valley Mills
12 Ironbridge Gorge
13 Blaenavon Industrial Landscape
14 Blenheim Palace
15 The City of Bath
16 Stonehenge, Avebury and Associated Sites
17 The Royal Botanic Gardens of Kew
18 Westminster Palace, Westminster Abbey and St Margaret's Church
19 Tower of London
20 Maritime Greenwich
21 Canterbury Cathedral, St Agustine's Abbey and St Martin's Church
22 Dorset and East Devon Coast
23 Liverpool
24 Cornwall and West Devon Mining Landscape

Management

The UK government is responsible for the sites and must work with the local authority and the owners of the land to ensure that the sites are protected. Management plans are prepared for each of the sites and usually last for five years. These plans help to ensure that the site is protected and that there is a framework for decisions that are taken. The plans identify a number of objectives and how they will be achieved. Every six years the UK government has to report to the World Heritage Committee on the state of conservation of the sites in their care.

The sites do not gain any funding from the British government or UNESCO although the British government does contribute around £130,000 to the Committee's World Heritage Fund every year which low income countries can apply for. They do get funding from the Lottery and private companies.

Figure 25 Lulworth Cove in Dorset – World Heritage Site

and means that resources are available to promote and manage tourism in the area. Special funds are available to landowners and certain restrictions apply on development.

Management

Much of the land in National Parks is owned by private individuals. It is not publicly owned like it is in other countries. The National Trust owns some of the land and therefore has a say in the management of these areas. Each of the National Parks is run by its own National Park Authority. The Authorities have two statutory purposes.

1   To conserve and enhance the natural beauty, wildlife and cultural heritage of the area.

2   To promote opportunities for the understanding and enjoyment of the park's special qualities by the public.

The main power of the National Park Authority is to control development. Their funding is mainly from central government. The Parks employ a number of people including rangers who are responsible for conserving and enhancing the natural beauty, wildlife and cultural heritage of the Park and improving opportunities for the public to use the park. If there is any conflict between conservation and enjoyment, conservation always takes priority. Each of the National Parks has its own management plan which states the objectives of the Park and the ways in which these objectives are to be met; it is the overarching vision of the Park. The plans last for five to ten years and are derived through consultation with all the stakeholders such as local authorities, National Trust and local landowners.

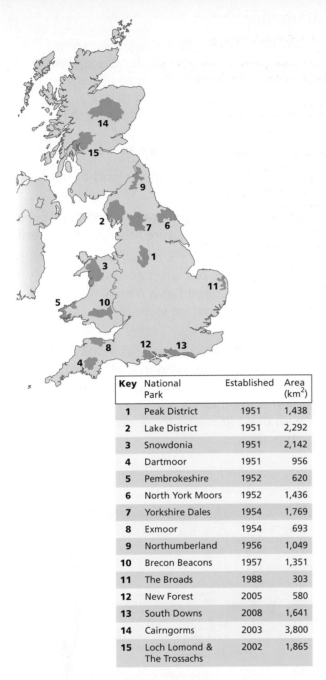

Key	National Park	Established	Area (km²)
1	Peak District	1951	1,438
2	Lake District	1951	2,292
3	Snowdonia	1951	2,142
4	Dartmoor	1951	956
5	Pembrokeshire	1952	620
6	North York Moors	1952	1,436
7	Yorkshire Dales	1954	1,769
8	Exmoor	1954	693
9	Northumberland	1956	1,049
10	Brecon Beacons	1957	1,351
11	The Broads	1988	303
12	New Forest	2005	580
13	South Downs	2008	1,641
14	Cairngorms	2003	3,800
15	Loch Lomond & The Trossachs	2002	1,865

Figure 26 National Parks in the UK

National Parks

Reasons for designation

National Parks are areas of land which have outstanding value in terms of their natural beauty, environment or recreational value. There are thirteen parks in the UK and two proposed parks, one of which being the South Downs, the other the Mourne area in Northern Ireland. The Norfolk Broads has the same status as a National Park but has never been designated. The designation as a National Park gives the area special protection

Figure 27 Buttermere, Lake District National Park

National Nature Reserves (NNRs)

Designation

The first NNR was designated in 1951 in Bienn Eighe in north-west Scotland. The first English sites were designated in 1952. There are now more than 215 NNRs covering over 87,000 hectares. NNRs are designated by Natural England. They are usually designated for their broad ecological value and not the presence of a particular species. There are, however, a number of sites which do have rare or endangered species. The NNR network represents almost every kind of vegetation type found in the UK. When they were first designated it was for conservation reasons only but more recently their role has changed and recreation has been recognised as an important part of their role.

Some sites which have endangered species may also have one of the following special designations:

- Special Protection Areas (SPA) under the EC Birds Directive

- Special Areas of Conservation (SAC) under the EC Habitats and Species Directive

- Ramsar sites under the Ramsar Convention.

Management

The majority of NNRs allow the public some access. School groups and students are given educational tours to help them to understand conservation management and to see a wide range of animals and plants in their natural habitat.

NNRs can be managed in a number of ways:

- Natural England may buy the land or the lease of the land.

- The land may be in private ownership but the owners may have a nature reserve agreement with Natural England.

- The land may be declared as a NNR which is owned and managed as a nature reserve by an 'approved body', for example, the Wildlife Trust.

Each NNR has a Site Manager and a number of estate workers who are paid to look after the site. Each site has a management plan which usually last for five years. It has a number of objectives and a plan of what needs to be done to achieve those objectives.

Figure 28 Oxwich Dunes, Gower Peninsula, South Wales – National Nature Reserve

Areas of Outstanding Natural Beauty (AONB)

This designation came into being in 1949 as part of The National Parks and Access to the Countryside Act. There are now 49 AONBs in England, Wales and Northern Ireland.

Designation

AONBs are designated by Natural England for England, and the equivalent bodies in Wales and Northern Ireland. (Scotland has national Scenic Areas which have different designation criteria.) AONBs are areas of countryside which have significant landscape value, the smallest being The Scilly Isles (16 km²) and the largest being the Cotswolds (2,000 km²).

AONBs have a number of aims; these are:

- to conserve and enhance the natural beauty of the landscape

- to provide an area for enjoyment of the countryside
- to look after the interests of the local people.

Management

They are managed much like National Parks through planning controls and practical countryside management which, unlike National Parks, is the responsibility of the local authority they are in. Some local authorities have set up Conservation Boards who manage the AONB such as for the South Downs and Mendip Hills. In other local authorities the AONB management is run by the local authority planning department. Each AONB has a management plan which includes its aims and how it will attempt to achieve those aims.

England:			
Arnside and Silverdale	Dedham Vale	Lincolnshire Wolds	Northumberland Coast
Blackdown Hills	Dorset	Malvern Hills	Quantock Hills
Cannock Chase	East Devon	Mendip Hills	Shropshire Hills
Chichester Harbour	East Hampshire	Norfolk Coast	Solway Coast
Chilterns	Forest of Bowland	North Devon	South Devon
Cornwall	Howardian Hills	North Pennines	Suffolk Coast and Heaths
Cotswolds	High Weald	North Wessex	Surrey Hills
Cranborne Chase and	Isle of Wight	Downs	Sussex Downs
West Wiltshire Downs	Isles of Scilly	Nidderdale	Tamar Valley
	Kent Downs		

Northern Ireland:
Antrim Coast and Glens
Causeway Coast
Lagan Valley
Lecale Coast
Mourne
Binevenagh
Ring of Gullion
Sperrin
Strangford Lough
Proposed AONBs:
Erne Lakeland
Fermanagh Caveland

England and Wales:
Wye Valley AONB/Dyffryn Gwy AoHNE

Wales:
Bryniau Clwyd AoHNE/Clwydian Range AONB
Gwyr AoHNE/Gower AONB
Llyn AoHNE/(Lleyn AONB)
Ynys Mon AoHNE/Anglesey AONB

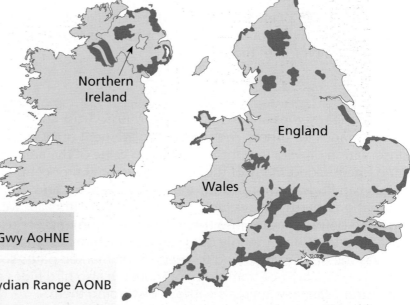

Figure 29 Areas of Outstanding Natural Beauty (AONB) in the UK

Environmentally Sensitive Areas (ESA)

Designation and management

These are agricultural areas which have been designated because they need special protection because of their landscape, wildlife or historical value. The scheme was introduced by DEFRA in 1987 in five areas of the country including the Cotswold Hills and the Essex Coast as it was felt that new farming methods were ruining the countryside. The following year five more areas were designated. In these areas farmers were given grants to protect the environment such as to retain hedges, replace or maintain field ponds and to repair stone walls. The farmers had to apply for the grants and DEFRA ensured that the farmers used the money appropriately. The scheme has now been replaced by the Environmental Stewardship Scheme which all farmers can be part of.

Wildlife reserves

Designation

Wildlife reserves or nature reserves are cared for by the Wildlife Trust. There are 2,200 nature reserves in the UK. Nature reserves are areas where wildlife is protected because of its own value. Little of the countryside of the UK is natural because it has been influenced by people for thousands of years. However, it is this evolved landscape that the nature reserves protect.

The reserves are very varied but fall into three categories:

- The 'natural environment' – this is the countryside part of the Wildlife Trust from coppiced woodland to chalk downland.

- The 'industrial environment' – these are the relics of our industrial past such as quarries, railway cuttings and canals.

- There are also planned reserves which are like planted gardens which have been set up to be a showcase for fauna and flora which are typical of the UK.

Management

Some of the reserves are owned by the Wildlife Trust and some the Trust manages for others. The prime management objective is conservation of wildlife but the recreation value of the areas is now being encouraged. Many of the reserves have a visitor centre where visitors can find out more about the reserve. Leaflets and information boards are available to ensure that visitors are well educated before they go into the reserve, refreshments are usually available and wildlife friendly gifts can be purchased. In the reserves the visitors are asked to keep to the marked paths so that fragile habitats are not trampled on. There are also bird hides so that visitors can view animals without disturbing them.

Sites of Special Scientific Interest

There are more than 4,000 of these sites in England, covering around 7 per cent of the country's land area. They are the country's very best wildlife and geological sites. They include some of the most spectacular and beautiful habitats in the country. More than half of these sites have other designations such as Special Protection Areas (SPAs) or National Nature Reserves (NNRs).

Management

The land is owned by private individuals and Natural England works with over 26,000 separate owners to try to conserve the sites. If the sites are to be conserved they need careful management such as controlling water levels, and only grazing animals at particular times of year. If there is poor management or neglect and Natural England cannot reach an agreement with the owner, Natural England may pursue more formal legal methods, such as imposing management schemes.

Figure 30 Englemere Pond

ACTIVITIES

Higher

1   The designation of World Heritage Sites is based on two criteria. What are they?

2   Describe how National Parks are designated and managed.

3   Describe and give reasons for the location of National Parks in the UK.

4   How are National Nature Reserves designated?

5   Other designations are AONBs, ESAs, wildlife reserves and SSSIs. Choose one of these designations and give reasons why it is important to protect these areas.

Foundation

1   Complete the following sentences:

   A place becomes a World Heritage Site if it is a building which ....

   Or a natural feature which

   ....

   The UK has .... World Heritage Sites.

   They are managed by the UK government working with .... and ....

   Plans are drawn up which last for .... years. Every .... years the UK must report to the committee on the state of the sites in its care.

2   What is a National Park?

3   How many National Parks are there in the UK?

4   How are National Parks managed?

5   Other designations are National Nature Reserves, AONBs, ESAs, wildlife reserves and SSSIs. Choose one of these designations and give reasons why it is important to protect these areas.

Case Study: How are the pressures and conflicts being managed in Dartmoor National Park?

Dartmoor National Park covers 853 km2 in the south-west of England. It became a National Park in 1951 and has more than 8 million visitors a year.

Visitors to National Parks can cause pressures on, and conflicts between, the different groups of people who use the Park. The pressures cause problems such as severe erosion of honeypot areas and traffic congestion. Therefore, recreation and tourism in Dartmoor NP have to be managed to retain the natural and cultural environment of the area. The National Park is run by the Dartmoor National Park Authority (DNPA) who employ a large workforce to ensure the smooth running of the Park. The Park Rangers are the people who have to ensure visitor enjoyment but also ensure that the local environment is maintained. They are the public interface of the National Park Authority as they communicate with locals, visitors and the NPA. There are a number of pressures on the Park which have been managed in order to achieve this aim.

Figure 31 Dartmoor National Park

A well-informed public will take more care of the Park

There are a number of information centres around the National Park – the High Moorland Visitor Centre, Princeton is open all year round. The four other centres open from April until March. The DNPA in 1996 set up its Moor Care Programme using funding from the EU to combat recreational erosion caused by visitor pressure on Dartmoor. The funding of £500,000 was used to repair existing damage and to make visitors aware of the damage that they cause. Guidelines were prepared to limit visitor damage to the Park (see Figure 32).

These guidelines are well publicised around the Park and local tourist attractions.

The DNPA organises guided walks which start from different car parks or villages throughout the park and ensure that visitors understand and get maximum benefit from the National Park. The walks are well documented on the National Parks website www.nationalparks.gov.uk.

Special interest groups are encouraged to talk to the NPA about their plans so that problems/conflicts can be sorted out before they occur. Such groups include the British Canoe Union and the South Devon Hang Gliding Club. Various codes of conduct and guidance for recreational activities have been produced by the NPA and all groups who use the Park must adhere to them.

- Plan your route carefully.
- Be careful with cigarettes and barbecues especially in dry weather.
- Some areas may be suffering from excessive erosion. Please avoid these areas whenever possible.
- Use hard surface car parks whenever possible and do not park on the grass verges.
- On paths walk in single file if necessary to avoid damaging the path or making it wider.

Figure 32 The Moor Care Programme

Visitors should be encouraged not to use their cars

In order to reduce visitor pressure on the park, the Dartmoor Freewheeler bike bus runs from April until the end of September, charging £5 for each journey. The scheme has been set up to allow people to cycle in the park rather than drive their cars. The service operates on a rota basis from Saltram to Princetown, Newton Abbot to Mardon Down, Plymouth to Okehampton and Buckfastleigh to Postbridge.

A speed limit of 40 miles an hour has been introduced on 90 miles of open moorland roads and there has been a decrease in traffic speed of about 5 mph. Mobile speed measuring equipment has been used to enforce the speed limit. Awareness has been raised by media campaigns and boards in car parks, and verges have also been improved to improve visibility on open moorland roads. This has decreased the incidence of animal deaths on the moorland roads and so lessened conflicts with farmers.

There has also been much signage introduced since 1994 to encourage through traffic to avoid the Park, notably the A382 by using the A38 and A30 instead. This has led to benefits to villages along the road particularly Moretonhampstead. Although the amount of traffic has not decreased there has been less of an increase. For instance, between 1985 and 1994 traffic increased by 42 per cent, but between 1995 and 2002 the increase was 1 per cent. The villagers are now less disturbed by visitor traffic.

The DNPA is also paying towards the provision of some public transport in the area which otherwise would be withdrawn as it is not economically viable, for example, the number 72 bus from Bovey Tracey to Newton Abbot and the number 82 Exeter to Plymouth transmoor link. A Sunday rover ticket has also been introduced with 10 per cent more passengers in 2004 than 2002. Okehampton train station has been reopened for passengers to encourage visitors to travel by train not by car.

The idea now being proposed is that Ivybridge, Bovey Tracey and Yelverton are used as gateway settlements to the park. People could park their cars there and use public transport to move around the park. The local communities would need to be supportive of this idea and are being consulted. There has also been a traffic calming scheme in Mary Tavy which has improved the quality of life for the local inhabitants.

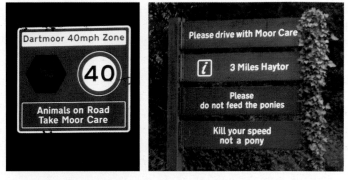

Figure 33 Signage warning drivers about careful driving and speed on Dartmooor

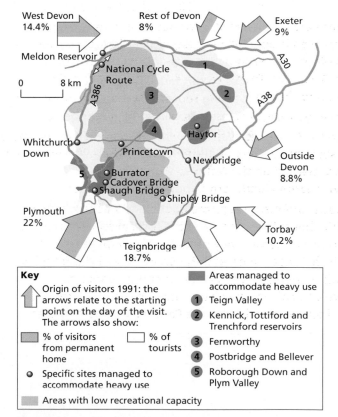

Figure 34 Origin of visitors and management of honeypot areas of Dartmoor National Park

Development conflicts and pressure are controlled by planning permission

Planning permission can cause many problems and conflicts. The local people will want to be treated like residents in other areas and not have restrictions put on them just because they live in a National Park. Outside of National Parks planning permission is granted by the local council. The process shown in Figure 35 has to be followed in a National Park which is much more complicated. This can cause resentment and bad feeling between the locals and National Park Authorities. However, in the long run it means that the aims of the NP are met.

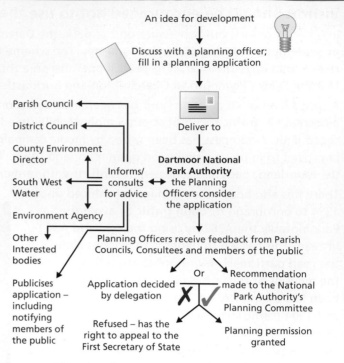

Figure 35 The planning process in Dartmoor National Park

The concentration of visitors at honeypot sites causes erosion problems

Most areas of the Park can cope with a certain amount of recreational pressure from walkers. The effect of recreation pressure is not evenly spread. It tends to be more intensive close to car parks, riverside picnic sites and on popular walking routes; for example, from a car park to a Tor. Erosion is caused by a number of factors such as hikers' boots, livestock grazing, tractors, mountain bikes and natural forces such as heavy rainfall (see Figure 36).

The amount of erosion in popular areas is monitored carefully. There are rangers who are responsible for an area of the Park. They monitor their areas by observation and photography and report any erosion problems. If the erosion problems are serious enough there will be money put aside to deal with the problems.

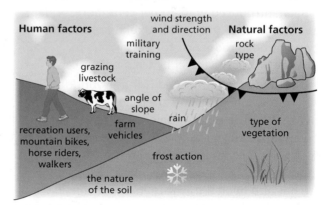

Figure 36 Factors that cause erosion in Dartmoor National Park

The gorse has been cut back on the hillside to allow the visitors room to wander. Not keeping them to a narrow path has lessened the erosion problem. In areas where the path is narrower erosion still occurs. The erosion gullies are regularly filled in and the turf/grass restored.

Haytor Moor is a very popular tourist honeypot which was suffering from a number of problems caused by visitor pressure. The ranger responsible identified the problems and reported them to the DNPA.

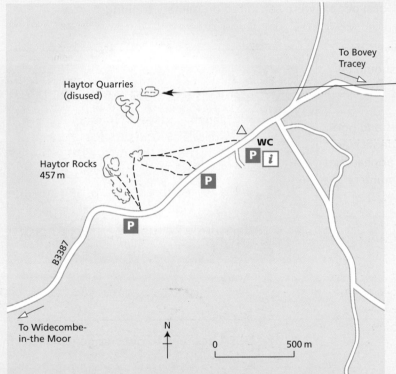

To Bovey Tracey

Haytor Quarries (disused)

Haytor Rocks 457 m

B3387

To Widecombe-in-the-Moor

WC
P i
P
P

The area close to the fence around the quarry was also trampled and bare.
Patches of bare earth have been reseeded with the National Park Authority's moorland grass seed mix.

N

0   500 m

Key
△   guided walks start point
P   parking
WC   toilets
i   information centre
- - -   footpaths

Vehicles had been driven onto the land beside the car park causing damage to the grass.
Low grassed banks have been created around the car parks to stop visitors from driving on the open areas beside the car parks. Granite blocks are used to block off some car parks. This restricts visitor numbers and allows the grass time to recover.

Figure 37 The problems and solutions at Haytor, a honeypot site

Other users of the National Park include the army

Dartmoor is also used by the army for training – approximately 11 per cent of the land area is owned by the army. This can cause conflicts with both local people and visitors. In order to minimise the problems a steering group has been organised which meets annually to discuss any issues that have arisen. Members of the steering group include the 43 Wessex Brigade and Commandant Commando Training Centre Royal Marines, Dartmoor National Park Authority, Natural England and the Duchy of Cornwall. The steering group is supported by a working party who record complaints and instigate the conservation and access projects agreed by the group; they also oversee all environmental monitoring.

Conflicts which may occur between the visitors and the army are minimised by making the public fully aware of when areas will be closed for military training. The military training areas are focused between Okehampton and Princetown and close to Yelverton. The areas are open for 245 days at Okehampton. The closed days are notified both on the internet, local newspapers and in the Dartmoor NP publications. Most of the training involves infantry work and therefore causes very little disruption to the local residents. The military does have a visual intrusion impact because of flags and notices, and vehicular access. There is also the noise of firing. When the new management plan was prepared, local people were consulted on military training.

The results showed:

- 52 per cent supported the stopping of live firing
- 1 per cent thought all military training should be stopped
- 48 per cent did not object to live firing.

The survey distinguished between residents and non-residents; a higher percentage of non-residents were opposed to live firing. Therefore it would appear that local residents are more supportive of the military training than the visitors.

Review

By the end of this section you should be able to:

- understand the reasons for the designation and the different ways of managing the UK countryside
- be able to recognise the pressures and conflicts in one UK National Park
- understand the management objectives in one UK National Park.

ACTIVITIES

Higher

1 Explain the pressures and conflicts that are occurring in Dartmoor National Park.

2 How has the Dartmoor National Park authority managed the problems?

Foundation

1 One of the aims of the National Park is to keep the public well informed. Describe one way that the DNPA has achieved this.

2 What is the Moor Care Programme?

3 The DNPA has tried to discourage people from using their cars.

   a Describe two forms of transport that the DNPA has provided for people so that they do not need to use their cars.

   b Figure 33 gives instructions to drivers. Can you explain why drivers are being asked to keep to these rules?

4 Haytor is a popular place for tourists to visit.

   a What problems have tourists caused in the area?

   b How has the DNPA dealt with these problems?

Extension

Use the Dartmoor National Park website to research guided walks and other events that are provided by the National Park Authority.

Sample Examination Questions

Higher tier

1 Study Figure 1 on page 183. Describe and explain the changes in primary employment. You should use data in your answer. **(4 marks)**

2 There has been a 'spiral of decline' in some rural areas of the UK. What is a 'spiral of decline'? **(3 marks)**

3 Supermarkets are now sourcing many of their products locally. What are the advantages and disadvantages of locally sourced produce? **(3 marks)**

4 State the disadvantages of using biofuel. **(2 marks)**

5 Study Figure 15 on page 194. It shows the amount of land farmed organically in the UK between 1995 and 2007.

  a Between 1995 and 2001 by how much did the land farmed organically increase? **(1 mark)**

  b Explain why the amount of land farmed organically increased so much. **(3 marks)**

  c After 2001 the amount of land farmed organically started to decrease.

    Suggest reasons why. **(3 marks)**

6 Choose a National Park that you have studied. Explain how conflicts in a National Park are being managed. **(6 marks)**

  Chosen national park

  ....

Total 25 marks

Foundation tier

1 Study Figure 1 on page 183. Describe the changes in the sectors of employment. You should use data in your answer. **(4 marks)**

2 There has been a 'spiral of decline' in some rural areas of the UK. What is a 'spiral of decline'?

Put the following statements into the correct order to explain a 'spiral of decline'. **(3 marks)**

  The shop cannot make a profit so closes down.

  People leave a rural area due to better facilities and employment chances in urban areas.

  More people leave the village because there is no shop.

  Less people are left in the village to buy goods from the local shop.

3 Supermarkets are now sourcing many of their products locally. What are the advantages and disadvantages of locally sourced produce? Put the following statements into the correct column.

  Adds less to carbon footprint of products.

  Provides a market for local farmers.

  Takes more time to source the products.

  More people have to be employed to source products, therefore wages bill increases.

Advantages	Disadvantages

(4 marks)

4 State three disadvantages of using biofuel. **(3 marks)**

5 Study Figure 15 on page 194. It shows the amount of land farmed organically in the UK between 1995 and 2007.

  a What was the number of hectares farmed organically in 1995? **(1 mark)**

  b After which year did the amount of land farmed organically begin to decrease? **(1 mark)**

  c Explain why the amount of land farmed organically increased so much. **(3 marks)**

6 Choose a National Park that you have studied. Describe how conflicts in a National Park are being managed. **(6 marks)**

  Chosen national park

  ....

Total 25 marks

Factors affecting settlements

> **Learning objective** – to study the factors affecting settlements.
>
> **Learning outcomes**
> * To be able to describe and explain the reasons for different settlement sites.
> * To recognise reasons why settlements have different shapes.
> * To explain what is meant by counter-urbanisation.
> * To know the effects of depopulation on remote rural areas.

Physical and human factors affecting the site and situation, growth and shape of settlements

Physical and economic factors affect the location, shape and growth of settlements. Settlements do not happen accidentally or grow by chance. There is always a good reason why a settlement is where it is. The land on which a settlement is built is called the site. The original decision to locate a settlement in a particular place would have been influenced by many factors. Most settlements were built by farming communities who would have needed a site that met all or as many as possible of their needs. The following factors were all important:

* access to a permanent supply of water
* well-drained land that was free from flooding
* land that was sheltered from strong winds and storms
* land that faced south to gain maximum warmth from the Sun
* fertile land for arable crops and pasture for livestock
* timber for fuel and building.

If a settlement grew, it was probably because it had many of the above factors as well as a good situation. (A settlement's situation is its location relative to its surroundings.) A good situation allows a settlement to grow and develop into a central settlement surrounded by other settlements. This central settlement is likely to grow into a market town as it is easily accessible from all the other settlements. Routes would focus on the central town and trade would develop, leading in turn to a growth in service industries.

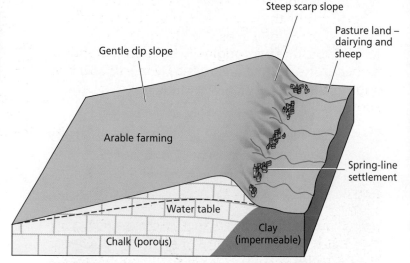

Figure 1 Diagram of spring-line settlements

Figure 2 Littondale, North Yorkshire, spring-line settlement

Water supply

Settlements that are located close to rivers, lakes or springs are called wet-point sites. Figure 1 shows how a line of villages has developed alongside springs at the base of the hill. These settlements are called spring-line settlements and are one type of wet-point site. As water infiltrates into the hillside, it percolates through the porous rock. When the water reaches impermeable rocks into which it cannot soak, it issues forth as a spring.

Those who live in settlements located close to rivers have to be careful to build their houses above the floodplain. If houses are built too close to the river, there is a chance that if the river floods, serious damage to property can occur. This was shown in many areas of England during the autumn of 2000. Settlements were flooded from York in the North to Uckfield in the South.

Settlements that are sited above the floodplain are called dry-point sites. The city of Ely in Cambridgeshire was originally built on a slightly higher area of land surrounded by marshland. The original medieval site of St Albans stands out above the floodplain of the River Ver.

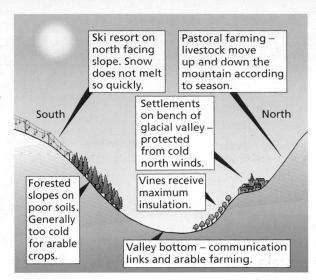

Figure 4 Land use in the Alps

Defence

Centuries ago, selecting a site for defence purposes was very important. A castle was often built on high ground overlooking the surrounding countryside. This is the case in Edinburgh and Lincoln. The town of Savignano in southern Italy was sited in a commanding position above a gap in the Apennine Mountains (see Figure 5).

Figure 3 An alpine valley in Zermatt, Switzerland

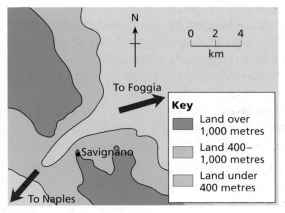

Figure 5 Map of Savignano

The original site of Paris was on the Ile de La Cité, an island in the middle of the river Seine. This protected the inhabitants from attack, as they were surrounded by water. Paris subsequently grew as it became a focus of routeways.

Venice is on the coast of north-east Italy, at the northern end of the Adriatic Sea. It is located at the mouth of the River Po which is a delta. The city is built on more than 100 islands, split up by canals.

Aspect and shelter

In the northern hemisphere, south-facing slopes receive more sun than the north-facing slopes and are therefore warmer. The south-facing slopes are also sheltered from the cold northerly winds. More settlements and agricultural land are therefore sited on the south-facing slopes (see Figure 4).

The canals act as 'roads' and are the only way, other than by foot, to travel around the city. The largest canal is the Canal Grande. Venice's site was chosen because it provided a good defensive position. It later became a rich port, trading with cities all around the Mediterranean and western Europe. It is still an important city today, but much of its wealth is now based on tourism.

Many settlements are located on the inside of river meanders because they would need to be protected in only one direction. Examples include Yarm, Durham, Shrewsbury and Warkworth (as indicated on Figure 6; also refer to the OS map on page 35).

Human factors affecting the site of a settlement

Communications

Settlements often grew where rivers could be easily crossed. This might be at fords (Oxford and Hertford) or at bridging points. The lowest bridging point (the nearest point to the sea that could be bridged) was a particularly favourable site. Many large cities were originally sited at the lowest bridging point; examples include London, Hamburg, Paris and Exeter.

Other favourable communication sites were at the junction of valleys or in gaps through hills. Montgenevre and Briançon are in cols (gaps) in the Alps and straddle the French–Italian border. Good communications often gave the settlement an advantage over others so it grew as a route centre. Traders would bring their goods to these accessible settlements and, in time, markets grew up there. Settlements also developed at favourable coastal locations. Ports such as Poole in Dorset and Sydney in Australia grew up around large natural harbours.

Resources

Early settlers relied upon timber for both fuel and building material. A site close to woodland was therefore an advantage. Stone was also used for building, so

Figure 6 Photograph of Warkworth

proximity to a quarry was also useful. During the Industrial Revolution, coal was in great demand as a power source for factories. Many mining towns sprang up on the coalfields of northern England. The existence of oil reserves in various parts of the world, such as the Middle East and Russia, has been the reason for mining settlements to grow in these areas. Aberdeen in Scotland saw considerable growth with the development of the North Sea oil industry.

Figure 7 Worcester – a bridging point on the River Severn

Settlement shapes

Settlements can be classified according to the arrangement of houses within them.

1 Nucleated or clustered settlements have the individual buildings grouped closely together. They often form at crossroads or route centres. They may have originally clustered close together for defensive purposes or because communal farming took place in the area.

2 Dispersed or fragmented settlements have individual buildings spread out. There is usually no obvious centre. They are often rural farming villages, where areas of woodland were gradually cleared.

3 Linear settlements have buildings on either side of a road, valley or the coast. Ribbon development is when housing grows out from a town along a main road.

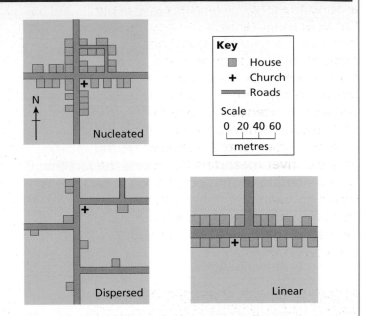

Figure 8 Diagram of settlement shapes

Changes to rural communities

Counter-urbanisation

Counter-urbanisation is the movement out of cities to rural areas. This process has been happening in MICs for the last 50 years. There are five main reasons for this movement.

1 Urban areas are becoming less pleasant places to live. This is because of an increase in pollution, crime and traffic.

2 There has been an increase in car ownership which has allowed people to live further from their place of work. There has also been an improvement in the road networks.

3 There has been an increase in the number of people working from home due to technological improvements such as email and video-conferencing.

4 There is an ageing population and people tend to move to the countryside when they retire.

5 Business parks on the edge of cities mean that people do not have to commute into the city to work and therefore can live in rural areas close by.

This movement of people has had an impact on both the area receiving the migrants and the area which has lost its population.

Negative impacts of counter-urbanisation on rural areas

- There can be conflict between the local residents and the 'newcomers' to the area.
- Many of the migrants still work in urban areas therefore the journey to work can cause congestion and pollution.
- House prices in rural areas may rise as demand increases. This may mean that local people cannot afford to buy a house and have to move away from their local area.
- Many of the migrants do not support local businesses and do their shopping in the urban areas where they work.
- The traditions of the village are not valued by the newcomers, therefore there can be a loss in community spirit.
- Villages become ghost towns during the day – loss of community spirit.
- Many church parishes have been amalgamated as the 'newcomers' do not go to church.

Positive impacts of counter-urbanisation on rural areas

- Local schools have an increase in pupils and are able to stay open.
- Some local services are supported such as public houses, local tradesmen (for example, builders).
- Old derelict farm buildings are turned into habitable dwellings which adds to the aesthetic value and community well-being.

Another effect of this movement is the fact that it has created an ageing population in rural areas.

The people who tend to move to rural areas are the more affluent who have a young family and the retired. The people who move out of the countryside are the young and single people who are looking for work and facilities that an urban area can offer. This is shown on the age–sex pyramid for 2005 in Figure 9. Between 1985 and 2005 there were major changes in the age structure of rural areas in the UK. In some rural areas there was a 30 per cent decrease in the population aged 15–29 and a 25 per cent increase in the numbers aged 40–59.

ACTIVITIES

1 What is meant by the term counter-urbanisation?

2 Describe two positive and two negative impacts of counter-urbanisation on rural areas.

3 What are the characteristics of an area which has suffered from rural depopulation?

4 Study Figure 9.

 a Describe the trends shown by the graph.

 b Give reasons for the trends you have identified.

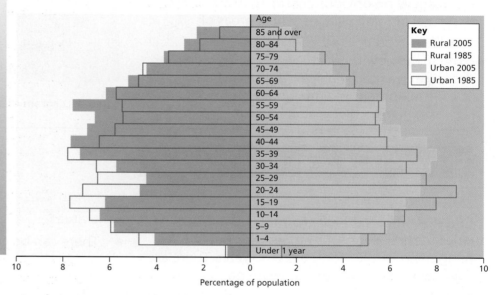

Figure 9 A population pyramid comparing rural and urban population in 1985 and 2005

Depopulation of remote rural areas

There has been a movement out of rural areas which are classed as remote rural areas although even in this category it depends on what is classed as remote. Some remote areas such as North Cornwall have seen an increase in population, whereas other remote areas such as the Highlands of Scotland have seen a decline in rural population. As can be seen from Figure 10 there has been a decline in population for the age bands up to 40 in all types of rural areas between the years 1985 and 2005. However, there has been an increase in all the age bands over 40 except 70–75 which has seen a small decrease.

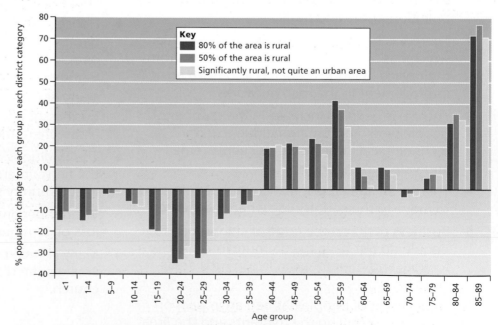

Figure 10 Changes to rural population profile 1985–2005

This movement out of remote rural areas has meant that the people who remain there have seen a decline in service provision. In 2001 there were 600,000 people living in what can be classed as remote rural areas; 45 per cent of these people did not live within 4 km of a doctors' surgery, 4 km of a Post Office and were also without a bus service.

This situation will continue to worsen as many Post Offices are closing in rural areas in the UK due to them not being profitable. In Cornwall 25 per cent, and in Devon 22 per cent, of Post Offices are set to close while the county average for the UK is 18 per cent.

Only 50 per cent of people in remote rural areas have a bank account because there were no local banks so they do not see the point. The decline in rural services has also seen the closure of many primary schools such as Satterthwaite and Rusland School and Lowick School, both near Ulverston in the Lake District. They were closed in 2006.

In Cornwall the only major hospital is situated in Plymouth which is actually in Devon! Therefore if you are a patient suffering from cancer you would have to travel up to 100 miles to receive treatment.

Key service	% without
Shop	70
Post Office	43
Daily bus service	75
School	50
GP	83
Village hall	28
Public house	29

Figure 11 The percentage of rural settlements without key services

Review

By the end of this section you should be able to:

- describe and explain the reasons for different settlement sites
- recognise the reasons for different settlement shapes
- explain what is meant by counter-urbanisation and know its effect on rural communities
- know the effects of depopulation on remote rural areas.

ACTIVITIES

1   Study Figure 6 on page 216 and the OS map extract of Warkworth on page 35. Find Warkworth on the OS map.
 a   What is the name of the farm marked A on Figure 6?
 b   What land use is marked B on Figure 6?
2   State the ways in which the houses in area C are different to the houses in area D.
3   Why have houses not been built on:
 a   area E?
 b   area F?
4   Give the name and a four figure grid reference for an example of each of the following. Do not use an example that has already been used in the text:
 a   a dispersed settlement
 b   a nucleated settlement
 c   a linear settlement.
5   Find Alnwick on the map. Give six figure grid references for the following features found in, or close to Alnwick:
 a   Alnwick information centre
 b   St Leonard's hospital
 c   Alnwick museum
 d   the roundabout where the A1(T) meets the A1086.
6   Name the features found at the following grid references:
 a   208 144
 b   192 145
 c   253 071
 d   237 117
7   Describe the physical factors that affect the site of settlements.
8   How can good communication links affect the growth of settlements?
9   Compare and describe the settlement shapes shown in Figure 8 on page 217.

Extension

Choose a town in your local area.
a   Describe its site.
b   Why did your town grow while other settlements remained as villages?

Changing land use in urban areas

Learning objective – to study how land use is changing in urban areas.

Learning outcomes
- To understand the reasons for the change in land use in urban areas.
- To recognise that there are a number of reasons why more housing stock is needed.
- To understand the consequences of deindustrialisation including redevelopment and renewal.
- To know the advantages and disadvantages of brownfield and greenfield sites.

Land use in urban areas

Land use in urban areas in the UK has shown a dramatic change over the last 30 years. This is due to two significant trends.

- There has been an increased demand for housing by the UK population.
- There has been deindustrialisation with manufacturing moving from urban areas in the UK to LICs where production costs are much lower.

The reasons for the increase in the demand for housing are social, economic and political. The UK has seen a steady growth in population over the last 30 years. There has also been a large influx of migrants since the beginning of the twenty-first century. All of these extra people need homes.

Social reasons

There have been major social changes in the life of people who live in the UK.

- People are now marrying later in life – the average age has gone up from 24 in 1960 to 30 in 2010.
- There has also been a rise in the number of divorces which means that a family is not living as a group but is living in two different dwellings.
- There is also the added problem of an ageing population. Many people now live on their own or with their spouse until they are in their 70s and 80s – this means that more houses are needed for the younger generation.

- British society has also changed in that 40 years ago many grandparents lived with their families because they were unable to look after themselves. Many now live alone and rely on the welfare state to provide carers and home helps.

All of these changes have meant that there is a greater demand for new homes, particularly those for single people or married couples. This has led to a large increase in the number of one- and two-bedroom properties being built or older buildings being split into flats. There has also been a great deal of redevelopment taking place with old office and industrial space being turned into houses or more usually apartments.

Figure 12 Large family homes which have been split into flats

Figure 13 The Met Office in Bracknell before redevelopment

Figure 14 The Met Office site after being redeveloped with apartments

Economic reasons

The population of the UK is now wealthier than ever before. It then follows that people can afford to buy or rent properties at an earlier age and no longer have to live with their parents. There has also developed an attitude of 'buy now and pay later' which means that many people in their 20s do not save money but spend it on rents and mortgages rather than saving up until they have a deposit. This has been encouraged by mortgage companies who offer 100 per cent mortgages with no deposit whereas 20 years ago a 10 per cent deposit was required. What also needs to be considered is the increase in house prices which has led to many people living in smaller dwellings and hence yet more of an increase in the demand for one- and two-bedroom properties.

The increase in the average age to get married, but more so the average age to have children, have also impacted on the types of housing being demanded. People are having fewer children and having them later in life which means that they require smaller houses or flats.

Political reasons

In 2000 it was predicted that the population of the UK would rise by 4.1 million between 2001 and 2021. This target is still on track; 600,000 of this increase will be in the south-east of England. Coupled with the changes in society mentioned earlier in this section, this means that there will be a need for more houses. The government has recognised this need and produced the Sustainable Communites policy. This promises that 3 million new homes will be built by 2020, 200,000 of these in the south-east. Certain areas of the south-east have been designated as growth areas; these are Ashford in Kent, the M11 corridor, Milton Keynes and the Thames Gateway area. There will also be significant developments allowed in other areas of the south-east. The housing development shown in Figure 18 is on former greenbelt land on the western edge of Bracknell in Berkshire. The government has stated that any greenbelt land that is lost by these developments will be made up for by new greenbelt land being designated. The government is also developing eco-towns; bids for these towns are just being accepted by the government and the 10 proposed sites are shown in Figure 15.

Figure 15 The sites of the proposed eco-towns

Development of brownfield and greenfield sites

There has been a major shift in employment in urban areas in the UK with manufacturing industry moving to LICs where production costs are lower. This has led to many buildings being left abandoned and derelict. These sites in urban areas in the UK are known as brownfield sites. The derelict buildings on these sites are either converted into a new use such as housing, known as renewal, or the buildings are knocked down and new ones built, which is known as redevelopment. This process has been occurring all over the UK and many new houses, shopping and entertainment facilities have been created in some of the UK's most run down and derelict areas.

A brownfield site that has experienced renewal and redevelopment is in Norwich. It is a large site comprising 17 hectares and is located south-east of Norwich City Centre, on the banks of the River Wensum close to the railway station and the football ground at Carrow Road. The site has been redeveloped over a number of years. The redevelopment has seen the building of an entertainment complex including a fourteen-screen cinema, a large shopping centre and more than 200 residential units, many of them apartments built along the river side. New foot and cycle bridges have been built across the river to give better access to the area.

Figure 17 Renewal on a brownfield site in Norwich

The demand for housing has also been met by building on greenfield sites around the edge of urban areas leading to urban sprawl. This concept is also mentioned in the section on political changes. There have been new housing developments in many areas of the country around urban areas. Bracknell in Berkshire is seeing significant growth with a large new housing development on a greenfield site to the west of the town. Peacock Farm estate is situated next to the A329M and is close to the M4 for easy access for residents. The development includes 14,000 new homes, 91 acres of country parkland, a doctors' surgery and two primary schools (see Figure 18).

Some areas have seen the development of 'gated suburbs'. This is the concept which originated in countries such as South Africa to protect residents. A number of housing developments, for example in the south-east and the north-west, now have gates to protect them from perceived threats such as burglars.

Figure 16 Redevelopment on a brownfield site in Norwich

Figure 18 New housing on the edge of Bracknell

Advantages	Disadvantages
Planning permission is easier to get, the government is actively encouraging the use of these sites.	Complete environmental survey needed because of past usage is costly and time consuming.
Infrastructure such as gas, electricity and water is already present.	Perception of contaminated environment puts off prospective buyers.
Easier to market because of access to entertainment and other facilities.	Cities may have social problems – such as anti-social behaviour and crime as well as higher levels of pollution and congestion which could make marketing more difficult.
No building on greenfield sites so lessens urban sprawl.	Brownfield sites have to be cleared and in some cases decontaminated which adds to the construction costs.
	Land costs are higher as it is closer to the city centre.

Figure 19 The advantages and disadvantages of brownfield sites

Advantages	Disadvantages
Originally unoccupied therefore developers can build as they wish.	Infrastructure such as gas, electricity and water will not be present.
Plenty of space for car parking and landscaping to improve the working environment.	Urban sprawl using up green spaces on the edge of urban areas.
Cheaper land due to being further from the city centre.	It is more difficult to get planning permission as the government tends to be against it.
Lower construction costs as there is nothing to knock down or renew.	Building could disturb natural habitats and wildlife.
Easy to market to potential buyers because of pleasant environment.	Living on the edge of the city may increase the commute for some people.
Access to the development is easier as roads are not congested.	Disruption to local area during construction.
	People may not want to live away from the city centre because of their social life.

Figure 20 The advantages and disadvantages of greenfield sites

Review

By the end of this section you should be able to:

- explain the reasons for the change in land use in urban areas
- recognise that there are a number of reasons why more housing stock is needed
- understand the consequences of deindustrialisation including redevelopment and renewal
- describe the advantages and disadvantages of brownfield and greenfield sites.

ACTIVITIES

1 There has been an increase in demand for housing stock. Explain the social, economic and political reasons for this increase in demand.
2 What is the difference between renewal and redevelopment?
3 Building on brownfield sites has a number of advantages and disadvantages. Discuss these advantages and disadvantages from the following points of view:
   a a builder
   b local residents
   c a young couple wishing to buy a property.

Extension

The government is going to develop a number of sustainable towns called eco-towns.

Find out the principles behind the idea of eco-towns.

Keywords

Redevelopment This is when buildings in a city, which are no longer of use, are demolished and replaced with buildings that are in current demand.

Renewal This is when old buildings are renovated and brought up to date, combining the best of the old with the new.

Brownfield site This is an area within a city which is no longer used. It may contain old factories and housing, or it may have been cleared ready for redevelopment.

Brownfield potential The number of brownfield sites which are available for redevelopment within a city.

Greenbelt This is an area around the city, which is composed of farmland and recreational land. There are strict controls on the development of this land. Its purpose is to control the growth of cities.

Greenfield site An area on the edge of the city, which has never been developed in any way.

Rapid growth in LICs

> **Learning objective** – to study the rapid growth of urban populations in LICs.
>
> **Learning outcomes**
> * To understand the reasons for the rapid growth of urban areas in LICs.
> * To describe and explain the effects of rapid growth on Cairo.

Reasons for the rapid growth in urban areas in LICs

Urban areas in LICs have experienced a rapid growth since the 1950s. There are two main reasons for this rapid growth:

1 The migration from rural to urban areas caused by:

* lack of jobs in rural areas because of population growth and mechanisation

* salaries, which are lower in rural areas

* the development of TNCs and other industry providing jobs in urban areas

* the perception of a better life, including education.

2 The high natural increase in population caused by:

* the youth of the migrants – many of them are of child bearing age

* better medical facilities in urban areas – infant mortality is lower in urban areas in LICs

* higher life expectancy due to better living conditions and diet

* the lack of contraception or knowledge about contraception.

Case Study: The effects of rapid growth on a LIC urban area – Cairo

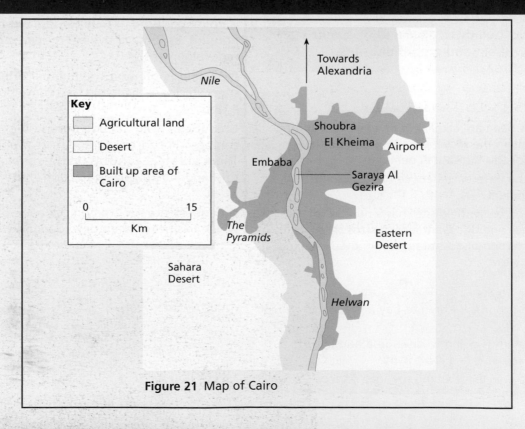

Figure 21 Map of Cairo

The effects of rapid growth on a LIC urban area – Cairo

Introduction

Cairo is the largest city in Egypt as well as its capital and is home to more than 25 per cent of the country's population. It is now one of the twenty most populated urban areas in the world and Cairo's population continues to grow at approximately 500,000 a year.

Cairo's growth has been greatest in the areas west of the Nile and to the north in Shoubra el Kheima. The population growth in Cairo is a direct result of people migrating there from rural areas and from increased life expectancy which went up from 41 years in 1960 to 70 years in 2010.

This rapidly growing population causes Cairo many problems. Housing is overcrowded and in short supply. This is not surprising with an average population density of 30,000 people per square kilometre which is higher than in Manhattan in New York. There are many other effects of this rapid growth in population. Pollution levels are high and there is continual congestion on Cairo's roads. There are also problems with rubbish collection and water supply.

Cairo, like many large cities in HICs, suffers from traffic congestion. This is caused by the 2 million cars which are driven around the streets along with 200,000 motorbikes, a few thousand buses and more than a million taxis. The effect of this congestion is noise and air pollution. The government is aware of the problems caused and it has responded by introducing low-emission gas buses and expanding the metro system. The metro at present has three lines but three more are planned by 2022.

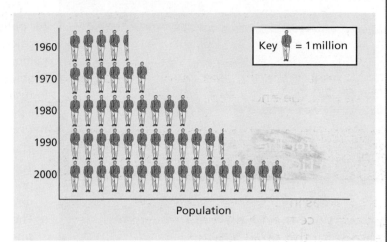

Figure 22 Cairo's population

Noise pollution

Noise pollution from the millions of vehicles, loud speakers calling Muslims to prayer and the noise of nightclubs on the River Nile cause many problems for the residents of Cairo. The noise is well above acceptable levels according to the World Health Organisation. It is particularly bad in the Saraya al Gezira district where the residents also have to cope with the nightclub boats on the river. Their Nileside rooms have noise from the nightclubs and their front rooms have the noise of the city.

Figure 23 Nightclub boats

Figure 24 Traffic congestion in Cairo

Air pollution

Air pollution is caused by the transport and industry. It is predicted that because of the poor air quality half a million of Cairo's residents will develop serious health problems which will result in premature death. In the industrial quarter Shoubra el Kheima, where many of the poor people live close to their work, 37 per cent of the residents suffer from lung problems.

The children in Cairo are faced with specific problems.
- The sun's rays are blocked by smog on the most polluted days which means that many suffer from a deficiency of vitamin D.
- The lead concentrations in the air from the lead smelters at Shoubra el Kheima cause a loss of intelligence, at an average of four IQ points.
- The concentration of lead in the air has also caused an 80 per cent rise in tooth decay.

A black cloud sometimes covers Cairo in a haze. It first appeared in 1999 and is most common in October and November. At this time of year straw is burnt after rice has been harvested adding to the already polluted air.

Figure 25 Air pollution

Land pollution

There is also a problem with land pollution. The huge population produces 10,000 tonnes of solid waste a day. Only 60 per cent is collected; the rest is left to rot in streets, canals, drains and neighbourhood dump sites. Rats and other vermin live in plague proportions on the waste dumps. Diseases are carried by the rats and can easily affect the inhabitants of Helwan. There are also large toxic stockpiles of hazardous waste, as much as 50,000 tonnes, from industry which has accumulated in Helwan, Shoubra and Embaba.

Figure 26 Zabaleen sorting rubbish

Water pollution

Water pollution is caused by both domestic and industrial waste water. Many small streams and old irrigation canals around Cairo are filled with plastic bags full of solid waste and are used for sewage disposal.

80 per cent of industrial waste water is discharged untreated into the Nile. This can be as much as 2.5 million litres a day. The effect of this is that Egypt's coastal fishing and tourist industry are being damaged. An example of this is the Shoubra el Kheima district to the north of the city which discharges its waste water straight into drains which are already heavily polluted and which flow into the Mediterranean.

It is estimated that 23 per cent of the population of Cairo does not have access to a fresh water supply and 25 per cent of the population is not connected to the public sewage system. Only 15 per cent of sewage water is treated properly; 60 per cent is carried raw through open canals to the Mediterranean.

Figure 27 City of the Dead

Housing problems

Due to the acute shortage of housing approximately 60 per cent of Cairo's population lives in shanty type dwellings. The most famous of these is the 'City of the Dead' or Arafa (cemetery) as it is called by the local residents. This is just one of the five cemeteries which used to be on the outskirts of the city in the Moqattam Hills but because of rapid urbanisation are now part of the city. This four-mile long cemetery in eastern Cairo is where people live and work among their dead ancestors. People live here illegally as it gives them shelter and they have nowhere else to go. The government has provided some electricity and water standpipes but there is no connection to the sewage system. It is not known how many people live among the gravestones in the 'City of the Dead' but estimates range from 30,000 to one million. The government has responded to the housing problem by building cities on the edge of Cairo in the desert, 6th of October and 10th of Ramadan, but many Cairo residents want to stay in the city where their jobs are. It has been estimated by David Sims, an American expert on housing in Cairo, that 'all of the new cities in the desert built over the last 25 years are equivalent to 6 months' worth of Cairo's natural growth.' Another effect of the housing shortage is that young professionals cannot marry because strong social rules say that couples cannot wed until the man can provide a home.

Positive effects of rapid growth

One of the positive effects is a large pool of workers. This means that Cairo is never short of people willing to do low paid, menial jobs. Many of these jobs involve people working in dirty environments; doing jobs that most of the population do not want to do. One example of this is the Zaballeen who collect and recycle waste.

Another positive effect is the purchasing power of such a large population which allows the economy to go faster. This will lead to an expansion in the manufacturing and retail sectors.

ACTIVITIES

1 Explain why urban areas in LICs have experienced rapid growth in the last 50 years.
2 Study the Cairo case study.
   a What percentage of Egypt's population lives in Cairo?
   b What is Cairo's population density?
   c Choose 4 problems that Cairo is experiencing due to rapid growth.
      Draw up a table which explains their causes and effects.

Extension
The 'City of the Dead' is a shanty town in Cairo.
Research eyewitness accounts of what it is like to live in the 'City of the Dead'.
Write your own 'eyewitness' account of life in Cairo's largest slum.

Review

From this section you should be able to:
- recognise the reasons for the rapid growth of urban areas in LICs
- describe and explain the effects of rapid growth on Cairo.

Sample Examination Questions

Higher tier

1   Study Figure 6 on page 216. It shows the village of Warkworth.

   a   State one physical factor which could have influenced the growth of Warkworth.   (1 mark)

   b   Explain the factors which have influenced the site of Warkworth.   (3 marks)

2   Study Figure 9 on page 218. It shows urban and rural population in 1985 and 2005.

   a   Do urban or rural areas have the highest number of people over 65 in 2005?   (1 mark)

   b   Describe and explain the changes in rural population between 1985 and 2005. You should use data in your answer.   (4 marks)

3   What is meant by the term rural depopulation? Use an example in your answer.   (2 marks)

4   The land use in urban areas in HICs is changing. Explain the social and political reasons for these changes in land use.   (4 marks)

5   Urban areas in LICs are growing rapidly. What are the effects of this rapid growth?   (4 marks)

6   Compare the advantages and disadvantages of building on brownfield and greenfield sites. Examples would assist your answer.   (6 marks)

Total 25 marks

Foundation tier

1   Study Figure 6 on page 216. It shows the village of Warkworth.

   a   State one physical factor which could have influenced the growth of Warkworth.   (1 mark)

   b   Describe the factors which have influenced the site of Warkworth.   (3 marks)

2   Study Figure 9 on page 218. It shows urban and rural population in 1985 and 2005.

   a   Do urban or rural areas have the highest number of people over 65 in 2005?   (1 mark)

   b   Describe the changes in rural population between 1985 and 2005. You should use data in your answer.   (4 marks)

3   a   What is meant by the term rural depopulation? Tick the correct statement.   (1 mark)

   A movement out of rural areas by the working population.   ☐

   A movement into rural areas by the working population.   ☐

   b   Give an example of an area where rural depopulation is occurring.   (1 mark)

4   The land use in urban areas in HICs is changing. Explain the social and political reasons for these changes in land use by completing the following sentences. Use the words below.   (4 marks)

   | later | rural | rise | grassy | ageing |
   | mixed | urban | earlier | youthful | fall |

   People are now marrying .... in life.

   There has been a .... in the number of divorces.

   There is an .... population.

   The government is allowing .... areas to expand onto greenbelt land.

5   Urban areas in LICs are growing rapidly. What are the effects of this rapid growth?

   The words in the box may help your answer.

   Examples would assist your answer.

   | air pollution | noise pollution | water pollution |
   | shanty towns | congestion | over-crowding |

   (4 marks)

6   What are the advantages and disadvantages of building on brownfield and greenfield sites? Examples would assist your answer.   (6 marks)

Total 25 marks

Population growth and distribution

> **Learning objective** – to study the changes in population growth and distribution.
>
> **Learning outcomes**
> - To be able to describe and explain the growth and distribution of global population.
> - To learn the reasons for changing patterns of birth rates and death rates and to understand the demographic transition model.
> - To recognise that there are physical and human factors which affect the distribution and density of population in China and the UK.
> - To understand what two countries are doing to cope with contrasting population problems.

Global population change

On 12 October 1999, the world's population reached 6 billion. Rapid population growth is a recent phenomenon in the history of the world. It is estimated that 2,000 years ago the world's population was about 300 million. For a very long time the world's population grew slowly and periods of growth were followed by periods of decline. It took 1,600 years for the world's population to double to 600 million.

In 1750 the world's population was estimated at 791 million. At this time 64 per cent of people lived in Asia, 21 per cent in Europe and 13 per cent in Africa. In 1900, the world's population had increased to 1.7 billion. The main growth areas at this time were in Europe, North America and South America. The percentage of people living in Asia had dropped to 57 per cent and in Africa to 8 per cent. The growth in the world's population started to rise quickly after 1900, increasing to 2.5 billion by 1950, an increase of more than 50 per cent in just 50 years. The really rapid growth in the world's population, however, took place between 1950 and 2000. In this period, the world's population increased to 6.2 billion, a 250 per cent increase. Figure 2 shows the year when the world's population reached each billion and the number of years it took to add each billion. By 2006 the population had reached 6.5 billion. And in 2008, the world's population reached 6.7 billion. You can see the estimated population at any time by going to www.popco.org/irc/popclocks which has regularly updated figures.

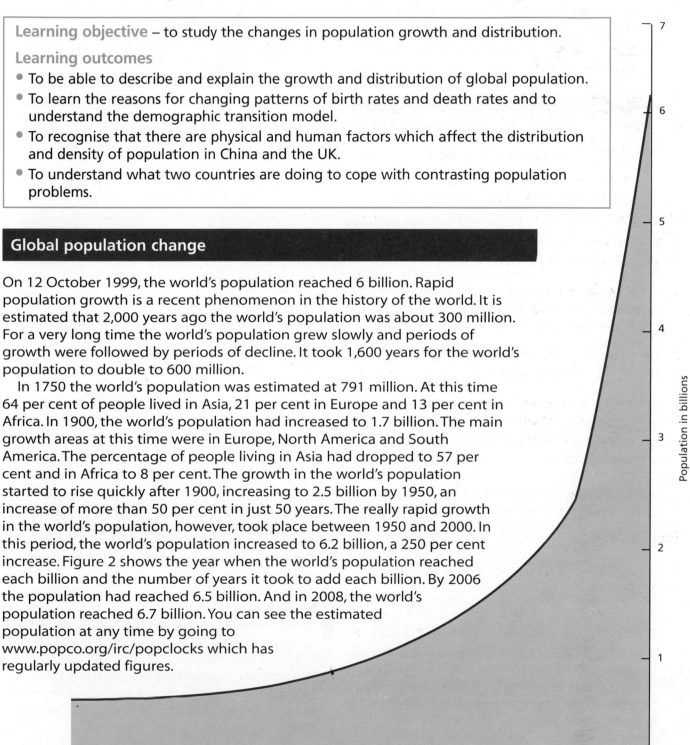

Figure 1 Graph of world population

Date	Billions	Years taken to add 1 billion
1804	1	
1927	2	123
1960	3	33
1974	4	14
1987	5	13
1999	6	12
2011 estimated	7	12

Figure 2 World population growth

Why is population growing rapidly?

The main reason for this rapid growth in population is the reduction in the death rate in LICs. The United Nations estimates that the world's population will reach 9 billion by 2050. At this time 60 per cent of the people will live in Asia, 20 per cent in Africa and 9 per cent in South America. The number of people in Europe will decline to 7 per cent, less than a third of its peak at the beginning of the twentieth century. In 1900 the population of Europe was three times that of Africa, by 2050 the population of Africa will be three times that in Europe.

How is population going to change in the future?

In 1900, 70 per cent of the world's population lived in LICs and MICs. This rose to 80 per cent by 2000 and is expected to rise to 90 per cent by the year 2050.

The world's population will continue to grow after 2050. The United Nations' long-range population projections indicate that the population will reach 9.7 billion by 2150 and stabilise at 10.5 billion after 2200. Some population experts suggest that the world's population will reach a peak of 12 billion before it starts to decline.

Predicting future population growth is a very difficult process. Some demographers suggest that the population will start to decline rapidly in 50 years' time due to falling birth rates. In the last 20 years, birth rates have been dropping in all countries. In western Europe and Japan, the average birth rate is eleven per thousand. If this continues over a number of years, then the total population of the world will begin to fall, as it has done recently in countries like Sweden and Italy.

It is possible, however, that birth rates might start to rise again in HICs because there will be a shortage of people to do the work.

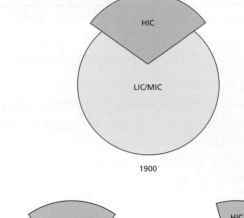

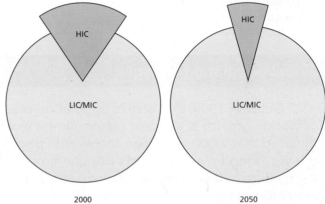

Figure 3 Pie charts showing the proportion of the world's population in LICs and HICs

ACTIVITIES

1 Use Figure 1 to estimate the world population in:
   a 1200
   b 1600
   c 2000
2 Describe the increase in world population shown in Figure 1.
3 The increase in world population after 1900 is often referred to as an explosion. Do you think this is a good description? Explain your reasons.
4 Draw a line graph to show the projected world population growth from 2000 to 2200. In which areas of the world do you think most of the growth will occur?
5 Draw a pictogram to show the percentage of people living in LICs and HICs in 1900, 2000 and 2050.

The distribution of global population

Population distribution means the pattern of where people live. World population distribution is uneven. Places which are sparsely populated contain few people. Places which are densely populated contain many people. Sparsely populated places tend to be difficult places to live. These are usually places with hostile environments, for example, Antarctica and the Sahara desert. Places which are densely populated are habitable environments, for example, Western Europe and the eastern coast of the USA.

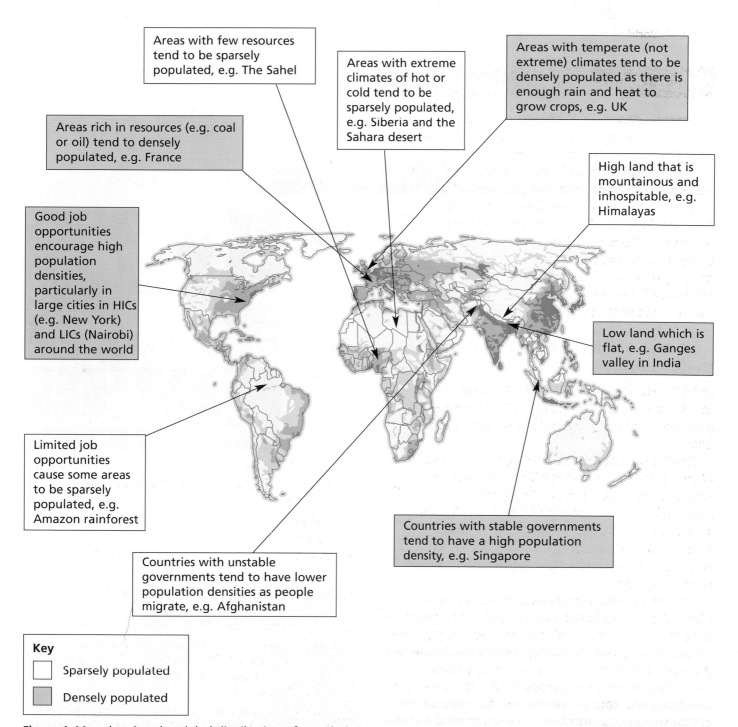

Areas with few resources tend to be sparsely populated, e.g. The Sahel

Areas with extreme climates of hot or cold tend to be sparsely populated, e.g. Siberia and the Sahara desert

Areas with temperate (not extreme) climates tend to be densely populated as there is enough rain and heat to grow crops, e.g. UK

Areas rich in resources (e.g. coal or oil) tend to densely populated, e.g. France

High land that is mountainous and inhospitable, e.g. Himalayas

Good job opportunities encourage high population densities, particularly in large cities in HICs (e.g. New York) and LICs (Nairobi) around the world

Low land which is flat, e.g. Ganges valley in India

Limited job opportunities cause some areas to be sparsely populated, e.g. Amazon rainforest

Countries with stable governments tend to have a high population density, e.g. Singapore

Countries with unstable governments tend to have lower population densities as people migrate, e.g. Afghanistan

Key

☐ Sparsely populated

▨ Densely populated

Figure 4 Map showing the global distribution of population

What are birth and death rates?

The major reason for population changes, whether in a particular country or the world as a whole, is a change in birth rates and death rates. The birth rate is the number of live babies born in a year for every 1,000 people in the total population. The death rate is the number of people in every 1,000 who die each year. The natural increase is the difference between the birth rate and death rate. If the birth rate is higher than the death rate, then the total population will increase. If the death rate is higher than the birth rate, then the total population will decrease.

Natural increase is usually expressed as a percentage per year:

$$\text{Natural increase (per cent)} = \frac{\text{Birth rate} - \text{death rate}}{10}$$

What causes birth and death rates to change?

Birth rate and death rate are affected by medical, economic, social and political factors.

Medical

In HICs new treatments, such as medicines to combat cancer, are continually being invented to combat diseases, which lead to longer lives.

Inoculations for childhood diseases have rapidly decreased the death rates in many LICs. Also in these countries improvements in medical care for children and pregnant mothers has dramatically decreased infant mortality rates which leads to families having fewer children as they know that they will grow into adulthood. In March 2006, The Health Foundation launched a three-year programme dedicated to improving the quality of health care for mothers and babies in Malawi. It aims to reduce the mortality rate among children under five by two-thirds by 2015.

Figure 5 Health care for mothers and babies reduces the mortality rate

Economic

It is now very costly to bring up a child in the UK. Increasingly in HICs couples do not want to change their lifestyle in order to have children. A typical family now pays an average of £186,032 to raise a child from birth to the age of 21, which amounts to £8,859 a year, £738 a month or £24.30 a day.

Death rate in the UK is strongly affected by poverty. Most of the areas with high death rates are classified as manufacturing centres, coalfields or ports, all areas with high unemployment. The death rate for people of all ages living in Glasgow is more than twice as high compared with that for their contemporaries in east Dorset. The male death rate in Glasgow was the highest in Britain at 1,420 per 100,000. The area of Dorset around Wimborne had the lowest death rate, at 700 per 100,000

Social

Educating women provides them with information on ways to control fertility. It also increases the time they spend in school and in further education; this leads to a greater chance of full-time careers, as education opens their eyes to life outside of the home. It also stimulates their curiosity so that they become easily bored at home. Consequently it is likely to raise the average age of marriage and delays their child bearing age. People are now marrying later in life and the average age has gone up from 24 in 1960 to 30 in 2010. Some religions such as Catholicism and Islam do not allow birth control which will generally lead to a higher birth rate.

Figure 6 Mural in China promoting the one-child family

Political

Some countries such as China and India have attempted to decrease birth rates through the introduction of family planning programmes. Other countries, such as France and Singapore are giving incentives to increase the birth rate because they are worried that the country is getting an ageing population and will not have a large enough workforce for economic growth in the future. As there will not be a large enough working population to support the dependent population, taxes will have to rise and pension entitlements fall.

Falling birth rates in Poland

In Europe, 2.1 children per woman is considered to be the population replacement level. In Poland the birth rate is just 1.23, one of the lowest in Europe. The country's population actually fell by half a million between 2000 and 2008. Estimates suggest there will be four million fewer Poles by 2030.

So why are Poles having fewer babies? It is because Polish society has undergone considerable changes in recent decades. First, more and more young people, especially women, are going to college and university. Women want to get a job and career first so they're not dependent on their husbands when they get married.

Another dramatic change came with the transition from communism to a market-based economy. Under communism unemployment officially didn't exist. Now, at 18 per cent, it's the highest in the European Union. This means there are concerns about getting and keeping a job. Couples are not prepared to have children if they do not have financial security. As well as concerns about job security, there is a housing shortage and many young people live with their parents because they cannot afford a flat. The cost of raising a family is also increasing. Many couples are not prepared to economise on things like food and holidays in order to afford having children.

Another reason why women are reluctant to break their career to start a family is because they fear they won't be able to get their jobs back after taking maternity leave.

The government has promised to build more flats for first-time buyers and introduce family-orientated legislation, which will include extending maternity leave by two weeks and improving public kindergartens. To encourage people to have more children the government has introduced a new law which pays couples a 'baby bonus' for each child they have, amounting to 1,000-zloty (£225).

The characteristics of the demographic transition model

The demographic transition model quite simply means 'population change model'. The demographic transition model shows population change in two ways:

1 Change over space: a number of countries at the same time can show the population characteristics of a different stage.

2 Change over time: a country will theoretically progress through the stages.

The model is based on what happened to the birth and death rates in western European countries.

Each of the stages of the demographic transition model has specific characteristics. These are the characteristics you can expect for each stage and possible reasons for the changes between stages:

Stage 1

There are no countries left in the world that are still at this stage when birth and death rates are very high. This stage is now confined to the poorest societies in the world like the tribes people in the Amazon. The birth and death rates can also go up and down from one year to the next, leading to a small growth or decline in the population. There are many reasons for this:

- little access to birth control
- because many children die in infancy (high infant mortality), parents tend to have more children to compensate in the hope that some will survive
- children are needed to work on the land to grow food for the family
- children are regarded as a sign of virility in some cultures
- religious beliefs (e.g. Roman Catholics and Hindus) that encourage large families
- death rates, especially among children, are high because of disease, famine, poor diet, poor hygiene, little medical science.

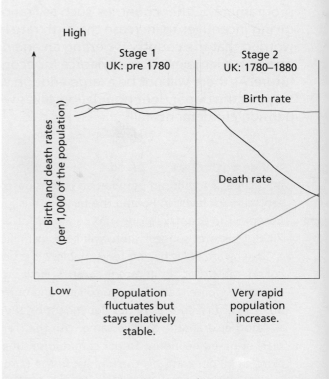

Figure 7 The demographic transition model

Stage 2

This is the stage of most rapid population growth; birth rates remain high, but death rates fall rapidly causing a high population growth. Many low income countries (LICs) are in this stage. The reasons for the death rate falling include:

- improvements in medical care, which have led to longer lives and a decrease in infant mortality
- improvements in sanitation and water supply
- the quality and quantity of food produced improves
- transport and communications improve the movements of food and medical supplies.

Stage 3

Birth rates now fall rapidly while death rates continue to fall. The total population increase slows. Many of the newly industrialised countries are at this stage. The reasons for this could be:

- increased access to contraception
- lower infant mortality rates means there is less need to have a bigger family
- industrialisation and mechanisation means fewer labourers are required
- as wealth increases, the desire for material possessions takes over the desire for large families. Equality for women means that they are able to follow a career rather than being pressurised into having a family.

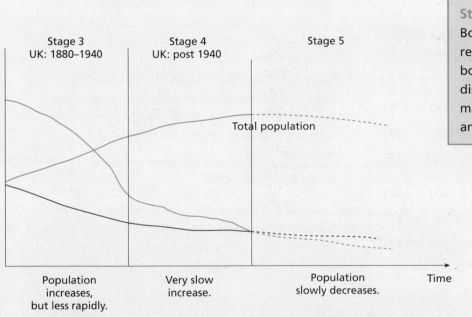

Stage 3
UK: 1880–1940

Stage 4
UK: post 1940

Stage 5

Total population

Population increases, but less rapidly.

Very slow increase.

Population slowly decreases.

Time

Stage 4

Both birth rates and death rates remain low, fluctuating with 'baby booms' and epidemics of illnesses and disease. This stage is characteristic of many of the high income countries and results in a steady population.

Stage 5

In this stage the death rate is higher than the birth rate, therefore there is a natural decrease so population falls. This stage was not on the model when it was first devised but has been added to show the recent developments in population change. This stage contains some countries in central and eastern Europe, such as Germany and Estonia where birth rates have dropped very low.

ACTIVITIES

Higher

1   Every ten seconds 45 people are born and 16 die somewhere in the world.

   a   How many more people are there in the world:

      i   every minute?

      ii   every hour?

      iii   every day?

      iv   every year?

   b   What will the long-term effects be on a country with a very low birth rate?

2   Study the following figures for birth and death rates per thousand for England and Wales between 1701 and 2001.

	1701	1721	1741	1761	1781	1801
b.r.	36	35	37	36	36	37
d.r.	34	36	36	32	29	22

	1821	1841	1861	1881	1901	1921
b.r.	34	31	32	33	30	21
d.r.	21	20	21	20	17	13

	1941	1961	1981	2001
b.r.	15	17	14	12
d.r.	13	11	12	11

   a   Use the figures to draw a graph for birth and death rates. Use the same axes.

   b   Draw vertical lines on the graph to divide it into the four stages of the demographic transition model.

   c   Which year shows the greatest natural increase in population?

   d   Which is the only year to show a natural decrease in population?

3   Draw a sketch of the demographic transition model. On your sketch extend the lines for the birth rate, death rate and total population to show what a fifth stage might look like.

Foundation

1   Every ten seconds 45 babies are born and 16 people die somewhere in the world. How many extra people are there in the world (the difference between those being born and those that die):

   a   every ten seconds?

   b   every minute?

2   Use the figures in the table (left) to draw a graph of birth and death rates for England and Wales between 1701 and 2001.

ACTIVITIES

1   Look at the table below. According to this table what will the population of the world be in 2050?

2   What factors might cause this estimation to be wrong?

3   Give two reasons why death rates are falling in LICs? Why are birth rates falling in HICs?

	Population 2000 (m)	Births per 1,000	Deaths per 1,000	Natural increase	Doubling time in years	Projected population 2025 (m)	Projected population 2050 (m)
World	6,067	22	9	1.4	52	7,810	9,000
HICs	1,184	11	10	0.1	809	1,236	1,200
LICs	4,883	25	9	1.6	42	6,575	7,800

What are the physical and human factors that affect the distribution and density of population in China and the UK?

Population distribution means the pattern of where people live. Places which are sparsely populated contain few people. Places which are densely populated contain many people.

Population density is a measurement of the number of people in an area. It is an average number. Population density is calculated by dividing the number of people by area. Population density is usually shown as the number of people per square kilometre.

Population is not evenly distributed. There are many reasons why people live in certain areas. These reasons can be physical or human.

- **Physical factors** include relief, climate and water supply. Flat lowland areas with a temperate climate and a reliable water source are usually densely populated and conversely areas with extreme climates are usually sparsely populated.

- **Human factors** include employment, industry and transport. The focus of communication networks will lead to high population densities because goods can be easily transported and industry will want to set up in these areas. Transport and trade mean that dense populations can be found at major ports.

The density of population in China

The distribution and density of population has been greatly influenced by physical and/or human conditions as can be seen by comparing the maps (Figures 8 and 9).

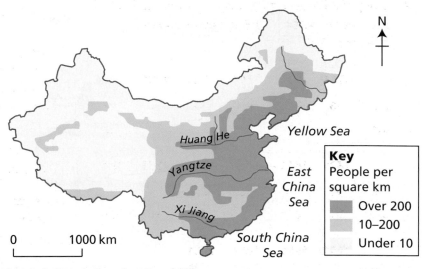

Figure 8 Population density of China

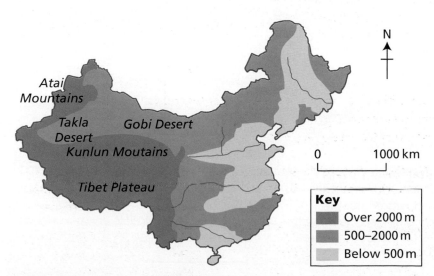

Figure 9 Physical features of China

The density of population in the UK

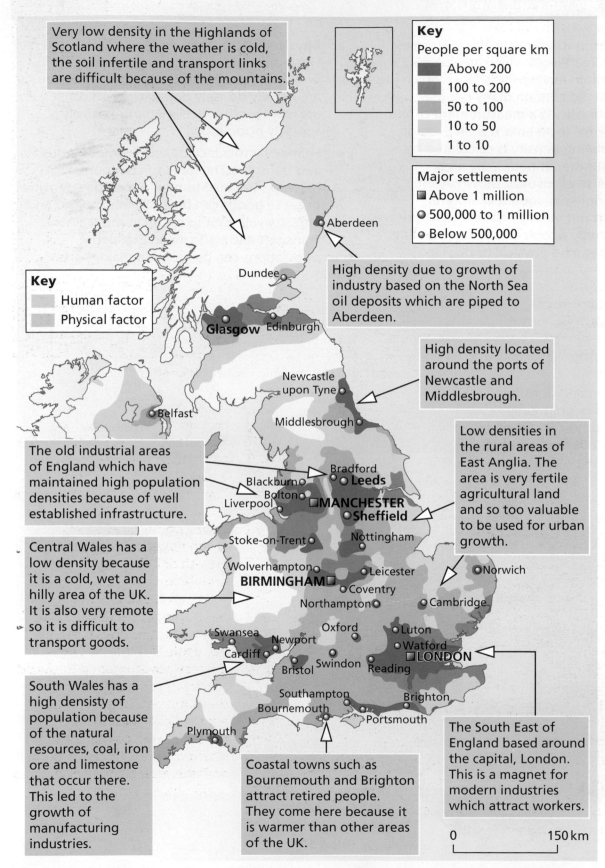

Very low density in the Highlands of Scotland where the weather is cold, the soil infertile and transport links are difficult because of the mountains.

Key
People per square km
- Above 200
- 100 to 200
- 50 to 100
- 10 to 50
- 1 to 10

Major settlements
- Above 1 million
- 500,000 to 1 million
- Below 500,000

Key
- Human factor
- Physical factor

High density due to growth of industry based on the North Sea oil deposits which are piped to Aberdeen.

High density located around the ports of Newcastle and Middlesbrough.

The old industrial areas of England which have maintained high population densities because of well established infrastructure.

Low densities in the rural areas of East Anglia. The area is very fertile agricultural land and so too valuable to be used for urban growth.

Central Wales has a low density because it is a cold, wet and hilly area of the UK. It is also very remote so it is difficult to transport goods.

South Wales has a high densisty of population because of the natural resources, coal, iron ore and limestone that occur there. This led to the growth of manufacturing industries.

Coastal towns such as Bournemouth and Brighton attract retired people. They come here because it is warmer than other areas of the UK.

The South East of England based around the capital, London. This is a magnet for modern industries which attract workers.

0   150 km

Figure 10 Reasons for density of population in the UK

The sparsest populated areas are the mountains over 2000 m and the desert areas. They all have population density of less than ten people per square kilometre, and are found in the west of China. The most densely populated areas are the coastal areas and the fertile floodplains of the major rivers, found in the east of the country. Climate is another important physical factor which affects the density of population. The climate of China is very diverse, from temperate to tropical and from arid to monsoonal. The large cities of Beijing and Shanghai do not get extreme climates and is one reason for their continued growth. There are no large settlements in the arid desert areas or the very wet and cold mountains.

Figure 11 Mountainous desert region, Xiniang Province, China

Figure 12 High density housing in Shanghai

Human factors are also very important in the distribution of population. In China the richer areas which have more industry have higher population densities. These areas are accessible with good communication links which has encouraged the growth of industry and population.

The level of economic development decreases from east to west, as does the population. In the 1970s the Chinese government introduced a strategy for coastal economic development. This led to rapid economic development along the south-east coastal area, which drew in workers, making it now the most densely populated region based around Shanghai.

Case Study: What has China done to reduce its birth rate?

Countries have contrasting population problems
Some countries want to reduce their birth rate and other countries are trying to increase their birth rate.

What has China done to reduce its birth rate?
In 1979 China had a quarter of the world's population. Two-thirds of its population was under the age of 30 years, and the largest cohort born in the 1950s and 1960s were entering their reproductive years. The government saw strict population control as essential to economic reform and to an improvement in living standards, so the one-child family policy was introduced.

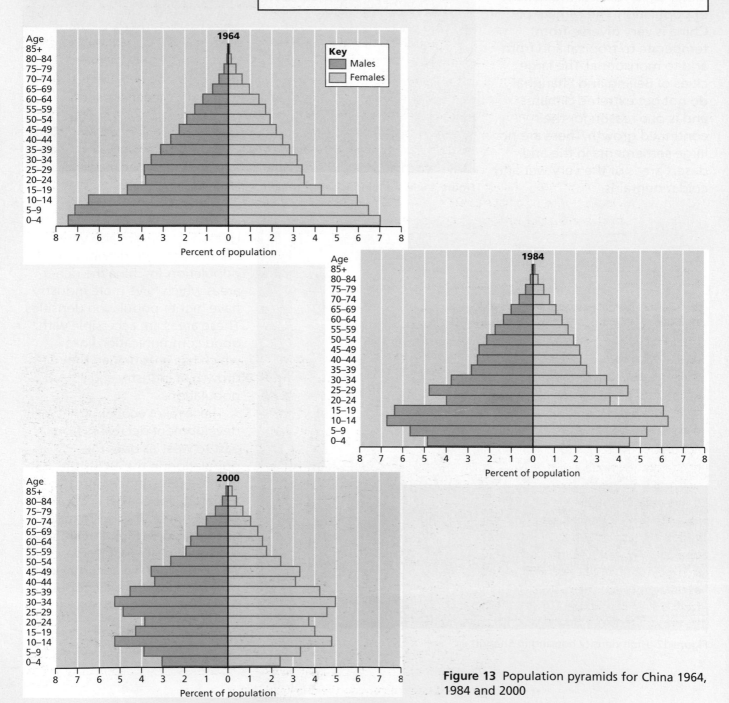

Figure 13 Population pyramids for China 1964, 1984 and 2000

Incentives

Couples with only one child were given a 'one-child certificate' entitling them to a package of benefits, including:

- cash bonuses
- longer maternity leave
- free education
- free medical care
- better child care
- preferential housing arrangements.

Disincentives

Couples were required to pledge that they would not have more children. If they had another child they lost all their privileges, could be sacked from their jobs and also received heavy fines.

People were monitored by the 'granny police'. These women made regular household visits to keep track of the status of each family under their jurisdiction and collected information on which women were using contraceptives, the methods used, and which had become pregnant. They then reported to the brigade women's leader, who collected the information and took it to a monthly meeting of the commune birth-planning committee. Each commune was allowed only a quota of births. To satisfy these quotas unmarried young people were persuaded to postpone marriage, couples without children were advised to 'wait their turn', women with unauthorised pregnancies were pressured to have abortions, and those who already had children were urged to use contraception or undergo sterilisation.

Recent changes to the one child policy

In rural areas, where approximately 70 per cent of the people live, a second child is generally allowed after five years, but this usually only applies if the first child is a girl. A third child is allowed among some ethnic minorities and in remote, underpopulated areas.

For urban residents and government employees, the policy is strictly enforced, with a few exceptions. The exceptions include families in which the first child has a disability or both parents work in high-risk occupations (such as mining) or are themselves from one-child families.

Figure 14 Mural promoting the one-child policy

Case Study: What has Singapore done to increase its birth rate?

What has Singapore done to increase its birth rate?

In the 1960s Singapore had a high birth rate and a lowering death rate being in stage 2 of the DTM. The government introduced a 'two is enough' policy. This policy was very successful and the birth rate fell considerably to a low of nine per thousand. In the late 1980s the government realised that if the birth rate continued to fall they would not have enough workers and the economy would stop growing. So in1987 they introduced the 'three or more policy' which gave people incentives to have more children. It has not been very successful.

Figure 15 shows that the birth rate is continuing to decline. In 2008 there were only 1.26 babies born per woman which compares with a rate of 5.8 in the 1960s. In December 2007 the Prime Minister of Singapore stated: 'To sustain growth and vitality in our economy, we need a growing population in Singapore with talents in every field.'

Figure 15 Changes in birth rates in Singapore

Incentives

Singapore now wants families to have more children and has implemented a series of incentives. Parents now get the following incentives:

- A cash gift of $3,000 each for first and second child.
- A cash gift of $6,000 each for third and fourth child.
- The second to fourth children can also have a savings account called a Children Development Account (CDA). This is a special savings account where any money that is saved will be matched by the government. Parents can save in the CDA any time until the day before the child's sixth birthday. The savings will be matched up to a total $6,000 for the second child and $12,000 each for the third and fourth child.
- 3 months' maternity leave for mothers.
- 3 days of paternity leave on the birth of the first four children for fathers.
- 5 days of paid childcare leave a year.
- With more children, parents are entitled to upgrade to a bigger flat. If couples have only one child then they can buy only a three-room flat. With two children they can buy a three- or four-room flat and so on. Couples with no children are not entitled to buy anything more than a three-room flat.
- Couples receive $95 for a maid if they have children under 12.

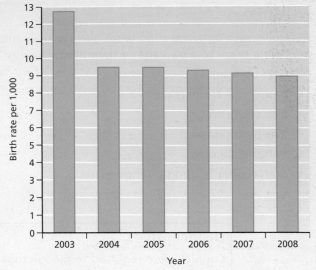

Figure 16 Some of the incentives

Review

By the end of this section you should be able to:

- describe and explain the growth and distribution of global population
- learn the reasons for changing patterns of birth rates and death rates and to understand the demographic transition model
- recognise that there are physical and human factors which affect the distribution and density of population in China and the UK
- understand what two countries are doing to cope with contrasting population problems.

ACTIVITY

Singapore has a slogan of 'three or more' to promote its population policy. Invent your own slogan for Singapore and incorporate it on a poster to promote their population policy.

Characteristics of population

Learning objective – to study how the characteristics and the structure of the population vary from place to place.

Learning outcomes
- To be able to understand population characteristics at a local scale.
- To be able to recognise and interpret different population pyramids.
- To understand the consequences of youthful and ageing populations.
- To know the advantages and disadvantages of an ageing population in one country.

The characteristics of population on a local scale

In the UK information about the population is collected in a Census which is a questionnaire that is delivered to all households once every ten years. The first Census was administered in 1801 and, apart from an interruption for the Second World War, there are accurate figures up to 2001.

Most nations in the world now conduct regular censuses. Figure 17 contains information on Welwyn Hatfield which shows characteristics of the population in 2001.

ACTIVITIES

Higher

Study Figure 17 on pages 244–245.

1 Draw population pyramids for Peartree and Welwyn North.

2 Describe the differences in the population structure of the two wards.

3 Suggest reasons for these differences.

4 Compare the ethnic structure of the two wards.

Foundation

Study Figure 17 on pages 244–245.

1 What percentage of the population is under 30 in:
   a Peartree ward
   b Welwyn North ward?

2 There are more elderly people in Welwyn North than Peartree. Suggest why.

3 Which is the most common ethnic group for both wards?

4 Compare the ethnic structure of the two wards.

Extension

Use data from National Statistics Online to produce a PowerPoint™ presentation for your area, comparing two different wards.

Ethnic stucture

Indicator	Peartree	Welwyn North
Ethnic structure	All People (Persons) Count 6,965	All People (Persons) Count 4,227
	White: British (Persons) % 90.55	White: British (Persons) % 91.08
	White: Irish (Persons) % 1.45	White: Irish (Persons) % 1.35
	White: Other White (Persons) % 2.20	White: Other White (Persons) % 2.84
	Mixed: White and Black Caribbean (Persons) % 0.69	Mixed: White and Black Caribbean (Persons) % 0.21
	Mixed: White and Black African (Persons) % 0.31	Mixed: White and Black African (Persons) % 0.40
	Mixed: White and Asian (Persons) % 0.62	Mixed: White and Asian (Persons) % 0.73
	Mixed: Other Mixed (Persons) % 0.30	Mixed: Other Mixed (Persons) % 0.14
	Asian or Asian British: Indian (Persons) % 0.70	Asian or Asian British: Indian (Persons) % 1.30
	Asian or Asian British: Pakistani (Persons) % 0.30	Asian or Asian British: Pakistani (Persons) % 0.09
	Asian or Asian British: Bangladeshi (Persons) % 0.06	Asian or Asian British: Bangladeshi (Persons) % 0.00
	Asian or Asian British: Other Asian (Persons) % 0.14	Asian or Asian British: Other Asian (Persons) % 0.38
	Black or Black British: Caribbean (Persons) % 0.56	Black or Black British: Caribbean (Persons) % 0.40
	Black or Black British: African (Persons) % 1.06	Black or Black British: African (Persons) % 0.19
	Black or Black British: Other Black (Persons) % 0.10	Black or Black British: Other Black (Persons) % 0.00
	Chinese or other ethnic group: Chinese (Persons) % 0.53	Chinese or other ethnic group: Chinese (Persons) % 0.45
	Chinese or other ethnic group: Other ethnic group (Persons) % 0.43	Chinese or other ethnic group: Other ethnic group (Persons) % 0.43
Explanation	The two wards show a similar ethnic structure although there is a significantly higher black population in Peartree. Information from the census on ethnicity might prove very useful for businesses interested in opening restaurants and clothing shops.	

Gender

Indicator	Peartree	Welwyn North
Gender	Males (Persons) Count 3,363	Males (Persons) Count 2,059
	Females (Persons) Count 3,622	Females (Persons) Count 2,169
Explanation	In both wards there are more females than males. This reflects the national pattern where 51.3% of the population is female. This is due primarily to females having a longer life expectancy and so there are a greater number of elderly women than men.	

Figure 17 Census data from Welwyn Hatfield, Hertfordshire

Occupational structure

Indicator	Peartree	Welwyn North
Occupational structure: Percentage in employment management and professional	20%	47%
Unemployed	Unemployed people aged 16–74: Aged 16–24 % 28.16	Unemployed people aged 16–74: Aged 16–24 % 16.33
	Aged 25–49 % 26.22	Aged 25–49 % 12.24
	Aged 50 and over (Persons) % 16.09	Unemployed people aged 16–74: Aged 50 and over (Persons) % 38.78
Explanation	The percentage of people claiming unemployment is high in Peartree for the two younger age groups. This could be due to a number of factors: • Poor academic qualifications. This is also reflected in the low percentage of people employed in management. • One parent families who have to look after children and can't go to work. • A lack of job opportunities. Therefore it would be advisable to try to create more jobs in Peartree to reduce the numbers claiming unemployment benefits. The percentage of unemployed in the Welwyn North ward in the over 50 age group is high. This could be caused by people in an affluent area retiring early. The relative affluence of the wards can be seen with the percentage employed in managerial and professional positions. Quite clearly there is likely to be a richer population in Welwyn North.	

Religion

Indicator	Peartree	Welwyn North
Religion	People stating religion as: Christian (Persons) % 62.39	People stating religion as: Christian (Persons) % 73.25
	People stating religion as: Buddhist (Persons) % 0.20	People stating religion as: Buddhist (Persons) % 0.24
	People stating religion as: Hindu (Persons) % 0.53	People stating religion as: Hindu (Persons) % 0.92
	People stating religion as: Jewish (Persons) % 0.29	People stating religion as: Jewish (Persons) % 0.83
	People stating religion as: Muslim (Persons) % 1.02	People stating religion as: Muslim (Persons) % 0.59
	People stating religion as: Sikh (Persons) % 0.04	People stating religion as: Sikh (Persons) % 0.26
	People stating religion as: Other religions (Persons) % 0.24	People stating religion as: Other religions (Persons) % 0.43
	People stating religion as: No religion (Persons) % 23.82	People stating religion as: No religion (Persons) % 16.23
Explanation	A higher percentage of the population in Welwyn North stated that they belonged to a recognised religion. All religions other than Muslim have a higher percentage in Welwyn north than Peartree. This information may be useful to religious groups when they decide where to build a new church or mosque.	

Population structure

Indicator	Peartree	Welwyn North
Population structure	All Persons; Aged 0–15 (Persons, Jun06) % 25.5	% 18.73
	All Persons; Aged 16–29 (Persons, Jun06) % 21.6	% 11.77
	All Persons; Aged 30–44 (Persons, Jun06) % 25.4	% 23.16
	All Persons; Aged 45–64 (Males), 45–59 (Females) (Persons, Jun06) % 16.7	% 29.40
	All Persons; Aged 65 and Over (Males), 60 and Over (Females) (Persons, Jun06) % 10.8	% 17.34
Explanation	Welwyn North has a much higher percentage of elderly people, therefore the council can use this information to provide better services for this age group, such as care homes. We can also see that Peartree has the highest percentage of children and young adults so the focus should be on schooling and the provision of facilities for young families.	

What are population pyramids?

The most important demographic characteristic of a population is its age–sex structure. Population pyramids (also known as age–sex pyramids) graphically display this information.

Population pyramids display the percentage or actual amount of a population broken down by sex and age. The five-year age groups on the Y-axis show the long-term trends in the birth and death rates but also reflect shorter-term baby booms, wars and epidemics.

Countries that are at different levels of economic growth have differently shaped pyramids.

Rapid growth: Philippines – a typical LIC

This pyramid of the Philippines (Figure 18) shows a triangle-shaped pyramid and reflects a high growth rate of about 2.1 per cent annually. The age–sex pyramid for the Philippines is typical of a low income country that is experiencing rapid population growth. The wide base indicates that there are large numbers of dependent children aged 0–14 in the total population, the result of high levels of fertility. The top of the pyramid is narrow and indicates that only a small proportion of the population lives to old age. This type of population pyramid can be compared with late stage 1/early stage 2 of the demographic

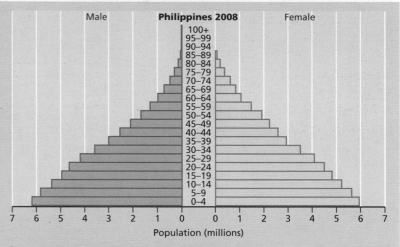

Figure 18 Population pyramid for the Philippines

transition model. This type of population structure is likely to have a number of important implications:

- Limited resources will be stretched to meet the needs of the large number of dependent children for schooling, nutrition and health care.
- As this group reaches working age, a large number of jobs will need to be created to enable them to support themselves and their families.
- As this group reaches child-bearing age, it is likely that fertility rates will remain high, with continued high rates of natural population increase.

Slow growth: Brazil – a typical MIC

The pyramid for Brazil shows a typical shape for a former LIC country experiencing economic growth. There is still a pyramid shape but the population steps do not decrease as rapidly as LICs. This is because of improvements in medicine and diet leading to a lower death rate (seven per thousand). The birth rate, however, is still high (eighteen per thousand) leading to continued population growth. The growth rate in 2008 was 1.33 per cent. This type of population pyramid can be compared with the early stage 3 of the demographic transition model. With continued improvements in living conditions

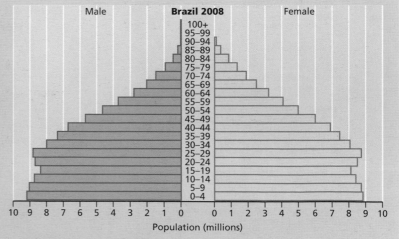

Figure 19 Population pyramid for Brazil

the elderly will live longer and the birth rate will decline, which eventually will lead to a pyramid that is shaped more like a bullet, with the population cohorts under age 60 of roughly equal size.

Negative growth: Germany – a typical HIC

Germany is experiencing a period of negative growth (–0.1 per cent). As negative growth in a country continues, the population is reduced. A population can shrink due to a declining birth rate and a stable death rate. Increased emigration may also be a contributor to a declining population. After the Second World War, workers from several southern European countries, especially Turkey, were encouraged to emigrate to Germany. The bulges in the 35–50 age groups in the 2008 pyramid show the children of these emigrants (see Figure 20).

Several European countries have begun to take on this shape and can be compared to the possible fifth stage of the demographic transition model.

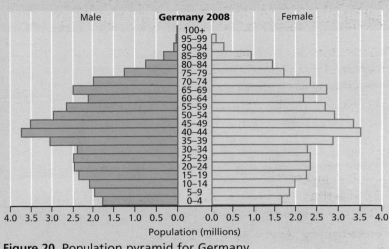

Figure 20 Population pyramid for Germany

ACTIVITIES

Higher

1   Study the population pyramids for the Philippines, Brazil and Germany in Figures 18, 19 and 20 on pages 246–247.

   a   Describe the population structure of the Philippines.

   b   What are the differences between the three pyramids? Use data in your answer.

2   a   Use the data in the table below to draw modified population pyramids. (Draw only four bars.)

   b   State whether each country is experiencing rapid growth, slow growth or negative growth.

Percentage of people in selected age groups for UK, Ethiopia and Ireland

Age	0–19		20–39		40–59		60+	
	M	F	M	F	M	F	M	F
UK	13	12	15	15	12	12	9	12
Ethiopia	28	28	13	13	6	6	3	2
Ireland	18	14	11	7	17	14	10	9

Foundation

1   Study the population pyramids for the Philippines, Brazil and Germany in Figures 18, 19 and 20 on pages 246–247.

a   Which country has the greatest percentage of its population in the age range:

   i   0–19   ii 60+   iii 20–59?

b   Describe three differences between the population pyramids for the Philippines and Germany.

2   Below are two population pyramids. One is for Sweden and the other is for Mexico.

   a   Which pyramid is for Mexico and which one is for Sweden?

   b   Give reasons for your answer.

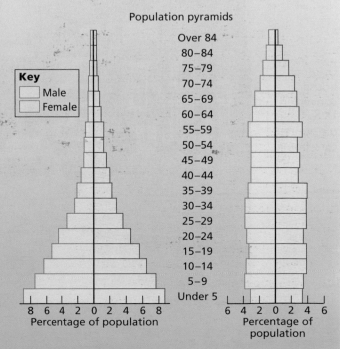

Figure 21 Population pyramids for Mexico and Sweden

What are the consequences of an ageing population?

Negative	Positive
In countries like the UK, the ageing of the population is an increasingly worrying problem. In 1950 there was only one pensioner for every five economically active people. Today this has increased to three pensioners for every five people of working age, which is causing a strain on the provision of state pensions as they are funded by the taxes of those people in work. It is obviously going to become increasingly difficult for the government to provide adequate pensions for the over 65s. Do the over 65s have a right to a state-funded pension? What can be done to ease the situation? These are possible solutions: ● Increase the taxes paid by the working population. ● Raise the age of retirement. This is set to change in the UK. In the year 2026 retirement age will be 66, increasing to 67 in 2036 and 68 in 2046. ● Abolish state pensions and make people pay for their own private pension plans.	The elderly can play an important part in the community by providing their time and expertise free of charge, such as working in charity shops.
With an increasing number of over 65s and life expectancy increasing all the time, there will be a much greater demand for health care and support services. At present hospitals are already short of bed space and specialist nursing for the elderly. The number of residential care homes is likely to increase dramatically, but they are very expensive (they can cost up to £2,000 a month and many people have to sell their homes to finance their own care).	With more people having leisure time there is a growth in the number of jobs in the leisure industry.
The amount of money spent on education might have to be cut to finance the elderly.	Unemployment rates will be low as the percentage of elderly increases.
With people living longer there is a large demand on housing using up large amounts of land.	

Original house converted to residential care home.

Modern extension built due to increasing demands of an ageing population.

Figure 22 A residential care home in Hertfordshire

What are the consequences of a youthful population?

Negative	Positive
The large numbers of children is one of the main problems facing governments of LICs. More than 40 per cent of the population of Africa is under fifteen. In The Gambia it has reached 50 per cent. This puts an enormous strain on the economies of these countries as they try to provide this huge number of children with education, health care and food. In many countries education is not free, especially at secondary level, although in The Gambia the government in 2004 made it free for girls to encourage them to stay at school and become educated rather than get married at an early age and have children. Attendance at secondary schools, especially in rural areas, is still very low which results in large numbers of unqualified workers, many of whom end up on the streets begging.	Children can look after their parents so less money needs to be spent on care for the elderly.
Disease among children is widespread with common (yet curable) complaints like measles and diarrhoea sometimes leading to death because of the lack of doctors and nurses and of necessary medical resources such as vaccines. Hospitals are non-existent in most rural areas.	There is a large, active workforce available for economic growth.

Figure 23 Children in The Gambia

ACTIVITIES

1 Draw typical population pyramids for the following areas:
   a an HIC
   b an LIC.
2 Define the terms 'youthful population' and 'ageing population'.
3 Explain the problems caused by an ageing population.

Case Study: The advantages and disadvantages of an ageing population in Japan

Introduction

Japan's population is ageing at an alarming rate, giving concern about economic growth and living standards. Below are some key facts about Japan's population:

● Japan's total population peaked at 127.8 million in 2005 and is forecast to fall by 30 per cent to just under 90 million by 2055.
● Japan's proportion of elderly is the highest in the world. In 2006, 20 per cent of Japan's people were 65 years or older. In the USA 12 per cent of people were over 65 and in the UK 16 per cent were older than 65.
● Japan has the fastest ageing population in the world.
● The number of people aged over 65 is predicted to rise sharply. The following are the projected figures.

Year	2015	2035	2055
Percentage	27	34	41

● The percentage of economically active will fall from 66 per cent in 2006 to 51 per cent in 2055.
● The birth rate hit a record low in 2005 of 1.29 children per woman. A rate of 2.07 is needed to keep the population from shrinking.

What are the disadvantages of an ageing population?

The results of an ageing population include a workforce too small to support the huge number of retirees, not enough tax money to pay for pensions and a dramatic increase in the cost of health care for the elderly.

Workforce

The biggest worry in Japan is economic growth and employment. Businesses already face difficulties finding new recruits. The labour force in the 15–24 age bracket, which stood at more than 8 million in 1990, will have shrunk to 5.3 million by 2015. Employment agencies are growth businesses in Japan these days. At Tokyo's Narita airport, the uniformed marshals who direct arriving passengers to the correct passport control queue are mostly of pensionable age. Taxi drivers and small-shop keepers are more likely than not to be grey-haired pensioners, as is the staff on the Tokyo subway.

Figure 24 shows how the proportion of workers to pensioners is dropping. Between 1990 and 2025 there will be only two workers paying taxes to support the pensioners compared with nearly six workers in 1990.

One solution to the shortage of workers is to bring in migrant labour. There are now 2 million foreigners living in Japan, 200,000 of them illegally. The IT sector in particular is looking outside Japan for new workers. Software engineers have been recruited in India, and Japanese companies have set up training schools in Beijing (China) and Ulan Bator (Mongolia) before bringing the graduates to Japan. Other solutions are to encourage men to work after retirement and to increase the number of women working which has historically been very low.

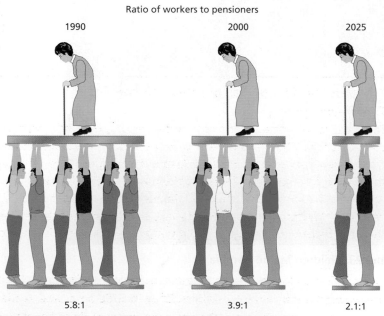

Ratio of workers to pensioners

1990   2000   2025

5.8:1   3.9:1   2.1:1

Figure 24 The changing ratio of workers to pensioners in Japan

Pensions

The state pension system will be the first to feel the negative effects of the ageing population. The government under Prime Minister Junichiro Koizumi introduced pension reforms in 2005 which included: the age of retirement rising from 60 to 65 by 2030; and higher pension contributions from the employers, employees and the government.

However, the reforms have not solved the problem of the pension burden and unless the birth-rate rises, which is unlikely, the amount of money that pensioners receive will have to fall.

Health care

Japan has a long tradition of honouring the old. Every year, National Respect the Aged Day is a public holiday. About 93 per cent of Japanese people who are over the age of 60 live at home, either on their own, with a spouse or with other family members. But traditions are changing; the number of people living in nursing homes or care homes is increasing. Paying for caring for the elderly accounts for half of Japan's health budget, and Japan has a huge financial deficit on the health budget. That is putting pressure on the nation's economy, and the expense of providing care facilities will go on rising as people live longer and the proportion of elderly people increases. In 2000, a tax on over 40s was introduced to help pay for equipment such as wheelchairs and send carers to private homes and retirement institutions to help the elderly.

More changes were added in 2006, including incentives to promote more independent living at home. Much more controversially a new health insurance scheme for the over 75s was introduced in 2008. It has already been nicknamed the 'hurry up and die' scheme, and has caused a political storm. Under recent changes the fee the hospital receives for a patient goes down after 100 days as an incentive to shorten hospital admissions which are long by international standards.

There has been an increase in the number of nursing homes but nowhere near enough have been built to house the numbers who need them.

At just one care home in Tokyo there are hundreds of people on the waiting list and to make matters worse one floor of the home is unused because they cannot get enough young staff to work there.

Figure 25 Elderly Japanese in a nursing home

What are the advantages of an ageing population?

The greying yen

Tetsuro Sugiura, chief economist at the Mizuho research institute in Tokyo, describes it as the 'grey boom'. It used to be that the elderly were anxious about the future and saved even into their old age. This is no longer true. Japan's pensioners are spend, spend, spending. They are buying luxury goods, travelling and indulging their taste for expensive foods. In the past they would try to leave as much as possible to their children who would have looked after them in old age. However, that unspoken family contract is nothing like as firm as it was. The children are doing less caring, and the parents have fewer inhibitions about spending the money they have saved. With so many old people spending their incomes this could lead to a growth in the economy.

Technology

The greying of Japan has led to a technological explosion. It has inspired an array of gadgets for people who are worried about elderly relatives. They include an online kettle that automatically sends emails to up to three people when it is switched on, and internet-linked sensors that can be attached to everyday items such as fridge doors and bathroom mats. These gadgets allow people to check up on their elderly relatives.

Review

By the end of this section you should be able to:

- understand population characteristics at a local scale
- recognise and interpret different population pyramids
- understand the consequences of youthful and ageing populations
- know the advantages and disadvantages of an ageing population in one country.

Sample Examination Questions

Higher tier

1 Study the graph of world population growth below (Figure 26).

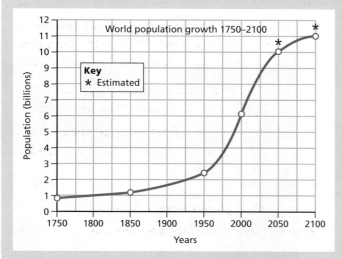

Figure 26 World population growth

   a When did the population reach 6 billion?

                                               (1 mark)

   b When is the population expected to reach 10 billion? **(2 marks)**

   c Describe the growth of world population. Use data in your answer. **(3 marks)**

2 Study the population pyramid for Germany in Figure 20 on page 247.

   a How many of Germany's female population were aged 10 to 14 years in 2008? **(1 mark)**

   b Give two of the changes to Germany's population structure that are likely to occur between 2000 and 2025. **(2 marks)**

   c Germany is an example of a country with an ageing population. Describe the problems this may cause. **(4 marks)**

3 Study the diagram which shows how population may change over time below (Figure 27).

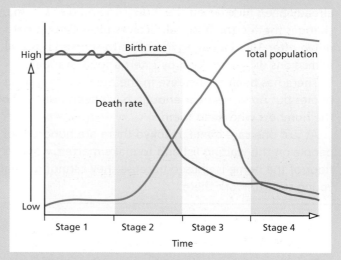

Figure 27

   a What is the name for this model? **(1 mark)**

   b Compare the birth rate, death rate and total population in stage 2 with those in stage 4. **(3 marks)**

   c Explain why the total population grew so rapidly in stage 2. **(3 marks)**

4 For one country that you have studied which is trying to increase its birth rate, describe the incentives and disincentives that have been used. **(5 marks)**

Total 25 marks

Sample Examination Questions

Foundation tier

1 Study the graph of world population growth (Figure 26 on page 252).

  a When did the population reach 6 billion?

    (1 marks)

  b When is the population expected to reach 10 billion? **(2 marks)**

  c Use the graph to complete the paragraph. Use some of the words in the box.

less	more	two	three
rapidly	slowly	2050	1850

In 1750 the population was .... than 1 billion. The population rose .... until 1950, at which stage the population was over .... billion. It then grew .... until 2000. It is estimated to continue growing rapidly until .... After this date growth will be less rapid, reaching 11 billion in 2100. **(5 marks)**

2 Study the population pyramid for Germany in Figure 20 on page 247.

  a How many of Germany's female population were aged 10 to 14 years in 2008? Tick the correct box.

    1.5 million ☐

    2.0 million ☐

    2.5 million ☐

    3.0 million ☐ **(1 mark)**

  b Using the population pyramid for Germany, complete the passage below which describes likely changes to Germany's population structure between 2008 and 2033. Choose the three correct answers from the box:

male	increase	stay the same
0 and 20 years		
female	decrease	40 and 59 years

The total number of people aged between .... will decrease.

The total number of people aged 65 and over will ....

There will be more .... aged over 70. **(3 marks)**

  c Germany is an example of a country with an ageing population. Describe the problems this may cause. **(4 marks)**

3 Study the diagram which shows how population may change over time (Figure 27 on page 252).

  a Which stages (1 to 4) are described below? **(2 marks)**

Description	Stage
Birth rate is high and death rate is falling	
Birth rate and death rate are both low	

  b In which stage (1 to 4) did the total population start to increase rapidly? **(1 mark)**

  c In which stage (1 to 4) could a country be described as an HIC? **(1 mark)**

4 For one country that you have studied which is trying to increase its birth rate describe the incentives and disincentives that have been used. **(5 marks)**

Total 25 marks

Population movement

Learning objective – to study population movement.

Learning outcomes
- To know the different types of population movement.
- To understand that migration can be classified in several ways.

Different types of population movement

The movement of people can be divided between migration and other short-term population movement.

Migration

Migration is the movement of people from one area to another, with the intention of remaining there permanently or semi-permanently. The United Nations defines permanent as a change of residence lasting more than one year. If people leave one country and go to another country, this will affect the number of people living in each country. People who leave a country are called emigrants and those entering are called immigrants.

People migrate to get away from something they do not like (a push factor), or may be attracted to another area that is of greater benefit to them (a pull factor).

Push factors include:	Pull factors include:
Natural disasters such as volcanic eruptions or floods. Harsh climates.	Hazard-free areas of the world.
War and political conflicts.	Political asylum, freedom of speech.
Lack of jobs leading to poverty.	Higher living standards and employment opportunities.
Poor or short supply of housing. Lack of medical facilities.	Plenty of available housing. Good medical and welfare services.

Short-term population movements

Short-term population movements can vary in time, usually less than a year. They involve a circulatory movement which involves a change of residence. This would include people going on holiday, students going to university, gap year students and commuters. A commuter is a person who lives in one area and travels to another area where they work. This movement could be between settlements, for example, from towns in the south-east of England to London; or within the settlement, for example, where people who live in the suburbs travel into the city centre for work.

A classification of migration

There are many reasons that cause people to migrate. Migrations can be classified as national or international, long-term or short-term, voluntary and forced. It is possible for a migrant to be a combination of these factors, for example, a refugee from Ethiopia who moved permanently to the neighbouring country of Sudan would be classified as a long-term, forced, international migrant.

National or international?

National migrants move from one part of a country to another part of the same country. This is important because it affects the distribution of the country's population. The past 50 years have seen a steady flow of people from the north to the south-east of England, mostly in the search for better paid jobs.

International migrants move from one country to another country. More than 70 million people migrate between countries each year. Although this is a large number it is less than the number of national migrants because the distances involved are often much longer and political controls make it difficult for migrants to move freely between countries. One of the largest international migrations is between Mexico and the USA. The most important feature of Mexican immigration is that most migrants enter the USA illegally. In 2004, there were an estimated 5.9 million illegal Mexican immigrants in the USA, which was more than the 4.4 million legal migrants. Large-scale illegal immigration in the USA is a relatively new thing to have happened. It has led to political debate about whether to provide public services like education for migrants, to grant them status as legal residents, or to increase the military presence on the border to prevent further illegal migration.

Long-term or short-term?

Some migrants intend to move permanently or long-term, such as many Americans who retire by moving from the north of the USA to the warmer areas of Arizona and Florida. Other people only intend to move somewhere for a short period, for example, students who move to university for three years; or seasonal workers such as fruit pickers. These are short-term or temporary migrants.

Voluntary or forced?

Voluntary migrations occur when the migrants themselves make the decision to move. Whereas forced migration occurs when the decision to move is made by people other than the migrants themselves.

The major reason for people to migrate voluntarily is to improve their standard or quality of life.

Examples of voluntary migration include:

- East Europeans moving to the UK in the first decade of the twenty-first century where they could earn considerably more money
- unemployed Mexicans illegally moving to the USA in search of unskilled work in agriculture
- Europeans moving to well-paid jobs in the oil-rich countries of the Middle East like Dubai
- families in the UK moving from cities to the countryside where pollution and congestion are much less
- elderly couples moving to the seaside for their retirement.

Figure 1 The Mexican border

Forced migration can be caused by human or physical causes. Examples of forced migration include:

- Natural disasters such as flooding, earthquakes or cyclones often force people to move from their homes because their lives are threatened.
- In many African countries there have been drought conditions when the crops have failed to grow and people have been forced to move to avoid starvation.
- Due to fighting in Rwanda in 1994 more than a million Rwandans left, to go to refugee camps in Burundi and Tanzania.
- In 1999 thousands of Kosovans fled their country because their homes were being burnt by Serbian police and armed soldiers.

ACTIVITIES

Higher

1 There are several push and pull factors which affect migrants. Outline the push and pull factors in the following cases:
    a Mexicans moving to California
    b migrants moving from rural areas of India to Mumbai
    c refugees escaping a war in Kosovo
    d an unemployed worker moving from the north of England to London.
2 What is the difference between migration and short-term population movements?

Foundation

1 a What is migration?
  b What are short-term population movements?
2 Say whether the following are migrations or short-term population movements:
    a unskilled workers moving from Mexico to California for the grape picking season
    b an office worker travelling daily from Wilmslow to central Manchester
    c a refugee from Ethiopia who moved permanently to the neighbouring country of Sudan
    d a British couple retiring to Spain.

Review

By the end of this section you should be able to:
- know the different types of population movement
- understand that migration can be classified in several ways.

Flows of population

Learning objective – to study the migration patterns into and within Europe since 1945 and the social and economic impact of these flows.

Learning outcomes
- To know what is meant by the European Union.
- To be able to describe the main flows into and within Europe.
- To understand the social and economic impact of these flows on the source country.
- To understand the social and economic impact of these flows on the host country.

The European Union (EU) was formed by a group of countries in Europe who share an economic and political vision.

By 2002, almost one in every ten people living in the more developed regions of the world was a migrant.

What have been the main migration flows into and within Europe since 1945?

Migration flows into Europe

Before 1960 Europe was a continent of zero net migration. During the 1960s emigration exceeded immigration. It took until the mid-1970s for this trend to be reversed. Net immigration into the EU is estimated to have been 1.7 million in 2005 which was slightly lower than in the previous four years. About 70 per cent of these migrants moved into Spain, Italy, Germany and the UK. The population of a number of countries in Europe is declining; migration will change this. This is due to the number of migrants and also because the migrants have higher fertility rates than the 'native' population due to their younger age. The total number of foreign-born residents in Europe is about 5.5 per cent of the total population. Figure 2 shows the percentage of foreign-born populations in the continent of Europe in 2005.

The migration flow patterns into Europe are many and varied. They also relate to the history of the individual countries being discussed. Many countries in Europe during the sixteenth and seventeenth centuries developed colonies. When these colonies were given their independence the residents were able to apply for passports for the 'mother' country and were given work permits. This greatly influenced the

flow of migrants into various European countries. The largest groups of international migrants to all European countries are from their original colonies. Figure 5 shows the reasons for migration into Europe in detail.

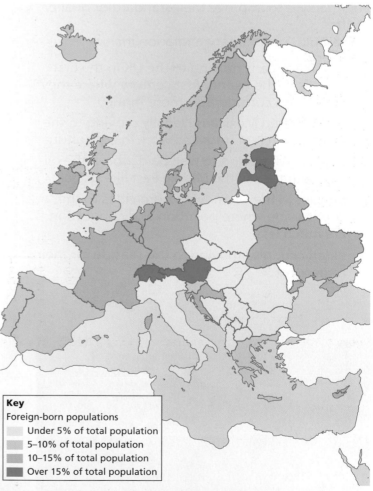

Key
Foreign-born populations
- Under 5% of total population
- 5–10% of total population
- 10–15% of total population
- Over 15% of total population

Figure 2 The percentage of foreign-born populations in Europe in 2005

Migration flows within Europe

More than half of the migrants to EU countries come from other EU countries. Since the EU was introduced there has been a relaxing of the boundaries between the member states which has meant that migrants can move freely between the member state countries. Many of these movements are not recorded. It is, however, known that a large number of migrants left the ten EU countries which joined in 2004 and moved to the UK as it was one of the few EU original countries which would allow the migrants entry as other countries closed their borders. The official figures state that between May 2004 and June 2006, 427,000 workers from eight EU accession states successfully applied for work in UK, 62 per cent of these migrants were Polish. By 2008, 700,000 Poles were working in the UK. Figure 4 has two graphs which show where the migrants to the UK came from and where they moved to. It must be remembered that this data is only for applicants who are registered.

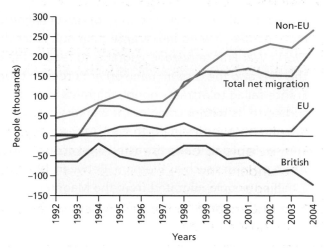

Figure 3 Net migration into the UK

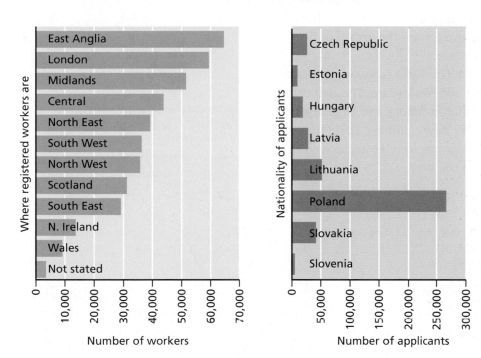

Figure 4 The source country and destination of migrants to the UK

France

France has always been a country of net immigration, with more people moving into France than out. After the Second World War France needed migrants to rebuild the country but this was also the case in many other European countries so France failed to attract enough migrants to fill the jobs. It turned to its former colonies for workers notably the 'Maghreb' countries in north-west Africa: Algeria, Morocco, Tunisia, Senegal. It also attracted workers from south-east Asian countries such as Vietnam. Between 1946 and 1990, 7 million people migrated from the Maghreb to France to fill vacancies in low-paid, low-esteem jobs.

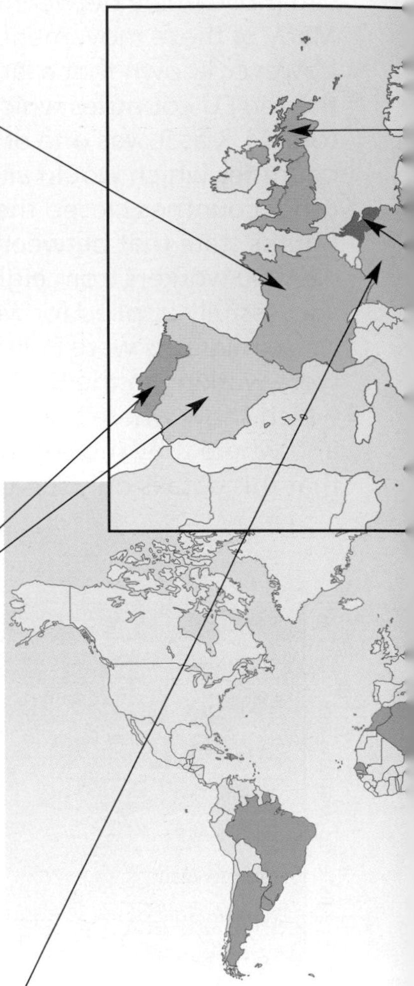

Spain and Portugal

Between the 1960s and 1980s many European countries received migrants who sought safety from political unrest in South American countries such as Argentina, Uruguay and Brazil. Many of these people were highly educated and easily found jobs in their new countries. For example, during the 1980s Spain benefited from the arrival of dentists from Argentina and Uruguay.

Many Brazilians migrated to Portugal (the main language of Brazil is Portuguese) finding jobs in marketing and health care. The past colonial links meant that there was already a shared culture and language which helped the migrants integrate into their new countries. Spain has also received large numbers of economic migrants from Morocco who risk their lives for the possibility of a life in the West.

Germany

After the Second World War Germany had a shortage of workers to rebuild its cities. It attracted workers from many countries by relaxing its immigration policy. The majority of migrants were from Turkey, although there were also considerable flows of people from Africa and Asia. These migrants were expected to return to their countries of origin once Germany was rebuilt. But many wished to stay and have gained citizenship. By 2005 there were 2.6 million Turks living in Germany which is 3 per cent of the population. They have brought with them their culture which has greatly enhanced life in Germany. They have also established economic links as many of them send money back to their families in Turkey.

Figure 5 The reasons for migration into Europe

United Kingdom

When the British Empire was at its most powerful, more than a third of the world's population lived under British rule. The vast majority of immigrants to the UK are from former colonies, most notably from the Caribbean and the Indian subcontinent. There have also been substantial flows from Kenya and South Africa. Examples of flows:

- Bangladeshis found work on public transport.
- West Indians found work in the health service as nurses and ancillary staff.
- Pakistani citizens were recruited to work in the textile mills in northern England.
- Indian citizens were recruited to work in the health service as doctors.

There were no language problems for these migrants due to the fact that English was the language of government and business within the colony. All of this immigration has given the UK a diverse culture with events such as the Notting Hill Carnival (a Caribbean celebration) being an established annual event.

The Netherlands

The Netherlands like all other European countries was short of workers after the Second World War. It recruited people from its colonies, notably Indonesia. In the 1960s The Netherlands changed from a country of net emigration to a country of net immigration. This was due to economic migrants from Surinam.

The social and economic impacts of international population movements on the country of origin and the host country

Social impact – The development of Polish shops on many British high streets adds to the cultural mix of the British society. There are also Polish bars, newspapers and internet radio stations.

Economic impact – There has been an impact on the welfare state as 27,000 child benefit applications have been approved. Some of these children do not live in the UK but migrant workers are allowed to claim benefit for them.

Social impact – There are now many Polish children in British schools especially Catholic schools. Some schools are teaching Polish history and culture to all students. The idea is to help British children better understand their new classmates.

A Polish food shop in the UK

Economic impact – They have had a positive impact on the labour market. The migrant workers are prepared to do jobs that British workers are not. For example, working on farms and in farming-related industries in Cambridgeshire.

Social impact – In Cambridgeshire the police force has to deal with 100 different languages. This has cost £800,000 for translators. They now employ community support officers to translate for the police.

Social impact – Polish migrants are having an impact on Catholic churches in the UK. In some parishes, masses in Polish are held with standing room only.

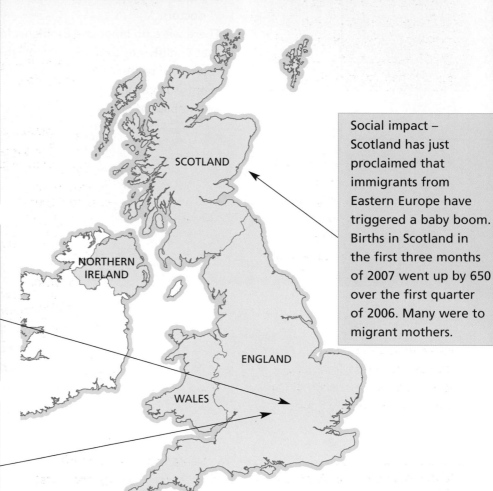

Social impact – Scotland has just proclaimed that immigrants from Eastern Europe have triggered a baby boom. Births in Scotland in the first three months of 2007 went up by 650 over the first quarter of 2006. Many were to migrant mothers.

Economic impact – The migrant workers add a considerable amount to consumer spending in the UK. The average migrant worker earns £20,000 per year of which £6,000–£7,000 is disposable income.

Social impact – The migrants are making the UK workforce younger; this has eased the pension burden. They also need housing which has helped to regenerate many inner city areas.

Figure 6 The impacts on a host country – The UK

Economic impact – The main Polish current affairs magazine, *Polityka*, has launched an incentive scheme called Stay With Us. This is to persuade the country's leading young academics to resist the pull to emigrate. About 100 scientists and researchers have each received a one-off payment of £5,000 to stay in Poland. This is equal to ten months' pay.

Economic impact – In Poland legislation is being drafted to try to encourage Poles to return home by offering them more lucrative salaries. This is due to a lack of workers in the country.

Social impact – The birth rate in Poland has decreased. This is due to the average age of migrants being in the reproductive age group.

Social impact – In some areas of Wroclaw a quarter of all anaesthetists have emigrated. The ones who remain are having to deal with more than one operation at the same time putting patients' lives at risk.

Social impact – Increase in salaries has meant that people have a higher standard of living and can afford luxury goods.

Economic impact – In 2005 10 per cent of jobs in the construction industry could not be filled. By early 2007 this figure had risen to 35 per cent due to a shortage of workers caused by migration.

Social impact – Many Polish villages are suffering from rural depopulation due to the number of migrants. It has also caused the breakdown of the traditional family unit, as the older generations are left behind in the country of origin.

Economic impact – In 2007 monthly salaries in Poland increased by 9 per cent due to a shortage of workers.

Figure 7 The impacts on a country of origin – Poland

ACTIVITIES

Higher

1 Study Figure 2 in page 256. It shows the percentage of foreign-born populations in Europe in 2005.

   a Describe the pattern of foreign-born populations in Europe in 2005.

   b Give one advantage and one disadvantage of using a choropleth map to display this type of data.

2 Choose three European countries. Explain the reasons which caused people to move into these countries.

3 Study Figure 4 on page 257.

   a From which source country did most people come?

   b Which area of the UK did most migrants settle in?

   c Why did most migrants settle in this area?

4 Draw a spidergram to show the effects of migration on the host country. You should use four different colours or write in four different fonts to distinguish between social positive and negative and economic positive and negative.

5 Draw a table to show the impacts on the source country. The columns should be headed with the terms:

   Social positive impact and social negative impact
   Economic positive impact and economic negative impact

   Use the statements provided below.
   You should use four different colours or write in four different fonts to distinguish between social positive and negative and economic positive and negative.

   • There has been an impact on the welfare state as 27,000 child benefit applications have been approved. Some of these children do not live in the UK but migrant workers are allowed to claim benefit for them.

   • The migrant workers add a considerable amount to consumer spending in the UK. The average migrant worker earns £20,000 per year of which £6,000–£7,000 is disposable income.

Foundation

1 Study Figure 2 on page 256.

   a Which countries have a foreign-born population of more than 15 per cent?

   b How many countries have a foreign-born population of less than 5 per cent?

   c Give one advantage and one disadvantage of using a choropleth map to display this type of data.

2 Complete the paragraph below using the section on reasons why people migrated to Europe to help you. Use some of the words in the box.

Morocco	Germany	Spanish
colonies	Turks	mother

   In many European countries such as .... workers were needed after the war to rebuild the cities. These migrants tended to be from the countries' .... These migrants have become a large percentage of the mother countries' populations, for example, by 2005 there were 2.6 million ...... living in Germany.

3 Study Figure 4 on page 257.

   a From which source country did most people come?

   b Which area of the UK did most migrants settle in?

   c Why did most migrants settle in this area?

4 Draw a spidergram to show the effects of migration on the host country.

   • In Cambridgeshire the police force has to deal with 100 different languages. This has cost £800,000 for translators.

   • The development of Polish shops on many British high streets adds to the cultural mix of the British society.

5 Draw a table to show the impacts on the source country. The columns should be headed with the terms:

   Social positive impact and social negative impact
   Economic positive impact and economic negative impact

Review

By the end of this section you should be able to:

• define the term European Union
• describe the main population flows into and within Europe
• explain the social and economic impact of these flows on the source country
• explain the social and economic impact of these flows on the host country.

Factors enabling population movement

> **Learning objective** – to study the factors which enable people to move.
>
> **Learning outcomes**
> - To be able to describe the technological factors which affect population movement.
> - To recognise that improved transport has led to greater population movement.
> - To be able to explain how the relaxation of national boundaries has increased movement of people within the EU.

How has the development of e-technology enabled people to move?

Over the past 30 years there has been a revolution in communications, which is due to developments in e-technology. E-technology is the use of the internet to link people across the world. In 1998 it was estimated that 9 per cent of UK households had access to the internet. By 2005, 53 per cent of UK households had internet access and this figure continues to rise. If we look at this figure on a global scale it is estimated that by 2010, 80 per cent of the planet will be on the internet. This linking of the world encourages and enables people to move.

There are a number of reasons for this:

- People now have a greater awareness of the world and want to experience different cultures and see different countries.

- People are able to look for work and to find accommodation in other countries very easily using the internet. Houses are advertised for sale on the internet therefore it is possible to live in Australia and buy a house from the UK ready for when you migrate.

- People can keep in close contact with family and friends when they are living abroad. It is far easier to sit at a computer at home using communication systems on the internet to keep in touch than to write letters. It also allows for visual contact using a webcam.

- People can book flights and other forms of transportation easily on the internet, thus making it easier to move around the world.

- People can still buy their favourite products on the internet, even if they are not available in the country they have moved to.

Figure 8 How long did it take these inventions to get a market of 50 million people?

How have developments in transport enabled people to move?

The availability of better transport infrastructure and cheaper and faster modes of transport has also enabled population movement. Places now do not seem as far away as they used to because the time to reach them has lessened due to excellent transport links. For example, 40 years ago the most common way to reach Australia was by boat which could take up to three weeks; nowadays it is 24 hours away by plane. Recently there has been the development of budget airlines. These have enabled people to move around the world much more cheaply and therefore more movements are occurring. This has had an impact on tourist movements. Many people now take two or three holidays a year due to cheap weekend breaks made available by the cheap budget airline flights.

Cheap flights have had an impact on economic migrants, for example, Polish workers commuting to the UK on Monday morning and returning on Friday evening. They have also allowed people who have retired abroad to regularly return home to see friends and family.

There has also been a major improvement in road and rail networks which have enabled people to move around more easily. The opening of the Channel Tunnel has made it very easy to drive or use the train to cross the Channel. This has meant many more people go to France, especially in the autumn for Christmas shopping trips, as it is far quicker to use the Channel Tunnel than a ferry crossing.

Prague opened up to tourists during the1990s but it wasn't until the low-cost airlines started to fly there in 2003 that tourist numbers took off. Many British people fly to Prague using easyJet or Ryanair and stay for three or four nights. There has also been a development in the stag- and hen-night market. Tourist numbers were 3.5 million in 2004 with Brits being the second largest at 650,000. Germany provided the largest group of tourists, many using its budget airline Germanwings. The figures continued to rise and in 2006 stood at 6.64 million.

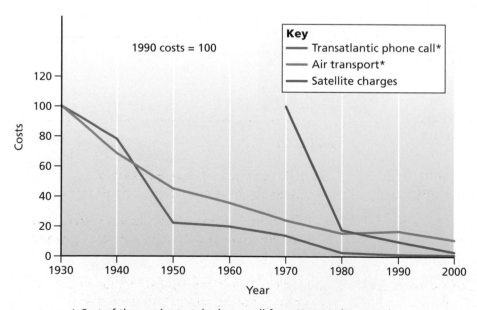

* Cost of three minute telephone call from New York to London
* Average air transport revenue per pasenger mile

Figure 9 The falling costs of communications

How has the relaxation of national boundaries enabled population movement?

The idea behind the EU is that there will be freedom of movement between the countries who are members. When the EU consisted of a small number of countries of equal economic development and similar GDP this freedom of movement was possible and did happen. Indeed this is still possible for the people who live in the first fifteen member countries of the EU. However, since the acquisition of the ten countries in 2004 the original member states at this time have been tightening their borders. For example, when Romania and Bulgaria joined the EU in January 2007 they were not allowed the free movement of labour that other countries were allowed; only Sweden and Finland allowed them to migrate freely.

The UK and other countries in the EU are tightening their immigration laws to all migrants. For example, the UK now does not allow unskilled migrants into the country at all except those from the 25 EU countries and skilled migrants have to fulfil a points quota as shown in Figure 10. Highly skilled economic migrants are still welcome in the UK, as they are in most countries of the world, as long as they reach the pass mark of 75 points.

Qualifications	Points	Previous earnings (£)	Points	Age	Points	Other	Points
Bachelor's degree	30	16,000–17,999	5	Under 28	20	If earnings/qualifications were gained in the UK	5
Master's degree	35	18,000–19,999	10	28–29	10		
PhD	50	20,000–22,999	15	30–31	5		
		23,000–25,999	20				
		26,000–28,999	25				
		29,000–31,999	30				
		32,000–34,999	35				
		35,000–39,999	40				
		40,000+	45				

Figure 10 UK entry points system for highly skilled migrants

ACTIVITIES

Higher

1 Give three ways that developments in e-technology have encouraged people to move.

2 Study Figure 8 on page 263. Suggest reasons why the internet took only four years to get a market of 50 million people.

3 How have developments in transport impacted on population movement?

Foundation

1 Give three ways that developments in e-technology have encouraged people to move.

2 Study Figure 8 on page 263. Suggest reasons why the internet took only four years to get a market of 50 million people.

3 Better motorways and budget airlines have enabled people to move. Give reasons why.

Extension

Choose a country in the EU you would like to migrate to.

What information did you need to make your choice?

What would you need to find out before you moved?

How would you find out this information?

Reasons for short-term population flows

> **Learning objective** – to study short-term population flows.
>
> **Learning outcome**
> - To understand the various reasons for short-term population flow.

There are a variety of reasons for short-term population flows. This section will look at medical, sport, tourism and economic population flows. A combination of push and pull factors will influence these short-term population movements.

Medical

It is becoming more common for UK residents to travel abroad to have operations, both medical and cosmetic. In 2007, 50,000 people left the UK to have medical treatments abroad. There are a number of reasons which cause people to travel abroad for medical care.

Push factors

- Unhappy with the National Health Service because waiting lists are lengthening and demand is not being met.
- Poorly maintained hospitals.
- British hospitals are perceived to be dirty and patients feel that they are not well cared for.
- Hospitals are closing down, therefore patients will have longer distances to travel.
- Patients feel that they are treated like a production line.
- Private health care is expensive in the UK.

Pull factors

- The treatment is much cheaper abroad.
- Modern medical facilities with state-of-the-art equipment which are clean and well stocked.
- Better patient care with more time spent by doctors and nurses with the patients.
- Can be done as part of a package holiday.

Cape Town, South Africa remains a premier destination for medical tourism, and plastic surgery in particular. The surgery is affordable, the care is highly professional and Cape Town remains a prime tourist destination. It is easy to travel to Cape Town for a holiday, have your surgery performed and return home refreshed. This is now a common procedure and patients travel from Europe, other parts of Africa and Australia to Cape Town for their plastic surgery.

Budapest, Hungary is a popular destination for people to have their teeth repaired. Figure 11 compares the prices for a selection of dental treatments in Budapest, the capital of Hungary, with the UK. It is obvious how great the savings can be especially when more complex treatments, such as implants are done. The relative cheapness of the treatment, and consequently value for money, is the major motive.

Although the major reason for these short term population flows is financial, there are many other push and pull factors involved. One of these is using the dental visit as part of a holiday. There are now several holiday companies who will arrange a package deal involving hotel accommodation, flights and dental work. This is proving to be very popular as it takes all the hard work out for the migrant. Dentist Abroad is a leading dental tour operator based in London. Dentist Abroad currently organises treatment for 80–100 people a month from all over the UK. They serve a significant 4–5 per cent of the growing dental tourism industry.

Dental Treatments in:	Budapest	UK	Savings
Implants without crown* (German)	£480	£1800	£1320
Porcelain veneer per tooth (from 8 teeth or more)	£279	£790	£511
Crowns (porcelain fused to metal, per tooth)	£199	£650	£451
Consultation	Free	£50	£50
Dental X-ray (small)	Free	£35	£35
Panoramic X-ray	£35	£75	£40

Figure 11 The price of dental treatments in Budapest and the UK
Source: Dentist Abroad

Other push and pull factors are:

- The introduction of budget airlines with direct flights to Budapest and other dental destinations.
- The development of the internet.
- A greater awareness of what is available due to advertisements.
- Ease of travel due to improved networks and relaxation of national boundaries.

Sport

There are different types of short-term flows in sport. These include circular flows such as athletes travelling to the Olympics or other sports that require their players to compete in countries around the globe. Figure 12 shows the movements of a female golf player competing on the European tour in 2008. If the player competed in every tournament she would visit 21 different countries. The players usually have a home in their own country but spend most of the year moving around the world.

Other sports such as football require players to stay in one country for the period of their contract. In the UK work permits are usually granted to players who have completed a number of matches for their national side, which has to be ranked in the top 70 countries by football's governing body FIFA. Figure 13 shows how global football has now become. Tottenham Hotspur had players from 17 countries playing for them in the 2008–2009 season.

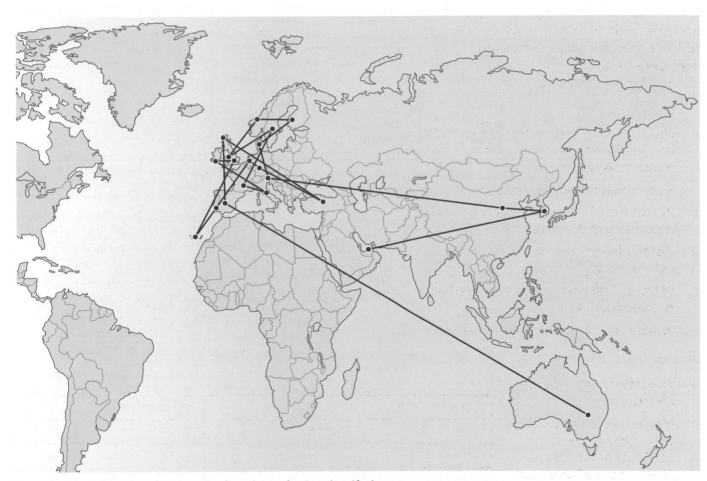

Figure 12 The migration pattern of a female professional golf player

What are the push and pull factors attracting these footballers to Tottenham?

The most important factor is probably money. Teams in the premiership pay the highest wages in Europe. The average annual wage for a premiership player in 2008 was £750,000. Signing-on fees paid when a player joins the club are often a six-figure sum, with payments usually spread over the term of a player's contract, for example, a £250,000 signing-on fee, spread over three years, would work out to an extra £1,603 per week. This is considerably more than players could earn in the majority of European countries.

Tottenham signed Roman Pavlyuchenko from Spartek Moscow, Russia in 2008.

The reasons why he moved were:

- Financial.

- He wanted to play with and compete against the best players in the world.

- He wanted to live in London, which is a major world city and could give him the entertainment and quality of life that his money could afford.

The push factors are often the opposite of the pull factors. Therefore low wages, poor competition and unsatisfactory quality of life led Roman Pavlyuchenko to leave his club for Tottenham.

One limiting factor was the effect the move would have on him and his family. He said 'The only thing that has kept me from moving before is my family. It was difficult for me to imagine how my wife and daughter could move from a place they are used to. I was also embarrassed that I could not speak English.'

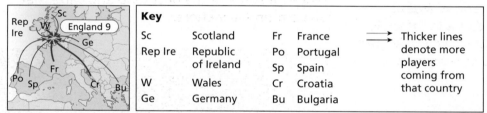

Key

Sc	Scotland	Fr	France
Rep Ire	Republic of Ireland	Po	Portugal
		Sp	Spain
W	Wales	Cr	Croatia
Ge	Germany	Bu	Bulgaria

⟶ Thicker lines denote more players coming from that country

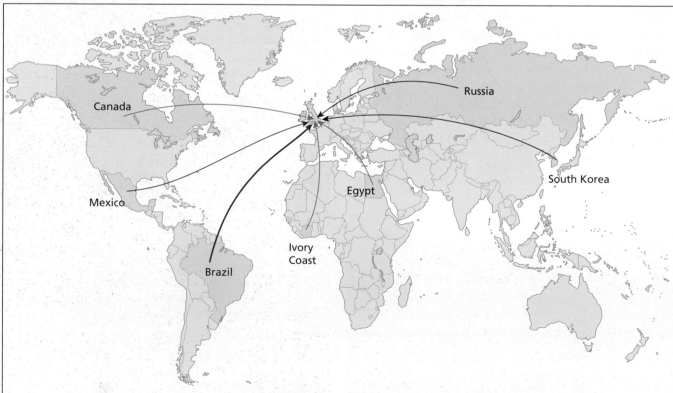

Figure 13 The source countries of Tottenham Hotspur players

Tourism

Tourism is travel for recreational, leisure or business purposes. Tourism can be defined as the temporary, short-term movement of people to a destination outside the places where they normally live and work, and their activities during their stay at these destinations.

What are the pull factors that attract people to France?

Climate

France has a wide variety of climates which attract tourists. The Mediterranean coast has hot dry summers (average temperatures of 25°C and virtually no rainfall in June, July and August). This climate is very appealing, particularly to those tourists from northern European countries with colder climates.

In the winter the weather in the mountain regions of France (Alps, Pyrenees and Massif Central) is very cold and produces a lot of snow. This attracts the adventure tourists who take part in winter sports like skiing, snowboarding and tobogganing.

Physical attractions

Many holidaymakers are attracted by the physical landscape. France has vast areas of stunning scenery, from the mountainous peaks of the snow capped Alps to the vast open vistas of the Camargue. France has hundreds of miles of coastline facing the Atlantic Ocean with wide sandy beaches and rolling waves, like The Vendee and the surfing centre of Biarritz. It also has beautiful beaches on the warm, shallow and tideless Mediterranean Sea where fashionable seaside resorts like Nice and Juan les Pins have developed.

Human attractions

Many holidaymakers are attracted by the human attractions on offer. France is the home of several theme parks like Parc Astérix, 35 km north of Paris, and Futuroscope in Poitiers – these are particularly popular with families. The largest theme park in France, Disneyland® Resort Paris, attracts 15 million tourists every year.

France also attracts cultural travellers to its numerous historic buildings such as the Pont du Gard, the chateaux of the Loire and the Roman amphitheatre in Nîmes. These attract visitors from all around the world; as do the famous buildings in Paris, such as the Louvre, the Eiffel Tower and the Sacré Coeur. Many tourists are attracted to France for some of the best food and wine that can be found anywhere.

Figure 15 One of the human attractions of France, the Eiffel Tower

Figure 14 The physical attractions of Biarritz

Transport

France is a very accessible country because there are first-class transport links with other countries in Europe and worldwide. Mass tourism depends on easy accessibility; tourists will always be attracted to places that they can reach easily. The Eurotunnel link under the English Channel means that tourists from London can now reach Paris in just over two hours. Many new airports, linked to Ryanair and easyJet, have developed in France in the last decade. This pulls tourists into the areas within close proximity to an airport. Tourism has grown rapidly in more remote areas that have been opened up by new airports and the comprehensive and expanding motorway network, for example, Bergerac airport connecting the Perigord region and the A75 autoroute (la Méridienne), which has opened up the Auvergne and Languedoc regions.

What are the push factors that make people leave the UK to go on holiday?

Climate

The British always perceive that their climate is very bad with lots of rain, and because of this they like to go to warm dry areas like the Mediterranean.

Economic

The average worker in the UK has increasingly more disposable income and can afford to have holidays. This increasing wealth is allowing them to often have several short trips a year. In 2007 and early 2008 the pound was very strong against the US dollar. This meant that it was cheap to buy things in America which further increased the desire to go on holiday there.

Media

There are now several TV programmes which are targeted towards tourists. Shows like 'Homes in the Sun' and 'Sky Travel' make people aware of where they can go and how easy it is to get there. Adverts for holidays appear in all the newspapers and on the radio. They make all the places sound very appealing and cause people who are often living in the fast pace of congested England to want the peace and tranquillity of an overseas holiday.

Figure 16 British holidaymakers at Lynmouth

Case Study: Economic migrants: A case study of a short term population flow – Poland to the UK

Introduction

Since 2004 there has been a large number of migrants coming from the ten EU states which joined the community in that year. According to official figures between May 2004 and June 2006 427,000 workers from those ten EU states successfully applied for work in the UK; 62 per cent of these migrants were Polish. By 2008, 700,000 Poles were working in the UK.

Motives for migrating

Obviously the main motive for economic migrants is an increase in wealth. Workers from East European countries such as Poland, Latvia and Romania have moved to the UK in search of better paying jobs. Some of the migrants only come for very short periods of time to coincide with seasonal jobs such as fruit or vegetable picking. They stay for a few months in the spring and summer and then go back to their families with enough money to see them through the winter. These migrants are very common in the rural areas of the UK like Norfolk and Lincolnshire. They do not have a great impact on the host country as they often live in caravans or tents set up by the farmers who take rent payments out of their wages. They also save most of their earnings to take home to their families.

Other migrants, normally the more educated, come for a longer period of time and look for full-time positions in jobs like health care and education. Anna is a typical example of an economic migrant, coming from Olkusz to London to get a teaching job. She explains the reasons for her move to the UK.

Mike's questions	Anna's answers
Why did you decide to come to London?	I came to London because I can speak English fluently; we learn English from year 1 (age 7).
Was there a problem getting a teaching job in Poland?	Unemployment in Poland is between 20 and 25 per cent. Some of my friends can't get a teaching job in Poland. There is more chance of working in England.
Was it easy to get a job in England?	I saw the advertisement on the internet. I applied by email. When I was offered an interview I organised a flight on easyJet.
How does the pay in England compare to Poland?	I am paid four times the amount of money in England for the same job.
Does that mean you have a better standard of living?	Yes. In Poland I only earned enough to pay for necessities like the rent for my flat and to buy food. In England I have enough money for luxuries like a car and for entertainment.
Has the changing exchange rate made any difference?	When I came to England in 2006 there were over 6 zloty to the pound, now (2008) there are only 4.5, which means it is more expensive when I go back home.

Figure 17 Reasons for economic migration

What are the problems that the migrant encounters and what solutions are there?

Problems for economic migrants	Solution to the problems
The less educated migrants often do not speak very good English and can be taken advantage of by unscrupulous employers who don't pay them a fair wage.	This would not happen if the migrant could speak English. There are classes available all over the country where they can learn basic English.
Poland is a much more rural country than England and the migrants often find it difficult to adjust to the noise and speed of English city life. This can lead to stress and many return to Poland because of homesickness.	Polish immigrants now comprise one of the largest ethnic groups in London. The Greater London boroughs of Acton, Balham, Brixton, Ealing, Earls Court and Hammersmith have become known as 'Polish towns'. This 'living together' helps new migrants to overcome their homesickness for rural areas.
Houses are generally much larger in Poland as there is not such a strain on space. When the Poles come to England they tend to live in flats or small terrace houses which they find very cramped.	As they integrate into English society they spend less time in their flats so don't notice the conditions so much. They put up with the cramped conditions so that they can save money to take back to Poland.
The exchange rate can fluctuate meaning that if the pound loses value to the zloty, as it did in 2008, then the money they earn in England is not worth as much in Poland as it was.	The exchange rate has been favourable in the past and might return to a favourable position in the future.
The education system in England is different from that in Poland and some children find it difficult to adjust. There are also cultural differences which can lead to ridicule and bullying at school.	There are now so many Polish children in British schools, especially Catholic schools where they are concentrated, that Polish history and culture may be taught to all students. The idea is to help British children better understand their new classmates. There are more than 50 Polish 'Saturday Schools' around the UK, organised and financed by the Polish Educational Society, with very little local or central government funding. Their purpose is to ensure that the children of immigrants maintain Polish language and cultural fluency in case they return to Poland and re-enter the education system.

ACTIVITIES

1 State four short-term population flows.
2 Why do people travel abroad for medical treatment?
3 Study Figure 13 on page 268.
   a How many Tottenham Hotspur players come from the UK?
   b Why do British football teams have so many players from other countries?
4 Many migrants move for economic reasons.
   a What are the motives for economic migration from Poland to the UK?
   b What are the problems that the economic migrants face?
5 Study Figure 12 on page 267. It shows the migration pattern of a female professional golf player.
   On a map of the world complete the PGA tour for a male professional golf player. These are the countries he visits.

China	Italy
Hong Kong	Republic of Ireland
Australia	England
South Africa	Wales
United Arab Emirates	Austria
Qatar	France
Thailand	Germany
USA	Scotland
Bali	Sweden
Portugal	Czech Republic
Spain	Netherlands
South Korea	Switzerland

Extension

1 Choose a medical procedure such as a face lift or having a tooth out. Research on the internet the best place to have the treatment carried out.
2 On a map of France mark and name all the places which are mentioned in the text about the short-term population flows relating to tourism.

Review

By the end of this section you should be able to:
• understand the various reasons for short-term population flow.

Learning objective – to study the reasons for and the consequences of retirement migration of UK citizens to Spain and retirement migration within the UK.

Learning outcomes
- To understand the reasons for retirement migration from the UK to Spain.
- To know the consequences on the destination.
- To understand the reasons for retirement migration from London to Norfolk.
- To know the consequences for the host region – Norfolk.

Retirement migration

Large numbers of British people every year decide to retire abroad. The country with the largest number of retired Brits is Canada, then the USA, Ireland and Spain. There are 80,000 retired Brits who live either full- or part-time in Spain. A number of studies have been carried out to ascertain why so many Brits choose Spain as their retirement destination. The results of these studies are shown in Figures 18 and 19 which show reasons for moving to the Costa del Sol.

Why do British people retire to Spain?

Mediterranean climate
The temperature in Spain is usually a constant 10°C warmer than in the UK. This is very important for retired people who are living on a fixed income and have to continually be aware of the cost of heating their homes.

Communication networks
The distance that Spain is from the UK is about 2,000 km. However, the time it takes to fly to Spain is less than the time it takes to drive from London to Manchester. It is also much cheaper to fly there, approximately £50, due to 'no frills' airlines like easyJet. Therefore it is easy for retired people to come back to the UK to visit their families. They are also able to keep in touch easily with cheap telephone calls and the internet.

Lifestyle
Many people who retire to Spain are attracted by the slower pace of life that they have witnessed when they have been on holiday in the country. They are also attracted by the lower crime rates and an absence of 'youth culture' in the Spanish areas that they have chosen to migrate to.

Most important reason for moving to the chosen destination	Percentage of respondents
Lower cost of living (including tax reasons)	6.2
Climate (including other environmental factors)	48.1
Health, slower pace of life	18.4
Antipathy to UK	6.8
Admiration of destination	5.0
Work or business connections	2.7
Family connections	8.9
Other	3.9

Figure 18 Reasons why UK citizens retire to Spain
Source: International Journal of Population Geography

Factor of attraction	Percentage of respondents
Mediterranean climate	90.4
Lifestyle of the Spanish people	52.7
Spain's lower cost of living	28.7
Better health conditions	17.0
Accessibility to home country	14.4
Interest in Latin and Mediterranean cultures	9.0
Community of foreign residents	11.2
Availability of leisure and recreational facilities	8.5
Spanish landscape	1.1

Figure 19 Reasons why British people are attracted to Spain
Source: International Journal of Population Geography

	Jan	Feb	Mar	Apr	May	Jun	Jul	Aug	Sep	Oct	Nov	Dec
Max temp	16°C	16°C	18°C	21°C	23°C	28°C	31°C	31°C	28°C	24°C	20°C	18°C
Min temp	9°C	9°C	11°C	13°C	15°C	19°C	21°C	22°C	20°C	16°C	12°C	9°C
Hrs sun	6	7	7	8	10	11	11	11	9	7	6	5
Ave rainfall	15 mm	14 mm	15 mm	16 mm	17 mm	21 mm	21 mm	23 mm	21 mm	18 mm	17 mm	14 mm
Sea temp	14°C	13°C	14°C	15°C	17°C	21°C	21°C	25°C	24°C	21°C	18°C	15°C

Figure 20 Climate information for Spain

Cost of living

People who retire to Spain receive their pension just as if they were in the UK. They are taxed by the Spanish authorities. However, the tax rates in Spain are lower than in the UK. The cost of living in Spain is also lower than in the UK. This is very important for pensioners who are on a fixed income. This means that they can buy food and drink more cheaply and have more disposable income.

Figure 21 Costa del Sol

Property market

There has been a boom in house prices in the UK. This has meant that many people now have the capital to buy a property in Spain which is less expensive. The retired people have some money left over to live on when they are not working.

Awareness of destination

Another reason for the boom in retirement migration is the awareness of what is available. The people who retire to Spain have experienced foreign countries through their holidays and believe that 'the grass is greener' in other countries. This has also been enhanced by the communications revolution and, of course, television programmes such as 'A Place in the Sun'.

Expatriate community

The network of other British people living in the area (expatriates, or informally known as expats) who can be of support is also important. This may not be important for the choice of country but could be for the place within the country that the migrants decide to live. If there are other people who speak the same language as you do and can help with problems as they have quite possibly experienced them, it is a strong pull factor for migrants.

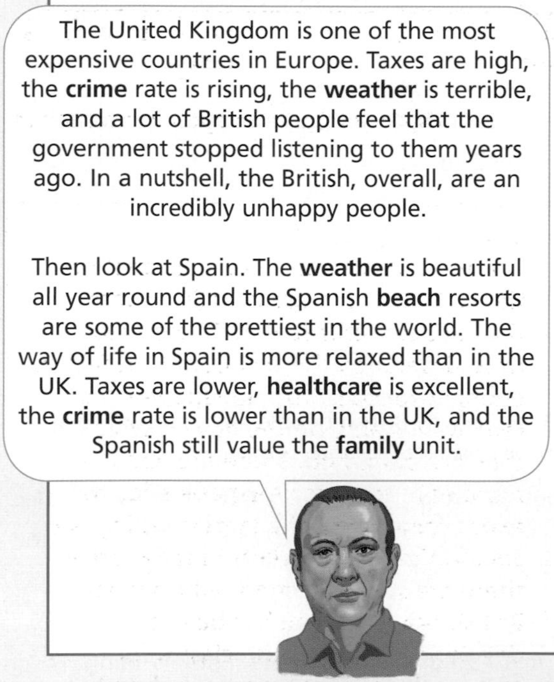

The United Kingdom is one of the most expensive countries in Europe. Taxes are high, the **crime** rate is rising, the **weather** is terrible, and a lot of British people feel that the government stopped listening to them years ago. In a nutshell, the British, overall, are an incredibly unhappy people.

Then look at Spain. The **weather** is beautiful all year round and the Spanish **beach** resorts are some of the prettiest in the world. The way of life in Spain is more relaxed than in the UK. Taxes are lower, **healthcare** is excellent, the **crime** rate is lower than in the UK, and the Spanish still value the **family** unit.

Leisure facilities

This is another set of factors that are important, not as much for choice of country, but for choice of location within a country. For some it may be the availability of sporting activities such as golf courses or bowling greens, for others it may be tea dances, coffee mornings and organised excursions. However, these sorts of activities are important as they are a way of further developing social networks.

Health care

In the past people did not migrate when they retired due to the lack of health care in other European countries. This is now not the case. If you receive a state pension in the UK you will be eligible for free state health care in Spain. This is due to the free movement of European people brought about by the EU. There are also many private hospitals in Spain which were not in existence 30 years ago. Therefore people feel confident that if they are ill there will be plenty of healthcare experts available to treat them.

Figure 22 The reasons given by one expat as to why he left the UK

The consequences of retirement migration on Spain

Population structure

Spain has an ageing population. This has been added to by the number of Brits and other nationalities, particularly the Irish, who have migrated there when they retire. This can be seen by looking at the population pyramids for 2000 and 2030. If the trend to retire to Spain continues and the Spanish birth rate remains low the imbalance in the population structure will continue. There will be pressure on the economically active due to the increasing dependant population. One of the problems will be the provision of health care for the elderly, retired population.

Housing developments

There has been a lot of development along the coast of Spain which has caused damage to the coastline. This prompted the government in 1998 to pass the Coastal Law to try to control beachfront development. The law stated that the Spanish government controls the coastal strip of 106 m in which no private housing is allowed. Technically, any property built within 106 m of the shore could be demolished. However, this is unlikely due to the complicated system of government in Spain.

Water

The areas of Spain where the expats live, such as the Valencia region, are known for their shortage of water. The expats buy properties with swimming pools and expect to be able to fill them; this is causing a major problem with water supply in the area. The rainfall in the area is low; it is not enough to supply the new housing developments which are taking place. There has also been an increase in demand for water due to the expats' leisure requirements.

In Murcia, south-east Spain, developers have been given permission to build golf courses; 54 of them in the last ten years and most of these in the last three. Many new housing developments have been built, both for holiday homes and for people to buy in their retirement. This was without thought for the lack of water in the area. The demand for water is now two and a half times the supply. The situation is becoming worse all the time as global warming changes rainfall patterns and many farmers have dug illegal wells in order to water their crops. Many people plant fig trees in their gardens and call their homes farms so that they qualify for irrigation water, but the water is usually used in swimming pools. The same has been occurring on the golf courses where the greens are called crops so that they can apply for irrigation water.

Health care

Many of the British who retire to Spain live on the Costa Blanca. This has caused the cost of health care there to increase dramatically. It is estimated that the British expats are costing the local government £800 million a year in health care costs. This has caused them to change the law. People who retire early to Spain will now have to pay for their own healthcare although people over the age of 65 will still be eligible.

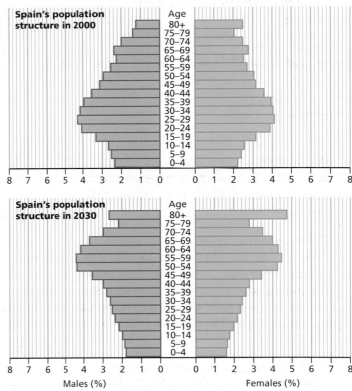

Figure 23 Spain's population structure

Culture

The expats have also had an impact on the culture of the areas of Spain that they are concentrated in. These areas have developed the services which British people expect. British newspapers are readily available on the day on which they are published. There are also a number of specific newspapers for the expat community, the largest selling is *El Sun*. In the supermarkets in these areas there are special sections which stock British brands. There has been a development in Spanish classes for expats and a willingness of the Spanish in the area to learn English to enable them to speak to their customers.

Case Study: Retirement migration to North Norfolk

Introduction

Increased longevity and improved levels of health and fitness mean that people are making lifestyle choices as they approach the end of their working lives. People are increasingly choosing to relocate to another area of the country which offers more attractive living conditions for retirement, usually in the countryside or near the coast. Internal migration figures for the UK back this up. Migration patterns for those aged over 60 in the year ending 2006 show a strong inflow into the South West and the East of England regions.

Place	Region	Retirees per 100
Christchurch	Dorset	33.0
Rother	East Sussex	32.1
West Somerset	Somerset	30.9
East Devon	Devon	30.3
Tendring	Essex	30.0
North Norfolk	**Norfolk**	**30.0**
East Dorset	Dorset	29.7
Arun	West Sussex	29.3
West Dorset	Dorset	28.2
Eastbourne	East Sussex	26.9

Figure 24 Top ten current retirement hotspots
Source: ONS

Where are the migrants coming from?

People aged 60 and over are migrating from the big cities into more rural areas. The biggest exodus by far is from Outer London (9,100 in 2005), followed closely by Inner London (8,400). However, these moves are closely followed by migration out of other large cities, namely Birmingham, Leeds, Manchester, Sheffield and Liverpool. Cities are being left with a relatively small proportion of their population being aged 60 or over. In the case of Inner London this is as low as 11 per cent, and in Manchester it is only 14 per cent, both of these are well below the UK average of 19 per cent. Many migrants start out buying a second home which they go to at weekends and then retire there full time when they reach retirement age.

Why do people retire to North Norfolk?

Property market

Older people are taking advantage of the fact that property prices are lower in those areas of the country which they wish to move to. The average house price in 2008 in North Norfolk, part of the East Anglia region, was approximately £200,000, whereas in greater London which supplies a high proportion of the migrants it was more than £335,000. This allows the migrants a considerable amount of extra money to live on when they stop working. The reasons why house prices are lower in North Norfolk is due to the remoteness of the area. Communication links are poor which means that the economically active population does not want to live in this area. This causes a lack of demand for housing which in turn lowers house prices. Fewer people living in the area makes the area more appealing to people when they retire.

Scenery

The natural beauty and the exceptional landscape of North Norfolk is seen as one of its most attractive qualities. Much of the area lies within the North Norfolk Area of Outstanding Natural Beauty (AONB) and the coastline is a designated Heritage Coast, including Ramsar sites. It acts as a powerful draw to in-migrants who wish to enjoy a rural lifestyle and take advantage of local activities such as bird watching, fishing and sailing.

Climate

Norfolk is one of the driest counties in England with the highest summer temperatures in the country and an average annual rainfall of only 625 mm. This compares favourably with the South West of England, the most popular retirement area in the UK, which has an average of 1,200 mm.

Lifestyle

Many people who retire to North Norfolk are attracted by the slower pace of life that is found in rural areas. They are also attracted by lower crime rates, particularly violent crime. Between April 2005 and March 2006, 330 fewer offences of violence were reported. Home burglaries were down by 6.7 per cent and vehicle-related crime dropped by 891 incidents. Chief Constable Carole Howlett said: 'Crime rates are down for the third year running across Norfolk. This is good news for the people of Norfolk especially regarding violent crime.'

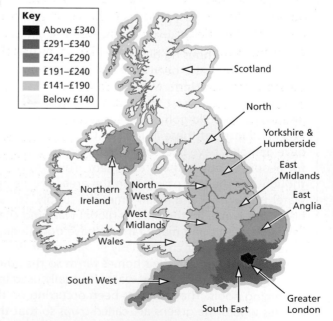

Key
- Above £340
- £291–£340
- £241–£290
- £191–£240
- £141–£190
- Below £140

Scotland
North
Yorkshire & Humberside
East Midlands
East Anglia
North West
Northern Ireland
West Midlands
Wales
South West
South East
Greater London

Figure 25 Average UK house prices by region

The consequences on the destination

Housing

The increase in the number of in-migrants has led to the creation of more demand for local housing than the market can supply. This increases competition, and prices for houses that do become available are pushed up. Furthermore, there is a strong view among local residents that in-migrants usually have more money to spend than local people, which also pushes up prices well beyond the reach of many residents. Local people, especially young people are unable to afford these artificially inflated house prices.

Many of the locals in the coastal, retirement villages of North Norfolk are unhappy that much of the new housing that is being built is executive homes which have been targeted at the top-end of the market for wealthy in-migrants rather than local people. In addition, the smaller traditional flint cottages are particularly attractive to people retiring to Norfolk.

Shops and facilities

Some of the villages in the area have benefited from the retired in-migrants because they support local services and want to be accepted in the local community. This means that they shop daily in the local village stores and drink in the local pub.

Other villages have changed in character due to the wealth of the retired in-migrants, for example, providing expensive, designer label clothes shops (Gunn Hill Clothing Company, Burnham Market) and Michelin starred restaurants (Morston Hall, Blakeney). As a result, many local people have to go outside the area for basic necessities. This is a problem because 80 per cent of people living in the Brancaster area are more than 6 km away from a supermarket. This is made worse by the poor communication links along winding, twisting roads and the inadequacy of the bus services. This makes getting the shopping time-consuming and difficult. It is easier for the retired migrants who have the time and transport to go into the local towns, Fakenham, King's Lynn and Norwich, to do their weekly shopping.

Population structure

North Norfolk has an ageing population. One of the major reasons for this is the steady influx of retirement migrants. The population pyramid in Figure 26 clearly shows the high percentage of all age groups over 50 in comparison with the UK average. Conversely, all ages below 50 are much lower than the UK average. The number of young adults aged 20–30 is particularly low. As these are potentially the next child-bearing generation there are likely to be even fewer children in the following years. This population structure will have massive consequences for North Norfolk. Due to the low number of young children several schools in the area are threatened with closure. The ageing population will put a great strain on the medical facilities. A new hospital has been planned for North Norfolk combining a doctors' surgery, an eight-bed dialysis unit, social services, day surgery, 24 beds and community health services under one roof. There has been a growth in age-related services such as chiropodists and alternative medicines.

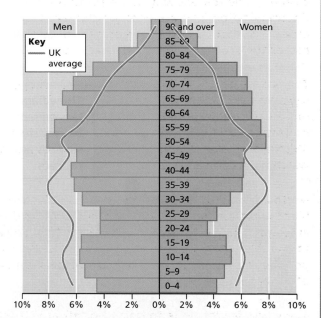

Figure 26 Population pyramid for North Norfolk

New, large detached houses owned by rich retirees having sold their properties in areas of high property value like Hertfordshire.

The village green with specialised butcher and bakery shop. These are services appreciated by retirees.

Typical retired inhabitants of Burnham which has 42% of it's population aged over 60. They are standing outside a tea room, catering for the retirees.

Figure 27 Burnham Market – an upper-class retirement area

The wide open, rural area with uncrowded country lanes that attracts retirees like Irene.

Traditional cottages built from local stone are very popular with retired people.

Irene retired to Burnham 17 years ago.

Why did you retire to Burnham Market?

Burnham Market, for me, has it all. Sometimes (unfairly) called Chelsea by the Sea it has a pretty village green overlooked by the church and surrounded by super little local shops – a proper butchers, bakers and fishmongers; there is a good fish restaurant, tearooms and busy, popular pubs selling food. Other types of shopping are well catered for as well. I love browsing in the boutiques where you can buy (or just look at!) gorgeous shoes and designer clothes as well as a great range of country clothing too.

The coast is only a couple of miles away at Holkham Beach, which has one of the most truly gorgeous beaches in England. It is a huge open space and you can walk for a mile or so to the sea when the tide is out. Even at the height of summer, it is never crowded. The winter is the most attractive and atmospheric time for me though; deserted, wild and beautiful.

Changing village character

The older, retired population in villages has caused a change in the character of village life. Facilities in the villages are changing to accommodate the older generation. New community halls have been built or original ones modernised with Lottery funding. In the past the halls would have been used for youth clubs and discos. Nowadays they are used in the evenings by clubs and societies which are geared towards the older generation such as whist drives and yoga.

Another change in the character to village life is that there are fewer families and young people settling in the area. This has caused village schools to be threatened with closure.

Retired people are buying up the houses and basically pricing people out of the market.

You've got all these shops in Burnham Market but you can't get any groceries, you can't get milk, you can't get bread.

There is nothing for me to do anymore because the youth club has closed and I am too young to go to the pub.

I have plenty of work because the rich, retired newcomers always want work done on their houses.

Figure 28 Consequences of retirement migrants on the host population

ACTIVITIES

Higher

1 a How many retired Brits live in Spain?

b Study Figure 20 on page 273.

  i What is the most important pull factor for migrants retiring to Spain?

  ii What is the least important pull factor for migrants retiring to Spain?

c Describe and explain 4 reasons why people retire to Spain.

d There are many consequences of this migration on Spain. Draw a spidergram to show the consequences.

2 Many people migrate to North Norfolk when they retire.

a Describe the reasons for this migration.

b Explain the consequences on the destination.

Foundation

1 a How many retired Brits live in Spain?

b Study Figure 20 on page 273.

  i What is the most important pull factor for migrants retiring to Spain?

  ii What is the least important pull factor for migrants retiring to Spain?

c Using some of the words from the word box, complete the sentences to explain why people retire to Spain.

| warmer | fixed | colder | high | | low |
| pension | post | lower | health care | | education |

The temperature in Spain is usually a constant 10°C .... than in the UK. This is very important for retired people who are living on a .... income and have to continually be aware of the cost of heating their homes.

People who retire to Spain receive their .... just as if they were in the UK. The cost of living in Spain is .... than in the UK.

In the past people did not migrate when they retired due to the lack of .... in other European countries.

d There are many consequences of this migration on Spain. Draw a spidergram to show the consequences.

2 Many people migrate to North Norfolk when they retire.

a Give three reasons for this migration.

b Explain the consequences on the destination.

Review

By the end of this section you should be able to:
- explain the reasons for retirement migration from the UK to Spain
- understand the consequences for the host country – Spain
- explain the reasons for retirement migration from London to Norfolk
- understand the consequences for the host region – Norfolk.

Sample Examination Questions

Higher tier

1 Read what the following people are saying and then classify their migration. **(4 marks)**

> **a** I travel from my home in Hertfordshire every day to work in the city.

> **b** I live in Spain and I play golf for a living. This month I will play in Dubai, South Africa and China.

> **c** I lived on a volcanic island which exploded. I was very frightened but fortunately I was rescued and taken to another country to live. I like my new country but I will soon go back to the island when the volcano has settled down.

> **d** I left Brazil in 1980 and went to live in Portugal. I live in Lisbon and work as a dentist.

2 **a** State one push factor for migration to Europe **(1 mark)**

   b State one pull factor for migration to Europe **(1 mark)**

3 Study Figure 5 on pages 258–259. Describe and explain the pattern of migration for British and European migrants. **(4 marks)**

4 Explain the social and economic effects of migration on the host country. **(4 marks)**

5 Complete the table below to show if the statement refers to economic effects or social effects of migration on the host country. The first has been done for you. Put a cross in the correct box. **(5 marks)**

Statement	Positive economic	Negative economic	Positive social	Negative social
Better salaries are being offered to encourage people to return.	✗			
Some anaesthetists have to deal with more than one operation at the same time putting patients' lives at risk.				
Jobs in the construction industry cannot be filled due to a shortage of workers.				
The birth rate has decreased. This is due to the average age of migrants being in the reproductive age group.				
Rural depopulation due to the number of migrants has caused a breakdown of the traditional family unit.				
Monthly salaries in Poland have increased by 9 per cent due to a shortage of workers.				

6 Many people migrate from the UK to another country.

For an international retirement migration you have studied, describe and explain the reasons for this retirement migration.

Chosen migration .... **(6 marks)**

Total 25 marks

Foundation tier

1 Read what the people opposite are saying and then classify their migration. **(4 marks)**

2 **a** State one push factor for migration to Europe **(1 mark)**

   b State one pull factor for migration to Europe **(1 mark)**

3 Study Figure 5 on pages 258–259.

   a Describe the pattern of migration for people moving into the UK. **(3 marks)**

   b Give one reason for the large increase in migrants from the EU in 2004. **(1 mark)**

4 Complete the following paragraph to explain the social and economic impacts of migration on the host country. Use some of the words in the box.

live	work	play	money	time
younger	older	fitter	languages	people

The migrant workers claim child benefit for children who do not …. in the UK.

The migrant workers spend a lot of ………. in the UK which helps the economy.

In Cambridgeshire the police force has to deal with 100 different …………….. This has cost £800,000 for translators.

The migrants are making the UK workforce ………….. **(4 marks)**

5 Complete the table below to show if the statement refers to economic effects or social effects of migration on the host country. The first has been done for you.

Put a cross in the correct box. **(5 marks)**

6 Many people migrate from the UK to another country.

For an international retirement migration you have studied, describe and explain the reasons for this retirement migration.

Chosen migration .... **(6 marks)**

Total 25 marks

Growth of the tourist industry

> **Learning objective** – to study the growth of the tourist industry.
>
> **Learning outcomes**
> - To explain the social, economic and political factors causing the growth of tourism.
> - To understand that holiday destinations offer a variety of physical and human attractions.
> - To describe different types of holidays.

What are the factors that have caused a growth in global tourism?

Tourism is one of the fastest growing industries in the world. It is becoming an important sector in both developed and especially developing world economies. Why is the industry growing at such a fast rate?

The growth can be attributed to a number of factors, including:

- social
- economic
- political.

Social factors

The social factors which have caused a growth in global tourism are the increase in the amount of leisure time available to people, the development of communications and information technology and the increase in the range of products available for tourists.

Increase in leisure time

The increase in available leisure time is due to the following factors:

- holiday entitlement
- shorter working week
- early retirement with pensions
- ageing population.

The amount of leisure time available to people has increased dramatically over the last 40 years

(Figure 1). This is because jobs come with holiday entitlement which is paid for. This paid holiday, as from 1 April 2009, is 28 days a year, an increase of 4 days since 2007. In 1981 there were only 15 paid days' holiday a year. This big increase in paid holidays allows people both the time and money to travel. In the UK we are also working shorter weeks. In the 1950s, a 50-hour, 6-day week was common for most workers. Most office workers now work between 35 and 40 hours a week, Monday to Friday. Some people now work flexitime which enables them to work longer days but have more time off at the weekend.

The number of people who are retired and are receiving pensions is also increasing in the developed world. This is a growth market for the tourist industry and is being exploited by many holiday firms.

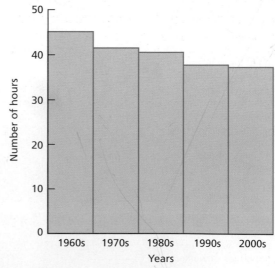

Figure 1 Working week hours table

Developments in communications and information technology

Developments in communication systems includes the development of computer reservation systems and the increasing availability of holidays advertised on the internet which facilitates online booking.

Computer reservation systems have totally changed the sale of air tickets and hotel accommodation. Global distribution systems such as Sabre, Galileo, Amadeus and Worldspan have made it possible for travel companies such as TUI to operate commercially on a world scale. These systems make it possible to obtain the latest information on an enormous range of travel and tourism products and services. Many customers now use Teletext and the internet to book holidays from their own homes. Most airlines and tour operators have recognised this potential and have developed online booking services and it is now possible to print your own tickets at home.

Product development and changing consumer needs, expectations and fashions

The travel and tourism industry has to continually come up with new products due to changing consumer tastes. One of the first products to be developed was Butlin's holiday camps in the 1950s. At the time, these were very successful, as they appealed to the British holidaymakers. More recently, there has been the development of theme parks, led by the Disney parks in the USA.

One of the most important product developments has been the package holiday which involved a tour company providing travel, accommodation and sometimes holiday activities. These evolved in the 1950s and were first run by Horizon Holidays. The most recent product developments include long-haul holidays to places like the Maldives and the specialist package holidays which cater for everybody's needs including wedding packages.

Many of these product developments are led by changing consumer needs, expectations and fashions.

Economic factors

The economic factors which have caused a growth in global tourism are greater wealth, currency exchange rates, and the developments in transport technology which has made places in the world seem closer together because it has shortened the time distance.

Greater wealth

The populations of most of the countries in the developed world are becoming increasingly wealthy. There are a number of reasons for this:

- more disposable income
- fewer children
- two-income families
- minimum wage.

The incomes of most people in HICs and MICs have increased at a greater rate than the cost of necessities (goods and services needed for everyday living). The average annual wage in 2008 was £23,000. This means that most people have more disposable income which they can spend on luxuries such as holidays. Therefore many people are taking two or even three holidays a year.

Most people also have fewer children than in previous generations, which gives them more disposable income and allows for the possibility of more frequent holidays or travel to more exotic places. The average family size in the UK was 2.4 children in 1971 and is now 1.8 children. This means that there is less money being spent on bringing up children and more on luxury items. Many families now have two wage earners. In 2008, 68 per cent of mothers had full- or part-time jobs. Consequently, families have proportionately more money to spend on luxuries of which holidays are one example. The minimum wage was raised to £5.73 per hour in October 2008. This means that the minimum wage has increased by 59 per cent since it was introduced in 1998. This allows low-paid workers more of an opportunity to go on holiday.

Currency exchange rates

Fluctuations in the currency of holiday destinations can make them very attractive. In 2007 and the first half of 2008 the USA saw a 20 per cent increase in the number of UK tourists visiting because the exchange rate was at $2 to the pound; the best exchange rate for many years. In the second half of 2008 the pound dropped against most of the world's currencies making it expensive for UK tourists to travel abroad. The weakening pound had the opposite effect on inbound tourists; encouraging more tourists from other countries to come to the UK.

Developments in transport

There have been many developments in transport which have impacted on the travel industry. These range from the increase in car ownership to the building of motorways and the greater use of air transport by the holiday industry.

Motorways allow holidaymakers to reach their destination much more quickly, saving time and often the expense of an overnight stay. Aircraft, ships and trains can now take large numbers of people to their destination safely and quickly. Economies of scale operate. The cost of flying a plane with 300 seats is not much more than one with 100 seats making the cost per person less. The same is true with the large cruise ships which can now carry more than 4,000 passengers.

The rise in budget airlines like easyJet and Ryanair has made air travel much cheaper and allowed tourists to make several short trips a year. Due to this there has been a considerable rise in the number of short break holidays for culture (for example, museums, art galleries) or entertainment like stag and hen weekends.

Political factors

There have been many changes in the policies that countries have towards tourism. Thirty years ago it would have been difficult to travel to countries such as China and East Germany because of the politics of those countries. They were communist countries that did not welcome tourists from other countries in the world. It is now easy to travel to most countries in the world although visas are still required for some countries such as Cuba and China. There are still some countries in the world that do not welcome tourists because of national security, for example, North Korea.

The relaxation of boundaries between the EU countries and the establishment of a common currency has made movement between these countries particularly easy. Many tourists have taken advantage of this and move freely between the countries for weekend breaks.

Holiday destinations offer a variety of physical and human attractions

People go on holiday for many different reasons and to locations which offer many different attractions. Holidays destinations can be popular because they have a range of physical attractions which people desire such as guaranteed sunshine, white sandy beaches and warm seas. Other tourists prefer to go on holiday in the winter months for a skiing break where guaranteed snow and excellent human facilities such as a range of ski lifts will be available. Holidaymakers are also attracted to destinations which can offer them the human attractions they wish to experience which can range from Disney themed parks to ancient monuments and museums.

A skiing holiday is an example of an adventure holiday. As well as skiing, other dangerous activities that holidaymakers can take part in are ice skating, tobogganing, ice climbing and paragliding

Village in the valley which will have hotels, chalets and facilities for aprés ski like sport centres and discos.

A large number of lifts transport skiers easily around the moutain.

Thick snow giving a long skiing season from November to April.

Bright, clear blue sky which looks beautiful and attracts tourists to the area.

Beautiful mountain scenery which attracts summer and winter tourists.

A variety of different slopes for skiers of all abilities, from very steep for experts to gentle for beginners.

Calm, warm blue sea ideal for watersports like speed boats and sailing and windsurfing.

Large port where cruise ships can stop and people can take boat trips to deserted islands and beaches.

Historic monument, the Acropolis, in a spectacular setting which attracts heritage tourists.

Busy city with shops and entertainment facilities like restaurants, cinemas and bars.

Hotels and restaurants in uncongested area making it quiet and relaxing for holiday makers.

Attractive parks providing shade from the hot sun. Frequented by locals and tourists taking a rest from shopping and site seeing.

Figure 2 Different types of holiday and tourist destinations

This hotel is used by the tour operator Libra as part of a package holiday. British families are flown to Athens airport and transported to the island by boat. They can stay at the hotel on half board basis for £650 for two weeks in July.

Hotels, bars and restaurants – all are facing the sea giving stunning views of the bay. Holiday makers can go to them without having to change out of their swimming costumes.

Rocky coastline which looks rugged and attractive. A good area for snorkelling because a wide variety of beautifully coloured fish will be there.

Bright blue sky. Hot and dry weather. Steep tree covered slopes make building difficult so the resort will not grow too large.

Sandy beach which is great for children to play on and for sunbathers.

Warm, shallow and calm sea, perfect for families.

Also good for watersports and volleyball. Banana boats and windsurfer boards are available.

Reclining chairs and sunshades lining the beach to give views of the sea whilst relaxing and maybe reading a book.

Shops selling tourist items. In this shop they are selling traditional hand made Spanish shawls and bags.

Backpackers often stay in cheap rooms which are let out by locals.

Pavement cafes where tourists can enjoy a relaxing drink or meal in the sunshine.

Group of backpackers on a tour of Europe after completing their exams. Their belongings are carried around in rucksacks.

This is Esmarelda Beach in Cuba. It is a beautiful location to get married. The temple looking out directly onto the white sandy beach is very romantic and popular for couples to have both their wedding and honeymoon at the nearby hotel.

Day trips to interesting places in the locality being advertised outside a travel agency

Narrow streets which are pedestrianised giving tourists attractive and car free areas to shop.

The fully inclusive hotels are just a short walk to the beach. Everything the tourists want is close together so they don't have to waste time in travelling from one place to another.

A whole variety of watersports take place in this shallow, safe protected bay. The picture shows catamarans, speed boats, windsurfers and pedaloes. There are also some people snorkelling amongst the coral reef.

The beautiful blue sky which brings hot dry weather makes the Caribbean Islands very popular with sun and sea tourists.

Warm, shallow sea and clean, white sand.

Warm, shallow sea and clean, white sand are the perfect place to relax on sun loungers and read a book or have a refreshing drink.

There is stunning scenery with the wide sweep of the bay and the tree clad hillsides which contrast against the azure blue of the sea.

Figure 2 Different types of holiday and tourist destinations continued

Different types of holidays

When mass tourism started in the 1960s most tourists were looking for a holiday which gave them sea, sand and sun. This was when package holidays were invented. A package holiday is one that has everything arranged by the tour company. The holiday includes in the price all transportation and accommodation, and usually offers some of the food such as breakfast and evening meal. The tour company would also offer the services of a representative in the resort to deal with any problems the tourist might have or to help them find out about the attractions in the area. The holidays are advertised in tour operator brochures and can be booked at travel agents, like First Choice and Thomas Cook, which are found on the high street in many towns. More commonly now, the holidays are advertised on the tour companies' websites and booked directly.

Figure 3 A selection of tour operator brochures

Jersey Tourism says niche market holidays are helping boost numbers, especially during off-season months. One hotel, which caters for Christian holidaymakers, said it is hoping to attract more visitors to Jersey this year. The Highlands Hotel specialises in offering Bible studies to their guests. Its manager, Alan Irving, said its location appeals to many Christians hoping to learn more about the Christian faith. The Highlands is one example of how some hotels on the island are targeting particular groups, which is a trend Jersey Tourism hopes will be developed further.

The range of holidays that people are taking has been rapidly expanding and there are now holidays catering for the hobbies and interests of different groups of people. Companies have introduced holidays for niche markets specialising in the unusual, such as trekking to Kathmandu or bird watching in The Gambia. An interesting example of a niche holiday is shown in the yellow box.

Adventure holidays

An adventure holiday is usually for the purpose of challenge, exploration, skills development or thrills, and probably appeals more to the younger market at one end of the scale and the active over 50s who have retired early. These are clearly not low-key holidays and may involve more than an element of risk, but that is why people go on them, for high activity, thrills and maybe spills. There are a lot of companies such as the adventure companies Exodus and Activities Abroad that specialise in adventure holidays.

Figure 4 An adventure holiday

Backpacking holidays

Backpacking is a term that has historically been used to mean a form of low-cost, independent international travel. Originally most backpackers would have gone camping or stayed in youth hostels but the backpacking tourist has become more sophisticated and now often stays in budget hotels. It is generally undertaken by younger travellers, particularly students on a gap year. It is becoming more common, however, for long-term workers to have a break in their careers and go on a 'gap year for grown-ups'.

Wedding holidays

It is now possible to get married in a number of exotic locations around the world. Many tour operators will arrange a package tour which includes the honeymoon and the marriage ceremony, often on a palm-fringed, white sandy beach. The advert on the right is from Virgin Holidays and shows what the tour company will provide to make the wedding run smoothly.

Your deluxe wedding package includes:

- Services of a Wedding Consultant
- Picturesque Ceremony Location
- Preparation of Documentation
- Certified Marriage Licence
- Marriage Officer
- Best Man/Maid of Honour or Witness (if required)
- Pre-recorded Musical Accompaniment
- Champagne and Chilled Hors D'oeuvres
- Reception for 30 min
- 2 Guests may attend the Ceremony and Reception
- Bridal Bouquet and Groom's Boutonniere
- Caribbean two-tier Wedding Cake
- Candlelit Dinner for Bride and Groom
- Continental Breakfast in Bed the Following Morning
- Just Married T-shirts
- One 7"×5" Wedding Photograph

Your Sandals Deluxe Wedding Package is FREE for stays of 7 nights or more. For shorter stays a charge of £579 applies. Promotional room categories not included.

Source: Virgin Holidays

ACTIVITIES

Higher

1 People now have greater leisure time available to go on holiday. Why?

2 Why do people who live in HICs now have more money to spend on holidays?

3 Communications networks have developed both in telecommunications and transport communications. How have these developments caused a growth in global tourism?

4 Study Figure 2 on pages 285–286. It shows a number of holiday destinations. Choose three of the photographs.

  a Describe the physical and human attractions of the area.

  b What type of holiday could occur in the area?

Foundation

1 People now have greater leisure time available to go on holiday. Use the terms in the box to explain why.

longer paid holidays	shorter working weeks
early retirement	

2 People who live in HICs now have more money to spend on holidays.

Complete the sentences to explain why. Use some of the words in the box. You may use a word more than once.

increased	decreased	more
less	work	play

Incomes have .... which means they have more money to spend on holidays.

Families have fewer children so have .... money available for holidays.

The minimum wage has increased and .... mothers go out to work.

3 Many families now have access to the internet. How has this caused a growth in global tourism?

4 There are now cheaper flights available. How does this affect the growth of tourism?

5 Study Figure 2 on pages 285–286. It shows a number of holiday destinations. Choose three of the photographs.

  a Describe the physical and human attractions of the area.

  b What type of holiday could occur in the area?

Review

By the end of this section you should be able to:

- explain the social, economic and political factors causing the growth of tourism
- understand that holiday destinations offer a variety of physical and human attractions
- describe different types of holidays.

Resort development

Learning objective – to study how tourist resorts change through time.

Learning outcomes
- To understand the Butler model of resort development.
- To know the development of Blackpool in relation to the Butler model.

The Butler model of resort development

In 1980 R.W. Butler developed a model for resort development. The model has seven stages which he believes resorts go through as they become tourist destinations. The model he devised is shown in Figure 5.

The model can be applied to many tourist destinations, both in HICs and LICs, but in this instance the example will be Blackpool, a resort on the north-west coast of the UK. The development of Blackpool in relation to the model is shown in Figure 6.

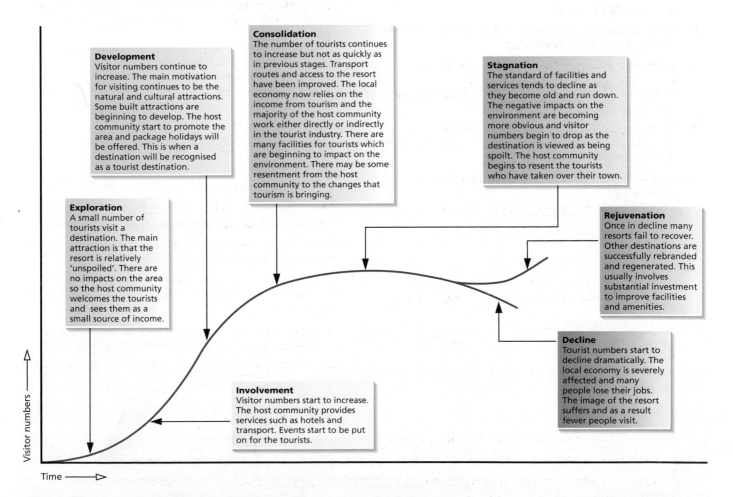

Development
Visitor numbers continue to increase. The main motivation for visiting continues to be the natural and cultural attractions. Some built attractions are beginning to develop. The host community start to promote the area and package holidays will be offered. This is when a destination will be recognised as a tourist destination.

Consolidation
The number of tourists continues to increase but not as quickly as in previous stages. Transport routes and access to the resort have been improved. The local economy now relies on the income from tourism and the majority of the host community work either directly or indirectly in the tourist industry. There are many facilities for tourists which are beginning to impact on the environment. There may be some resentment from the host community to the changes that tourism is bringing.

Stagnation
The standard of facilities and services tends to decline as they become old and run down. The negative impacts on the environment are becoming more obvious and visitor numbers begin to drop as the destination is viewed as being spoilt. The host community begins to resent the tourists who have taken over their town.

Exploration
A small number of tourists visit a destination. The main attraction is that the resort is relatively 'unspoiled'. There are no impacts on the area so the host community welcomes the tourists and sees them as a small source of income.

Rejuvenation
Once in decline many resorts fail to recover. Other destinations are successfully rebranded and regenerated. This usually involves substantial investment to improve facilities and amenities.

Decline
Tourist numbers start to decline dramatically. The local economy is severely affected and many people lose their jobs. The image of the resort suffers and as a result fewer people visit.

Involvement
Visitor numbers start to increase. The host community provides services such as hotels and transport. Events start to be put on for the tourists.

Visitor numbers

Time

Figure 5 The Butler model of resort development

1720	The only visitors were the landed gentry who would ride on the beach and bathe in the sea.
1735	Blackpool's first guest house was created by Edward Whiteside, specifically for visitors to Blackpool.
1780	There were 4 hotels, for example Bailey's now called The Metropole. The working classes stayed in small guesthouses in the area. There were bowling greens and facilities for archery. The main attraction was the sea or walking/riding along the sea front to 'take the air'. Many people bathed in the sea as it was seen as healthy to do so. A bell was rung when it was time for the ladies to bathe, and any gentleman found on the shore was fined a bottle of wine.
1781	Thomas Clifton and Sir Henry Houghton built 1st private road into Blackpool. Stage coaches ran from Manchester and Halifax. This allowed people from the mill towns of northern England access to cheap transport to the resort. However it took a day to reach Blackpool from Manchester and two days from Yorkshire.
1819	Henry Banks bought the Lane's End estate, which included the Lane's End Hotel. He built the first holiday cottages on this site during the 1820s.
1837	Dr John Cocker, Henry's son-in-law built the first assembly rooms where the tourists could meet and enjoy events. This was the Victoria Parade which also had six shops below.
1840	The first railway in the area opened in 1840 but it only ran as far as Poulton in the Fylde. Trippers completed their journey by waggonette.
1846	Branch line was built from Poulton to Blackpool. Thousands of day trippers now visited.
1856–1870	Promenade was built along the sea front.
1860	Still very little entertainment for the visitors who came to Blackpool.
1863	North Pier opened.
1868	Facilities started to be developed – Talbot Road Assembly rooms and Theatre Royal open.
1870	Central Pier opened with open-air dancing for the working classes. New promenade was opened to the South which linked the different areas of Blackpool together.
1872	The Raikes Hall Pleasure Gardens which included a lake, racecourse, football and cricket ground, skating rink, aviary, monkey house, ballroom, theatre and many other attractions were built.
1872	850,000 visitors.
1878	Winter Gardens opened – Blackpool's first large indoor entertainment venue.
1885	There was a developing problem with transport systems within the town. The council responded by building the country's first permanent electric tramway along the seafront. The first stage being from Cocker Street to South Shore.
1889	Opera House was built in the Winter Gardens complex.
1890	Blackpool at this time had 7,000 dwellings which could accommodate 250,000 holiday makers and a permanent population of 35,000.
1891–1894	Blackpool Tower was built. This included a circus and ballroom.
1893	South Pier opened.
1893–1899	North Promenade was built.
1894	Grand Theatre opened on Church Street.
1895	The Empire Theatre opened.
1896	A 'Gigantic Wheel' was built at the corner of Adelaide Street and Coronation Street. It was 220 feet high and had 30 carriages. The Winter Gardens added to its facilities with the Empress Ballroom and Indian Lounge.
1897	Traders on the beach were banned and they moved into the gardens of houses on the Promenade which saw the beginning of the Golden Mile.
1898 and 1900	The towns railway stations were rebuilt to deal with the increasing numbers of visitors who were arriving by train.
1902–1905	The present promenade between the North and South Piers was built at a cost of £114,700.
1904	Grand Theatre was built. Pleasure beach opened – it took 3 years to build.
1912	Blackpool illuminations were first switched on. They were put on hold during the First World War but were switched on again in 1925.
1923	The first Blackpool Carnival. The world's largest open-air baths opened at South Shore.
1926	Stanley Park opened.
1928	Olympia complex built on the site of the Great Wheel.

Figure 6 The development of Blackpool

1929	Louis Tussaud's Waxworks opened. Municipal aerodrome was opened.
1930	Visitor attractions such as Harrowside Solarium, Derby Baths were built along with transport facilities such as the Talbot Road Bus Station. Pleasure Beach was modernised.
1931	3,850,000 visitors.
1939	New Opera House opened which was Britain's largest cinema and Theatre.
1972	Blackpool Zoo opened.
1975	M55 opened between the M6 and Blackpool which made it easier to reach Blackpool by road. The car park at the end of the motorway built on the site of the old railway station can accommodate 6,000 cars. There are now 3 railway stations in Blackpool – North, South and in 1987 the new Pleasure Beach Railway Station.
1980	The Hounds Hill Centre opened. This was the first indoor shopping centre in Blackpool with 40 shop units.
1986	The Sandcastle opened.
1987	• Visitor nights have declined from 16m to 10.5m • The average annual hotel occupancy rate has reduced to 22% • Annual day visits have declined from 7.4m to 3.9m • The seasonal economy has shortened, the peak has become less pronounced. • Annual spend by overnight visitors has declined from £800m to £500m at 2004 prices.
1990	Blackpool Sea Life Centre opened to try to rejuvenate the town.
2003	Rejuvenation project started. • 26,700 new jobs to be created. • £2.2bn of capital to be invested. • 400,000 square metres of retail, casino, leisure, conference, office and airport development. • 5,700 new homes to be built. • 7m additional visitors per year. • 127 hectares of brownfield sites will be re-development.
2003	New art centre on the South Shore. The Solaris centre built which is a centre for environmental education and the promotion of sustainable tourism developed by Lancaster and Blackpool Universities.
2004	11,000,000 visitors.
2005	A widened road and new parking facilities have been built. There will be a new parkland area with rock climbing towers and all weather games pitches.
2008	The Bond Hotel, on Bond Street, is to have a £14m upgrade. The existing building will be demolished and replaced with a bigger hotel, with 142 bedrooms, compared to 65 in the current premises.
Autumn 2008	The council have recently approved the Talbot Gateway project. This will see the building of a new business district which will include offices, shops, a food store, cafes and restaurants, along with residential apartments and town centre parking.
2009	New coastal defence scheme will be completed costing £80m along 3.2km of Blackpool seafront.

Key

Exploration
Involvement
Development
Consolidation
Stagnation
decline
Rejuvenation

Figure 7 Blackpool in the 2000s

Review

By the end of this section you should be able to:
- understand the Butler model of resort development
- understand the development of Blackpool in relation to the Butler model.

ACTIVITIES

Higher

1 What is the Butler model of resort development?

2 Explain the seven stages of the Butler model.

3 Study Figure 6 on pages 290–291. Choose three features on the figure from each stage of the seven stages of the Butler model. Produce your own mini timeline for Blackpool.

Foundation

1 There are seven stages in the Butler model of resort development. State the names of the seven stages and give a brief description of what happens in each stage. You should start with exploration and end with rejuvenation.

2 Complete the table on the right by putting the words and statements in the correct box in the table. Use Figure 6 on pages 290–291 to help you to find out the dates that the event occurred.

- Stagnation
- Involvement
- Decline
- Development
- Consolidation
- 11,000,000 visitors
- The only visitors were the landed gentry who would ride on the beach and bathe in the sea

- Annual day visits have declined from 7.4 million to 3.9 million.
- Henry Banks bought the Lane's End estate, which included the Lane's End Hotel. He built the first holiday cottages on this site during the 1820s.
- The Sandcastle opened.
- Central Pier opened with open-air dancing for the working classes. New promenade was opened to the south which linked the different areas of Blackpool together.
- Blackpool illuminations were first switched on in 1934. They were put on hold during the First World War but were switched on again in 1925.

Stage of model	Date	Event or fact
Exploration		
Rejuvenation		

Extension

Choose another tourist destination in the EU. Draw your own timeline to show its development through the stages of the Butler model.

The effects of tourist industry growth

Learning objective – to study the social, economic and environmental effects of tourism in countries at different levels of development.

Learning outcome

- To know the positive social, economic and environmental effects of tourism.
- To know the negative social, economic and environmental effects of tourism.

The growth of tourism is having an effect on popular tourist destinations in countries at different levels of development. These effects can be either positive or negative. The effects can be economic due to the increase in jobs in primary, secondary and tertiary sectors, or social due to the impact on entertainment facilities or environmental, for example, due to footpath erosion.

The effects of tourism on Ayia Napa, Cyprus

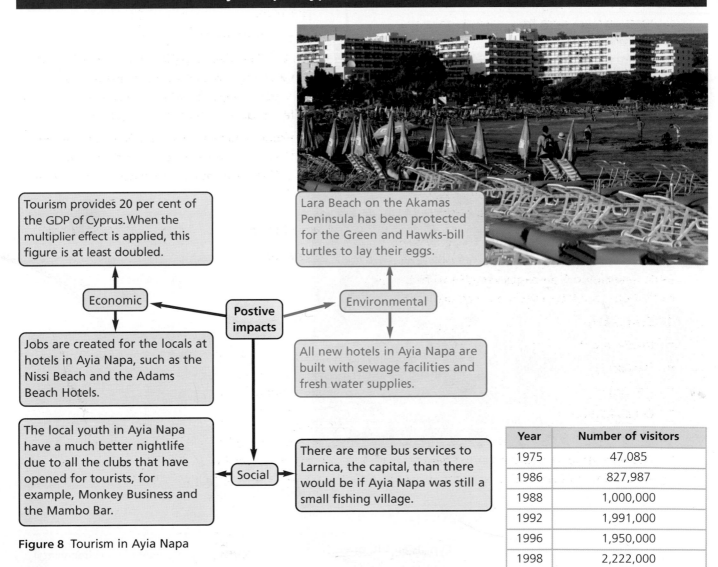

Tourism provides 20 per cent of the GDP of Cyprus. When the multiplier effect is applied, this figure is at least doubled.

Lara Beach on the Akamas Peninsula has been protected for the Green and Hawks-bill turtles to lay their eggs.

Economic

Postive impacts

Environmental

Jobs are created for the locals at hotels in Ayia Napa, such as the Nissi Beach and the Adams Beach Hotels.

All new hotels in Ayia Napa are built with sewage facilities and fresh water supplies.

The local youth in Ayia Napa have a much better nightlife due to all the clubs that have opened for tourists, for example, Monkey Business and the Mambo Bar.

Social

There are more bus services to Larnica, the capital, than there would be if Ayia Napa was still a small fishing village.

Figure 8 Tourism in Ayia Napa

Year	Number of visitors
1975	47,085
1986	827,987
1988	1,000,000
1992	1,991,000
1996	1,950,000
1998	2,222,000
2000	2,223,000

Figure 9 Tourist numbers for Cyprus

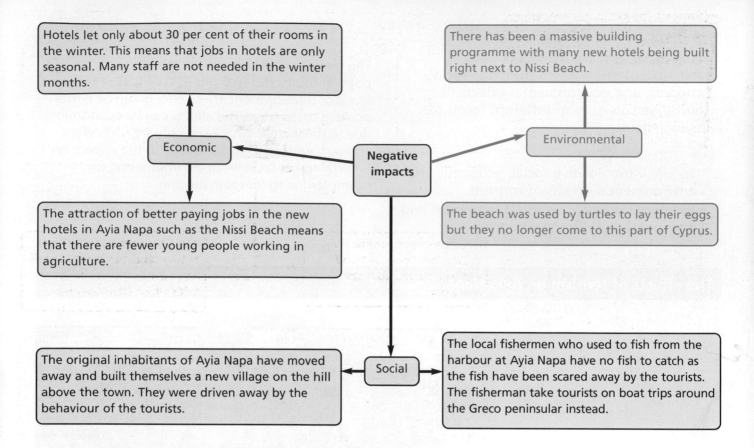

Hotels let only about 30 per cent of their rooms in the winter. This means that jobs in hotels are only seasonal. Many staff are not needed in the winter months.

There has been a massive building programme with many new hotels being built right next to Nissi Beach.

Economic

Negative impacts

Environmental

The attraction of better paying jobs in the new hotels in Ayia Napa such as the Nissi Beach means that there are fewer young people working in agriculture.

The beach was used by turtles to lay their eggs but they no longer come to this part of Cyprus.

The original inhabitants of Ayia Napa have moved away and built themselves a new village on the hill above the town. They were driven away by the behaviour of the tourists.

Social

The local fishermen who used to fish from the harbour at Ayia Napa have no fish to catch as the fish have been scared away by the tourists. The fisherman take tourists on boat trips around the Greco peninsular instead.

Figure 10 Clubbing in Ayia Napa

ACTIVITIES

1 Is Cyprus an HIC or LIC?
2 Complete the table below to show the effects of tourism on Cyprus. There should be two effects in each box.

	Social	Economic	Environmental
Positive			
Negative			

The effects of tourism on Zanzibar

Figure 11 Palace museum and walls surrounding Stone Town

1980	15,700
1985	19,000
1990	40,000
1995	50,000
2000	70,000
2005	115,000

Figure 12 Zanzibar tourist numbers

Figure 13 Scuba diving off the coast of Zanzibar

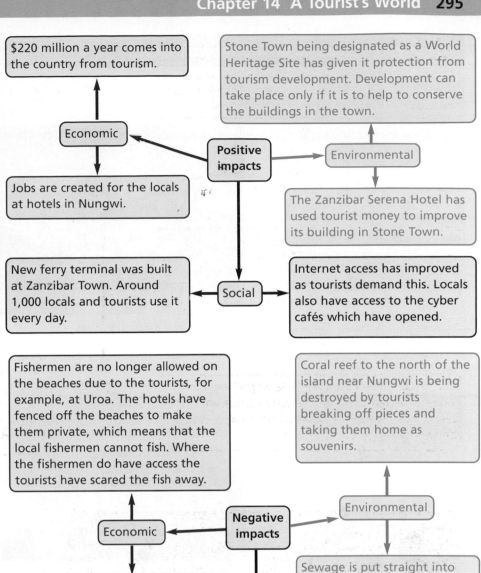

$220 million a year comes into the country from tourism.

Economic

Jobs are created for the locals at hotels in Nungwi.

Stone Town being designated as a World Heritage Site has given it protection from tourism development. Development can take place only if it is to help to conserve the buildings in the town.

Positive impacts

Environmental

The Zanzibar Serena Hotel has used tourist money to improve its building in Stone Town.

New ferry terminal was built at Zanzibar Town. Around 1,000 locals and tourists use it every day.

Social

Internet access has improved as tourists demand this. Locals also have access to the cyber cafés which have opened.

Fishermen are no longer allowed on the beaches due to the tourists, for example, at Uroa. The hotels have fenced off the beaches to make them private, which means that the local fishermen cannot fish. Where the fishermen do have access the tourists have scared the fish away.

Coral reef to the north of the island near Nungwi is being destroyed by tourists breaking off pieces and taking them home as souvenirs.

Economic   **Negative impacts**   Environmental

The jobs in the hotels, for example, the Serena Hotel in Stone Town, are menial and low paid.

Sewage is put straight into the sea. At Zanzibar Town tourists walk around the sewage as it trickles onto the beach.

Zanzibar is a Muslim country. Tourists have different moral codes, for example, they do not cover their shoulders. This insults the local inhabitants.

Social

Tourists are wealthier than the local people. This has led to an increase in muggings on the east coast near the hotels at Uroa and Matemwe.

ACTIVITIES

1 Is Zanzibar an HIC or LIC?
2 Complete the table below to show the effects of tourism on Zanzibar. There should be two effects in each box.

	Social	Economic	Environmental
Positive			
Negative			

The effects of tourism on Machu Picchu, Peru

Negative	Impact	Positive

Economic

The hotels such as the Sanctuary lodge at the entrance to Machu Picchu and the train line to the site are owned and run by The Orient-Express Hotels group, based in Bermuda. Therefore, a lot of the profit made from tourism leaves the country because the hotels are not owned by Peruvians.

The best jobs and, therefore, the high paying jobs are done by foreigners not local people, who are brought in to work by the foreign hotel company.

Figure 14 The market at Pisac

Tourists spend money in the area, which has a positive impact on the incomes of local residents. At the local market in Pisac on a Sunday morning, for example, a handicraft market has developed just for tourists. (Figure 14)

The porters are paid $10 each day for the four-day trip. The more reputable tour companies also request that their clients tip the porters. A tip of $12 is given by each member of the tour party and shared between the porters. This amounts to considerably more than hotel workers are paid. Machu Picchu generates $40 million a year in income for the Peruvian government.

Environmental

Garbage is thrown into rivers, such as the Urubamba, or left close to the trail. This includes human excreta.

Erosion is beginning to occur on the Inca Trail due to the pressure of 500 tourists a day. In 1998, 53,500 tourists walked the trail.

Tourists pick orchids which grow among the ruins and along the side of the trail.

The rubbish bins along the trail are picked up by park wardens and simply dumped, usually in an open pit about 50 m from the trail.

The large number of tourists at the ancient site in brightly coloured coats causes visual pollution (see Figure 15).

Figure 15 Tourists causing visual pollution

No plastic bottles are allowed on the trail, since 2000, only canteens.

The tourists pay $50 dollars each to travel the Inca Trail, which contributes to the upkeep of the area.

The numbers of people on the trail are being limited to 500 a day to reduce the rate of erosion.

Machu Picchu has been designated a World Heritage Site to protect it from large numbers of tourists.

Year	Trekkers on the Inca Trail
1992	5,000
1994	14,500
1996	30,500
1998	53,500
2000	82,000

Figure 15 Number of people on the Inca Trail

Social

The local villagers who are employed as porters are not treated well by some of the tour companies or some of the tourists. They are made to carry bags weighing up to 50 kilos. This can give them a false impression of all visitors.

The local villagers are affected by the clothes of the western visitors and wish to dress like them rather than in native garments (see Figure 16). The native ponchos are being worn with western style trousers by porters on the trail. This causes a breakdown in the local culture.

Figure 16 Porters on the Inca Trail

Numbers of people on the trail are limited to 500. This should allow for areas of quiet reflection due to fewer visitors.

Porters since 2000 have been limited to carrying a load of 25 kg.

The extra income coming into the area, as tourism provides jobs and opportunities to sell souvenirs, has improved the standard of living for the local people.

The effects of tourism on Malham, UK

Social effects

Tourism can be beneficial in creating more demand for local services such as banks and public transport. The bus service to Skipton, the local town, is more frequent in the summer months due to the tourists' use of it. The National Trust also runs a shuttle bus service from Settle to Malham on weekends and Bank Holidays throughout the summer. It costs £2 return. It runs every hour from 10.30 a.m. until 4.30 p.m. This service has two impacts: it releases pressure on the car park at Malham, and it can be used by local residents to get into Settle to do their shopping.

Figure 17 Parked vehicles in Malham (main street)

Visitors tend to park in the narrow village streets causing congestion. The local residents are prevented from going about their necessary activities and access for emergency vehicles is severely restricted. Figure 17 was taken on the main street of Malham in August. Due to the parked vehicles, cars have to wait if another vehicle is coming in the other direction. On the right of the photograph the grass has been eroded as this is the main route from the car park to Janet's Foss waterfall and the Pennine Way. If the cars were not parked on the road the visitors would walk on the road and not erode the grass verge.

Figure 17 also shows the large number of billboards that are still displayed in the main street even though the National Park authority has banned them because they ruin the authenticity of the village.

Traditional village public houses, such as The Buck Inn shown in Figure 18, have become 'themed', destroying their authentic nature as well as discouraging the locals. However, The Buck Inn opens one of its bars, known as the Hikers Bar, all day in the summer months, which generates income for the pub and enables the locals to have access to longer opening hours.

Figure 18 The Buck Inn

Figure 19 Town Head Farm

Economic effects

In 1991, 55 per cent of the houses in Malham were used for holiday purposes. There is a trend towards buying holiday cottages rather than hiring accommodation. The demand for second homes has meant that the prices of houses in the area have risen dramatically. Their prices are approximately 15 per cent higher than properties in less popular rural areas of Yorkshire. This makes it very difficult for the locals, especially young couples, to buy property in the area.

Tourism provides new employment opportunities in an area suffering from the depression in farming. The farmer at Town Head Farm has opened a campsite charging £10 a night per tent (Figure 19). He also allows people to park their cars in his farmyard for £3 a day.

There are also numerous cafés and shops in the village which cater for the tourists, such as The Cove Centre (see Figure 20). These provide employment opportunities for the local people. The employment is, however, seasonal and poorly paid.

Figure 20 The Cove Centre

Environmental effects

In 1994 the creation of the open access area and additional footpaths (Figures 21 and 22) through the Countryside Stewardship scheme in partnership with local farmers and landowners, means that locals as well as tourists have more rights to roam over their local area. However, this has caused problems for some farmers as tourists do not stay on the path causing erosion; they climb on the stone walls and their dogs worry the farmers' sheep.

Figure 21 Path to Malham Cove

Figure 22 Entrance to path to Malham Cove

Malham is in the Yorkshire Dales National park. This means that it is protected by the laws of the park which restrict development that is not in keeping with the natural environment. For example, any new houses have to be built using local stone.

The Malham area is very popular with between 75,000 and 100,000 visits per year. This causes erosion of footpaths, especially the footpath to Janet's Foss waterfall which is one of the closest attractions to the village. Figure 23 shows how, even though the path has been replaced with limestone slabs, it has not been made wide enough and erosion is still occurring.

Figure 23 Path leading to Janet's Foss waterfall

Review

By the end of this section you should be able to:
- explain the positive social, economic and environmental effects of tourism
- explain the negative social, economic and environmental effects of tourism.

ACTIVITIES

Higher

1 Describe one social, one economic and one environmental effect of tourism on Machu Picchu.

2 The number of tourists on the Inca Trail and visiting the ruins at Machu Picchu has been limited to 500 a day. Discuss the implications of this on the people and environment of the area.

3 Draw a graph to show the information on tourist numbers in Figure 15 on page 296.
   a Work out the figure for 2004, which is 500 people a day for 190 days (which is the tourist season).
   b Decide what type of graph you think is appropriate.
   c Draw the graph remembering to give it a title and label the axes.
   d Justify why the graphical technique you chose was appropriate.
   e Describe and give reasons for the changes that your graph shows.

4 Read the information on Malham. Draw spidergrams of the social, economic and environmental effects of tourism. You should include both positive and negative effects.

Foundation

1 Describe one social, one economic and one environmental positive effect of tourism on Machu Picchu.

2 Describe one social, one economic and one environmental negative effect of tourism on Machu Picchu.

3 Draw a graph to show the information on tourist numbers in Figure 15 on page 296. Include the figure of 95,000 for 2004.
   a Decide what type of graph you think is appropriate.
   b Draw the graph remembering to give it a title and label the axes.
   c Say why the graphical technique you chose was appropriate.
   d Describe and give reasons for the changes that your graph shows.

4 Read the statements below. Complete the table by putting each statement in the correct box.

   More frequent buses to Skipton.

   Visitors tend to park in the narrow village streets causing congestion.

   Billboards cause visual pollution.

   The Buck Inn is a 'themed' pub, destroying its authentic nature and discouraging the locals.

   In 1991, 55 per cent of the houses in Malham were used for holiday purposes.

   Local farmers have camping fields.

   Shops provide souvenirs for tourists.

   Shops provide jobs for locals.

	Social	Economic
Positive		
Negative		

Ecotourism

Learning objective – to study an ecotourism destination.

Learning outcomes
- To know the meaning of sustainable tourism and ecotourism.
- To know that tourism can protect the environment and benefit the local community.

Ecotourism

The World Tourism Organisation defines sustainable tourism as: 'Tourism which leads to the management of all resources in such a way that economic, social and aesthetic need can be fulfilled while maintaining cultural integrity, essential ecological processes, biological diversity and life support systems.'

In more simple terms this means that sustainable tourism is a process which meets the needs of present tourists and host communities while protecting and enhancing the needs of future generations.

Ecotourism is a branch of sustainable tourism. The International Ecotourism Society gives the following definition that is widely accepted:'Ecotourism is responsible travel to natural areas that conserves the environment and improves the well-being of local people.'

The Ecotourism Resource Centre gives a slightly more complex but broadly similar definition:'Ecotourism involves visiting natural areas with the objectives of learning, studying or participating in activities that do not bring negative effects to the environment; whilst protecting and empowering the local community socially and economically.'

The principles of ecotourism

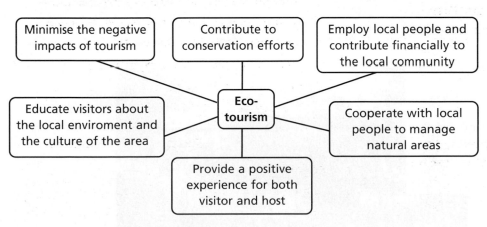

Figure 24 Principles of ecotourism

'Footsteps' is an ecotourism destination in The Gambia. It is built in the style of a traditional African village compound, with nine accommodation huts. It is located close to the village of Gunjur and is open all year round. Most of the tourists come from the UK.

The huts are made from local wood and materials. The furniture is made by craftsmen from Gunjur from local wood. The original buildings had straw roofs, but were destroyed in a fire in January 2007. The new huts have concrete roofs which are fire resistant; the reception, bar and restaurant have retained their straw roofs.

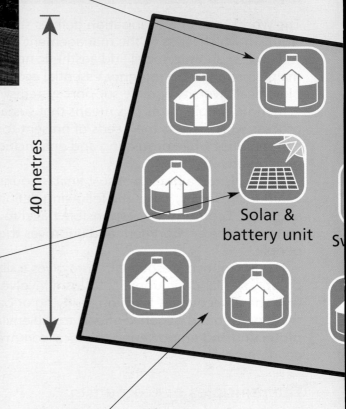

The wind and the Sun are used to produce electricity (see Unit 2 Chapter 7). The wind turbine has high maintenance costs and so the main source of power is solar energy. The solar powered freezer has considerably reduced the use of propane gas.

Solar & battery unit

40 metres

At the lodge guests can see local women creating 'tie dye' and batik or see how a Jembe drum is made using skills handed down over centuries. There is a shop on site which sells the work of these skilled craftspeople. Footsteps informs its guests about local markets and craftspeople. Footsteps also gives 20 per cent of its profit to the local community.

Figure 25 Footsteps Eco-Lodge

Footsteps has its own vegetable gardens and plant life. There are banana trees outside every hut as well as cashew, papaya, mango, orange and grapefruit trees. The gardens grow all of the vegetables, salad and herbs required by the lodge. Ducks are kept which provide eggs. The Gambians who run the gardens recycle everything that they have a use for.

All the toilets at Footsteps Eco-Lodge are composting toilets. This means that all harmful substances are removed, which allows the waste to be used as compost.

Water is a precious commodity. The water for the huts comes from tubewells and is stored in water tanks. Solar powered pumps are used to fill up the water tanks.

The water used by guests in sinks, baths and for washing clothes, known as grey water, is filtered and then used to irrigate the fruit and vegetables grown in the gardens.

Hot water for showers is provided by a coil of black pipe, full of water, built into the roof and heated by the Sun. The really hot water lasts approximately five minutes which ensures guests do not waste hot water supplies.

Bar & restaurant

Bantaba

Public toilet block

Gardens

Swimming pool

Large hut

Accommodation huts

Reception

0 metres

The water for the swimming pool is filtered through reed beds to get rid of impurities.

The company employs all 22 of their staff from the local village of Gunjur. The local Gambian employees receive training and are paid for the whole year, unlike most locally employed staff who are laid off out of season. They get medical and dental care and the opportunity for promotion and furthering their careers either within Footsteps or in the wider tourism industry.

Review

By the end of this section you should be able to:

- define sustainable tourism and ecotourism
- describe and explain how tourism can protect the environment and benefit the local community.

Sample Examination Questions

Higher tier

1 Study Figure 2 on pages 285–286 which shows the attractions of a number of holiday destinations. Look particularly at the sun, sea and sand holiday on Aegina, Greece, at the top of page 286.

   a Describe the physical attraction of this area. (3 marks)

   b Would this area be appropriate for an adventure holiday? (1 mark)

   c Give reasons for your answer to part b. (2 marks)

2 Define the term package holiday. Use an example in your answer. (3 marks)

3 Study Figure 9 on page 293. It shows tourist numbers for Cyprus. Describe the changes shown in the number of tourists visiting Cyprus. Use data in your answer. (4 marks)

4 Consolidation is one of the stages in the Butler model of tourism development. What happens to the resort in the consolidation stage? (2 marks)

5 Tourism has both positive and negative effects on areas. Explain the negative economic and environmental effects of tourism. Use examples from areas you have studied. (4 marks)

6 Ecotourist destinations protect the environment and benefit the local people. Choose an ecotourist destination you have studied.

   Chosen ecotourist destination ....

   Describe and explain how the environment has been protected. (6 marks)

Total 25 marks

Foundation tier

1 Study Figure 2 on pages 285–286 which shows the attractions of a number of holiday destinations.

   Look particularly at the sun, sea and sand holiday on Aegina, Greece, at the top of page 286.

   a State two physical attractions of this area. (2 marks)

   b State one human attraction of the area. (1 mark)

2 Adventure holidays are for challenge, exploration, skills development or thrills.

   a Would Aegina be appropriate for an adventure holiday? (1 mark)

   b Give reasons for your answer to part b. (2 marks)

3 What is a package holiday? Use an example in your answer. (3 marks)

4 Study Figure 9 on page 293. It shows tourist numbers for Cyprus. Describe the changes shown in the number of tourists visiting Cyprus. Use data in your answer. (3 marks)

5 The Butler model of resort development has seven stages. Complete the timeline below to show the stages in the correct order. Use the words in the box. (3 marks)

Exploration	Development	Stagnation

Stage 1	
Stage 2	Involvement
Stage 3	
Stage 4	Consolidation
Stage 5	
Stage 6	Decline
Stage 7	Rejuvenation

6 Tourism has both positive and negative effects on areas. Describe the negative economic and environmental effects of tourism. Use examples from areas you have studied. (4 marks)

7 Ecotourist destinations protect the environment and benefit the local people. Choose an ecotourist destination you have studied.

   Chosen ecotourist destination ....

   Describe and explain how the environment has been protected. (6 marks)

Total 25 marks

UNIT 4
Investigating Geography

15 Controlled Assessment

Learning objective – to study the requirements of controlled assessment.

Learning outcomes
- To understand what controlled assessment means.
- To consider the route to enquiry.
- To discover what you need to do.
- To understand how the different sections of controlled assessment will be marked.

Controlled assessment is a new form of assessment which in some ways is very like coursework but in other ways is like an examination. Controlled assessment is an enquiry based on primary data which you have collected on a field trip. The enquiry is then written up, some of it under the direct supervision of a teacher.

The route to enquiry

What do I have to do?
- The place you are going to study will be decided by your teacher.
- A question will be given to you by your teacher.
- You should try to devise mini hypotheses which break up the original question. This will make it easier for you to focus on what you need to do.
- The methods you use to answer your question will be devised through discussion with your teacher.
- All students can do the same methods and collect the information on their field trip in groups.
- Any secondary evidence that is needed should be collected at this stage.
- You should introduce your topic.

What does the information show me?
- This part of the controlled assessment must be done under direct teacher supervision.
- Describe your results in detail.
- Make analytical comments which draw your results together.
- Draw conclusions which answer all of your mini hypotheses and your original question.
- Make sure you have used evidence from your study when drawing conclusions.

What am I going to do with all this information?
- Describe and explain your methods of data collection.
- Collate all of the information that you and your group have collected. It should be presented in spreadsheets and charts.
- Draw a range of graphs using the information you have collected. Some of the graphs should be more sophisticated.
- Your graphs should be well presented with axes labelled and titles.
- You should also include other types of presentation techniques such as photographs and field sketches.

How well did I do?
- Were the methods you used to answer the question appropriate?
- How appropriate were the methods of presentation; have you justified why you used the presentation techniques that you used?
- How well were you able to analyse and conclude your study given the primary evidence you had collected?
- How could you have improved your study?

Does it all make sense?
- Does your work have a logical sequence?
- Are your diagrams linked to the text?
- Have you used geographical terminology?
- Have you checked your spelling and grammar?

Figure 1 The route to enquiry

What do I need to do to?

If you want to achieve high marks on controlled assessment you must follow the mark scheme, including all of the items that it mentions. If you do this your teacher will have to give you top marks! Below are grids you can use to ensure you have covered everything you need to achieve top range marks.

Purpose of investigation (6 marks)	Yes	No
Question is clearly stated and understood.		
Mini hypotheses which break the question down.		
There is a general and more focused statement about the location of the study. The area of study is also shown using maps and aerial photographs.		
Have I stated briefly how I am going to answer the question?		

Methods of collecting data (9 marks)	Yes	No
Have I described what I did?		
Have I explained why I used the methods in the way that I did?		
Have I stated where and when I used each technique?		
Have I stated why I used the techniques that I did?		
Have I included all of the results in neat tables and charts?		

Methods of presenting data (11 marks)	Yes	No
Have I used a range of graphical techniques, for example, line graphs and bar charts?		
Have I used a range of cartographic techniques?		
Have I made use of techniques such as location maps, choropleth maps, flow line maps? (These are usually classed as more sophisticated techniques and will show off your geographical skills.)		
Have I used visual techniques, for example; photographs and field sketches? (If annotated these are also classed as more sophisticated techniques.)		
Have all my graphs got labelled axes?		
Have I put a title and a scale on all my presentation techniques?		
Have I drawn my presentation techniques neatly?		

Analysis and conclusions (9 marks)	Yes	No
Have I described my results in detail; written about all the presentation techniques and included information (data) from them?		
Have I made analytical comments?		
Have I made any comparisons between the graphs/results?		
Have I answered all of my mini hypotheses and my original question?		
Have I used evidence from my study when I answered my question and mini hypotheses?		
Have I referred to the theory that my study is based on?		

Evaluation (9 marks)	Yes	No
Did the methods I used in my study help me to answer the question? Were they appropriate?		
Have I justified why I used the presentation techniques that I used? Were they appropriate?		
Was I able to answer my original question given the primary/secondary evidence I collected?		
Could I have improved my study?		

Planning and organisation (6 marks)	Yes	No
Have I included a contents page, page numbers, titles and headings?		
Have I integrated (written about) diagrams and figures in the text?		
Have I checked my spelling, punctuation and grammar?		
Is my work organised and does it have a logical sequence to the enquiry?		
Is my work fewer than 2,000 words long?		

How will my work be marked?

There follow some examples of how to achieve the top range of marks for your controlled assessment. These are exemplars of what students have written with examiner comments beside them. All examples fall in the top range of marks band. This piece of controlled assessment is based on the theme of tourism but the same question could have been asked on the environment theme.

The purpose of the investigation

> Question is clearly stated. The following paragraph shows understanding of the problem that is being investigated.

Introduction

The question I have been set to answer is:

Has the development of Lulworth Cove as a tourist destination ruined the landscape?

When areas of coastline become popular with tourists it can change the nature of the area. This study is going to look into the changes that take place and the effect they have on both the human and physical environment.

I have broken the question down into a set of mini hypotheses/ statements which I will try to answer. This should help me to focus my study on certain techniques and help me to draw conclusions on the evidence I have collected.

Mini hypotheses

Since the development of Lulworth Cove as a tourist destination:

- The high street has become full of tourist shops.
- The footpaths have been eroded badly.
- There are too many tourists which has ruined the peaceful atmosphere of the area.
- The car park and other development at Lulworth are visually intrusive.
- There is more litter and other types of pollution.

> Mini hypotheses help you focus your study.

The study will take place at Lulworth Cove in Dorset (see maps on next page). Lulworth Cove is a small village that is sited on the coast next to the World Heritage Site of Lulworth Cove. Weymouth is 20 miles to the west of Lulworth and Swanage is 17 miles to the east. The study will take place in Main Road, the car park, on the beach and on the footpaths leading to Stair Hole, Lulworth Cove and Durdle Door. The area attracts visitors because of the spectacular coastal features; these can be seen on the photographs and field sketches on pgs 12–16. In order to complete my study and answer the mini hypotheses I have stated I will need to complete a number of techniques. These will include traffic and pedestrian counts, an Environmental Impact Analysis (EIA), a questionnaire and quadrat analysis across several footpaths. These techniques will be carried out over the weekend the 11–13 May.

> There is a general and focused statement of location and maps.

> This section helps you with the sequence for your report.

The location of Lulworth Cove Village

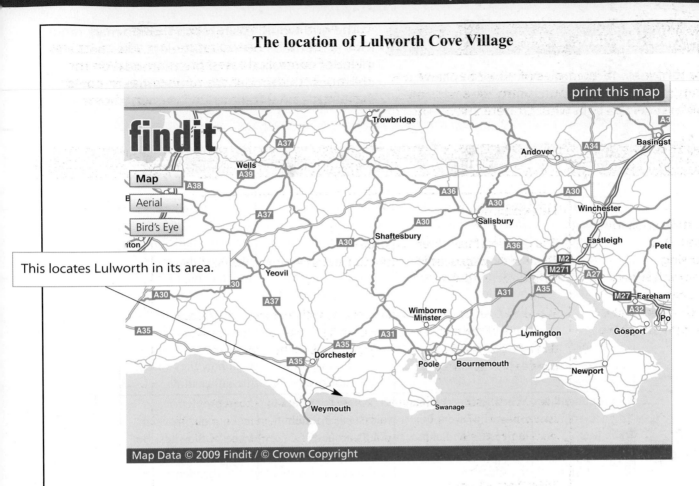

print this map

findit

Map
Aerial
Bird's Eye

This locates Lulworth in its area.

Map Data © 2009 Findit / © Crown Copyright

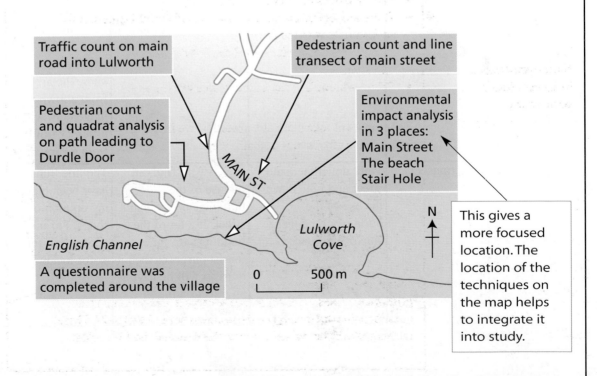

Traffic count on main road into Lulworth

Pedestrian count and line transect of main street

Pedestrian count and quadrat analysis on path leading to Durdle Door

Environmental impact analysis in 3 places:
Main Street
The beach
Stair Hole

MAIN ST

English Channel

Lulworth Cove

A questionnaire was completed around the village

0   500 m

N

This gives a more focused location. The location of the techniques on the map helps to integrate it into study.

Methods of collecting data

The techniques grid below describes, explains and evaluates two of the techniques which were carried out on the field trip.

The grid would easily reach the top mark range for the methods of collecting data. The chart also includes an evaluation of the methods of collection; this is one way of ensuring that this section is completed.

Clear description of how the technique was carried out.

This explains why the methods were done in the way that they were.

Technique Where? When?	Method and explanation	Purpose/ justification	Evaluation
Traffic count on main road 12.30-3.30 11.5.08	Recorded on a tally sheet how many vehicles went in and out of the car park. Each group took a half hour slot. This meant that every group had time to do their other techniques and people did not get bored.	To work out how many people visited and when were the busiest times and which day was the busiest. To record the types of vehicles to work out which was the most popular form of transport to Lulworth Cove.	The traffic count is a simple way of obtaining data on numbers of vehicles which come to Lulworth Cove. It can, however, be inaccurate if some people in the group do not take care with how they record the information.
Environmental Impact Analysis. This was completed at different points around Lulworth marked on the map.	When first arriving at Lulworth I went to a high point and chose my sites. Walked to the specified site and assessed the environment using my prepared grid. I tried to do these at about the same time.	To assess the effect of tourists at different points around Lulworth using the grid that I had worked out with my group before we left Reading. The grid had criteria such as amount of litter and amount of dog fouling.	I had problems making decisions at some of the sites. Be more decisive. My judgements may have been affected by the different weather conditions on the two days which weren't really part of the assessment. I may not have chosen the best sites because I don't know the area. Being from a town my judgement will be different from a person from a rural area.
Line transect	Walk down the main street and note down the use of the buildings on either side of the road.	This was to find out the use of the buildings on the main street. If a lot of the buildings are for tourist purposes then tourism will be having an effect on the village.	The line transect may have been biased by my opinion of the shops. For instance is a local pub for tourists or for locals?

Justification provided and linkage to the focus of the study.

Evaluation of the method.

Methods of presenting data

If top range marks are to be achieved then a range of appropriate graphical, cartographic and visual techniques should be used. They should be well presented with labelled axes and titles.

The graphs do not have to be constructed using a computer although sometimes the use of a computer can enhance the presentation skills.

A wide range of data presentation techniques should be used. Data presentation techniques could include: any type of graph such as bar graphs and line graphs, pie charts or pictorgrams, field sketches and photographs should also be used. More sophisticated techniques could involve using a base map with the techiques displayed in the appropriate areas.

Some examples of the presentation techniques which could be used for each method in the methodology table are mentioned below.

Technique	Suggested display technique
Traffic and pedestrian counts	Flow line maps. This could be drawn on a map of the area which shows the road where the techniques were carried out.
Environmental Impact Analysis	Bi-polar analysis, star/kite diagrams.
Line Transect	Map of the main street drawn out by hand. Map of main street completed on computer with photographs inserted to show different facilities.

Line graph constructed on a computer used to display pedestrian count information.

Graph has a title.

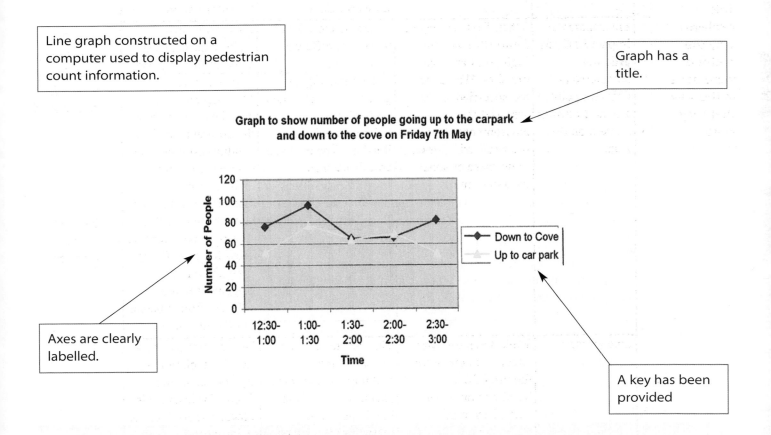

Graph to show number of people going up to the carpark and down to the cove on Friday 7th May

Axes are clearly labelled.

A key has been provided

Analysis and conclusions

The analysis and conclusions below are a top of the mark range answer for one of the mini hypotheses. A number of techniques are used to come to a conclusion on the first hypothesis.

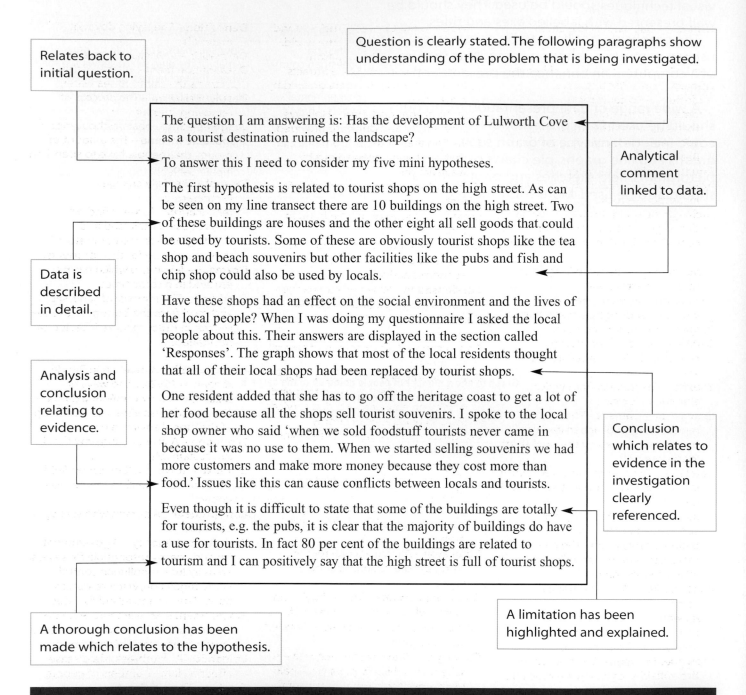

Relates back to initial question.

Question is clearly stated. The following paragraphs show understanding of the problem that is being investigated.

Analytical comment linked to data.

Data is described in detail.

Analysis and conclusion relating to evidence.

Conclusion which relates to evidence in the investigation clearly referenced.

The question I am answering is: Has the development of Lulworth Cove as a tourist destination ruined the landscape?

To answer this I need to consider my five mini hypotheses.

The first hypothesis is related to tourist shops on the high street. As can be seen on my line transect there are 10 buildings on the high street. Two of these buildings are houses and the other eight all sell goods that could be used by tourists. Some of these are obviously tourist shops like the tea shop and beach souvenirs but other facilities like the pubs and fish and chip shop could also be used by locals.

Have these shops had an effect on the social environment and the lives of the local people? When I was doing my questionnaire I asked the local people about this. Their answers are displayed in the section called 'Responses'. The graph shows that most of the local residents thought that all of their local shops had been replaced by tourist shops.

One resident added that she has to go off the heritage coast to get a lot of her food because all the shops sell tourist souvenirs. I spoke to the local shop owner who said 'when we sold foodstuff tourists never came in because it was no use to them. When we started selling souvenirs we had more customers and make more money because they cost more than food.' Issues like this can cause conflicts between locals and tourists.

Even though it is difficult to state that some of the buildings are totally for tourists, e.g. the pubs, it is clear that the majority of buildings do have a use for tourists. In fact 80 per cent of the buildings are related to tourism and I can positively say that the high street is full of tourist shops.

A thorough conclusion has been made which relates to the hypothesis.

A limitation has been highlighted and explained.

Evaluation

There should be an evaluation of three of the sections of the study:

- The methods to collect the data (as shown on the techniques grid).
- The techniques to display the data.
- The evidence found – how useful was it in answering your original question?

Top level marks will only be achieved in this section if all of these elements have been covered.

GLOSSARY

Acid rain – Rain with acidic gases dissolved in it, can prove harmful for plants and fish.

Aesthetic – An appreciation of beauty.

Afforestation – Planting trees.

Andesite – A volcanic rock.

Anomaly – An irregularity. Something that is different from the trend.

AONB – Area of Outstanding Natural Beauty.

Aquatic – Relating to water.

Aquifer – Underground store of water in permeable rock.

Arch – An opening through a headland.

Archipelago – A group of islands.

Aspect – The direction that a slope faces.

Baby boom – An increase in the birth rate, often after a war.

Bar – A sand and/or shingle ridge, which extends right across a bay.

Barge – A flat-bottomed boat.

Batik – A method of producing coloured designs on textiles using wax.

Bauxite – The mineral from which aluminium is made.

Beach replenishment – The replacement of beach material that has been removed by the process of longshore drift.

Betel nut – The fruit of the Betel Palm. It is chewed and spat out. It acts as a mild stimulant.

Biodegradable – The ability of a substance to break down by biological means into the raw materials of nature and disappear into the environment.

Black market – An illegal trade in commodities.

Breakwater – A wall built along a coastline to protect a harbour or area of land from the sea.

Brownfield potential The number of brownfield sites which are available for redevelopment within a city.

Brownfield site This is an area within a city which is no longer used. It may contain old factories and housing, or it may have been cleared ready for redevelopment.

Budget airlines – Cheap air transport such as easyJet.

CARE – Cooperative for Assistance and Relief Everywhere. This organisation works to fight poverty and respond to emergencies around the world.

Catchment area – The area from which a shopping centre attracts its customers. Or the area drained by a river basin.

Catered accommodation – Holidays where food and drink are provided.

Cave – An area at the bottom of a cliff that has been hollowed out by wave action.

Chiropodist – A person who cares for feet.

Cohort – A group of people banded together.

Communist country – A country where the state plans and runs most economic activities.

Condensation – When water changes from a gas to a liquid as it cools.

Coniferous – Trees which stay in leaf all year round.

Consortium – An association of several businesses.

Consumer society – A society in which individuals are encouraged to spend money on new products and services so as to benefit the economy.

Contraception – A means of stopping pregnancy.

Convection current – Movement within the Earth, which moves tectonic plates.

Coppice – The process of cutting trees back to ground level to stimulate growth.

Coral atoll – A circular coral reef or string of coral islands around a lagoon.

Coral reef habitats – The animals and plants which live on a coral reef.

Corrie – An armchair-shaped hollow left after glaciation.

Countryside Stewardship Scheme – A scheme in which farmers were paid to improve the natural beauty of the countryside.

Crust – The name given to the outer layer of the earth.

Deciduous – Trees which lose all their leaves, usually in winter.

DEFRA – Department for Environment, Food and Rural Affairs.

Demography – The study of population.

Deposition – The laying down of materials.

Dermatitis – A disease of the skin.

Desalination plant – A factory that extracts the salt from sea water.

Desulphurisation – The process of removing sulphur.

Dinghies – Small boats without motors.

Disposable income – The amount of money that people have to spend on luxury goods.

Diurnal – The daily change in temperature.

Diversification – Farmers find other ways of using their land and buildings due to the poor return they are getting for their products.

Dormant – A volcano which has not erupted in historic times.

Dredging – The removal of sand, silt and mud from the bottom of the sea or river in order to make it easier for navigation.

Earth Summit – A meeting in Rio de Janeiro in 1992 to find ways of dealing with environmental damage. The agenda was aimed at a clean up of the global environment.

Eco-lodge – A tourist bungalow that is run sustainably.

Ecotown – Towns built on brownfield sites that are based on low carbon impact.

Entrepreneur – A person who sets up a business.

Environment Agency – A government-funded agency responsible for several areas including pollution control, waste regulation, water resources, flood defence and inland fisheries.

Environmental Stewardship Scheme – Grants paid to farmers who protect a certain percentage of their land.

Epidemic – An outbreak of a disease affecting large numbers of people.

Erosion – The wearing away of materials by a moving force, such as a river, the sea or ice.

Ethnic – Relates to a group of people who have a common national or cultural tradition.

Evacuation – Leaving home and moving to a safer location.

Evapotranspiration – All the moisture removed from an area by evaporation and transpiration.

Expat – Short for expatriate; a person who lives outside their native country.
Export – A good or service which is sold to another country.

Faulting – The fracturing of the Earth's crust.
Fauna – The animals of a region.
Favela – The name given to a shanty settlement in Brazil.
Fertiliser – A substance put onto crops to increase their yield.
Fertility rate – The average number of children each woman in a population will have.
Fetch – The length of water over which wind has blown.
Floodplain – The flat area of land that the river spills onto when it bursts its banks.
Flora – The plants of a region.
Folding – The bending and crumpling of layers of rock.
Footloose – An industry that can locate anywhere.
Fortification – A large defensive building like a castle.
Fuelwood – Trees cut down for firewood.
Fungi – Includes moulds, yeast, mushrooms and toadstools.
Furrows – The lines in a field made by a plough.

Gap year – A year off taken by students before or after university.
Garbage – Another name for rubbish.
Gastric – Relates to the stomach.
GDP – Gross domestic product – The total amount of money earned by a country in a year.
Geostationary satellite – These have a fixed position over a point on the Earth's surface, and therefore monitor only that part of the surface.
Geothermal energy – Energy produced by heat from inside the Earth.
Globalisation – The way that companies, ideas and lifestyles are increasingly being spread around the world.
Global warming – An increase in the temperature of the Earth's atmosphere.
Greenbelt This is an area around the city, which is composed of farmland and recreational land. There are strict controls on the development of this land. Its purpose is to control the growth of cities.
Greenfield site An area on the edge of the city, which has never been developed in any way.

Greenhouse gases – Gases that trap heat within the Earth's atmosphere.
Grey pound – The spending power of the elderly population.
Gridlocked – Roads that are so full of traffic that there is very little movement.
Groundwater – Rainwater that has moved through the ground to fill up spaces in the rock.

Hard engineering – The building of coastal or river defences using man-made materials such as concrete, or wood.
Hectare – A measurement of land.
Heritage coast – A stretch of undeveloped coastline managed for its landscape and recreation value.
HIC – High income country. See LIC.
Holiday entitlement – The number of days' holiday that a person is allowed.
Honeypot – A place that attracts large numbers of visitors.
Hydrocarbons – A compound of hydrogen and carbon in a liquid, solid or gas form. Coal gas and petroleum are two examples.
Hydroelectric power – Energy produced by running water turning a turbine.

Impermeable – A rock that does not allow water to pass through it.
Import – A good or service that is bought by a country.
Incinerator – A furnace for burning rubbish.
Indigenous – The original people or plants to colonise an area.
Informal sector – Employment which is not registered with a government for tax purposes, e.g. street sellers.
Infrastructure – This is the name given to communication links, sewage and telephone systems, and other basic services, which provide a network that benefits business and the community.
Interception – This is when precipitation is trapped by the leaves of trees or vegetation before it reaches the ground.
Irrigation – Water added to crops to help them grow in dry periods.

Jetty – A pier in a harbour which boats can dock at.
Jobs related directly to tourism – Jobs in the tourist industry such as waiters.
Jobs related indirectly to tourism – Jobs which are created by the tourist industry such as laundry services to hotels.

Kindergarten – A school for young children.

Lahars – An Indonesian word for a rapidly flowing mixture of rock debris and water. Sometimes referred to as mudflows.
Landfill – Waste material that is emptied into a man-made hole in the ground. It is then covered with soil when full.
Landslide – A type of mass movement. Large amounts of water in the soil cause large areas to slide down a slope.
Leukemia – A type of cancer of the blood cells.
LIC – A low income country. See HIC.
Limestone pavement – A bare area of limestone rock.
Load – The material transported by a river.
Long profile – Shows the changes in the height of a river's course from its source to its mouth.
Lubricant – A liquid substance such as oil, which allows objects to flow more easily.

Magma – Molten rock under the surface of the Earth.
Magnitude – A measurement of the strength of an earthquake.
Malnutrition – The lack of essential vitamins and foods required for good health.
Mantle – The layer of the Earth between the crust and the core.
Maritime – Relates to the sea.
Mass tourism – Large numbers of holidaymakers.
Mechanisation – The use of machinery.
Mercalli scale – A scale for measuring the effects of earthquakes.
Meteorologist – A person who studies the weather.
MIC – A middle income country.
Migration – The movement of people or animals.
Millet – A cereal crop.
Minimum wage – The least amount of money that can be paid to an employee by law.
Monsoon – A climate with one very rainy season.
Multiplier effect – The knock-on effect of an activity causing spending in other areas.

National Grid – A high-voltage electric power transmission network in Great Britain, connecting power stations and major substations, making sure that electricity generated anywhere in Great Britain can be used to satisfy demand elsewhere.

National park – An area of countryside which is being protected because of its beauty and also managed for visitor recreation.

Natural decrease in population – This occurs if the death rate of a country is higher than the birth rate.

Outskirts – The edges of a built-up area.

Overhang – A piece of rock, which juts out over a plunge pool or a cliff.

Ox-bow lake – A horseshoe shaped lake that is formed from a cut-off meander bend.

Pension – Money a person receives when they retire.

Percolation – The downward vertical movement of water within the soil.

Percussion gun – A gun used in ski resorts to artificially trigger an avalanche.

Permeable – A rock that allows water to pass through it.

Pesticide – A chemical that is sprayed onto crops to kill insects that eat the crops and therefore reduce the yield.

Photosynthesis – The process by which green plants take in sunlight, carbon dioxide and water and convert them into oxygen and energy.

Photovoltaic cells – a device that converts solar energy into electricity

Pill box – Small concrete buildings used as fortification and defence.

Political asylum – A political refugee given protection by the country they have moved to.

Porcelain – A fragile type of china.

Porous – A rock that allows water to collect in its pore spaces.

Precipitation – All forms of moisture reaching the ground (e.g. rain, drizzle, snow and sleet).

Prefabricated concrete – Manufactured sections of concrete that are easy to assemble on site.

Prevailing wind – The most common wind.

Promontory – A headland or cliff protruding into the sea.

Pumice – A spongy, light volcanic rock.

PVC – Polyvinyl chloride – A type of plastic.

Pyroclastic flow – An avalanche of hot ash, pumice, rock fragments and volcanic gas that rushes down the side of a volcano at speeds of up to 150 km per hour.

Ramsar – The convention on wetlands signed in Ramsar, Iran, in 1971 to conserve and wisely use wetlands and their resources.

Redevelopment This is when buildings in a city, which are no longer of use, are demolished and replaced with buildings that are in current demand.

Refugee – A person who is forced to move to another country usually as a result of war, religious persecution or a natural disaster.

Renewal This is when old buildings are renovated and brought up to date, combining the best of the old with the new.

Relief – The shape of the land.

Relocation – When a business moves from one area to another.

Residential care homes – Places that elderly people pay to stay in and be looked after.

Richter scale – A scale to measure the magnitude (size) of an earthquake.

Rural – Countryside.

Rural depopulation – The movement out of rural areas by people either looking for better employment opportunities or for a better provision of facilities.

Saga – An organisation for people aged over 50.

Saturated – When rock or soil can hold no more water.

Seasonal jobs – Jobs which exist only at certain times of the year.

Seiche – A temporary disturbance in the water level of a lake or partially enclosed body of water.

Seismograph – A machine which measures earthquakes.

Self-catering accommodation – Holidays where food and drink is not provided.

Sewage – Liquid waste from urban areas.

Shanty towns – An unplanned settlement often without any services.

Slip plane – An area between two different rock types, which can become saturated and therefore allows the rock to move.

Smog – A mixture of fog and dirt particles from car exhausts and industrial smoke. Can cause breathing difficulties.

Sniffer dogs – Dogs trained to search out particular smells.

Soft engineering – Building of coastal and river defences using natural materials such as sand.

Spit – A ridge of sand and/or shingle joined to the land at one end; the other end tapers into the sea.

SSSI –Site of Special Scientific Interest which is protected against damaging operations.

Stable – Not easily altered.

Stack – A piece of rock that stands in the sea. It used to be joined to the headland.

Standpipes – Central water taps used by a community.

Sterilisation – An operation to make it impossible to conceive.

Stump – A piece of rock that used to be a stack but is now covered by water at high tide.

Subduction zone – The place where one tectonic plate sinks below another plate.

Synthetic fibres – Man-made materials.

Tarn – A small mountain lake in a corrie.

Telecommunications – Communicating by cable telephone.

Tenements – A large building split into flats or single rooms.

Terracettes – Small terraces seen on grassy slopes.

Thaw – Snow melt.

Tie dye – A method of producing patterns on cloth.

Toxic – Poisonous.

Transpiration – The process by which water is lost to the atmosphere through the leaves of plants and trees.

Tributary – A minor river joining on to the main river.

Tubewells – Small wells often built in villages in an LIC.

Undercutting – The process by which a cliff or a river bank is undermined.

Urban – Built-up areas.

Urbanisation – The growth in the proportion of people living in towns and cities.

Vermin – Animals that cause damage to crops (e.g. mice).

Vigilante – A member of the public who takes the law into their own hands.

WaterAid – An international organisation that helps people escape poverty and disease caused by a lack of drinking water.

Wildfowl – Aquatic birds, such as ducks.

World Heritage Site – Set up to protect natural and cultural properties of outstanding universal value against the threat of damage in a rapidly developing world. At the end of 2000 there were 690 sites in 122 countries.

WTO – World Trade Organisation.

Zloty – The currency in Poland.

Sample Examination Answers

UNIT 1

Chapter 1 Geographical Skills

Higher tier

1 a Oldfield and Punch farm, both for 1 mark. **(1 mark)**
b Horningsea **(1 mark)**
c *Point marked*. Seven A roads (1) join in the centre (1) They meet at a ring road (1) There is a radial pattern (1) They come into Cambridge from all directions (1) **(3 marks)**

2 a 231111 **(1 mark)**
b south **(1 mark)**
c 4 km 800 m. Allow 100 m either way. **(1 mark)**
d along the river **(1 mark)**
e *Point marked*. One mark for each characteristic e.g. there are dunes in the south/2605 (1) The beach is widest in grid square 2510 (1) it is 300 m wide (1) There is a rock outcrop at Birling Carrs (1) There are many other examples. **(3 marks)**

3 1 mark for each sector plus 1 mark for completing key. **(4 marks)**

4 a Either Windsor Castle or Thames Street **(1 mark)**
b 5 mm **(1 mark)**
c Information can be shown on a map
Shows the information visually.
Busiest routes clearly shown. **(1 mark)**
d Accept any appropriate technique such as pictogram, bar graph or table. (1) Explanation for extra mark will focus on clarity of data.
Line graph and pie charts would be inappropriate. **(2 marks)**

5 Mention of different skills at 1 mark each to a maximum of 3 e.g. graphs, research from internet, Google Maps™, photographs, keyboard.
Maximum of two marks on how it can be enhanced **(4 marks)**
(Total 25 marks)

Foundation tier

1 a 2 **(1 mark)**
b Any one of church (with tower), public house or telephone. **(1 mark)**
c There are SEVEN A roads that join in the centre of Cambridge. Cambridge has a ring road on the west and NORTH of the city. The ring road on the west is the M11 **(3 marks)**

2 a 231111 **(1 mark)**
b south **(1 mark)**
c 5 km **(1 mark)**
d along the river **(1 mark)**
e *Point marked*. One mark for each characteristic e.g. there are dunes in the south/2605 (1) The beach is widest in grid square 2510 (1) it is 300 m wide (1) There is a rock outcrop at Birling Carrs (1) There are many other examples **(3 marks)**

3 This type of graph is called a **divided/compound bar graph**. The percentage of people working in primary industry is 20% in **Taiwan**. In Taiwan there is **45%** working in tertiary industry. In Mali only 3% work in **secondary** industry. **(4 marks)**

4 a 112 **(1 mark)**
b 1 cm **(1 mark)**
c Information can be shown on a map
Shows the information visually.
Busiest routes clearly shown. **(1 mark)**
d Accept any appropriate technique such as pictogram, bar graph or table. **(2 marks)**

5 Mention of different skills at 1 mark each e.g. graphs, research from internet, Google Maps™, photographs, keyboard. **(4 marks)**
(Total 25 marks)

Chapter 2 Challenges for the Planet

Higher tier

1 a 4000 BC **(1 mark)**
b *Point marked*. Allow a maximum of three if no data is used.

The temperature rose rapidly (1) for 1200 years (1) The climate has fluctuated (gone up and down) (1) The lowest temperature was 10000 years ago (1) when it was 5°C lower than now (1) There have been warm and cold periods (1) The little ice age lasted 600 years (1) **(4 marks)**
c Earth movements in space. Expect these two, although the wobble is also acceptable. There must be some explanation for full marks. Only one movement needs to be covered.
The shape of Earth's orbit around the Sun varies (1) from nearly circular to elliptical and back to circular (1) again every 95,000 years (1) Cold, glacial periods have occurred when the earth's orbit is circular (1) and warmer periods when it is more elliptical (1)
The tilt of the earth's axis varies over time (1) from 21.5° and 24.5° (1) This variation occurs over a 41,000 year time span (1) The greater the angle of the tilt the hotter are the summers and the winters are colder (1) When the angle is greater the earth usually experiences warmer periods (1) **(4 marks)**

2 Any two points at 1 mark each. Examples:
This rise will threaten large areas of low lying coastal land including major world cities such as London, New York and Tokyo (1)
Many islands in the Pacific Ocean are already covered with sea water (1) People are also leaving other low lying coral atolls (islands) before they become engulfed by the sea (1) **(2 marks)**

3 One aim well described or two simple statements relating to the aims of the meeting. Descriptive comments about the successes of a meeting to a maximum of 2 marks. There must be an explanation to gain full marks. **(4 marks)**

4 Both ways need to be explained. Two marks for each.
The first shows recycling in the office (1) this means that materials are not thrown away and can be used again (1)
The second way shows a way that a hotel can become more sustainable by not having to wash towels so frequently (1) this means that water is saved (1) and less detergents are needed (1) **(4 marks)**

5 Sustainable points about Traffic management in Cambridge.
Can limit traffic entering the city centre (1) Less pollution from exhausts (1) Double decker buses can take equivalent to 70 cars drivers (1) Parks are at the edge of the city keeping cars well away from centre (1) Improves traffic flow so less petrol being used (1).
Sites so easy access from all routes (1)
At least one point relating to Cambridge needs to be made for full marks.

Level	marks	
0	0	No acceptable response.
1	1–2	Descriptive comments about traffic management that could relate to any urban area.
2	3–4	Either specific points about an urban area. Or explanation as to how the management is sustainable to reach level 2.
3	5–6	Both specific points and explanation to reach level 3.

(6 marks)
(Total 25 marks)

Foundation tier

1 a 5°C **(1 mark)**
b From 8000BC the temperature rose **rapidly** for 1200 years. The climate has fluctuated. The **lowest** temperature was 10,000 years ago when it was 5°C lower than the present temperature. There have been warm and cold periods. **4000** years BC was a warm period. The little ice age lasted **600** years. **(4 marks)**

c

statements	true	false
The shape of Earth's orbit around the Sun varies.	✓	
The Earth's orbit around the sun is star shaped		✓
Cold, glacial periods have occurred when the Earth's orbit is circular.		✓
The Earth tilts on its axis. ✓		

(4 marks)

2 Simple impacts at 1 mark each. E.g. coast flooded (1) houses ruined (1) islands submerged (1) farming land lost (1) **(2 marks)**

3 a One aim well described or two simple statements relating to the aims of the meeting. **(2 marks)**
b Descriptive comments about the successes of a meeting to a maximum of 3 marks. There must be an explanation to gain full marks. **(4 marks)**

4 a Recycling materials **(1 mark)**
b This shows a way that a hotel can become more sustainable by not having to wash towels so frequently (1) this means that water is saved (1) and less detergents are needed (1) which is more environmentally friendly (1). **(3 marks)**

5 a 5 **(1 mark)**
b A special lane for the buses **(1 mark)**
c 3 **(1 mark)**
d less cars in city
less pollution
1 bus takes 70 people
Many other possibilities **(1 mark)**
(Total 25 marks)

UNIT 2

Chapter 3 Coastal Landscapes

Higher tier

1 a Expect to be able to recognise the drawing of the feature. One mark per 2 correct features. **(2 marks)**
b Low **(1 mark)**
c Low tide because the stump is visible (1) Stumps can only be seen when the tide is out (1) **(1 mark)**

d One mark for first answer, rock or chalk.
Terminology: slumping (1).
Two marks for description of slumping. It fell from the cliff (1). **(3 marks)**

2 a Geology, rock type.
Rock structure.
Coastal processes: cliff face – weathering and mass movement; cliff foot – erosion by the sea. **(3 marks)**
b Build up of beach material on one side. Dissipates wave energy due to build up of material. Material no longer moves along the coast. Waves break before they reach the cliff. **(3 marks)**
c Any soft engineering techniques can be explained. Look for more than descriptive comments about what they look like and their advantages and disadvantages. An explanation for groynes would be that they stop LSD. **(3 marks)**

3 The Met Office predicts the likelihood of a coastal flood and gives information to the public through weather forecasts and news broadcasts on the television. These advise householders to be proactive and either ring a flood hotline number or go onto the Environment Agency website to check the likelihood of a flood in their area. On the Environment Agency website there will be information on the likelihood of a flood. This will be identified by a system of warning codes; they are flood watch, flood warning, severe flood warning and all clear. **(3 marks)**

4

Indicative content
Effects to include houses lost, cost of this loss. May be some discussion on the results of the effects – the management. Must be a range of examples for level 3.

Level	Mark	Descriptor
1	1–2	Simple descriptive statements about the effects of coastal recession.

2 3–4 Level two is reached by either using specific material or explanation of the effects. The top of the level requires both specific detail and explanation.

3 5–6 A good understanding is shown of the effects of coastal recession on a range of examples.

(6 marks)

(Total 25 marks)

Foundation tier

1 a True, false, true, true. (4 marks)

b Low. (1 mark)

c Low tide because the stump is visible (1). Stumps can only be seen when the tide is out (1). (2 marks)

d One mark for first answer.
Rock or chalk.
Terminology: slumping (1).
Two marks for description of slumping. It fell from the cliff (1). (3 marks)

2 a Weathering
Corrasion (2 marks)

b Groynes – a fence going down the beach from the cliff to the sea. Prevents longshore drift by building up a beach. (3 marks)

c (2 marks)

Soft engineering technique	Description
Beach replenishment	The coastline is built up with sand and pebble from elsewhere.
Managed retreat	The land by the sea is made into a gentle slope instead of a steep one.
Cliff regrading	The sea is allowed to flood areas which were once defended.

d Levels mark (2 marks)
Expect soft engineering techniques such as:
Beach nourishment provides a beach is easily washed away.

3 Indicative content
Effects to include houses lost, cost of this loss.

May be some discussion on the results of the effects – the management

Level	Mark	Descriptor
1	1–2	Simple descriptive statements about effects of coastal recession.
2	3–4	Level two is reached by either using some specific material or clear descriptive comments of the effects.
3	5–6	A good understanding is shown of the effects of coastal recession. A number of examples are used of varying depth or one example is used in great depth.

(6 marks)

(Total 25 marks)

Chapter 4 River Landscapes

Higher tier

1 a All statements to be credited at one mark. Biological weathering – This is the action of plants and animals on the land (1) Seeds that fall into cracks in rocks (1) will start to grow when moisture is present.(1) The roots the young plant puts out force their way into cracks (1) and, in time, can break up rocks (1) Accept comments about animals, such as rabbits, can also be responsible for the further break-up of rocks (1) Allow 1 mark for the sketch and 3 for the annotations. (4 marks)

1 b One mark for each type e.g. soil creep and slumping. (2 marks)

2 Little usage in the in the upper stage (1) some hill farming (1) More usage as you move into middle and lower stage (1) such as tourism and industry (1) (3 marks)

3 *Point marked.*
The answer will focus on depth of water and friction.
Inside of bend has shallow water (1) lots of friction between bed and bank and the water (1) slows movement (1) Opposite statements for outside of bend. (4 marks)

4 Three marks for each technique. Use examples from chapter. (6 marks)

5

Level	marks	
0	0	No acceptable response
1	1–2	Descriptive comments that could relate to any river management scheme.
2	3–4	Descriptive comments that relate to a chosen river management scheme and some explanation.
3	5–6	Good description of the chosen river management scheme and a range of explanations relating to a case study.

(6 marks)

(Total 25 marks)

Foundation tier

1 a **Biological weathering is the action of** plants and **animals** on the land. Seeds that fall into cracks in rocks will start to grow when **moisture** is present. The roots the young plant puts out force their way into cracks and, in time, can break up the **rocks**. (4 marks)

1 b One mark for each type e.g. soil creep and slumping. (2 marks)

2 a Two at 1 mark each. Examples tourism, forestry and farming. (2 marks)

b meanders/bendy river (1 mark)

3 The outside of a meander bend has the **deepest** water because this is where the greatest erosion takes place and forms a river cliff. The water is moving **fastest** at this point and therefore erodes the bank using corrasion. The water moves more quickly on the outside due to the lack of **friction** because of the river's depth and consequent lack of contact with the bed and banks. **Deposition** occurs on the inside because the water is moving more slowly and is shallower. (4 marks)

4 a Afforestation is the planting of trees (1) this is a form of soft engineering (1) it slows surface runoff (1). (2 marks)

b Use examples from chapter (4 marks)

5

Level	marks	
0	0	No acceptable response.
1	1–2	Descriptive comments that could relate to any river management scheme.
2	3–4	Descriptive comments that relate to a chosen river management scheme.
3	5–6	Good description of the chosen river management scheme with an explanation.

(6 marks)
(Total 25 marks)

Chapter 5 Glaciated Landscapes

Higher tier

1 a plucking and abrasion – 1 mark each **(2 marks)**
   b As a glacier moves down a valley, it puts pressure on the valley sides and bottom (1) This pressure creates heat (1) The heat causes a small amount of ice to melt (1) the water runs into cracks in the valley sides and refreezes (1) As the glacier moves, it then pulls away some of the rock face (1). **(3 marks)**
2 Some possible answers on the diagram. There are others.

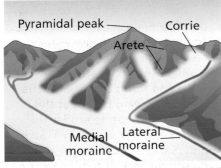

(5 marks)

3 Simple diagram showing lateral moraines merging to form a medial moraine. Allow max of 1 mark without a diagram. **(3 marks)**
4 All that is required here are examples of appropriate leisure activities, a description of the activity and areas where they are found. E.g. In winter, parts of Scotland become skiing destinations (1) as the glaciated hills take on a

covering of snow (1). Aviemoor, for example, survives on its winter tourist income (1). The question asks for activities, so two or more have to be named for full marks. **(4 marks)**
5 Only one design is required. Zoning is likely to be the most popular answer. One or two marks depending on the quality of the answer. **(2 marks)**

6

Level	marks	
0	0	No acceptable response.
1	1–2	Descriptive comments that could relate to any avalanche.
2	3–4	Descriptive comments that relate to a chosen avalanche and some explanation of effects.
3	5–6	Good description of the chosen avalanche and a range of explanatory effects relating to a case study.

(6 marks)
(Total 25 marks)

Foundation tier

1 a

Statement	Correct order
The water runs into cracks in the valley sides and refreezes.	4
As a glacier moves down a valley, it puts pressure on the valley sides and bottom.	1
As the glacier moves, it then pulls away some of the rock face.	5
The heat causes a small amount of ice to melt.	3
This pressure creates heat.	2
This process is known as plucking.	6

(5 marks)

   b abrasion **(1 mark)**
2 See diagram in Higher tier, question 2. The diagram shows some possibilities. There are other correct answers. **(5 marks)**
3 Glaciated landscapes can be used for leisure and **recreation**. Two examples of this are skiing and **hiking**.

The most common type of farming in glaciated landscapes is hill **sheep** farming. This is because the soil is **poor**. **(4 marks)**
4 Allow 1 mark for naming a way and 1 mark for a description. Allow 3 + 1
Examples
Snow shed or avalanche shed (1) is a structure that provides avalanche protection for roads and railway tracks (1). They are built of wood or reinforced concrete (1).
Snow fences (1) are built to stabilize snow (1). They usually have gaps between the beams (1) and are built perpendicular to the slope (1), with reinforcing beams on the downhill side (1).
Avalanche control experts create smaller, controlled avalanches (1) to break up heavy masses of snow (1) and prevent larger, uncontrolled avalanches (1). **(4 marks)**

5

Level	marks	
0	0	No acceptable response.
1	1–2	Descriptive comments that could relate to any avalanche.
2	3–4	Descriptive comments that relate to a chosen avalanche.
3	5–6	Good description of the chosen avalanche with an effect explained.

(6 marks)
(Total 25 marks)

Chapter 6 Tectonic Landscapes

Higher tier

1 a Antarctica or Africa **(1 mark)**
   b *Point marked.*
   They are found in lines (1) down the centre of the Atlantic (1) On the edges of the continent (1) west edge of North and South America (1) On plate boundaries (1).
   An excellent answer:
   Earthquakes occur in long narrow bands on all three types of plate boundary, both on the land and in the sea. The largest belt runs around the Pacific Ocean. Other major belts travel along the middle of the Atlantic

Ocean and through the continents of Europe and Asia from the Atlantic Ocean to the Pacific Ocean. **(3 marks)**

c The answer will focus on destructive plate boundaries. At a destructive plate boundary (1), two plates move towards one another (1). Where they meet, one plate is subducted (slides) below the other (1). The cause of this subduction is the difference in density between the two plates (1), with the heavier one being subducted below the lighter one (1). The plate melts as it subducts (1) the melted plate erupts through a crustal weakness (1). **(4 marks)**

d

Level	marks	
0	0	No acceptable response.
1	1–2	Some simple comments about earthquake prediction e.g. earthquake areas are monitored with machines.
2	3–4	More clear comments that relate to earthquake prediction and some attempt at success for top of level. E.g. tilt metres measure tiny changes in slope angle.
3	5	Good description of earthquake predictions and a clear attempt at saying how successful are these attempts.

(5 marks)

2 a fertile soils
tourist industry
lava can be diverted. **(3 marks)**

3 *Point marked*. Several ways to a maximum. The Mercalli Scale gives an indication of the intensity of an earthquake (1) while the Richter Scale refers to its magnitude/ strength (1). The Mercalli Scale is determined by the effects the earthquake has on humans, buildings and the local landscape (1). The Richter Scale is designed to allow easier comparison of earthquake magnitudes (1). Using this scale it is much easier to compare the power of two earthquakes regardless of their location (1). **(3 marks)**

4

Level	marks	
0	0	No acceptable response.
1	1–2	Descriptive comments that could relate to the impacts of any earthquake.
2	3–4	Descriptive comments that relate to the impacts of a chosen earthquake. For top of level the impacts need to be both on the community and the environment.
3	5–6	Good description of the impacts of the chosen earthquake and an evaluation of the impacts on the community and the environment.

(6 marks)
(Total 25 marks)

Foundation tier

1 a 1999 **(1 mark)**
b Africa **(1 mark)**
c *Point marked*.
They are found in lines (1) down the centre of the Atlantic (1) On the edges of the continent (1) west edge of North and South America (1) On plate boundaries (1). **(3 marks)**
d See answer to Higher tier question 1(c). **(4 marks)**
e Seismometers, tilt meters, monitoring crustal movement, seismic gap theory **(2 marks)**
f A variety of methods are being used by scientists to predict earthquakes (1) but they are not completely accurate (1). Despite sophisticated monitoring equipment it still remains very difficult to pinpoint exactly when earthquake will happen (1). They are improving techniques (1) there is no set pattern to earthquakes (1). **(3 marks)**
2 fertile soils
tourist industry
lava can be diverted. **(3 marks)**
3 *Point marked*.
4 a *Point mark* effects on the people at one mark each.
Three marks can only be awarded if a case study example is used. **(3 marks)**

b *Point mark* effects on the environment at one mark each. Three marks can only be awarded if a case study example is used. **(3 marks)**
(Total 25 marks)

Chapter 7 A Wasteful World

Higher tier

1 The USA produces a large percentage of the world's waste. (1) There seems to be a correlation between population numbers and waste collected (1), countries with large population like China have a large percentage of the world's waste (1) however, it is not as large proportionally as the USA (1).
(3 marks)

2 a Garden, kitchen, paper and board **(1 mark)**
b i electrical goods **(1 mark)**
ii because of the consumer society, people are wealthy and therefore can afford to buy electrical goods. It is seen to be trendy to continually have a new mobile phone etc. computers are updated continually with a better model. Media and advertising making people aware of the products available. **(4 marks)**

3 Any type of renewable fuel is acceptable. Use figures 14–17 for answers. **(6 marks)**

4 a This is a way of turning off appliances that have been left on standby. All appliances are plugged in to an adapter. A BBSB button needs to be located somewhere in the house. As you go to bed or leave your home simply press the button and all of your appliances will go off. This will save energy while you are out or in bed. **(1 mark)**

b This is one example from the textbook, any would be suitable. Must be at a local level and contain specific points to achieve full marks:
Penwith Housing Association Penzance Cornwall the project was completed in 2004. It was the first of its kind because it involved supplying fourteen bungalows with ground source heat pumps. This provided the householders with heating via

radiators and hot water. There is no mains gas in this area and therefore although the houses were well insulated their bills were high due to having to use solid fuel heating systems. The cost of the project was £200,000 much of which was obtained through grants. Due to the success of this scheme there are now 700 schemes across the country which are either running or being installed. **(3 marks)**

5 Levels mark

Indicative content
Waste collection from houses and collection points such as bottle banks at supermarkets. Specific detail would be the box schemes used by a particular council or the names of the recycling centres such as Longshot Lane in Bracknell.
The reuse of recycled materials such as where the glass is reused and what is made.

Level	Mark	Descriptor
1	1–2	Simple descriptive statements about waste collection and recycling schemes.
2	3–4	Level two is reached by some specific information about either recycling schemes or how the waste is reused. The top of the level requires more in-depth information about the recycling of the waste.
3	5–6	A good understanding is shown of recycling schemes and how the waste is reused. Case study material is convincing.

(6 marks)
(Total 25 marks)

Foundation tier
1 The USA produces a **large** percentage of the world's waste. There seems to be a link between population **numbers** and waste collected. Countries with large population like **China** have a large percentage of the world's waste. **(3 marks)**

2 a Garden **(1 mark)**
b i e-waste stands for waste from electrical goods. **(1 mark)**
ii See answer to Higher tier, question 2(b) (i). **(3 marks)**
3 Any type of renewable fuel is acceptable. Use figures 14–17 for answers. **(6 marks)**
4 a See answer to Higher tier, question 4(a). **(2 marks)**
b See answer to Higher tier, question 4(b). **(2 marks)**
5 Levels mark

See answer to Higher tier question 5.

Level	Mark	Descriptor
1	1–2	Simple descriptive statements about waste collection and recycling schemes.
2	3–4	Level two is reached by clear descriptive comments about either recycling schemes or how the waste is reused. The top of the level requires more in-depth information about the recycling of the waste. Some of the information should be specific information.
3	5–6	A good understanding is shown of recycling schemes and how the waste is reused. Case study material is evident.

(6 marks)
(Total 25 marks)

Chapter 8 A Watery World

Higher tier
1 a i 5 is being used for agricultural purposes (1), watering/ irrigating crops (1) 7 is being used for domestic purposes (1) to wash clothes (1) **(2 marks)**
ii crops are being watered because there is not enough rain **(1 mark)**
b Any number of appropriate ways but at least one must be explained to reach full marks. Disease, pollution, sewage.
Open sewers run into the rivers (1) people drink from these (1)
People wash their clothes in the river (1) they drink from the same river (1). **(4 marks)**
2 a Both lines drawn correctly (1) Sectors labelled (1) **(2 marks)**
b Either two simple statements or one expanded point e.g.
More domestic appliances (1)
People bath more (1) because there is mains water (1). **(2 marks)**
c 1 mark is given for the method and 1 to describe it. Two ways at two marks each e.g.
Metering (1) people have to pay for more water use (1) Short flush toilet (1) only half the amount of water is used. **(4 marks)**
3 a Permeable **(1 mark)**
b One mark per correct point
Rain falls on the mountains soaks into permeable rocks
The rainwater flows through the rock due to gravity.
The water is stored in the rock
If a well is built water can be pumped to the surface. **(3 marks)**

4

Level	marks	
0	0	No acceptable response.
1	1–2	Descriptive comments that could relate to any scheme.
2	3–4	Descriptive comments that relate to a chosen scheme and some explanation of effects.
3	5–6	Good description of the chosen scheme and a range of explanatory effects relating to a case study.

(6 marks)
(Total 25 marks)

Foundation tier
1 a

	domestic	industrial	agricultural
Photograph 5	✓		
Photograph 7			✓

(2 marks)
b At least two ways for full marks. Pollution, disease will be the most common. Either of these two points expanded plus the other stated will receive full marks **(3 marks)**
2 a Both lines drawn correctly (1) Sectors labelled (1) **(2 marks)**

b In Africa **85%** of water is used on farming. In Europe only **30%** is used on farming. This shows that the HICs use **less** water on farming than LICs (3 marks)

c 1 mark is given for the method and 1 to describe it. Two ways at two marks each e.g.
Metering (1) people have to pay for more water use (1) Short flush toilet (1) only half the amount of water is used. (4 marks)

3 a permeable (1 mark)

b Answers in the correct order
Rain falls at area V.
The rainwater flows through the rock due to gravity.
The water is stored in the rock
If a well is built water can be pumped to the surface. (4 marks)

4

Level	marks	
0	0	No acceptable response.
1	1–2	Descriptive comments that could relate to any scheme.
2	3–4	Descriptive comments that relate to a chosen scheme.
3	5–6	Good description of the chosen scheme and a clear indication of benefits.

(6 marks)
(Total 25 marks)

UNIT 3

Chapter 9 Economic Change

Higher tier

1 Secondary industry is the manufacturing of goods using the raw materials from primary industry. Example – car manufacture. (2 marks)

2 Mechanisation, cheap imports and depletion of raw materials are 3 reasons. Could be two reasons, one more developed. (3 marks)

3 23% (1 mark)

4 In 1850 48% of the population was employed in the secondary sector. By 1900 this had increased. It then decreased to 45% in 1950. The percentage continued to decreased by 19% in 2000. (3 marks)

5 Cheaper production in LICs and globalisation. (3 marks)

6 China has a great wealth of natural resources having vast reserves of coal, oil and natural gas. Human reasons include – education, government policy, large workforce. (4 marks)

7 Factors affecting the location of tertiary industry. Excellent transport system including wide roads, bus route, cycle and pedestrian lanes, Modern design to attract potential health club clients. Modern flats which house young single people who account for a high proportion of the club's clients. (3 marks)

8 Levels mark

Indicative content
Example could be China Clay Pit in Cornwall now the Eden project. Expect some descriptive points such as – the pit is 60 m deep and the area of 35 football pitches.
Benefit – it is now a tourist attraction. It is run in a sustainable way and there are many information boards which inform about sustainable development. There is also a building which is called The Core which teaches how to be more aware of the damage we are causing to the planet in a user friendly way. Much of the energy for the Eden Project is produced by sustainable means.

Level	Mark	Descriptor
1	1–2	Simple descriptive statements about rural areas and how they have been improved. Not clear if discussing rural de-industrialised areas.
2	3–4	Level two is reached by there being clear reasoning about the benefits of de-industrialised areas or the area is clearly identifiable from the text. The top of the level requires both specific points and reasoning about the benefits of de-industrialisation.
3	5–6	A good understanding of the benefits of de-industrialisation all in a case study framework.

Foundation tier

1 The manufacturing of goods using the raw materials. (1 mark)

2 Mechanisation, cheap imports and depletion of raw materials are 3 reasons. Could be two reasons, one more developed. (3 marks)

3 23% (1 mark)

4 In 1850 48% of the population was employed in the secondary sector. By 1900 this had increased. It then decreased to 45% in 1950. The percentage continued to decreased by 19% in 2000. (4 marks)

5 Cheaper production in LICs and globalisation. (2 marks)

6 See answer to Higher tier, question 7. (4 marks)

7 See answer to Higher tier, question 6. (4 marks)

8 Levels mark (6 marks)

See answer to Higher tier, question 8.

Level	Mark	Descriptor
1	1–2	Simple descriptive statements about rural areas and how they have been improved. Not clear if discussing rural de-industrialised areas.
2	3–4	Level two is reached by there being clear statements about the benefits of de-industrialised areas. The top of the level requires both specific points and reasoning about the benefits of de-industrialisation
3	5–6	A number of descriptive points about the benefits of de-industrialisation all in a case study framework.

(6 marks)
(Total 25 marks)

Chapter 10 Farming and the Countryside

Higher tier

1 Only 2 marks if no data is present
The numbers employed in Primary industry have decreased (1) from 7% to 2% (1). This is because farming is seen as a 'dirty' job (1) (4 marks)

2 As people leave an area due to better facilities and employment chances in urban areas. Less people

are left in the village to buy goods from the local shop. The shop cannot make a profit so closes down. More people leave the village because there is no shop.

(3 marks)

3 1 mark for each point
Adds less to carbon footprint of products (1) Customers trust the local farmers and will buy their produce (1) Provides a market for local farmers (1) Takes more time to source the products (1) More people have to be employed to source products therefore wages bill increases (1).   (3 marks)

4 The grain required to fill the petrol tank of a Range Rover with ethanol is sufficient to feed one person per year.
Rapeseed, pointing to research showing the crop generates copious amounts of nitrous oxide – an even more powerful global warming gas than CO_2.
A land area twice the size of Britain is needed to get enough biofuel crops to halve our greenhouse gas emissions.
37 countries across the world are facing food shortages.
The global food price index rose 40 percent this year to the highest level on record.
Scrapping of set-aside for growth of biofuels will cause problems for birds, insects and biodiversity.

(2 marks)

5 a 605,000   (1 mark)
   b Organic food contains more vitamins and minerals (1) People became more aware of the chemicals being used on farms (1) The fact that farmers wear protective clothing to apply the chemicals (1) People became aware of the conditions animals were being kept in on traditional farms (1) such as battery hen cages (1).
(3 marks)
   c Some of the land was set aside (1) Farmers decided that they were not making enough profit and went back to using chemicals to increase yields (1) Some farmers discovered that they did not have enough land to make a profit as organic farming is less intensive (1).   (3 marks)

6 Levels mark

Indicative content
Conflicts between farmers and motorists
Tourists and Park Rangers due to erosion, parking facilities
More specific comments would be farmers have had sheep killed on roads through the open moorland on Dartmoor. The DNPA has introduced the Moor care programme

Level	Mark	Descriptor
1	1–2	Simple descriptive statements about conflicts in National Parks.
2	3–4	Level two is reached by either using case study material or explanation of the conflicts. The top of the level requires both case study detail and explanation of either conflicts or management.
3	5–6	A good understanding is shown on the conflicts experienced in National Parks between different groups of people and how they are being managed. Case study material is convincing.

(6 marks)
(Total 25 marks)

Foundation tier

1 Only 3 marks if no data present
The numbers employed in Primary industry have decreased (1) from 7% to 2% (1). There has been an increase in the numbers working in tertiary industry (1) the numbers employed in secondary decreased until 2001 (1) and then stayed at the same level (1).   (4 marks)

2 The shop cannot make a profit so closes down.
People leave a rural area due to better facilities and employment chances in urban areas.
More people leave the village because there is no shop.
Less people are left in the village to buy goods from the local shop
(3 marks)

3 1 mark for each point   (4 marks)

Advantages	Disadvantage
Adds less to carbon footprint of products	Takes more time to source the products
Provides a market for local farmers	More people have to be employed to source products therefore wages bill increases

4 See answer to Higher tier, question 4.   (3 marks)
5 a 45,000   (1 mark)
   b 2001   (1 mark)
   c Organic food contains more vitamins and minerals (1) People became more aware of the chemicals being used on farms (1) The fact that farmers wear protective clothing to apply the chemicals (1)   (3 marks)
6 Levels mark   (6 marks)

See answer to Higher tier, question 6.

Level	Mark	Descriptor
1	1–2	Simple descriptive statements about conflicts in National Parks.
2	3–4	Level two is reached by either using some case study material or clear descriptive comments of the management.
3	5–6	A good understanding is shown on the conflicts experienced in National Parks between different groups of people and how they are being managed. Case study material is convincing.

(6 marks)
(Total 25 marks)

Chapter 11 Settlement Change

Higher tier

1 a River or meander bend   (1 mark)
   b Meander bend – defence
      River – water supply
      Flat fertile land – farming
(3 marks)
2 a Rural   (1 mark)
   b Only 2 marks if no data is present. The numbers living in rural areas have decreased (1) in the age groups from 10–40 between 1985 and 2005 (1).
(4 marks)

3 The movement out of rural areas which are classed as remote rural areas. Remote areas such as the Highlands of Scotland have seen a decline in rural population. The population leaving are usually of working age. **(2 marks)**

4 Social:
People are now marrying later in life, the average age has gone up from 24 in 1960 to 30 in 2010. There has also been a rise in the number of divorces which means that a family are not living as a group but are living in two different dwellings.
There is also the added problem of an ageing population. Many people now live on their own or with their spouse until they are in their 70s and 80s this means that more houses are needed for the younger generation.
British society has also changed in that 40 years ago many grandparents lived with their offsprings' families due to being unable to look after themselves. Many now live alone and rely on the welfare state to provide carers and home helps.
Political:
Sustainable communities policy and building on greenbelt land. **(4 marks)**

5 Effects could be for any urban area. If specifics are given credit up to 2 marks.
Effects such as air, land, noise pollution or housing problems such as shanty towns. **(4 marks)**

6 Levels mark

Indicative content
Brownfield sites advantages
Planning permission is easier to get, the government is actively encouraging the use of these sites.
Infrastructure such as gas, electricity and water is already present
Easier to market because of access to entertainment and other facilities
No building on Greenfield so lessens urban sprawl
See textbook for details on other sites

Level	Mark	Descriptor
1	1–2	Simple descriptive statements about development. Not clear if discussing greenfield or brownfield sites.

| 2 | 3–4 | Level two is reached by there being clear reasoning about either greenfield or brownfield sites. The top of the level requires both advantages and disadvantages of one of the site types. |
| 3 | 5–6 | A good understanding and comparison is made between the two different sites and their advantages and disadvantages. If case study material is used it is convincing. |

(6 marks)
(Total 25 marks)

Foundation tier

1 a River or meander bend **(1 mark)**
  b If explanation is given, credit.
    Meander bend – defence
    River – water supply
    Flat fertile land – farming **(3 marks)**

2 a Rural **(1 mark)**
  b Only 3 marks if no data is present
    The numbers living in rural areas have decreased (1) in the age groups from 10–40 between 1985 and 2005 (1). **(4 marks)**

3 a A movement out of rural areas by the working population. **(1 mark)**
  b Remote areas such as the Highlands of Scotland **(1 mark)**

4 People are now marrying **later** in life.
There has been a **rise** in the number of divorces.
There is an **ageing** population.
The government is allowing **urban** areas to expand onto greenbelt land. **(4 marks)**

5 See answer to Higher tier, question 5. **(4 marks)**

6
See answer to Higher tier, question 6.

Level	Mark	Descriptor
1	1–2	Simple descriptive statements about development. Not clear if discussing greenfield or brownfield sites.

| 2 | 3–4 | Level two is reached by there being clear information about either greenfield or brownfield sites. The top of the level requires both advantages and disadvantages of one of the site types |
| 3 | 5–6 | A good understanding of greenfield and brownfield sites and their advantages and disadvantages. If case study material is used it is convincing. |

(6 marks)
(Total 25 marks)

Chapter 12 Population Change

Higher tier

1 a 2000 **(1 mark)**
  b 2050 **(1 mark)**
  c 3 × 1 mark e.g. the population rose rapidly between 1950 and 2050 slow/steady growth until 1950 maximum 2 marks without data **(3 marks)**

2 a 2 million **(1 mark)**
  b 2 × 1 marks. 2 × 1 0–39 decreases, 55+ increases, etc. Description of individual bars e.g. 0–4 years, 45–49 (except 100+) = Max 1. Not just gender – reject 'the number of males will increase'.
    Accept 'older increases', 'younger decreases'.
    Reject changes to birth rate/death rate. **(2 marks)**
  c 4 × 1 pressure on health services, care homes, social services, isolation after the death of a partner, pressure on relative carers, tax burden, smaller economically active population, ageism, governments unable to pay for pensions, additional housing needs, entertainment/ recreation geared towards needs of elderly. People working longer before they retire. Go to (1+1) for developed points. Reject 'it will become overpopulated'.
    Pure list with no development/ description = Max 2. **(4 marks)**

3 a Demographic transition model
(1 mark)
b 3 × 1 mark BR in Stage 2 high, Stage 4 low (1)
DR in Stage 2 falling, Stage 4 low (1)
Total population in Stage 2 low, Stage 4 high (1)
Or starting to rise/explosion in Stage 2, levelling out/declining slightly in Stage 4 (1). **(3 marks)**
c Allow one mark for the comment that the birth rate is much greater than death rate. It then requires reasons why the death rate dropped and the birth rate remained high. So expect answers to focus on improvements in medicine, hygiene, food and transport.
(3 marks)

4 Levels mark

Indicative content
Description only required so mark will depend on the quality of the descriptions and the range of examples used.

Level	Mark	Descriptor
1	1–2	Simple descriptive statements about ways that birth rate is rising. Not clear if discussing a particular country.
2	3–4	Level two is reached by there being clear description of policy relating to a named country. The top of the level requires both incentives and disincentives of the policy.
3	5–6	There are a range of incentives and disincentives relating to a named country. Case study material used is convincing.

(6 marks)
(Total 25 marks)

Foundation tier
1 a 2000 **(1 mark)**
b 2050 **(1 mark)**
c 5 × 1 mark slowly, two, rapidly, 2050 **(5 marks)**

2 a 3.5 million. **(1 mark)**
b 3 × 1 marks 0–39, increase, female. **(3 marks)**
c 4 × 1 mark pressure on health services, care homes, social services, isolation after the death of a partner, pressure on relative carers, tax burden on smaller economically active population, ageism, governments unable to pay for pensions, additional housing needs, entertainment/recreation geared towards needs of elderly. 1+1 for developed points. Reject 'over populated'. Pure list with no development/description = max 2 **(4 marks)**

3 a

Description	Stage
Birth rate is high and death rate is falling	2
Birth rate and death rate are both low	4

(2 marks)
b 2 **(1 mark)**
c 4 **(1 mark)**

4 Levels mark
See answer in Higher tier, question 4.

Level	Mark	Descriptor
1	1–2	Simple descriptive statements about ways that birth rate is rising. Not clear if discussing a particular country.
2	3–4	Level two is reached by there being description of policy relating to a named country. The top of the level requires clear descriptions.
3	5–6	This level requires both incentives and disincentives of the policy. Case study material used is convincing.

(6 marks)
(Total 25 marks)

Chapter 13 A Moving World

Higher tier
1 a voluntary, national, short term population movement – commuter

b voluntary, international, short term population movement – sportsperson
c forced, international, short term migration – refugee
d international, voluntary, long term migration – Brazil to Portugal **(4 marks)**
2 a Political unrest in countries **(1 mark)**
b Countries needed workers to fill jobs after the war **(1 mark)**
3 Numbers very low in the early 1990s peaked in 1998 with 40,000, it then declined and was low until 2004. Rose in 2004 to 70,000 due to new countries joining the EU. There seems to be no correlation between the two lines.
Low numbers in 1994, 1998, 1999 approximately 25,000 British people migrated but there has been a steady increase in numbers since this time. Reasons for this are many people migrating abroad and moving to other HICs such as Australia and New Zealand for a better standard of living. **(4 marks)**
4 Negative economic – There has been an impact on the welfare state as 27,000 child benefit applications have been approved. Some of these children do not live in the UK but migrant workers are allowed to claim benefit for them. Positive economic – The migrant workers add a considerable amount to consumer spending in the UK. The average migrant worker earns £20,000 per year of which £6,000–£7,000 is disposable income.
Negative social – In Cambridgeshire the police force has to deal with 100 different languages. This has cost £800,000 for translators. Positive social impact – The development of Polish shops on many British High Streets adds to the cultural mix of the British society. **(4 marks)**

5 See table below. **(5 marks)**

Statement	Positive economic	Negative economic	Positive social	Negative social
Better salaries are being offered to encourage people to return.	X			
Some anaesthetists have to deal with more than one operation at the same time putting patients' lives at risk.				X
Jobs in the construction industry cannot be filled due to a shortage of workers.		X		
The birth rate has decreased. This is due to the average age of migrants being in the reproductive age group.				X
Rural depopulation due to the number of migrants has caused a breakdown of the traditional family unit.				X
Monthly salaries in Poland have increased by 9 per cent due to a shortage of workers.	X			

6 Levels mark

Indicative content
Example could be UK to Spain
Reasons such as climatic, lifestyle, improved communication networks.

Level	Mark	Descriptor
1	1–2	Simple descriptive statements about why people retire. Could be about any country. For example, they move there because it its warmer.
2	3–4	Level two is reached by there being clear reasoning about why the migrants moved or specific points are made. The top of the level requires both specific points and reasoning about the migration.
3	5–6	A good understanding is shown of the reasons for migration all within a case study framework.

(6 marks)
(Total 25 marks)

Foundation tier

1 a short term population movement – commuter
  b short term population movement – sportsperson
  c short term migration
  d long term migration Brazil to Portugal **(4 marks)**

2 a Political unrest in countries **(1 mark)**
  b Countries needed workers to fill jobs after the war **(1 mark)**
3 a The number of people from non-EU countries is always higher than the number of people from EU countries. Between 1997 and 2000 there was a large increase in the number of people from non-EU countries. The EU countries rose between 1997 and 1998 but then declined. It rose again in 2003. **(3 marks)**
  b Ten new countries joining the EU and having the right to free movement between the member states. **(1 mark)**
4 live
money
languages
younger **(4 marks)**
5 See table in answer to Higher tier, question 5. **(5 marks)**
6 Levels mark

See answer to Higher tier, question 6.

Level	Mark	Descriptor
1	1–2	Simple descriptive statements about why people retire. Could be about any country. For example, they move there because it its warmer.
2	3–4	Level two is reached by there being clear reasoning about why the migrants moved or

specific points are made. The top of the level requires both a specific point and some weak reasoning about the migration.

Level	Mark	Descriptor
3	5–6	A fair understanding is shown of the reasons for migration specific points are also made.

(6 marks)
(Total 25 marks)

Chapter 14 A Tourist's World

Higher tier

1 a Sandy beach
Warm, shallow and calm sea
Rocky coastline which looks rugged and attractive
Bright blue sky
Hot and dry weather. **(3 marks)**
  b No **(1 mark)**
  c There is not the correct environment. An adventure holiday needs thrills such as mountain climbing or cave diving. If yes is given and it is justified here correctly to adventure holiday definition allow. **(2 marks)**
2 Definition must involve elements such as transport (1) and accommodation (1). The other mark is for the example
Sun, sea and sand holiday on Aegina, Greece This hotel is used by the tour operator Libra as part of a package holiday. British

families are flown to Athens airport and transported to the island by boat. They can stay at the hotel on half board basis for £650 for two weeks in July.   **(3 marks)**

3 1 mark per point Up to 2 marks for data.
There were less than 50,000 in 1975. By 1988 there was 1million the figure then increased greater by almost 100,000 in 4 years. This trend continued but between 1998 and 2000 the numbers only increased slightly by 1,000 tourists.   **(4 marks)**

4 The number of tourists continues to increase but not as quickly as in previous stages. Transport routes and access to the resort have been improved. The local economy now relies on the income from tourism and the majority of the host community work either directly or indirectly in the tourist industry. There are many facilities for tourists which are beginning to impact on the environment. There may be some resentment from the host community to the changes that tourism is bringing.   **(2 marks)**

5 Any level of development would be acceptable. Must be more than one example for full marks. Both negative economic and environmental effects must be included for full marks. There must be explanation and specific points to achieve more than 2 marks.
One mark per point.
Footpath erosion on the footpath from Malham village to Janet's Foss waterfall.
Locals in Zanzibar have the menial low paid jobs in the hotels such as cleaners.   **(4 marks)**

6

Indicative content
Example such as footsteps in The Gambia
A number of management techniques should be developed.

Level	Mark	Descriptor
1	1–2	Simple descriptive statements about the management initiatives. Could be about any country. For example, they recycle the water.

2	3–4	Level two is reached by there being clear reasoning about the way the initiatives are protecting the environment or specific points. The top of the level requires both specific points and reasoning about the initiatives
3	5–6	A good understanding is shown of the management techniques all within a case study framework.

   (6 marks)
   (Total 25 marks)

Foundation tier

1 a Sandy beach
  Warm, shallow and calm sea
  Rocky coastline which looks rugged and attractive.
  Bright blue sky
  Hot and dry weather   **(2 marks)**
 b Reclining chairs and sunshades lining the sea to give views of the sea whilst relaxing and maybe reading a book.   **(1 mark)**

2 a No   **(1 mark)**
 b There is not the correct environment. An adventure holiday needs thrills such as mountain climbing or cave diving.
  If yes is given and it is justified here correctly to adventure holiday definition allow.   **(2 marks)**

3 Definition must involve elements such as transport (1) and accommodation (1). The other mark is for the example
Sun, sea and sand holiday on Aegina, Greece. This hotel is used by the tour operator Libra as part of a package holiday. British families are flown to Athens airport and transported to the island by boat. They can stay at the hotel on half board basis for £650 for two weeks in July.   **(3 marks)**

4 1 mark per point
Up to 2 marks for data.
There were less than 50,000 in 1975. By 1988 there was 1million the figure then increased greater by almost 100,000 in 4 years. This trend continued but between 1998 and 2000 the numbers only increased slightly by 1,000 tourists.   **(3 marks)**

5   **(3 marks)**

Stage 1	Exploration
Stage 2	Involvement
Stage 3	Development
Stage 4	Consolidation
Stage 5	Stagnation
Stage 6	Decline
Stage 7	Rejuvenation

6 Any level of development would be acceptable. Must be more than one example for full marks. Both negative economic and environmental effects must be included for full marks. There must be specific points to achieve more than 3 marks.
One mark per point.
Footpath erosion on the footpath from Malham village to Janet's Foss waterfall.
Locals in Zanzibar have the menial low paid jobs in the hotels such as cleaners.   **(4 marks)**

7

Indicative content
Example such as footsteps in The Gambia
A number of management techniques should be developed.

Level	Mark	Descriptor
1	1–2	Simple descriptive statements about the management initiatives. Could be about any country. For example, they recycle the water.
2	3–4	Level two is reached by there being clear reasoning about the way the initiatives are protecting the environment or specific points. The top of the level requires both specific point and some weak reasoning about the initiatives
3	5–6	A fair understanding is shown of the management techniques, specific points are also made.

   (6 marks)
   (Total 25 marks)

Index